MAX-PLANCK-GESELLSCHAFT

Universität Augsburg University

TECHNISCHE UNIVERSITÄT MÜNCHEN

THE GEORGE WASHINGTON UNIVERSITY LAW SCHOOL WASHINGTON DC

MIPLC Studies

Volume 19

Hyewon Ahn

Second Generation Patents in Pharmaceutical Innovation

Nomos

MIPLC Munich Intellectual Property Law Center
Augsburg München Washington DC

The Deutsche Nationalbibliothek lists this publication in the Deutsche Nationalbibliografie; detailed bibliographic data is available in the Internet at http://dnb.d-nb.de .

a.t.: Augsburg, Univ., Diss., 2013

ISBN 978-3-8487-0874-1

1. Edition 2014

Acknowledgements

This dissertation was accepted by the University of Augsburg for the degree of doctor juris in July 2013. The study takes into account statutory and case law available until the end of 2013.

It would not have been possible to write this doctoral thesis without the help and support of people around me, to only some of whom I can give particular mention here.

First and foremost I would like to express my heart-felt gratitude to my supervisor Prof. Dr. Christoph Ann for his continuous support of my PhD study, endless encouragement, patience, and scholarly input. He has always made himself available to clarify my doubts and has been willing to help me to move forward whenever I faced obstacles throughout the whole period of research. Under his constant and invaluable guidance I could successfully overcome many difficulties. For all these reasons and many more, I am eternally grateful.

I would also like to sincerely thank Prof. Dr. Ulrich M. Gassner for his insightful critique and interest in my research and for being the second referee of this thesis.

I will forever be thankful to my second supervisor Prof. Dr. Nari Lee who indeed had recommended that I should pursue the PhD study and always stood beside me, for her guidance, insights and integral view of my research. Her enthusiasm and love for research and teaching has been contagious. I feel privileged to be associated with a person like her during my life.

I am very much indebted to Prof. Dr. Joseph Straus who kindly shared with me his immense knowledge no matter whether he was in his office or even on a cruise, especially for his extensive discussions around my work. And I will remember one of many pieces of advice from him which speeded my research up greatly, i.e. "Well, a PhD thesis is not supposed to save the whole globe."

I owe Prof. Martin Adelman lots of gratitude for his valuable advice, many thoughtful and detailed comments, as well as constructive criticism throughout the study. He always supported and enlightened me and knew how to make a person moved with one sentence, i.e. "So, how's your thesis going?".

I am also thankful to Chief Judge Randall R. Rader across the Atlantic who provided me with a great chance to experience and learn how the court system works in the CAFC. I was very much privileged to learn from him and grateful for his encouragement, advice and deep insights into U.S. and comparative patent law.

My sincere gratitude is extended to Prof. Dr. Joseph Drexl for the academic support to carry out the research work at the Institute. I also take this opportunity to acknowledge the Max-Planck Institute for the Intellectual Property and Competition Law that provided a scholarship and thus made my Ph.D. work possible.

I am also thankful to the MIPLC program director, Dr. Gintare Surblyte, who made available her support in many ways.

My time at MPI was made enjoyable in large part thanks to the many friends that now become a part of my life. Ilho Lee deserves special mention here for his constant support and helping me when I faced difficulties or queries throughout my study. I also would like to thank Max Wallot and Eugenio Hoss for their support, helpful discussions and listening to my academic woes. Special thanks must go to Dr. Monica Donghi and Dr. Jörg Habermann for their support for my PhD study as well as kind proofreading with their technical and legal knowledge. I am also grateful to my office colleagues, Nicole van der Laan, Rachel Alemu, Kan He, Magdalena Kolasa, and Seyhan Ugurlu, who went through hard times together, cheered me on, celebrated each accomplishment, and made a stimulating and fun filled environment.

I extend my deep thanks to Kyounghee Paek, Yeonhee Kim, and Jeongeun Lee who helped me to update the development of Korean Jurisprudence and have been there for me as always. Their support, friendship, and belief in me were a treasure and will always be remembered.

Lastly, I would like to thank my parents and my sister. Their love and support all the way from Korea allowed me to finish this journey. I owe them everything and just wish I could show them how much I love and appreciate them.

December 2013 *Hyewon Ahn*

Inhaltsverzeichnis

List of Abbreviations

AB	Appellate Body
ABPI	Association of the British Pharmaceutical Industry
Adv. Genet.	Advances in Genetics
aff'd	affirmed
AIPLA Q. J.	AIPLA Quarterly Journal
Aliment Pharm. Ther.	Alimentary Pharmacology & Therapeutics
Am. U. L. Rev.	American University Law Review
Art.	Article
B. C. L. Rev.	Boston College Law Review
BeckRS	Beck-Rechtsprechung
Bell J. Econ.	Bell Journal of Economics.
Berkeley Tech. L. J.	Berkeley Technology Law Journal
BGH	Bundesgerichtshof, Federal Supreme Court of Germany
Bioorgan. Med. Chem.	Bioorganic & Medicinal Chemistry
Biotechnol. Law Rep.	Biotechnology Law Report
BOA	Board of Appeal of the European Patent Office
BPatG	Bundespatentgericht, Federal Patent Court of Germany
BpatGE	Entscheidungen des Bundespatentgerichts
Brit. Med. J.	British Medical Journal
Brookings Paper on Econ. Activity	Brookings Paper on Economic Activity
B. U. L. Rev.	Boston University Law Review
Cal. L. R.	California Law Review
Case W. Res. L. Rev.	Case Western Reserve Law Review
cert.	certiorari
C.F.R.	Code of Federal Regulations
CIPA	Chartered Institute of Patent Attorneys
CJEU	Court of Justice of the European Union
Clin. Chem.	Clinical Chemistry
Clin. Dermatol.	Clinical Dermatology
Clin. Infect. Dis.	Clinical Infectious Diseases

Clin. Microbiol. Infec.	Clinical Microbiology & Infection
Clin. Pharmacokinet.	Clinical Pharmacokinetics
Clin. Pharmacol. Ther.	Clinical Pharmacology & Therapeutics
Colum. L. Rev.	Columbia Law Review
Conn. J. Int'l L.	Connecticut Journal of International Law
Cornell L. Rev.	Cornell Law Review
Discov. Med.	Discovery Medicine
DPMA	Deutsches Patent- und Markenamt, German Patent and Trademark Office
Drug Discov. Today	Drug Discovery Today
Drug Info. J.	Drug Information Journal
Duke L. J.	Duke Law Journal
Econ. J.	The Economic Journal
e.g.	exempli gratia, for example
EFPIA	European Federation of Pharmaceutical Industries and Associations
EIPR	European Intellectual Property Review
Epilepsy Res.	Epilepsy Research
EPO	European Patent Office
Eur. J. Drug Metab. Ph.	European Journal of Drug Metabolism and Pharmacokinetics
Eur. J. Health L.	European Journal of Health Law
FDA	U.S. Food and Drug Administration
Fed. Law.	Federal Lawyer
Food & Drug L.J.	Food and Drug Law Journal
Fordham Int'l L. J.	Fordham International Law Journal
Fordham L. Rev.	Fordham Law Review
FTC	Federal Trade Commission
Geo. L. J.	Georgetown Law Journal
Geo. Mason L. Rev.	George Mason Law Review
GPA	German Patent Act
GRUR	Gewerblicher Rechtsschutz Und Urheberrecht
GRUR Int	Gewerblicher Rechtsschutz und Urheberrecht Internationaler Teil.
GRUR-Prax	Gewerblicher Rechtsschutz und Urheberrecht, Praxis im Immaterial- und Wettbewerbsrecht

GSK	GlaxoSmithKline
Harv. Int'l L. J.	Harvard International Law Journal
Harv. L. Rev.	Harvard Law Review
Health Affair.	Health Affairs
High Tech. L. J.	High Technology Law Journal
Hist. & Tech.	History and Technology
Hous L. Rev.	Houston Law Review
Hum. Psychopharm.	Human Psychopharmacology
ICTSD	International Centre for Trade and Sustainable Development
IDEA	IDEA: The Journal of Law and Technology
IDSA	Infectious Diseases Society of America
IG Rule	The rule established in the I.G. Farbenindustrie's A.G.'s Patent case
IIC	International Review of Intellectual Property and Competition Law
Ill. L. Rev.	Illinois Law Review
IMD	Incrementally Modified Drugs
In Vivo: Bus. Med. Rep.	In vivo: The Business and Medicine Report
INN	International Non-proprietary Name
Int. J. Health Care Fi.	International Journal of Health Care Finance & Economics
Int. J. Ind. Organ.	International Journal of Industrial Organization
Intell. Prop. Q.	Intellectual Property Quarterly
IP	Intellectual Property
IPR	Intellectual Property Right
IR	Infrared
J. Chem. Inf. Comp. Sci.	Journal of Chemical Information and Computer Sciences
J. Copyright Soc'y U.S.A.	Journal of the Copyright Society of the USA
J. E. C. L. & Pract.	Journal of European Competition Law and Practice
J. Econ. Behav. Organ.	Journal of Economic Behavior & Organization
J. Econ. Manage. Strat.	Journal of Economics & Management Strategy
J. Econ. Perspect.	Journal of Economic Perspectives
J. Financ. Econ.	Journal of Financial Economics
J. Generic Med	Journal of Generic Medicine
J. Health Econ.	Journal of Health Economics

J. Ind. Econ.	Journal of Industrial Economics
J. Law Econ.	Journal of Law & Economics
J. Legal Stud.	Journal of Legal Studies
J. Manage.	Journal of Management
J. Marketing Res.	Journal of Marketing Research
J. Med. Chem.	Journal of Medicinal Chemistry
J. Pat. & Trademark Off. Soc'y	Journal of the Patent and Trademark Office Society
J. Pat. Off. Soc'y	Journal of the Patent Office Society
J. Pharmaceut. Marketing Manage.	Journal of Pharmaceutical Marketing and Management
J. Tech. L. & Pol'y	Journal of Technology Law & Policy
J. Technol. Transfer	Journal of Technology Transfer
Lancet Infect. Dis.	Lancet Infectious Diseases
LJ	Lord Justice
Manage. Decis. Econ.	Managerial and Decision Economics
Manage. Sci.	Management Science
Mich. Telecomm. Tech. L. Rev.	Michigan Telecommunications and Technology Law Review
Minn. L. Rev.	Minnesota Law Review
Modern Drug Discov.	Modern Drug Discovery
Nat. Rev. Drug Discov.	Nature Reviews Drug Discovery
NBER	National Bureau of Economic Research
New Eng. J. Med.	New England Journal of Medicine
NIHCM	The National Institute for Health Care Management Research and Educational Foundation
NME	Mew Medical Entity or New Molecular Entity
NMR	Nuclear Magnetic Resonance
Nw. U. L. Rev.	Northwestern University Law Review
N.Y.U. L. Rev.	New York University Law Review
OECD	Organisation for Economic Co-operation and Development
Open Access J. Clin. Trials	Open Access Journal of Clinical Trials
OTC	Over-The-Counter
Para	paragraph
PCT	Patent Cooperation Treaty

PHC	Paroxetine hydrochloride
PHOSITA	The person having ordinary skill in the art
PLOS Med	Plos Medicine
Probl. Perspect. Manage.	Problems and Perspectives in Management
R&D	Research and Development
RAND J. Econ.	RAND Journal of Economics
reh'g	rehearing
Res. Policy	Research Policy
San. Diego L. Rev.	San Diego Law Review
Santa Clara Computer & High Tech. L. J.	Santa Clara Computer and High Technology Law Journal
SAR	Structure-Activity Relationship
Sci. & Pub. Pol'y	Science and Public Policy
Sec.	Section
Seton Hall L. Rev.	Seton Hall Law Review
SME	Small and Medium Enterprise
SMU L. Rev.	SMU Law Review
Soc. Philos. Policy	Social Philosophy & Policy
SPC	Supplementary Protection Certificate
St. John's J. Legal Comment.	St. John's Journal of Legal Commentary
Stan. Tech. L. Rev.	Stanford Technology Law Review
Sup. Ct. Rev.	Supreme Court Review
Tenn. L. Rev.	Tennessee Law Review
Tex. Intell. Prop. L.J.	Texas Intellectual Property Law Journal
Tex. L. Rev.	Texas Law Review
TFEU	Treaty on the Functioning of the European Union
THC	Terazosine hydrochloride
Trademark Rep.	Trademark Reporter
TRIPS	The Agreement on Trade Related Aspects of Intellectual Property Rights
Tul. J. Tech. & Intell. Prop.	Tulane Journal of Technology & Intellectual Property
U. Chi. L. Rev.	University of Chicago Law Review
UC Irvine L.R.	UC Irvine Law Review
U. Dayton L. Rev.	University of Dayton Law Review
U.K.	United Kingdom
UNCTAD	United Nations Conference on Trade and Development

U. Pa. J. Int'l Econ. L.	University of Pennsylvania Journal of International Economic Law
U.S.	United States
U.S.C.	United States Code
USPTO	U.S. Patent & Trademark Office
Va. L. Rev.	Virginia Law Review
Vand. L. Rev.	Vanderbilt Law Review
Wake Forest L. Rev.	Wake Forest Law Review
Wash. U. J. L. & Pol'y	Washington University Journal of Law and Policy
Wash. U. L. Rev.	Washington University Law Review
WHO	World Health Organization
Wid. L. Symp. J.	Widner Law Symposium Journal
WIPO	World Intellectual Property Organization
Wm. & Mary L. Rev.	William and Mary Law Review
World Pat. Info.	World Patent Information
WTO	World Trade Organization
XRPD	X-ray powder diffraction
Yale J. Health Pol'y L. & Ethics	Yale Journal of Health Policy, Law, and Ethics
Yale L. J.	Yale Law Journal

I. INTRODUCTION

A. Overview

> "Over the past two decades, the pharmaceutical industry 'has moved very far from its original high purpose of discovering and producing useful new drugs. Now primarily a marketing machine to sell drugs of dubious benefit, this industry uses its wealth and power to co-opt every institution that might stand in its way, [...]."[1]

This is the much-quoted statement of Dr. Marica Angell, the former editor-in-chief of the New England Journal of Medicine. It is a sobering reflection on the operational reality that the development of new medications and improvements to those medications play a crucial role in ensuring continued gains in health and longevity. The need for new medicines is never-ending. To spur the investment needed for the continued research and development ("R&D") of new medicines, economic incentives are essential prerequisites. These incentives can also be provided by intellectual property protection -- particularly patents -- government funding, or other administrative policies. However, achievements of R&D are not enough to provide a constant and efficient flow of new medicines to the market. The pressure exercised by competitors such as generic companies leads to a reduction in drug prices and this too is necessary.

The following purposes of the patent system have been discussed: i) Providing motivations for making useful inventions,[2] ii) disclosing and disseminating information and inventions to the public,[3] and iii) allowing for more efficient exploration of the possibilities inherent in prospective inven-

---

1 *Angell*, 2004, xvii-xviii.

2 *Luski/Wettstein*, 1 Probl. Perspect. Manage. 31, 31 (2004); *Ann*, 2009, 361; *Crouch*, 16 Geo. Mason L. Rev. 141, 141 (2008); *Graham v. John Deere Co.*, 383 U.S. 1, 9 (1966) ("The patent monopoly was not designed to secure to the inventor his natural right in his discoveries. Rather, it was a reward, an inducement, to bring forth new knowledge."); *Crouch*, 39 Seton Hall L. Rev. 1125, 1134 (2009); *cf. Kamien/ Schwartz*, 1982, 190-91 (noting "[t]he monopolist [...] chooses to spend less on development than would a social planner because his reward from innovation is smaller than the total social benefit.").

3 *Friebel et al.,* 2006, 21; *Eisenberg*, 56 U. Chi. L. Rev. 1017, 1028-30 (1989).

tions.[4] The patent system can be used as a way of creating prior art and preventing others from obtaining a patent that an original inventor might later infringe.[5] More importantly, the patent system encourages investment in potentially risky commercialization activities[6] and turns inventions into new goods and services[7] by providing the opportunity to recoup that investment.[8] In other words, it creates the incentives to develop nascent inventions into marketable products, since the prospect of a patent provides greater efficiency in the development of inventions.[9] Jerome Frank J noted in 1942:

> "The controversy between the defenders and assailants of our patent system may be about a false issue – the stimulus to invention. The real issue may be the stimulus to investment."[10]

This function of the patent system can be clearly seen in the responses to the Court of Justice of the European Union ("CJEU") decision,[11] in which the

---

4 *Kitch*, 20 J. Law Econ. 265 (1977); *Mazzoleni/Nelson*, 27 Res. Policy, 273, 275-80 (1998); *Pfaff v. Wells Electronics, Inc.*, 525 U.S. 55, 63 (1998), *reh'g denied* (acknowledging two purposes of the patent system, i.e. "creating and the publicly disclosing new inventions.").

5 *Jaffe*, 29 Res. Policy 531, 539-40 (2000); *Levin et al.*, 1987 Brookings Paper on Econ. Activity, 783, 798 fn. 29 (1987). However, if this was the purpose, it will be the cheaper and easier way to publish the invention to the proper media. *See e.g. Lichtman/Baker/Kraus*, 53 Vand. L. Rev. 2175, 2175-76 (2000).

6 *Roin*, 87 Tex. L. Rev. 503, 509 (2009); *Merges*, 7 High Tech. L. J. 1, 69-70 (1992) ("[P]atents may spur development more than invention per se. […] this may in fact be such an important function that it more than outweighs the contribution patents make to incentives to invent."); *Jaffe/Lerner*, 2004, 43 ("Patents protect an individual's or firm's investment in the development of an idea, as much as they protect the invention itself."); *Svatos*, 13 Soc. Philos. Policy 113, 114 (1996); *Scherer*, 1984, 22-25 (with the example that an investor entered into partnership with the inventor of the steam engine owing to the patent); *Duffy*, 71 U. Chi. L. Rev. 439, 440 (2004).

7 *Kieff*, 85 Minn. L. Rev. 697, 707-12 (2001); *Merges*, 7 High Tech. L. J. 1 (1992).

8 *See e.g., Eisenberg*, 56 U. Chi. L. Rev. 1017, 1036-46 (1989); *Blair/Cotter*, 10 Tex. Intell. Prop. L. J. 1, 78-80 (2001); *Hoffman*, 89 Cornell L. Rev. 993, 1022 (2004) (noting a patent gives an opportunity to recoup R&D costs, thereby providing incentives to invest in further research); *Svatos*, 13 Soc. Philos. Policy 113, 119 (1996) (noting "[j]ust as there is no guarantee that patents will not allow "monopoly" profits, there is also no guarantee that a patent will help capture even normal profits, even if the invention socially useful; this can result from a lack of marketing know-how, excessive litigation costs, etc.").

9 *Kitch*, 20 J. Law Econ. 265, 276 (1977).

10 *Picard v. United Aircraft Corp.*, 128 F.2d 632, 643 (2nd Cir. 1942).

11 C-34/10, *Oliver Brüstle v. Greenpeace e.V.*, 2011.

Court held that human embryonic stem cells were not patentable subject matter in Europe. Among the many concerns and objections voiced regarding the decision, the major worries were the impediments to competition in the international market for new disease therapies,[12] and the lack of incentive for innovative companies to invest in this field of R&D in Europe.[13]

The Board of Appeal of the European Patent Office ("BOA") noted in one case that it must be assumed that inventors invent not out of idle curiosity, but with some concrete technical reason in mind.[14] However, it is often observed that inventions may arise as a result of felicitous curiosity, by serendipity, as a result of a flash of insight, or simply due to human nature without recourse to specific grounds.[15] It follows that inventions may arise without patent protection. However, the necessary investment needed to develop such innovation is unlikely to follow without patent protection. With strong protection, companies will invest hundreds of millions of dollars in their R&D in anticipation of substantial reward.[16] Thus, although the patent system is subject to criticism with regard to the high prices that may be entailed by patent protection, there is little doubt that it is crucial to spurring pharmaceutical innovation.[17]

Specifically, the pharmaceutical industry may be regarded as one of those industries in which the economic rationale for patents works best to protect inventors from imitators, provides the incentive for bearing the cost of innovation,[18] as well as ensuring essential protection.[19] However, in spite of this protection, the number of innovative new medicines per year has decreased or remained the same.[20] This seem to undermine the above arguments[21] that patent protection provides incentives for real innovation and promotes the progress of technological development in this field. In addition,

12 *Abbott*, 471 Nature 280 (2011) (citing Dr. Brüstle's own word, namely "if we are not allowed to protect our inventions in Germany, we won't be able to compete in the international market for new disease therapies.").

13 *Smith*, 472 Nature 418 (2011).

14 *Agrevo/Triazoles*, T 939/92, OJ EPO 1996, 309, 320.

15 *Crouch*, 39 Seton Hall L. Rev. 1125, 1134 (2009); *Burk/Lemley*, 89 Va. L. Rev. 1575, 1581 (2003).

16 *Scherer*, 20 Health Affair. 216, 220 (2001).

17 *Cohen/Nelson/Walsh*, 2000, 3.

18 *Bessen/Maskin*, 40 RAND J. Econ. 611 (2009).

19 *Roin*, 87 Tex. L. Rev. 503, 513-15 (2009); *Bessen/Meurer,* 2008, 88-89.

20 See subsection III.B.2.

21 See subsection III.A.3.b).

the pharmaceutical industry is facing numerous challenges, such as major capital losses in revenue as the patent terms on some blockbuster drugs have expired, spiralling costs for the development of new drugs, particularly in running clinical trials, more stringent regulatory requirements, and increasingly cost-constrained healthcare systems.[22]

Consequently, the focus has shifted towards alternative strategies of revenue generation. Such strategies may include a move away from creating innovative new medicines in favour of lower-risk solutions, such as improvements or applications. These second generation inventions are also referred to as blocking patents, incremental improvement patents, surrounding patents, fencing patents, and second-tier patents. The strategies used to develop these second generation inventions are referred to as life cycle management, evergreening patenting, patent thicketing, and patent clustering. This increase in the number of second generation inventions in the pharmaceutical industry is particularly worrisome in light of the concomitant dearth of innovative medications and it is questionable whether the movement toward second generation inventions and products is well aligned with the health needs of societies.[23] In addition, second generation patents may adversely impact competition by preventing generic companies from entering into the market or at least making them hesitant to do so.

Since superior new medications are essential to maintaining and improving the health of a society, these concerns about the dearth of new medications and the increase in the number of second generation patents are important and serious. This dissertation will analyze and review whether these concerns are justified, and, if so, whether or how patent law could help to eliminate or lessen these concerns. Amongst others, the following issues will be addressed: Whether the patent system is associated with the dearth of new medications, whether the patent system sufficiently encourages manufacturers to invest in new medications, whether there is a correlation between the increased number of second generation patents and any change in patent law, whether there has been any change in the patentability requirements of second generation inventions, whether all kinds of second generation inventions retain the same value, whether second generation inventions hinder true innovation, such as new medicines, whether second generation inventions delay or prevent the entry of generic products, and, if so, whether and

22 *See e.g., Federsel*, 18 Bioorgan. Med. Chem. 5775, 5775 (2010); *Paul, et al.*, 9 Nat. Rev. Drug Discov. 203, 203 (2010).

23 *Avorn*, 309 Science 669, 669 (2005).

how the patent system can improve the situation that confronts pharmaceutical companies and society in general.

B. Outline of the dissertation

This dissertation approaches and analyzes the above issues from various perspectives, mainly within the patent system, and is structured as follows:

Chapter 1 presents a short introduction to the dissertation. Chapter 2 defines the nature of inventions, considers the definition of inventions and innovations in the pharmaceutical art, discusses the range of products in the pharmaceutical market, and explores second generation inventions in pharmaceutical technology along with their backgrounds. Chapter 3 examines the specificities of pharmaceutical development procedure and of the drug markets as well as the central role of the patent system in the industry. It further presents recent challenges, such as the dearth of new medications and efforts to overcome this problem. Chapter 4 revisits the patentability requirements of selection inventions, reviews recent court cases and amended patent examination guidelines and explores the changes therein. Based on the findings in chapter 4, chapter 5 examines concerns about the changes in patentability requirements and assesses the implications thereof with consideration of the scope and the duration of patent protection conferred by second generation patents. Further, an understanding of the implications for competition in the market of generic versions engendered by second generation patents is sought. After reviewing different natures of selection inventions, chapter 6 seeks to formulate proposals on the scope, terms, and patentability requirements of species selection inventions and other selection inventions, to remove uncertainties for private players and users of the patent system and to provide greater benefits to society. Finally, chapter 7 provides a summary and a conclusion.

C. Scope of the dissertation

In the discussion of second generation inventions, the focus will mainly be on chemical selection inventions, such as species selection inventions, optical isomers, metabolites, and crystalline forms. These inventions are chosen not only because they are characteristic examples of second generation inventions, but also because species selection invention can represent features of a basic invention. Therefore, they provide a good basis for further discussion of pharmaceutical inventions and innovations. Subsequently, this research results reported in this dissertation could be applied to all other second generation inventions insofar as they also originate from basic inventions.

Jurisdictions are selected based upon an evaluation of the extent of patenting activity and of the pharmaceutical market. Firstly, patenting activity is considered. According to the World Intellectual Property Organization ("WIPO") report,[24] the top five countries for originating Patent Cooperation Treaty ("PCT") filings in 2011 were the United States, Japan, Germany, China, and the Republic of Korea. The combined shares of these five countries accounted for 73.1% of total PCT filings.[25] Furthermore, the top five countries for originating PCT applications in the field of pharmaceuticals in 2011 were the United States, Japan, Germany, France and the Republic of Korea.[26]

The market for pharmaceuticals is further considered, and the number of national phase entries per relevant patent office is analyzed as an indicator of the commercial attractiveness of the country or region. The top five patent offices showing the highest number of national phase entries in 2011 were the offices of the United States, Europe, China, Japan and Republic of Korea.[27] In addition, the actual size of market is considered. According to one report on the pharmaceutical industry, the North American market was the world's largest with a 41.8% share, followed by Europe, accounting for 26.8%, and Japan for 12%, in 2011.[28] In addition, the most highly developed pharmaceutical markets in 2011 were reported to be the United States, Japan, Germany, France, Italy, Spain, Canada, the United Kingdom and the Republic of Korea.[29]

Thus, based on the patenting activities and the importance of the pharmaceutical markets, Germany, the United Kingdom, the United States, and Korea were selected as representative. In addition, the practice before the European Patent Office ("EPO") will be analyzed.

---

24 *WIPO*, 2012.
25 *WIPO*, 2012, 26-27.
26 *WIPO*, 2012, 44.
27 *WIPO*, 2012, 55.
28 *European Federation of Pharmaceutical Industries and Associations ("EFPIA")*, 2012, 14.
29 *IMAP*, 2012, 16.

This paper takes into account the fact that there are other regimes supporting the progress and development of pharmaceutical innovation and securing sustainable access to medicines for the public. Examples would be regulatory exclusivities in pharmaceutical law, prizes, or government funding for research in this area. Nevertheless, this paper will focus exclusively on the patent system. Furthermore, while issues in the area of competition law are not treated exhaustively, such issues will be discussed to the extent that second generation inventions are involved.

II. PHARMACEUTICAL INVENTIONS, INNOVATIONS & PRODUCTS

A. *Cumulative nature of inventions*

Most inventions have been developed based on previous inventions.[30] This has never been so accentuated as in the current evolution of high technologies.[31] The cumulative nature of technological innovation poses a problem for operating an optimal patent system,[32] namely, today's patent can hinder tomorrow's innovations.[33] Thus, every potential inventor can be a potential infringer,[34] although this is not always immediately obvious.[35]

The literature on law, economics or patents is inconsistent in its use of terms to describe previous inventions and subsequent inventions.[36] Representative terms would be first/second generation, earlier/later inventions,[37]

---

30 *E.g.*, "[d]*warfs standing on the shoulders of giants,*" in Latin: *nanos gigantium hemeris insidentes*, Wikipedia, available at: http://en.wikipedia.org/wiki/ Standing_on_the_shoulders_of_giants; it is a Western metaphor meaning "one who develops future intellectual pursuits by understanding the research and works created by notable thinkers of the past. (Last accessed on December 20, 2013).

31 *Scherer/Ross*, 1990, 264 (noting "growth of technology is cumulative and richly interactive"); *Scotchmer*, 5 J. Econ. Perspect. 29 (1991) (stressing the importance of the cumulative nature of innovation); *Arrow*, 1962, 616-619 (noting that today's invention is the input for future innovations); *Vossius*, 59 J. Pat. Off. Soc'y 180, 180 (1977) (noting "[a] completely pioneer invention is a rare occurrence in today's world.").

32 *Scotchmer*, 5 J. Econ. Perspect. 29, 30 (1991).

33 *Luski/Wettstein*, 1 Probl. Perspect. Manage. 31, 31 (2004).

34 *Merges/Nelson*, 90 Colum. L. Rev. 839, 916 (1990); *O'Donoghue*, 29 RAND J. Econ. 654, 655 (1998); *Heller/Eisenberg*, 280 Science 698 (1998) (noting strong IP right would rather impede research than promote it).

35 *Scotchmer*, 27 RAND J. Econ. 322, 329 (1996).

36 *Cf. Janis*, 40 Harv. Int'l L. J. 151, 151-152 (1999) (using "second tier patent" as a generic label encompassing utility models, petty patents, and so on which is different from the regular patent system.).

37 *Gallini/Scotchmer*, 2002, 65.

primary/secondary patents, basic inventions/applications,[38] pioneer/subsequent patents,[39] broad/subservient patents,[40] dominant/subservient patents,[41] and basic/future inventions. [42] Similarly, terms that refer to the inventors of both inventions include first/second inventors, initial/later inventors, or original developer/subsequent improvers.[43] The earliest invention or patent has been referred to as the original invention, the breakthrough invention, the initial patent, [44] the originating patent, or the parent patent. Another comparable notion is upstream invention and downstream invention.[45] The terms will be disambiguated in the following sections, and "basic invention" and "second generation invention" will be adhered to in this paper.

1. Basic and second generation inventions

An invention that is a breakthrough or pioneering invention, which provides the roots and routes for future innovations, is often called a **basic invention**.[46] In contrast to basic inventions, second generation inventions are generally improvements and applications of the basic inventions. A class of invention called a "selection invention" is particularly relevant in pharmaceutical and chemical inventions and is discussed in detail below.

---

38 *Matutes/Regibeau/Rockett*, 27 RAND J. Econ. 60, 60-61 (1996); cf. basic/applied research: *Eisenberg*, 56 U. Chi. L. Rev. 1017, 1017 (1989). (basic research which directed solely toward expanding human knowledge vs applied research which directed toward solving practical problems),.

39 *Merges/Nelson*, 25 J. Econ. Behav. Organ. 1, 13 (1994).

40 *Merges/Nelson*, 25 J. Econ. Behav. Organ. 1, 21 (1994).

41 *Chang*, 26 RAND J. Econ. 34, 49 (1995).

42 *Friebel et al.,* 2006, 26.

43 *Lemley*, 75 Tex. L. Rev. 989 (1997).

44 *Matutes/Regibeau/Rockett*, 27 RAND J. Econ. 60, 60-61 (1996).

45 *Heller/Eisenberg*, 280 Science 698 (1998).

46 *Friebel et al.,* 2006, 26-29.

a) Improvement inventions

An improvement invention refers to an invention that essentially builds upon a basic invention,[47] or to an invention that could not have occurred until the basic invention was available.[48] Thus, improvement inventions can only occur in the wake of basic inventions are the outcome of research activities directed to improvements or applications of previous inventions.[49] In the context of patent law, an improvement invention may be referred to as a dependent invention, which may not be used without infringing the basic patent, until it expires.[50] Improvement inventions are ubiquitous as most technological progress builds upon previous inventions.[51] They are most commonly found in the software industry, where incremental improvement is endemic for various reasons.[52]

b) Selection inventions

Improvements can also be achieved through selection in some technical fields. Although it is difficult to find a statutory definition, a "selection invention" is generally understood as an invention that has a particular concept which is selected from a prior broader or larger generic concept of an invention and that presents superior or advantageous properties compared to

---

47 *Bessen/Maskin*, 40 RAND J. Econ. 611, 612 (2009) (improvement inventions as an example of sequential inventions).

48 *Denicolò/Zanchettin*, 20 Int'l. J. Indus. Org. 801, 804 (2002).

49 *Gallini/Scotchmer*, 2002, 65.

50 See e.g., Korean Patent Act, Art. 98 (Relation to Patented Invention etc. of Another Person) *Jackson*, 9 J. Tech. L. & Pol'y, 117, 119 (2004); *Gallini/Scotchmer*, 2002, 65.

51 *CFMT, Inc. v. Yieldup Intern. Corp.*, 349 F.3d 1333, 1340 (Fed. Cir. 2003).

52 *See in general, Burk/Lemley*, 89 Va. L. Rev. 1575, 1620-24 (2003).

the broader concept, which were not disclosed in the prior art.[53] It is an invention that falls under the scope of the prior art disclosure, but has not been individually disclosed in the prior art.[54] A patent document from which a selection invention is derived is referred to as a dominant patent.[55]Selection inventions are also referred to as "improvement inventions" since they usually provide some unexpected results or benefits, which also help to overcome challenges to patentability based on assertions of the obviousness thereof.[56] Selection inventions can be generally categorized into three types, according to the selection of an individual element, sub-sets, or sub-ranges respectively.[57]

Selection inventions can be found in various technical fields. When a class of a mechanical invention is a group of structural elements, one of which is

---

53 *Bayer/E-Isomers of N-alpha-(2-Cyan-2-alkoximino-acetyl)-amino acid derivatives and peptides*, T12/90 (1990), point 2.7 (stated "the term 'selection' is the singling out of a narrow portion from a relatively broad scope immanent.", quoting *Bayer/ Diastereomer*, T 12/81 OJ EPO 1982, 296, 301); *see also Nastelski*, Review of Intellectual Property and Competition Law ("IIC") 1972, 267, 291 (describing a selection invention as an invention providing a particular representative (or a subgroup) of already disclosed product group by the first inventor which showing particularly distinguishing effects when used as indicated by the first inventor or has the possibility of a different type of use.); *see also Vossius*, Gewerblicher Rechtsschutz Und Urheberrecht ("GRUR") 1976, 165, 165 (describing that a chemical selection exists when an second inventor has select one or more representatives from a group of substances, one component from a mixture, or a narrower range of alloy components from a [broader] alloy area.); *see also Grubb/Thomsen*, 2010, 232 (describing selection invention as an invention that is the selection of a particular compound or relatively small group of compounds from the larger group previously disclosed in broader terms, and the compound or the small group of compounds are individually new but fall within an earlier discloser.); *see also, Blanco White,* 1983, 104-106 (noting "[a] special case arises where, although the subject-matter of the claim concerned has never specifically been disclosed before, there has been a prior publication covering that subject-matter in general terms; or (in other words) there is an earlier document which "contains a broad description or claim covering the whole area within which the subsequent selection falls.").

54 *See, e.g., Agranat/Caner*, 4 Drug Discov. Today 313, 313-314 (1999).

55 *Miller/Evans*, 2010, 14-15.

56 *Miller/Evans*, 2010, 14, fn12.

57 Guidelines for Examination in the European Patent Office, June 2012, (herein after "EPO Examination Guidelines"), G-VI, 8 ("Selection inventions deal with the selection of individual elements, sub-sets, or sub-ranges, which have not been explicitly mentioned, within a larger known set or range").

selected as being particularly useful, it is a selection invention.[58] Examples of such inventions can be found in the field of alloys, where a specific range of compositions are chosen, or in the field of engineering and manufacturing, where specific operating conditions are selected. Selection inventions are typically encountered in pharmaceutical and chemical technologies. In the field of chemistry, any competent researcher who invents one compound and discovers its usefulness, can enumerate derivatives that may be equally useful, even though it remains beyond the power of the researcher to manufacture more than a few of those compounds at the time of filing.[59]

Although second generation patents can be found in all technological fields, this thesis will focus on those in the pharmaceutical industry. Pharmaceutical selection inventions could be a selection of a compound or of compounds, the use of a compound, a chemical process, dimensions, a range of values, parameters, crystal forms,[60] nanoscales, dosage regimes, and so on.[61] A more extreme case of a selection invention would be claiming a known compound with a very high level of purity.[62]

B. Inventions and innovations in pharmaceutical field

1. Inventions and patents in pharmaceutical field

Categories of pharmaceutical patents are not generally different from patents in different fields of technology. Compounds and processes can be subject to patent protection, but a new use of a known compound can be patented depending on the particular jurisdiction. Typical pharmaceutical patents can protect active ingredients and their metabolites, hydrates, salts, esters, intermediates and the like combinations of more than two active ingredients, methods of manufacturing the active ingredient and its intermediates, different methods or uses of medical treatment of known medications (includ-

---

58 *Grubb/Thomsen*, 2010, 64.

59 *See e.g., Blanco White,* 1983, 104.

60 *Smith Kline & French Laboratories v. Evans Medical* [1989] Fleet Street Report ("F.S.R.") 561,563 (Aldous J. noted "the *polymorph patent is said to be a selection patent*, in that the [basic] patent disclosed Cimetidine makes no mention that it can exist in A, B or C [crystal] form."[Emphasis added]).

61 *See generally Miller/Evans*, 2010, 14-15; for the dosage regime, refer *Abbott Respiratory/Dosage Regime*, G 2/08 (2010), para 6.3.

62 *Grubb/Thomsen*, 2010, 237.

ing dosage regimes), and formulations of a drug, including new dosage forms, devices such as patches, drug delivery systems.[63] These inventions and patents will be explained in detail in chapter II.C. The protection covers various aspects of pharmaceutical innovation. It is possible to form a hierarchy among compound, use or process claims of patents based on the scope of protection that the patents provide.

a) Product invention and the absolute character of its protection

A claim to structures rewards patentees with exclusive rights to all properties and manufacturing processes thereof, regardless of whether properties or processes discovered subsequently were acknowledged by the applicant at the time of filing. If the product is a compound, this is called "absolute compound protection",[64] which differs from "purpose-limited protection", where the patent can cover only the purpose of the compound as indicated in the patent application.[65] Regarding the broader scope of the exclusivity of the product, Jacob LJ noted:

> "[A]ny product claim is apt to give the patentee "more than he has invented" – and in two ways. Firstly such a claim will have the effect of covering all ways of making the product including ways which may be inventive and quite different from the patentee's route. Secondly it will give him a monopoly over all uses of the patented compound, including uses he has never thought of."[66]

Although there are arguments for purpose-limited protection,[67] the Federal Supreme Court of Germany ("BGH") clearly addressed the effect of absolute chemical protection on the pharmaceutical industry. In the *Klinische Ver-*

---

63 *Voet*, 2011, 59.

64 *Kraßer*, 2009, 130 *et seqq.*; *Bacher/Melullis* in: Benkard *et al.*, 2006, § 1 Rdns 12 and 16; *Deutsches Patent- und Markenamt* ("DPMA"), 2008, 29; *Merges/Duffy*, 2011, 393; *cf.* Case C-428/08, *Monsanto Technology LLC v. Cefetra BV and Others*, E.C.R. 2010, I-06765 (holding the Art. 9 of Council Directive 98/44/EC of 6 July 1998 on the legal protection of biotechnological inventions did not confer absolute protection to the patented product, i.e. a patented DNA sequence, when it was contained in soy meal, where it did not perform the function for which it was protected); *see also Kilger/Feldges/Jaenichen*, 87 J. Pat. & Trademark Off. Soc'y 569 (2005) (for the German perspectives of purpose-limited compound protection for the sequences of human genes in German Patent Act).

65 DPMA, 2008, 29.

66 *Lundbeck v. Generics Ltd.* [2008] EWCA Civ 311, para 54.

67 *Domeij*, 2000, 85 *et seqq.*; *Merges/Duffy*, 2011, 399.

suche case, the BGH held that as a consequence of dependent patents, the product patent kept its economic value, since in order to exploit the use patent, the later patentee would need the approval of the product patentee. Accordingly, the earlier patent retained its full validity with respect to third parties regarding the use protected by the later patent. [68] This increases the value of the product patent and allows the holder to exploit the exclusive right of the earlier patent.[69]

b) Hierarchy of pharmaceutical patents

The hierarchy of pharmaceutical patents can be established according to the scope of patents. The most valuable is *a compound patent*, because it affords absolute compound protection in that it covers a product independent of its formulation, manufacture, or use and without regard to how much of the patented compound it contains, as long as it contains an active ingredient covered by the compound patent.[70]

A medical use patent covers the (un)approved second or further medical use of a previously patented compound with a first medical use.[71] Since this type of patent also covers any product claiming the protected medical use, it is the second most valuable patent. However, given the problems of enforcement associated with this type of patent, it is not easy to encourage pharmaceutical manufacturers to invest their R&D resources in this new use of old drugs. [72] Induced infringement can be found only when a drug product has an instruction for the other's patent-protected medical use. The off-label

---

68 *BGH/Klinische Versuche (Clinical Trials)*, GRUR 1996, 109, 115. Since official translations of materials in language other than English are not always available, the author did it by consulting other's translation or by herself. For accuracy, please check its original version.

69 *BGH/Klinische Versuche (Clinical Trials)*, GRUR 1996, 109, 115.

70 *Nastelski*, IIC 1972, 267, 271-72 (noting an unlimited protection provided to the patented product which has no definite external form, and only the patentee is authorized to make the product or the chemical substance commercially, to bring it into commerce, to offer it for sale or to use it.); *Grubb/Thomsen*, 2010, 77' *Voet*, 2011, 60; *SmithKline Beecham Corp. v. Apotex Corp.*, 403 F.3d 1331, 1341-42 (Fed. Cir. 2005) (holding no matter how small the amount is, as long as the product contains a compound protected by a patent, it infringes the compound patent.).

71 *Voet*, 2011, 60.

72 *Eisenberg*, 5 Yale J. Health Pol'y L. & Ethics 717, 724-25 (2005).

use by the doctors[73] - the prescription of a medication in a manner different from that approved by regulatory authorities - can be a serious problem for the patentee of a new medical use seeking to enforce his patent right.

The remaining types of patents can be ranked below the previous two. The scope of these patents is normally narrow, and sometimes excessively specific. Consider, for example, the scope of a patent covering a product manufacturing process. As the Imperial Supreme Court of Germany held in 1888, the protection of a manufacturing process included those products made directly by the protected process.[74] However, it cannot prevent anyone from making the same products by a completely different method, if any.[75] In addition, a patent might be less useful for a process than a product, because it is more difficult to prove patent infringement for a process.[76] A process patent can be enforceable when the use of that process invention can be determined from the end-product or from other evidence, such as trace impurities.[77] For this reason, TRIPS requires that the onus of proof is reversed and imposed upon the alleged infringer of the patented process if the compound is novel.[78]

This narrow but overly specific claim often makes it very difficult to design around the patent. A patent with a very narrow scope of protection can therefore be extremely valuable in preventing the market entry of generic versions.[79] As patents for compounds, new uses and processes offer different strategic values to the patent holder, industries often recognize the hierarchical differences and strategically seek protection accordingly.

---

73 *Stafford*, 358 N. Engl. J. Med., 1427 (2008).

74 *Methylenblau*, 22 Reichsgericht in Zivilsachen 8 (holding "the product manufactured by means of the (protected) process does not fall outside of subject-matter of invention, and constitutes the end-point as characterized by patent law. Thus the process comprises the product manufactured by the by said process as part of the subject-matter of the invention.").

75 *Grubb/Thomsen*, 2010, 77-78; *Nastelski*, IIC 1972, 267, 272 (a third party patent on method of preparation or forms of use of the product is dependent on the product patent, and he cannot practice his patent commercially without the approval of the holder of the product patent.).

76 *Cohen/Nelson/Walsh*, 2000, 10.

77 *Grubb/Thomsen*, 2010, 245.

78 TRIPS Art. 34 (Process Patents: Burden of Proof), In other words, the court would assume that it has been produced by the patented process unless the alleged infringer would prove otherwise.

79 See subsection V.D.3.d).

2. Innovations in pharmaceutical field

The pharmaceutical industry has been referred to as one of the best examples of an industry for which patents are regarded as socially desirable, since incentives arising from patents appear to be prerequisites for the vast majority of pharmaceutical innovations. If there is an invention that cannot be categorized as such, however, its protection might be unjustified. Therefore, it will be helpful to define what pharmaceutical innovation is and what it is not.

a) Invention v. innovation

The distinction between invention and innovation returns us to Schumpeter's Theory of Economic Development.[80] Schumpeter distinguishes the act of innovation, which is a new combination of known and/or unknown means of production, from the act of invention, which creates a new means of production.[81] He further argues that invention of itself does not produce an economically relevant effect.[82] In contrast, innovation brings incessant changes in economics through a so-called "process of creative destruction."[83] Eisenberg notes that an innovation may be defined as putting existing inventions to practical use.[84] Svatos argues that the innovation is the final product that appears on the market and is different from the invention for which a patent was granted.[85] He further argues that patents therefore stimulate a combi-

80 *Nelson/Winter*, 1982, 263.

81 *Schumpeter*, 1964, 100-101 (Innovation comprises: (1) the introduction of a new good or of a new quality of a good; (2) the introduction of a new method of production which includes a new way of handling a commodity commercially; (3) the opening of a new market for the good, irrespective of the prior existence of the market; (4) the conquest of a new source of supply of raw materials or half-manufactured goods; (5) the carrying out of the new organization of any industry, such as the creation of a monopoly position or the breaking up of a monopoly position.); *Schumpeter*, 1942, 139-140 (mentioning the competition of these types of innovations); He distinguished these two without mentioning "innovation," which appears in his later publication, *Business Cycle*, 1939, 84).

82 *Schumpeter*, 1939, 80.

83 *Schumpeter*, 1942, 137-38.

84 *See e.g., Eisenberg*, 56 U. Chi. L. Rev. 1017, 1036-37 (1989).

85 *Svatos*, 13 Soc. Philos. Policy 113, 122 (1996).

nation of invention and marketing skill.[86] Merges similarly holds that "[a]n invention refers to the practical implementation of the inventor's idea. [...] An innovation is the 'debugged' and functional version of the invention: the version first offered for sale."[87] He further contends that the innovation significantly differs from the invention because of the changes necessary to turn the invention into a commercial product.[88] While the distinction between invention and innovation is somewhat simplified, since the process of development is a continuum,[89] the two ends, i.e. invention and innovation are relatively easy to distinguish.

Chronologically, once an invention has been made, substantial investment is often needed to ready the invention for the market.[90] Such investment can involve the construction of a new plant or equipment, promotion or advertisement.[91] Indeed, innovation, in conjunction with investment and development, is more sensitive to economic variables than invention.[92] Converting inventions into innovations is a core feature of technological progress.[93]

b) NMEs as the core of pharmaceutical innovation

Every product available on the pharmaceutical market which is developed from an invention can be considered an innovation. However, the significance of an innovation can vary substantially between a second generation product and new medical entities ("NMEs").[94] In other words, for some products, such as NMEs, substantial investment in preclinical and clinical trials to meet regulatory requirements must be made to bring the invention to market, in contrast to second generation products. More importantly, NMEs are basic inventions that bring constant changes in market economics

---

86 *Svatos*, 13 Soc. Philos. Policy 113, 122 (1996).

87 *Merges*, 76 Cal. L. R. 803, 807 (1988).

88 *Merges*, 76 Cal. L. R. 803, 807 (1988) (also noted this distinction between invention and innovation has been criticized as a simplified dualism by some economists, who argue that the process of development is actually much more of a continuum).

89 *Nelson/Winter*, 1982, 263-64; *Merges*, 76 Cal. L. R. 803, 807 (1988).

90 *See e.g., Eisenberg*, 56 U. Chi. L. Rev. 1017, 1037 (1989).

91 *See e.g., Eisenberg*, 56 U. Chi. L. Rev. 1017, 1037 (1989).

92 *Scherer*, 1984, 26.

93 *Chandy, et al.*, 43 J. Marketing Res. 494 (2006).

94 See subsection II.D.1.

through various second generation products. Thus, NMEs are the really valuable innovations in the pharmaceutical industry. In this context, we must question whether current patent protection for pharmaceuticals incentivizes R&D of truly valuable innovation.

C. Second generation inventions and patents in pharmaceuticals

As noted above, some evidence in the cases involving second generation inventions is complicated.[95] After a basic research period, leading to the identification of a "lead compound", the typical procedure in developing a medicine can be briefly summarised as follows: "With the selection of the lead compound, the chemist and biologist embark on an extensive program to improve its potency, the specificity of biological effect with concomitant reduction in toxicity, oral absorption, duration of action, metabolic profile and pharmacokinetic pattern. This typically involves extensive structure-activity relationship ("SAR") studies."[96]

The lead compound or the lead compound series are to be patentable,[97] and generally, the outputs from subsequent developments are also the objects of patent protections. Using the concept of basic and second generation inventions, the lead compound will be the *basic invention*, and the following inventions will be *second generation inventions.* The second generation inventions from the lead compound can be salts, esters, ethers, polymorphs, metabolites, pure form, particle size, isomers, mixtures of isomers, com-

95 *Laboratoires Servier v. Apotex*, [2008] EWHC Civ 445, para 41.

96 *deStevens*, 1990, 266; *Domeij*, 2000, 26.

97 *deStevens*, 1990, 266; *Domeij*, 2000, 26.

plexes, combinations and other derivatives of known substance, and the like. These inventions are eligible for patent protection in most jurisdictions.[98]

Beyond second generation, there can be (n+2) generation inventions, such as, a new crystal form of a known salt of a basic medication,[99] a new use of a known metabolite, [100] solvates or hydrates of a known salt form, and the like. However, all of these types of invention will be comprehensively referred to as second generation inventions in this dissertation since all such inventions arise subsequent to the basic invention.

The relevant inventions, patents and types of claims for second generation inventions are explained briefly here, according to the three types, i.e. product patents, use patents, and process patents.

1. Product inventions and patents

a) Species selection inventions

In the U.S., the United States Patent and Trademark Office ("USPTO") defines *a species selection invention* as an invention that is a different embodiment or a species that could fall within the scope of a generic invention.[101] Further, a generic invention should require no material element ad-

---

98 In some jurisdictions, such as India, these cannot be patent eligible if these second generation inventions are regarded as the mere discoveries of new properties or new uses for a known substance. *See* Sec. 3(d) of Indian Patents Act, 1970 ("The mere discovery of a new form of a known substance which does not result in the enhancement of the known efficacy of that substance or the mere discovery of any new property or new use for a known substance or of the mere use of a known process, machine or apparatus unless such known process results in a new product or employs at least one new reactant."); *see further* Manual of Patent Office Practice and Procedure in India, 08.03.05.04 (Ver. 01.11, as modified on March 22, 2011) ("Explanation: For the purposes of this clause, salts, esters, ethers, polymorphs, metabolites, pure form, particle size, isomers, mixtures of isomers, complexes, combinations and other derivatives of known substance ***shall be considered to be the same substance, unless they differ significantly in properties with regard to efficacy***." [Emphasis added]).

99 *E.g., Laboratoires Servier v. Apotex*, [2008] EWHC Civ 445 (crystalline forms of tert-butylamine salt of perindopril were claimed).

100 *E.g., Teva v. Merrell* [2007] EWHC 2276 (Ch) (the new uses of a metabolite of a known substance were claimed).

101 U.S. Patent & Trademark Office, Manual of Patent Examining Procedure (8th ed 2010) ("MPEP"), § 806.04; *see also Chisum*, 2012, § 12.03[3].

ditional to those required by a species invention and each species invention must require all of the limitations of the generic invention.[102] Similarly, in Europe, EPO considers that a selection invention deals with the selection of individual elements, which have not been explicitly mentioned within a larger known set as a selection invention.[103]

Markush type claim

The use of a Markush type claim[104] was first reported in a U.S. case involving Eugene Markush, who filed a patent application in 1924 for pyrazolone dyes where a generic structure was claimed.[105] This type of claim is used when no generic term describes the desired individual species that share common significant features, similar properties or activities, or at least one common function, or which have an equivalent basis for categorization in the same group.[106] The scope of this kind of claim in chemistry is limited by the compounds that can be manufactured by combining various alternatives mentioned for the different positions in the formula. One famous example is a claim in respect of a cheese cigarette filter, which reads: "A cigarette filter according to claim1 in which the cheese comprises grated particles of cheese selected from a group comprising Parmesan, Romano, Swiss and Cheddar cheeses."[107]

Although there are some downsides to using it,[108] this type of claim is very popular and common as it has several advantages. It may offer broader protection for the patentee and it is easier to file as one multinational patent

---

102 MPEP § 806.04 (d).

103 EPO Examination Guidelines"), G-VI, 8.

104 Markush type claims are one of the formats of claiming, such as Jepson type claims, product-by-process claims, means-plus-function claims, step-plus-function claims, and the like.

105 *Fitt*, 20 Biotechnol. Law Rep. 17, 18 (2010).

106 *See e.g., Durham*, 1999, 57; *Valance*, 1 J. Chemical Documentation, 87, 87-88 (1961); *Miller/Evans*, 2010, 146-48.

107 U.S. Patent No. 3,234,948 (February 15, 1966, under the title of "Cheese-Filter Cigarette").

108 These disadvantages could be the difficulty to search through the normal database, increased prosecution time and examination errors, undermining their status as the prior arts, and being unclear in their scope of protection, *see e.g. Brown*, 31 J. Chem. Inf. Comp. Sci. 2, 3-4 (1991) (also noting "it is unreasonable to expect that so many compounds will exhibit activity similar to the activity shown by substances for which practical data is supplied.").

application rather than several separate patent applications. Furthermore, it can provide the licensor with a stronger basis for cross-licensing agreements with licensees, who own improvement (selection) patents that use the licensor's invention.[109]

The following is an example of a Markush type claim in U.S. Patent No. 4,115,574,[110] which can also be referred to as a "*genus" claim.*

1. A thieno[2,3-b][1,5]benzodiazepine compound of the formula

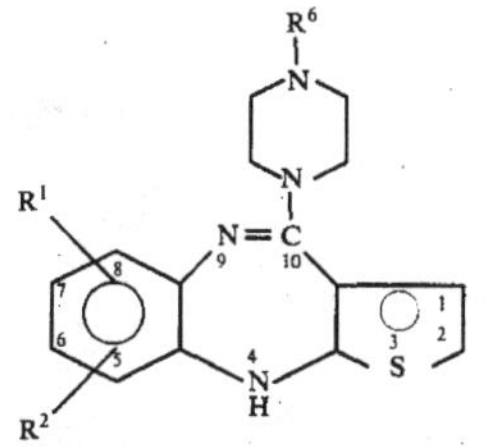

or a pharmaceutically acceptable acid addition salt thereof, wherein R[1] and R[2] independently represent hydrogen, C_{1-4} alkyl, halogen, C_{1-4} haloakyl, nitro, amino, C_{1-4} alkoxy, C_{1-4} alkylthio or a group of the formula $—SO_2N(R^4)_2$ where R^4 is C_{1-4} alkyl; wherein R^6 is hydrogen, phenyl, halophenyl, C_{1-4} alkyl, C_{1-4} carbalkoxy or $—(CH_2)_nOH$ where *n* is 2 or 3; and wherein the thiophene ring is unsubstituted or is substituted by a C_{1-4} alkyl group in the 2-position.

(Underlines added).

109 *Brown*, 31 J. Chem. Inf. Comp. Sci. 2, 2-3 (1991); *see also Miller/Evans*, 2010, 146-48 (noting "the power of Markush claiming is most evident when combinations of Markush groups are all used within the same claim. The number of possible embodiments of the invention multiplies in a combinatorial fashion not practically reproduced by drawing all of the embodiments separately.").

110 U.S. Patent No. 4,115,574 (September 19, 1978, under the title of "Benzodiazepine derivatives"), this claim was simpler than the correspondent claim of a U.K. patent, and is a good example of a basic invention.

A species claim

About 15 years after U.S. Patent No. 4,115,574 was granted, a combination of the optional variables mentioned above, such as R^1, R^2, and the substitution in the thiophene ring, was filed by the same applicant as follows:[111]

1. 2-Methyl-10-(4-methyl-1-piperazinyl)-4H-thieno[2,3-b][1,5]benzodiazepine, or an acid addition salt thereof.

This is referred to as a *"species" claim* because it is a claim directed to a specific species from a genus.

The compound named above has the following chemical formula:

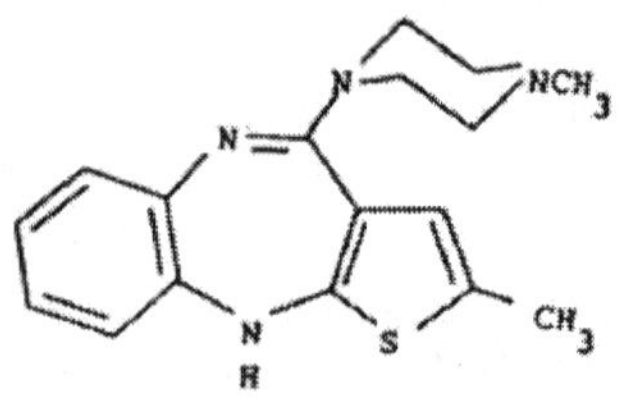

One can arrive at this formula *by selecting the underlined groups from the above "genus" claim* 1 of the U.S. Patent, i.e., C_1 alkyl(-CH_3) group for R^6; hydrogens for both R^1 and R^2; and the thiophen ring, which is substituted by a C_1 alkyl (-CH_3) group in the 2-position. This compound was later named "Olanzapine". It is evident that the structure of the compound itself was already disclosed in the prior art as one of the possible combinations, although it was not disclosed specifically. This kind of invention, like the invention of "Olanzapine" is achieved through a specific and particular selection from a group disclosed in the prior art, and thus is referred to as a species selection invention.

111 U.S. Patent No. 5,229,382 (July 20, 1993, under the title of "2-methyl-thieno-benzodiazepine").

b) Optical isomers

Organic chemical compounds contain carbon atoms ("C"s) which are covalently bonded to other atoms. Each carbon atom normally forms four bonds.[112] If a carbon atom has four single bonds, the four other atoms around the carbon atom usually form a tetrahedral spatial arrangement (See Figure 1).[113] Compounds with the same molecular formula or atomic composition, but with a different spatial arrangement are called *stereoisomers*. *Optical isomers*[114] are one type of stereoisomers and can be classified further into enantiomers and diastereomers.[115] *Enantiomers* are a pair of stereoisomers that differ only in their spatial arrangements and have at least one "stereocenter," which is a carbon atom (C) with four different groups attached.[116] The spatial structure is the nonsuperimposable mirror image of the other, designated "chiral," which is derived from the Greek *cheir*, meaning "hand."[117] Its three dimensional molecular structure is depicted with wedges and dashes and the enantiomers of the amino acid alanine are presented in Figure 1 as an example. Various naming conventions are used to distinguish between the enantiomers, such as "(+)" or "(-)", "(d)" or "(l)", "(D)" or "(L)",

---

112 *William* 1999, 18.

113 *Macomber*, 1996, 97 (Further noting the study of this kind of three-dimensional structure of molecule and the spatial relationship among the atoms is called stereochemistry. *Macomber*, 1996, 189).

114 This is because a pure enantiomer rotates plane-polarized light in a particular direction, such as clockwise, or counterclockwise.

115 ***"Diastereomers"*** are the optical isomers which occur when there are more than one chiral centers in the compound and which are non-superimposable, non-mirror images of others. And ***"epimers"*** are diastereomers that differ in configuration of only one stereogenic center.

116 For example, two different mirror-imaged forms are a "right handed form" and a "left-handed form." In Figure 5, the carbon atom in the center is a stereocenter to which four different groups has been attached, namely –COOH, -NH_2, -CH_3, and H. The solid wedge is used to indicate that the methyl group (–CH3) is projecting out of the page (toward to the viewer), while the hashed line indicates that the hydrogen atom (H) is behind the page (away from the viewer). Some compounds having more than two chiral centers result in multiple possible three-dimensional arrangements which are known as diastereomers.

117 *See generally William* 1999, 612-613; *see also Ortho-McNeil Pharm., Inc. v. Mylan Labs., Inc.*, 348 F. Supp. 2d 713, 720 (N.D.W.Va. 2004), *aff'd*, 161 Fed.Appx. 944 (these kinds enantiomeric compounds are thus often analogized to a person's left and right hands).

and "(R)" or "(S)",[118] and for the racemates, "(±)" or "(dl)" or (RS) are used.[119] A "*racemic mixture*" or a "*racemate*" refers to an equal mixture of R and S enantiomers.[120]

Figure 1: Example of an enantiomer - an amino acid, alanine.

(*S*)-alanine mirror plane (*R*)-alanine

Research into drug chirality has been underway since 1874.[121] Although enantiomers have nearly identical physical properties, they often have different activities and side effect profiles. This has long been recognized both by academia, by industry and by regulatory authorities.[122] These are the medications that are separated from the racemate mixtures; the components obtained are responsible for beneficial pharmacological action, while other components that are usually responsible for side effects are excluded.[123] More than half of the drugs listed in the *Pharmacopoeia*[124] are chiral

118 These systems are not interchangeable.

119 Unless otherwise indicated, R/S system is used in this paper.

120 Racemates are normally produced through a chemical reaction which prepares a chiral compound from an achiral compound in normal conditions.

121 *Mansfield/Henry/Tonkin*, 43 Clin. Pharmacokinet. 287, 287 (2004).

122 *Caldwell*, 16 Hum. Psychopharm. S67, S67, S70 (2001) (noting the existence of optical enantiomer was recognized in 1848, and the research into enantiomers has become to be more active since 1980s according to the technical progresses on separation, analysis, and production on an industrial scale of enantiomers); *Darrow*, 2 Stan. Tech. L. Rev. 1, para 7 (2007) (noting enantiomers can exhibit substantially different biological, pharmacological, or toxicological activity).

123 *The National Institute for Health Care Management Research and Educational Foundation ("NIHCM")*, 2002, 5.

124 *Pharmacopoeia* is a book containing directions for the identification of samples and the preparation of compound medicines, and published by the authority of a government or a medical or pharmaceutical society.

molecules,[125] including many of the world's best-selling products, such as Lipitor®, Plavix® and Nexium®.[126] Other well-known chiral drugs include Ibuprofen, Claritin®, Allegra®, Prilosec®, Zyrtec®, and even thalidomide.[127]

Enantiomer patents claim selected individual enantiomers of racemic mixtures that were previously disclosed in the prior art, mainly, their basic patents. For this reason, an enantiomer patent may be categorized as a selection invention. The importance of enantiomer patents is reflected in the "patent cliff"[128] threat by the expiration of enantiomer patents on blockbuster chiral drugs.[129] Knowledge of the structure of one enantiomer, or of a racemate, necessarily furnishes a person skilled in the art with knowledge of the structure of the other or both enantiomers.[130] This leads to a fundamental inquiry regarding the novelty or obviousness of enantiomer inventions.[131] The validity of enantiomer patents has often been challenged, mostly by generic pharmaceutical companies on the grounds of lack of novelty, lack of inventive step, lack of utility, double patenting, and insufficiency of disclosure.[132]

---

125 *Ariëns/Wuis*, 42 Clin. Pharmacol. Ther.361, 361-62 (1987) (showing 949 out of 1675 drugs listed in the *Pharmacopoeia* were chiral, 461 of the 469 natural or semisynthetic chiral products (98.3%) are single enantiomers, but only 58 of 480 synthetic chiral products (12.1%) are single enantiomers).

126 *IMS Health*, 2010 (the top three best-selling global drugs from 2007 to 2009 and top three out of top four best-selling global drugs in 2010 are single enantiomers).

127 *Darrow*, 2 Stan. Tech. L. Rev. 1, para 2 (2007).

128 *See* chapter III.B.3; *See also Mansell*, 1 Scrip Executive Briefing 1, 1–16, (2008) (explaining that "patent cliff" is a term for the loss of revenue which occurs when the monopoly granted by patents is lost and the generic versions of drugs enter into the market. It is expected that the patent cliff reaches its peak in 2010-2011 as patents of many blockbusters including SanofiAventis' Clopidogrel, Pfizer's Atorvastatin, and others expire.).

129 *Agranat/Wainschtein*, 15 Drug Discov. Today, 163, 169 (2010).

130 *Darrow*, 2 Stan. Tech. L. Rev. 1, paras 5-6 (2007).

131 *See e.g., Darrow*, 2 Stan. Tech. L. Rev. 1, paras 5-6 (2007).

132 *Agranat/Wainschtein*, 15 Drug Discov. Today, 163, 163 (2010); *Darrow*, 2 Stan. Tech. L. Rev. 1, para 3 (2007) (noting the patentability of chiral molecules has taken on increased significance and is a subject of litigation.).

c) Crystalline forms

Polymorphs are different crystalline forms of the same compound. Polymorphism denotes the ability of a material to exist in more than one form or crystal structure. It was discovered in the 19th century that many substances could be crystallized into solids with different melting points and crystal habits.[133] The molecules in the crystalline form are arranged in an organized pattern called a "lattice"; which is different from an amorphous form, in which the molecules are randomly distributed.[134] Among the substances that exist in crystalline form, some can be in one crystalline form, which is referred to as a monomorphic substance, for example, wax or common window glass. Others that exist in more than one organized pattern, such as the cocoa butter in chocolate,[135] are referred to as polymorphs. According to the shape of the crystals, polymorphs can often exhibit different physico-chemical properties, such as stability, solubility, hygroscopicity,[136] and hardness,[137] although their chemical composition is identical in all forms. Examples among drugs include Ranitidine (Zantac®), Paroxetine (Deroxat®), and Cefnidir (Omnicef ®). A patent for a polymorph can be extremely valuable when the patent covers the most stable form at ambient conditions, considering that less stable forms may spontaneously convert to the most stable form.

Co-crystals such as solvates or hydrates are called *pseudo-polymorphs*. If the substances are dissolved in a solution, they are normally recovered by evaporation of the solvent. [138] If this evaporation is conducted with carefully controlled parameters (e.g. "in water solvent," such as humidity, or drying / evaporating), some substances can retain a certain number of water

---

133 *Brittain*, 2009, 1.

134 *Giron*, 73 J. Thermal Analysis & Calorimetry 441, 441-42 (2003).

135 Cacao butter could exist in six different crystalline forms; the most thermodynamically stable form (form VI) has a dull surface and soft texture; however, form V is the most appreciated by consumer and shows the crispy hardness and glossy surface. In order to make chocolates crystallize exclusively in the preferable form (form V), the crystallization process must be controlled by a sophisticated temperature regime, *see in general, Von der Freien*, 39 Chemie in Unserer Zeit, 416, 423 (2005).

136 "Hygroscopicity" means the readiness of a substance to absorb moisture from the atmosphere.

137 *Brittain*, 2009, 2-3.

138 *Seager/Slabaugh*, 2010, 279.

molecules as part of the solid crystalline structure.[139] This type of crystalline form is called a "*hydrate.*"[140] If the same procedures are followed "in a solvent other than water," the resulting crystalline form is called a "*solvate*".[141]

Claims to polymorphs can be suitably drafted by using their physicochemical parameters, which are determined by Single crystal X-ray diffraction (SXD), X-ray powder diffraction (XRPD), Infrared(IR)- or Raman spectroscopy, solid state 13C-Nuclear Magnetic Resonance (NMR) spectroscopy, and the like. Thus, in a properly drafted claim for polymorphs, many figures are listed.[142]

d) Metabolites and prodrugs

Metabolites are substances produced in the body through the metabolism of other substances and in some cases are responsible for the pharmacological effects observed. The *metabolism* of substances absorbed in the body makes the ingested substance more water-soluble and readily excreted by the kidney.[143] This is one of the major pathways by which a xenobiotic substance, such as a medication, is inactivated.[144] However, it is not uncommon to find that a metabolite itself has pharmacological effects, while the parent medication that is metabolized to it does not.

Prodrugs are bioreversible derivatives of active drugs. The active ingredients exerting the pharmacological effects are released through biotrans-

---

139 *Seager/Slabaugh*, 2010, 279.

140 *Seager/Slabaugh*, 2010, 279 (the retained water in the crystalline structure is called the water of hydration, and according to the number(n) of water molecules in the crystalline structure, they are called anhydrate (n=0), ***hemihydrates*** (n=1/2), monohydrate (n=1), dihydrate (n=2), and the like.).

141 *Giron*, 73 J. Thermal Analysis & Calorimetry 441, 442 (2003) (further noting solvates were new crystalline compounds formed with the solvent, i.e. were the combination of solvent molecules with the compound molecules).

142 Claim 1 of GB Patent No. 1,543,238 (March 28, 1979, under the title of "Polymorph of Cimetidine")
A substantially crystallographically pure polymorphic form of Cimetidine (Cimetidine A) which is characterised by an infra red spectrum (1% KBr disc) having very strong, broad peaks at 1400 and 1385cm^{-1}, a strong, sharp peak at 1205 cm^{-1} and a medium-sharp peak at 1155 cm^{-1} and having no peak at 1180 cm^{-1}.

143 *Ionescu/Caira*, 2005, 3.

144 *Ionescu/Caira*, 2005, 41.

formation in the body. Prodrugs account for 5-7% of the drugs approved worldwide.[145] Prodrugs are chemicals with little or no pharmacological activity, but they are used to improve the efficacy of established drugs.[146] Through this approach, one can improve the bioavailability of the active drugs or make oral administration possible by overcoming poor solubility, instability, insufficient oral absorption, local irritation, and the like.[147] Examples of prodrugs include the well-known proton pump inhibitor[148] Omeprazole, the ACE inhibitor[149] Enalapril, and the antibiotic Hetacillin.[150]

Figure 2: A simplified representative illustration of the prodrug concept[151]

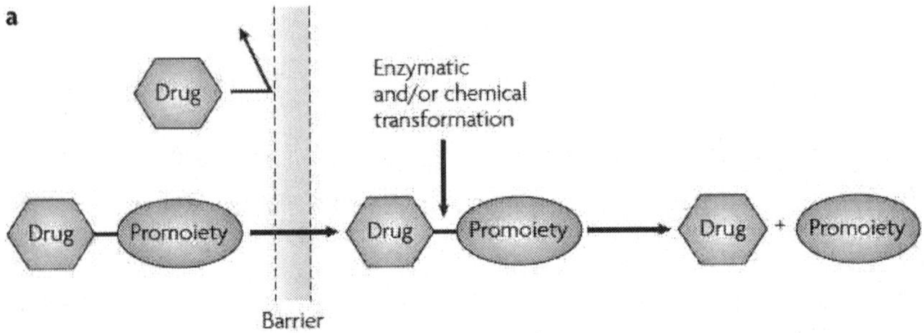

a | The drug–promoiety is the prodrug that is typically pharmacologically inactive. In broad terms, the barrier can be thought of as any liability or limitation of a parent drug that prevents optimal (bio)pharmaceutical or pharmacokinetic performance, and which has to be overcome for the development of a marketable drug. The drug and promoiety are covalently linked via bioreversible groups that are chemically or enzymatically labile, such as those shown here. The 'ideal' prodrug yields the parent drug with high recovery ratios, with the promoiety being non-toxic.

---

145 *Rautio, et al.*, 7 Nat. Rev. Drug Discov. 255, 255 (2009); *Oellerich/Armstrong*, 47 Clin. Chem. 805, 805 (2001).
146 *Ionescu/Caira*, 2005, 372.
147 *Rautio, et al.*, 7 Nat. Rev. Drug Discov. 255, 255 (2009); *Oellerich/Armstrong*, 47 Clin. Chem. 805, 805 (2001).
148 A proton pump inhibitor has long-lasting effect to reduce the gastric acid production and used for the treatment of a couple of disorders related to the over-secretion of gastric acid, such as gastritis or peptic ulcer disease.
149 An ACE inhibitor is an "angiotensin-converting-enzyme" inhibitor and used for the treatment of hypertension and congestive heart failure.
150 *Hansen/Hirsch*, 1997, 342.
151 *Rautio, et al.*, 7 Nat. Rev. Drug Discov. 255, 256 (2009).

How substances are categorized depends on when their characteristic is identified. Two main cases may be distinguished. If the pharmacological effect of a medication is due to the transformation of a drug into a metabolite, the medication may be called “a drug” and an “active metabolite”. If, on the other hand, said effect is due to the release of the drug from a larger chemical entity, then the medication may be called “a drug” and “a prodrug”.

e) Esters and salts

Esters are chemical compounds that react with water to produce alcohols and organic or inorganic acids. Thus, when a medication is in alcohol form, it can be converted to its ester form via reaction with acids. In turn, when this ester form is administered to the patient, it will be hydrolyzed in the physiological condition to yield alcohols or acids that will have pharmacological effects.[152] Aspirin, which is remarkably versatile, is an acetyl *ester* of salicylic acid.[153]

Salts are compounds that result from the neutralization reaction of a base and an acid. Salts are composed of positively charged ions (cations) and negatively charged ions (anions); and can be organic or inorganic (metallic).[154] Salt forms may enhance absorption in the body or the stability of product, or they may be formulation-friendly.

f) Dosage forms

A dosage form is the entity administered to patients in order that that they receive an effective dose of a drug, such as tablets, capsules, injections, and transdermal patches.[155] These kinds of inventions may include different strengths, an extended release form, or another delivery system such as an inhaler, or implanted device.[156] A sustained release drug delivery system, for example, aims to maintain therapeutic blood levels of the drug for an extended period by controlling the rate of release of the drug from the dosage

152 *Seager/Slabaugh*, 2010, 481-82.
153 *Seager/Slabaugh*, 2010, 481.
154 *Seager/Slabaugh*, 2010, 278-79.
155 *Mahato/Narang*, 2012, 15-16.
156 *NIHCM*, 2002, 5.

form.[157] This can be achieved by providing multiple doses of a drug within a single dosage form, which are released at periodic intervals, or by delaying the timing of the first release.[158] Over the past forty years, the sustained release drug-delivery system has attracted considerable attention, since it can reduce the frequency of dosing, increase effectiveness of the drug by reducing the dose required, reduce the incidence of adverse effects, provide uniform drug delivery, and simplify dosing regimes.[159]

g) Combinations of active ingredients

A new product can be provided by combining the active ingredient of an approved drug with one or more other active ingredients.[160] As in other technical fields, a mixture of known substances can be patentable if it meets the requirements of patentability. For example, the combination of aspirin and another pain-killer, such as Naproxen,[161] can be created to enhance their analgesic or anti-inflammatory therapeutic effect; or a combination of two diuretics (amiloride and hydrochlorothiazide) with different mechanism of action can exhibit more than additive effects. Thus, said combinations can be claimed.[162]

2. Use inventions

a) New Use/New method of treatment

A medical indication is a symptom or particular circumstance indicating the advisability or necessity of a specific medical treatment or procedure. The nature of a medical use invention is based on a newly identified effect, and

---

157 *Jantzen/Robinson*, 2002, 748.
158 *Jantzen/Robinson*, 2002, 748.
159 *Jantzen/Robinson*, 2002, 747; *see also Actavis UK Ltd v. Novartis AG* [2010] EWCA Civ 82, para 62 (Jacob LJ noted a sustained release might provide better efficacy or fewer side effects or better compliance).
160 *NIHCM*, 2002, 5.
161 *E.g., Willkens/Segre*, 19 Arthritis & Rheumatism 677, 680-81 (2006).
162 *Merck & Co., Inc. v. Biocraft Laboratories, Inc.*, 874 F.2d 804 (Fed. Cir. 1989), *cert. denied,* 493 U.S. 975 (1989) (holding the patent was invalid because of lack of inventive step over prior art).

is a new teaching that results from that discovery.[163] Often, pharmaceuticals have several different indications. For example, aspirin was discovered as a highly effective pain-killer in 1897 by Hoffmann, Eichengrün and Dreser at Bayer. However, the mechanism of its action, namely the inhibition of the biosynthesis of prostaglandins from arachidonic acid, was first discovered by John Vane at the Royall College of Surgeons as late as 1971.[164] Since then, it has turned out to have many more additional therapeutic indications, especially in preventing heart attacks and strokes.[165] Revisiting old drugs in this way may lead to therapeutically interesting new discoveries, and new benefits to the patients. The industry has coined this repositioning approach "teaching an old drug new tricks."[166]

Patent law deals with medical treatment differently from other methods or use claims related to medicines. Medical treatment and procedures are often excluded subject matter for patenting, as is the case in Europe.[167] If a previously unknown substance is proven to have a novel therapeutic or diagnostic effect, a patent applicant can obtain an exclusive right to all uses of the substance.[168]

The prohibition in Europe has been relaxed by the introduction of the new provision of Art. 54(5) of the European Patent Convention ("EPC") 1973 regarding *first medical use*. The first medical use of a known substance can be patented, and has come to be regarded as a product patent. Moreover, if one can prove a second medical use for a substance, which was known to have a first therapeutic effect, it is possible to claim a second medical use as well. For a second medical use, the applicant would have exclusivity only on the *second medical use* in Europe.[169] The practice was derived from the EPO's G 5/83 decision[170] and various technical board of appeal cases regarding second medical use, is now finally based on the statutory language of the Art. 54(5) of EPC 2000. In the United States, however, patents on uses

---

163 *Klöpsch*, IIC 1982, 457, 467.

164 *Dutfield*, 2009, 17-20.

165 *Dutfield*, 2009, 20.

166 *Scudellari*, The Scientist, April 1, 2011.

167 European Patent Convention, Art. 53 (c).

168 Cf. However, in the past, if the substance was known, a patent could be granted neither on the product, which would be lacking in novelty, nor on the new use, as the patent grant would contravene the provision banning patents for medical procedures.

169 *Eisai/Second medical indication*, G 5/83, OJ EPO 1985, 64.

170 *Eisai/Second medical indication*, G 5/83, OJ EPO 1985, 64.

are limited to a particular "method-of-use", which does not protect the product as such.[171]

b) Dosage regime

Dosage regime provides instructions for the proper way to take a medication, such as "three times per day after a meal," "once a day before sleep," or "40 mg once a day in the morning for 4 to 8 weeks." For example, if the single novel feature of an invention is the direction "once a day prior to sleep" of a well-known substance to cure the same illness, the Enlarged BOA held that this use was not excluded from patentability under the EPC. [172]

3. Process inventions

a) Process

A chemical process invention denotes the invention of a process to manufacture a product. In Germany, since the *Kongo-Rot* decision in 1889,[173] so-called "analogous chemical processes"[174] are also patentable if the product resulting from the process demonstrates unexpected and advantageous characteristics or effects in comparison to known chemical products.[175] In the United Kingdom and under EPO practice, if a compound is patentable, both the claims directed to the compounds and to the process for the manufacture

---

171 *LabCorp v. Metabolite, Inc.*, 548 U.S. 124 (2006); *UNCTAD-ICTSD,* 2005, 356.

172 *Abbott Respiratory/Dosage Regime*, G 2/08 (2010) (a referral to the Enlarged Board of Appeal for the decision that a feature of a claim relating to a specific dosage regime reflected a medical activity which was excluded from patentability under Art. 52(4) EPC 1973, *Kos Lifesciences/ Dosage regimen*, T 1319/04, OJ EPO 2009, 36).

173 *Kongo-Rot*, Decision of the Reichsgericht (Imperial Supreme Court) of May 8, 1889, Patentblatt 1889, 209, 212.

174 "Analogous chemical processes" are processes for making a new chemical product. These processes are neither chemically new nor unusual, have different starting materials but with an analogous constitution, interacting with one another in the same procedural manner (or same starting analogous procedural manner) to obtain definite new chemical products of a new constitution corresponding to specific expectation.

175 *Nastelski*, IIC 1972, 267, 269-70.

of that compound are patentable, even if the starting material and the process are already known.[176] In the United States, this type of analogous process patent is considered to be obvious,[177] unless it is a biotechnological process.[178]

b) Intermediates

Intermediates are compounds that normally have no pharmaceutical activities on their own, but can be used in a chemical process to manufacture an active pharmaceutical ingredient. They are patentable either by their function in a chemical method of production or by the novel properties of the new end product.[179] A patent on an intermediate essential to produce the basic medicine could effectively prolong the control of the resulting drugs' markets.

D. Pharmaceutical products in the market

Although the value and size of innovation vary, every product available on the market developed from an invention, can be an innovation. Pharmaceutical innovations, namely, pharmaceutical products – more commonly known as medicines or drugs – are a fundamental component of both modern and traditional medicine.[180] It is essential that such products are safe, effective, and of good quality, and that they are prescribed and used rationally.[181] For this reason, they are heavily regulated and influenced by the types of pharmaceutical products that are already on the market. Incentives for a new innovation in this market need to account for market regulations. Accordingly, this chapter will explore the types of marketed products.

176 *Grubb/Thomsen*, 2010, 246.
177 *In re Durden*, 763 F.2d 1406, 1410 (Fed. Cir. 1985).
178 35 U.S.C. (2007) § 103(b).
179 *Hansen/Hirsch*, 1997, 345.
180 *WHO*, Pharmaceutical products, available at: http://www.who.int/topics/pharmaceutical_products/en/. (Last accessed on December 20, 2013).
181 *WHO*, Pharmaceutical products, available at: http://www.who.int/topics/pharmaceutical_products/en/. (Last accessed on December 20, 2013).

1. New medical entities, new molecular entities

An NME is an active ingredient that has never been marketed before in any form, or in the product containing it.[182] Thus, the manufacturers must prepare all of the efficacy and safety data through experiments and trials.[183] The first product with an International Non-proprietary Name ("INN") of an active ingredient can also be regarded as an NME. An INN is a unique name that is globally recognized; it is public property;[184] and it is given to a pharmaceutical substance as designated by the World Health Organization ("WHO"). The significance of NMEs and the current status of new drug development will be further elaborated in chapter III.B.2.

2. Similar or equivalent "me-too" products

Once a new medical structure with interesting pharmacological properties has been reported to the public, many other companies perform their own research around said identified structure, and the research that they undertake regarding the new medical structure is sometimes called "me-too" research.[185] A product resulting from this research is often derogatorily called a "me-too" product, because it follows the research prospects that others have already successfully identified. A "me-too" product can be any drug entity that is in the same class and is used for the same main indication as the prototype drug.[186] These may be also NMEs, and they will be subject to all preclinical and clinical trials to prepare the data necessary to meet the regulatory requirements.

In the sense that the research follows a relatively easier path of a previously identified medical structure, the follow on research leading to similar

---

182 *Paul, et al.*, 9 Nat. Rev. Drug Discov. 203, 203 (2010); *FDA*, Drugs@FDA Glossary of Terms, available at: http://www.fda.gov/Drugs/informationondrugs/ucm079436.htm#M (Last accessed on December 20, 2013); *Pisano*, 2006, 119 (noting "new molecular entities (NMEs)-both small molecules and biologics-").

183 *NIHCM*, 2002, 4.

184 *WHO*, International nonproprietary name, available at: http://www.who.int/medicines/services/inn/en/ (Last accessed on December 20, 2013); this INN can be also called as a "generic name" that is contrasting to the "brand name," however, in order to avoid any future confusion, this term is not used in this thesis.

185 *Hansen/Hirsch*, 1997, 324.

186 *Wertheimer/Santella/Chaney*, 17 J. Pharmaceut. Marketing Manage. 25, 29 (2005).

or equivalent products are viewed negatively. Furthermore, with regard to the efficacy of me-too products, some argue that a me-too drug has diminished value, serving merely to increase a pharmaceutical company's profits.[187] However, they provide several advantages. Firstly, they may offer wider choice for physicians and patients and can contribute to cost-containment in pharmaceutical care.[188] They enable physicians to treat diverse patients with precision and provide options when the first medicine treated is either ineffective or not tolerated.[189] In addition, they have been also associated with overall cost savings, especially through competition among drugs in a therapeutic class.[190]

Secondly, a me-too product differs from second generation products in that it is a product that is based on an NME. As they are based on new molecules, the improvement through me-too products is sometimes more valuable than improvement through second generation products. This is mainly because analogous studies provide molecules which have different characteristics. These molecules "are as different from the parent molecule as a recent car compared to a 40-year-old model."[191] Furthermore, once the drug is on the market, more people will be exposed to it. This may reveal rarer side effects, which sometimes cause the manufacturer to withdraw the drug from the market. However, it may also lead to the identification of further medical uses of the drug, such as in the cases of Minoxidil[192] or Sildenafil.[193]

Thirdly, they may manifest entirely new properties, which can lead a therapeutic derivative to become a new lead structure. A representative example of this is Imipramine synthesized as an analogue of the antipsychotic drug Chlorpromazine. Imipramine demonstrated antidepressive activity and has provided an effective therapy for the treatment of depression since

---

187 *See e.g.*, *Angell*, 2004, 75-76, 80-83; *Avorn*, 309 Science 669, 669 (2005).

188 *Wertheimer/Levy/O'Connor*, 2001, 79-82.

189 *Wertheimer/Levy/O'Connor*, 2001, 80-81.

190 *Wertheimer/Levy/O'Connor*, 2001, 100-105.

191 *Wermuth*, 2008, 129; *see also Wertheimer/Levy/O'Connor*, 2001, 78-79 (arguing that it was better to have multiple drugs in the same class).

192 *Zins*, 6 Clin. Dermatol. 132 (1988), minoxidil's hair growth activity was observed on the patents who took it for the treatment of hypertension.).

193 *Ghofrani/Osterloh/Grimminger*, 5 Nat. Rev. Drug Discov. 689 (2006); *Kling*, 1 Modern Drug Discov. 31 (1998), The sildenafil, an active ingredient of Viagra® was initially synthesized and studied for use in the treatment of hypertension and then of angina pectoris (a symptom of ischaemic heart disease).

1954.[194] Thus, a new drug that may seem similar to an older one can provide a major advance in pharmaceutical technology[195] and can become a true pharmaceutical innovation.

3. Second generation products

Second generation products result from follow-up R&D essentially based on an existing product (an NME) and have essentially the same mode of action.[196] These second generation products may have the same INN as the first product (e.g., second products involving *inter alia* new formulations, crystalline forms, particle sizes or medical uses) or a different one (e.g. combinations, individual stereoisomers separated from mixtures or metabolites of an existing INN).[197] They are also called Incrementally Modified Drugs ("IMDs"), which either rely on an active ingredient present in a drug already approved for the market, a closely related chemical derivative of such an ingredient,[198] or have been modified by the manufacturer, such as new formulations, combinations, salts or esters, and the like.[199] Although some commentators use different definitions for second generation products,[200] or for follow-on products,[201] this thesis will use the term "second generation products" according to the definition set out above.

194 *Wermuth*, 2008, 129.

195 *Wertheimer/Santella/Chaney*, 17 J. Pharmaceut. Marketing Manage. 25, 29-30 (2005) (reporting 81% of the drugs in the list of essential medicines by the World Health Organization were me-too products).

196 *DG Competition*, 2009, 351; *in general, Scotchmer*, 27 RAND J. Econ. 322, 329 (1996) (defining "improvements" as a new version of the patented product with greater commercial value).

197 *DG Competition*, 2009, 351.

198 Such as new salts or esters.

199 *NIHCM*, 2002, 4.

200 *Den Exter*, 17 Eur. J. Health L. 125, 131 (2010) (noting second generation drug as me-too products).

201 *Wertheimer/Santella/Chaney*, 17 J. Pharmaceut. Marketing Manage. 25, 29 (2005) (considering "follow-on drugs" as those that had approved indication in addition to their originally approved indication).

Re-evaluation of old drugs, such as single enantiomers, can be successful on occasions,[202] which can lead some companies specializing in chiral synthesis to develop single isomers and, subsequently, to enter into licensing agreements with the originators of the racemate.[203] These second generation products can certainly provide a high return on investment. The development of a medicine using an active ingredient, the safety and efficacy of which have already been established, is normally less time consuming, less expensive, and less risky than using a compound about which little is known. The high cost potential for IMDs can make modifying older products attractive.[204]

4. Generic drugs

A generic drug, or a "generic", is identical to or bioequivalent to a brand name drug in dosage, safety, strength, route of administration, quality, performance, and intended use. [205] A generic drug product must contain identical amounts of the same active ingredient(s) as the brand name product and have equal effect and little difference when substituted for the brand name product.[206] Although generic drugs are chemically identical to their branded counterparts, they are typically sold at substantially discounted prices from the branded prices. The U.S. Food and Drug Administration ("FDA") has noted that generic drugs save consumers an estimated $8 to $10 billion a year at retail pharmacies, and billions more can be saved when hospitals use generics.[207]

---

202 *Hutt/Valentová*, 50 Acta Facultatis Pharmaceuticae Universitatis Comenianae 7, 14 (2003) (noting failure of developing single enantiomers, such as dilevalol, sotalol, and fluoxetine).

203 *Tucker*, 355 Lancet 1085, 1085 (2000) (providing Sepracor as an example of these specialized companies); *see also Darrow*, 2 Stan. Tech. L. Rev. 1, para 113 (2007) (noting Sepracor obtained patents on single enantiomer versions of sixteen chiral drugs previously sold as racemates by other firms.).

204 *NIHCM*, 2002, 4.

205 *FDA*, available at: http://www.fda.gov/Drugs/ResourcesForYou/Consumers/QuestionsAnswers/ ucm100100.htm (Last accessed on December 20, 2013).

206 *FDA*, available at: http://www.fda.gov/Drugs/ResourcesForYou/Consumers/QuestionsAnswers/ ucm100100.htm (Last accessed on December 20, 2013).

207 FDA, Generic Drugs: Same Medicine, Lower Cost, available at: http:// www.fda.gov/downloads/ ForConsumers/ConsumerUpdates/UCM340458.pdf (Last accessed on December 20, 2013).

E. Summary

Since no invention can occur in a vacuum, today's technology depends upon yesterday's.[208] The path of invention and innovation in pharmaceutical technology is no exception. Inventions in pharmaceuticals can thus be divided into basic inventions and second generation inventions. When there is investment, these inventions become innovative products that reach the market.[209]

In this chapter, we have explored the disctinction between basic and second generation invention. As seen above, basic inventions can be developed into NMEs, which can then lead to second generation inventions, and the products that usually follow successful NMEs. Among the second generation inventions, species selection inventions have been shown to be different. Unlike other second generation inventions, a species selection invention can be another basic invention, in the sense that it can also be developed into an NME, which can in turn lead to other second generation inventions. In this sense, a species selection invention has a dual nature – it can be both a basic and a second generation invention.

In the product market, in addition to NMEs and second generation products, there are "me-too" products and generic drugs in the pharmaceutical market place. A me-too product is a drug entity that is in the same class and used for the same medical purposes as the prototype drug. However, these are also NMEs, since they are active ingredients that are marketed for the first time. In contrast, generic products are the bioequivalents of a reference drug in dosage, safety, strength, route of administration, quality, performance, and intended use, but are sold at a much lower price.

The definitions and concepts of inventions and products are crucial to understanding the law on the patentability of inventions, the market situation where the products a play role, and the phenomena that we are facing.[210] As presented in chapter I.C, selection inventions will be the focus of the discussion as representatives of second generation inventions.

---

208 *Luski/Wettstein*, 1 Probl. Perspect. Manage. 31, 31 (2004).

209 *Chandy, et al.*, 43 J. Marketing Res. 494 (2006).

210 See chapter III.B.

III. SPECIFICITIES IN PHARMACEUTICALS AND RECENT DEVELOPMENTS

A. *Innovating and inventing in pharmaceutical industry*

While the cumulative development of knowedge and path of innovation may still be the same, each industry has different and specific characteristics. These characteristics include the ease with which inventions can be imitated, the need for cumulative innovation rather than stand-alone development, the speed and cost of R&D. The extent to which patents cover an entire product or a mere component thereof, are all dependent on the industry.[211] The pharmaceutical industry has attracted attention among regulators and policy makers, because it is one of the most profitable and innovative industries and because its products are directly connected to public health. This chapter will explore the specific factors that distinguish the process of R&D and innovation in the pharmaceutical industry from that of other technological industries.

1. Specificities in the drug development process

a) Highly regulated industry

Few industries bear such high regulatory burdens on initial innovations as the pharmaceutical industry.[212] Without regulatory approval, any exclusivity is worthless since the product cannot be marketed. [213] The mission of the drug regulatory authority is to ensure that drugs marketed in a country are safe and effective. To do so, they review the evidence produced and submitted by the companies that seek to market drugs. This rigor on the part of regulatory authorities intensified in the aftermath of scares such as the adul-

---

211 *Burk/Lemley*, 89 Va. L. Rev. 1575, 1577 (2003).

212 *Bessen/Meurer,* 2008, 89; *Roin*, 87 Tex. L. Rev. 503, 516 (2009) (raising examples such as agricultural-chemicals and medical-equipment industries which are governed by regulatory regimes.).

213 *Teece*, 15 Res. Policy 285, 300 (1986).

terated sulfamilamide case in the United States and regulation became even more stringent following the thalidomide tragedy in the late 1950s and early 1960s.[214] The Vioxx®' withdrawal in 2004 was one of the most recent events that alarmed authorities.[215]

In order to ensure the safety of the public, it is right and proper that drugs be thoroughly tested and that information regarding safety and efficacy be produced before the drugs are marketed. This demanding requirement, however, typically leads to prolonged preclinical and clinical trials.[216] Moreover, the regulation has become ever more stringent over time.[217]

b) R&D – a costly and lengthy road to a medicine

The process of developing a drug typically is sequential. First, a compound is identified which may have promising therapeutic efficacy throughout lead compound identification and repeated chemical optimizations in the laboratory. Next, the selected compound must pass preclinical testing in vitro and in animals, a new drug application must be filed with the administrative authority, three phases of clinical trials in humans must be completed,[218] and

---

214 *Scherer*, 2007, 22; *William*, 1999, 87 (noting after the prescription of thalidomide for pregnant women to treat morning sickness, it was found that thalidomide was responsible for the fetal defects, and that one of enantiomers was responsible for the beneficial effect and the other was for the side effect.); *Mann/Andrews*, 2007, 3 (also mentioning after this thalidomide disaster, drug regulatory mechanisms of today had been established).

215 *Horton*, 364 Lancet 1995, 1995 (2004).

216 Clinical development accounts for around 63% of the costs for developing each NME, and 53% of the costs are incurred from Phase II to launch. *See e.g., Paul, et al.*, 9 Nat. Rev. Drug Discov. 203, 205 (2010).

217 *Dutfield*, 2009, 295-96; *Federsel*, 18 Bioorgan. Med. Chem. 5775, 5777 (2010).

218 Phase I trial is performed on a small number of (usually) healthy volunteers to obtain information on toxicity and safe dosage ranges in human. In phase II trial, the drug is administered to a large number of individuals who were selected from the patients for whom the drug is intended to be beneficial. In final phase III trial, many patients are enrolled and it is tried to detect adverse reactions which less frequently occur in patient populations. During these clinical trial phases, extensive toxicology experimentations on animals, long term stability testing, additional dosage formulation work, process development to supply enough compounds for the clinical testing also often occur in parallel. *See e.g., DiMasi/Hansen/Grabowski*, 10 J. Health. Econ. 107, 110 (1991); *See e.g., Scherer*, 2007, 5-8.

a drug must survive a final administrative authority's review.[219] The considerable increase in the duration of clinical and pre-clinical studies is due to an escalation in the obligatory numbers of subjects for the clinical trials,[220] the increased requirement of mandatory analytic, pharmacologic, toxicological, and clinical trials,[221] and the increased number of studies on the treatment of chronic conditions, such as cancers, immunological disorders,[222] and cognitive disorders. This whole process currently takes 10 to 13 years, significantly longer than it was 40 years ago, when the average period was 8 years.[223] Figure 3 shows a recent example.

Figure 3: R&D, a long and costly process[224]

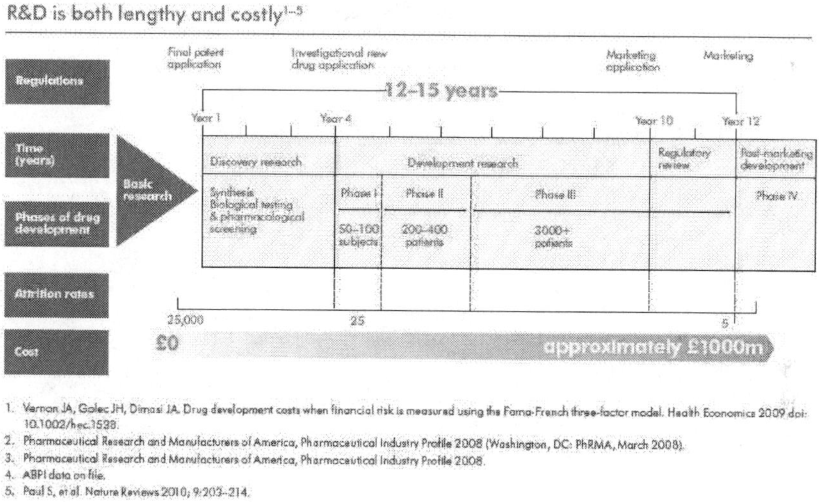

219 *See generally, DiMasi/Hansen/Grabowski*, 10 J. Health. Econ. 107, 109-11 (1991); *Schuster/Laggner/ Langer*, 11 Current Pharmaceutical Design 3545, 3545 (2005).

220 *DiMasi/Hansen/Grabowski,* 22 J. Health Econ. 151, 177 (2003).

221 *Brandt*, 1996, 129; *Dickson/Gagnon*, 3 Nat. Rev. Drug Discov. 417, 420 (2004) (e.g.: more extensive regulatory requirements to mandate to include women and children in the test).

222 *Dickson/Gagnon*, 3 Nat. Rev. Drug Discov. 417, 420 (2004).

223 Dickson/Gagnon, 4 Discov. Med. 172 (2004); *see also EFPIA*, 2012, 6 (reporting 10 years of R&D period and 2~3 years of administrative procedure); *Grabowski/ Kyle*, 2008, 275 (noting the R&D process of a medication from the synthesis of a compound synthesis to marketing approval of it typically takes more than a decade.).

224 *Association of the British Pharmaceutical Industry ("ABPI")*, 2011, 10.

The process is of course costly.[225] However, just because something is expensive does not mean that it is good, and there is no reason that the cost should be maintained at this level. In this respect, the figures sometimes speak for themselves. Though the process of estimating the cost of NMEs largely varies by therapeutic indications and is complicated, since the money spent on R&D is regained in revenue over several years, studies have shown a dramatic increase in cost. The average cost of preclinical and clinical studies for traditional products (small chemicals) was estimated at 0.8 billion USDs in 2000,[226] which was double the cost of the previous fifteen years.[227] An updated estimate of the same type of products was 1.3 billion USD in 2010.[228] The introduction of new drugs to the market is financed almost entirely by the private sector, even though the result of investment is regarded as a public benefit.[229] Some scholars have argued that the initial stages of high risk projects could be subsidized by government, since basic research projects often involve high costs and potentially high but uncertain rewards.[230] A contrasting example is the computer industry, where two pro-

---

225 *ABPI*, 2011, 10; *Schuster/Laggner/ Langer*, 11 Current Pharmaceutical Design 3545, 3545 (2005); cf. *Cockburn*, 2006, 13, 25 (noting the trend of increasing R&D expenditure was "to some degree" overstated however admitting the growth in R&D spending was "substantial.").

226 *DiMasi/Hansen/Grabowski,* 22 J. Health Econ. 151, 166-67 (2003).

227 *Anonymous*, 418 Nature 353 (2002).

228 *Federsel*, 18 Bioorgan. Med. Chem. 5775, 5777 (2010), in 2009, the average cost of R&D to bring an NME to the market by large pharmaceutical companies is estimated to be up to around 1.8 billion USD. *See Paul, et al.*, 9 Nat. Rev. Drug Discov. 203, 204 (2010); *See also O'Hagan/Farkas,* Bain Insights [online] 1 (2009) (noting "Bain's drug-economics model shows that the situation is untenable. In the late 1990s, pharma companies spent $1.1 billion, on average, to develop and launch a new drug. Today, just a decade later, the investment has doubled to $2.2 billion."); Recently Forbes even has reported the average drug developed by major pharmaceutical companies costs at least 4 billion USDs and could come to 11 billion dollar, *see Herper*, Forbes, February 2, 2012 (introducing Eli Lilly's average cost of bringing a new drug to market is 1.3 billion USDs which is the price that would buy 371 Super Bowl ads, 16 million official NFL footballs, two pro football stadiums, pay of almost all NFL football players, and every seat in every NFL stadium for six weeks in a row).

229 *Dickson/Gagnon*, 3 Nat. Rev. Drug Discov. 417, 427 (2004); *see also Tuominen*, 2011, 4; *see also U.S. Department of Commerce International Trade Administration,* 2004, vii.

230 *Merges*, 7 High Tech. L. J. 1, 47 (1992); *Nelson*, 2000, 98.

grammers could develop a commercial software program in a garage.[231] Even though the cost of writing code for operating systems has increased, this takes considerably less time and is cheaper than developing a new drug.

Even the figures given above may represent an underestimate of the real costs of drug discovery.[232] Significantly, the figures do not include costs incurred prior to the target validation.[233] The research required to identify and validate a given target varies by subject, which makes the underlying parameters difficult to quantify.[234] Most importantly, these figures do not include the R&D costs for products that cannot be launched on the market,[235] which is the main expense in the industry. It has been reported that 75% of the fully capitalized cost of developing a new medication is the average cost of failures.[236] As Jacob LJ puts it simply: "*The few winners must pay for all the losers.*"[237] These failures are also based on uncertainty in developing a drug.

---

231 *Burk/Lemley*, 89 Va. L. Rev. 1575, 1582 (2003) (e.g. Steve Jobs and Steve Wozniak for Apple Computer; Bill Hewllet and David Packard for Hewlett-Packard started in a garage).

232 Some scholars also argued expenditure for marketing support or cost for post-market surveillances, line extensions, development of new indications, and the development of new formulations, dosage forms and so on must be added., *see Federsel*, 18 Bioorgan. Med. Chem. 5775, 5777 (2010); *see Munos*, 8 Nat. Rev. Drug Discov. 959, 962-63 (2009); *See also Pisano*, 2006, 120.
However, these are mainly not the cost to bring a NME to the market, thus it would not be proper to include them.

233 *Paul, et al.*, 9 Nat. Rev. Drug Discov. 203, 205 (2010); In the drug discovery, a "target" can mean a target protein which plays key role in the function of normal and abnormal cells, which leads to the formation of hypothesis that the modulating the function of this protein which linked to disease could be a route to a new medication. This kind of disease-linked protein is referred to as a target, and the process of confirming such hypothesis is usually referred as "target validation." *See Knowles/Gromo*, 2 Nat. Rev. Drug Discov. 63, 63 (2003).

234 *Paul, et al.*, 9 Nat. Rev. Drug Discov. 203, 205 (2010).

235 *Paul, et al.*, 9 Nat. Rev. Drug Discov. 203, 205 (2010).

236 *Cockburn*, 2006, 17.

237 *Jacob*, December, CIPA 711 (2008).

c) Uncertainties in post-invention development

"*A hallmark of medical decision-making is choice under uncertainty.*"[238] "*[D]rug development remains part science and part art.*"[239] These statements reflect the uncertainty of even post-invention development in this field. At least three levels of risk are are derivable from scientific, regulatory, and economic uncertainty respectively.[240]

(1) Scientific uncertainty: Unpredictability of substances

Firstly, scientific uncertainty arises because of the unpredictability of substances. Owing to this unpredictability, only one of every 10,000 new substances reaches market approval.[241] It is well established that the properties of chemical compounds are substantially contingent upon their chemical structures. However, it is no longer disputed that a small structural modification may result in major differences in biological activity,[242] which is to say, reasonable predictions of relations between structure and activity can be found in general with some limit beyond which no such prediction can be validly made.[243] This unpredictability is also clearly demonstrated by the reasoning of the courts, which require higher disclosure in this field than in other technological fields.[244] In other words, since there is less room for the

238 *Frank*, 2004, 9.

239 *Bartfai/Lees*, 2006, 258.

240 *Dickson/Gagnon*, 3 Nat. Rev. Drug Discov. 417, 419-420 (2004).

241 *Hansen/Hirsch*, 1997, 326; *ABPI*, 2011, 10 (reporting pharmaceutical industry has an attrition rate of NMEs, from discovery to product, of 25,000:5); *see also Heilman*, 4 Quality Assurance, 75, 75 (1995); *see also EFPIA*, 2012, 6 (reporting one or two out of every 10,000 substances may successfully become marketable medicines); *see also Kola/Landis*, 3 Nat. Rev. Drug Discov. 711, 712 (2004) (reporting 62 percent of drug candidates that made it through Phase I failed to pass Phase II, and 45percent of those that did fail to pass Phase III); *see also* Figure 3.

242 *Agrevo/Triazoles*, T 939/92, OJ EPO 309, 325 (1996), point 2.6.2.

243 *Agrevo/Triazoles*, T 939/92, OJ EPO 309, 325 (1996), point 2.6.2.; *see also Ciba-Geigy/Benzothiopyran derivatives*, T 20/83, OJ EPO 1983, 419, 421 (noting "[a]s a rule, prediction by persons skilled in the art is no longer possible where the substances whose properties have to be assessed have been theoretically synthesized, by interchanging all the structural elements from compounds forming the state of the art and having the same kind of effect. Such is the case in this instance.").

244 *Brandi-Dohrn*, Gewerblicher Rechtsschutz und Urheberrecht Internationaler Teil ("GRUR Int") 1995, 541, 543; *see also infra* 899.

person skilled in the art to be able to know possession of an invention, more variants need to be enabled to meet the disclosure requirement in the pharmaceutical art. Thus, when many compounds are disclosed in the prior art, it would be unreasonable to expect that these compounds would exhibit similar technological effects to those shown by substances for which practical data are provided.[245]

(2) Regulatory and market uncertainties

During the long period of acquiring regulatory approval, the high probability of failure in each clinical trial phase and thus failing to acquire regulatory approval risks the business in this sector.[246] Many failures occur in the later stages of development such as during clinical trials.[247] Indeed, 78% of NMEs that survive all of the phases of clinical trials are never marketed.[248] Across the entire process of the product development path, therefore, pharmaceutical companies need to review the status of development and make a so-called "Go/No-Go" decision, namely, a decision about whether to continue to develop or not at several points until the final decision to launch the end product.[249]

Even after a launch, there are some uncertainties in the market environment, such as the acceptance of a new medical product not only by the patient but also by physicians who show a high degree of loyalty to familiar medications.[250] Furthermore, information generated by the pharmaceutical companies after the launch can indicate that the drugs are unsafe or not sufficiently effective.[251] This information can cause sales to plummet,[252] or cause

245 *Brown*, 31 J. Chem. Inf. Comp. Sci. 2, 3-4 (1991).

246 *Dickson/Gagnon*, 3 Nat. Rev. Drug Discov. 417, 419-420 (2004).

247 *Cockburn*, 2006, 17-18.

248 *Frank*, 22 J. Health Econ. 325, 327 (2003); *DiMasi/Hansen/Grabowski*, 22 J. Health Econ. 151, 165 (2003).

249 *DiMasi/Hansen/Grabowski*, 10 J. Health. Econ. 107, 109 (1991) (noting these decisions would be dependent upon potential therapeutic efficacies, frequency and severity of adverse drug reactions, marketing, distributing, productions costs, patent protectability, and the like.).

250 *Dickson/Gagnon*, 3 Nat. Rev. Drug Discov. 417, 419-420 (2004).

251 *Eisenberg*, 5 Yale J. Health Pol'y L. & Ethics 717, 718 (2005); this is also partly because that some side effects can be only found after disclosing the medication to a larger population than that of clinical trials.

252 *Eisenberg*, 5 Yale J. Health Pol'y L. & Ethics 717, 718 (2005).

the product to be removed from the market.[253] The most famous case in point is Vioxx®, which revealed a serious adverse cardiovascular effect after FDA approval.[254] This caused Merck to remove the product from the market and resulted in a catastrophic loss of value, including high litigation costs thereafter.[255]

d) Information rich chemicals

Information is, by nature, expensive to produce, cheap to reproduce, and difficult to profit from.[256] Unlike other chemicals, such as organic solvents, drugs are information-rich chemicals. This is partially because regulation demands production and disclosure of the huge amount of information that is necessary to meet the regulatory authorities' standards must be accumulated and disclosed.[257] This information concerning the use of chemicals is expensive to produce as discussed in chapter III.A.1.b). Once produced and disclosed, however, it is easy to reproduce and difficult to keep exclusive. Risks surrounding the information and its non-excludability further contribute to the uncertainty of the drug development process.

---

253 *Schuster/Laggner/ Langer*, 11 Current Pharmaceutical Design 3545 (2005) (noting "[o]ver 90% of the market withdrawals were caused by drug toxicity.").

254 *Bresalier, et al*, 352 New Eng. J. Med. 1092, 1098 (2005).

255 Litigation costs were 4.85 billion USDs funding to the expected settlement to resolve roughly 50,000 lawsuits in 2007, or 58 million USDs to settle allegations advertising Vioxx® with 30 US states in 2008. *See Martinez, et al.,* Wall St. J., Oct. 1, 2004, at A1; *see also Merck*, Merck Press Release, Nov. 9, 2007.

256 *Nordhaus*, 1969, 70.

257 *Eisenberg*, 5 Yale J. Health Pol'y L. & Ethics 717, 717 (2005); see also *DiMasi/ Hansen/Grabowski,* 22 J. Health Econ. 151, 166 (2003) (estimates average costs to develop a new drug at $802 million in 2003); *Burk/Lemley*, 54 Case W. Res. L. Rev. 691, 726-728 (2003); creating the information can be risky considering some information generated during or after the R&D procedure of a drug can make the medication withdrawn from the market.

2. Specificities in the market for pharmaceuticals

a) Imitation with negligible cost and much reduced risk

Imitation is a typical example of information spillover.[258] The risk of imitation, of course, haunts all investments in any field of R&D.[259] Imitation follows closely and only on the heels of successful innovation.[260] The innovator's R&D returns can be maximized by an intermediate delay between his own invention and the successful imitation thereof.[261]

The relative ease of imitation with or without patent protection is one of the main factors that differentiates the pharmaceutical industry from others.[262] Sherer takes the aircraft industry as an example, which also utilizes sophisticated technology and spends billions of dollars to develop new products.[263] Even without patent protection, however, in attempting to imitate anAirbus A380, a firm would spend nearly as much as Airbus did to develop its own A380. Moreover, by the time the imitator had completed its rival A380, Airbus would be a decade ahead in sales and would enjoy a substantial production cost advantage. The software industry is another example. Even after a product embracing the invention is available on the market, reverse engineering is both difficult and time consuming.[264]

In contrast, in the pharmaceutical industry, much R&D is directed to securing information,[265] and, once the required knowledge is accumulated, if there is no protection, it *ipso facto* becomes available to any interested party. With such information, it is relatively cheap and quick for an imitator to

---

258 *Dasgupta*, 98 Econ. J. 66, 74 (1988).

259 *Jaffe/Lerner*, 2004, 41; *cf. Bessen/Maskin*, 1999, 2 (noting, however, for industries like software and semiconductors, imitation promotes innovation and long patents of broad scope would inhibit it, because the innovation in these industries are both sequential and complementary.).

260 *Cadot/Lippman*, 1995, 1; *see also Christie, et al*, 8 PLoS Med 1 (2013) (In addition to these imitating activities, there are patenting activities by the companies other than the drug's originator to seek monopoly control over innovations to blockbusters).

261 *Cadot/Lippman*, 1995, 15-17.

262 *Scherer*, 2007, 33-34.

263 *Scherer*, 2007, 33-34.

264 Johnson-Laird, 19 U. Dayton L. Rev. 843, 843-44 (1994); *Burk/Lemley*, 89 Va. L. Rev. 1575, 1584 (2003).

265 See subsection III.A.1.

identify the composition of a new medication and to manufacture it.[266] In addition, the knowledge of an innovator's success itself reduces the risk of failure for the imitator. The knowledge of success, in other words, reduces a great deal of an imitator's uncertainty,[267] which cannot be compared with that of innovator. Thus, there are few barriers to imitation, without patent protection.[268] This can be clearly observed in the quick and vast market erosion once the patent term of a product expires and generic versions of that product enter the market.[269]

b) Prescription based purchase: A disconnection between choosers and payers

As in other industries, medicines are produced by pharmaceutical companies and consumed by end-users, i.e. patients. However, unlike other consumer products, medicines are often chosen and/or prescribed by medical doctors and normally paid for or reimbursed by insurance companies or the relevant health system.[270] This is especially true of prescription drugs that cannot be sold without a doctor's prescription. Consequently, the person who prescribes the drug, the purchaser, and the end-consumer of the drug may in fact be different in most cases. This disconnection between the person who selects and the person who pays and consumes causes the demand for prescription drugs to be more price-inelastic than that of over-the-counter

---

266 *Mansfield/Schwartz/Wagner*, 91 Econ. J. 907, 913 (1981); mentioned in *Roin*, 87 Tex. L. Rev. 503, 511 (2009) (noting generic drug manufacturers spend on average about $2 million on the approval process).
267 *Kieff*, 85 Minn. L. Rev. 697, 709 (2001).
268 *Teece*, 15 Res. Policy 285, 300 (1986); *Roin*, 87 Tex. L. Rev. 503, 516 (2009) (raising examples such as agricultural-chemicals and medical-equipment industries which are governed by regulatory regimes.).
269 The asymmetry between pharmaceutical innovators and imitators was not as glaring before the regimes like Hatch-Waxman Act or Regulation on SPC with Bolar exceptions were introduced. Until early 1980s, generic drug providers could have invested nearly as much as the original companies did. *See Scherer*, 2007, 34-35; *see also Bond/Lean*, 1977.
270 *DG Competition*, 2009, 21-22 (see also Figure 2 in page 22).

("OTC") drugs, which may be sold without prescription.[271] In contrast, for prescription drugs, the prescribers do not pay for the drugs that they order.[272] As this disconnection causes prescription drugs to be cost-insensitive, demand curves can be easily manipulated through advertisement and promotion.[273]

c) Information asymmetry and high loyalty to a medicine

Markets for medical care are also characterized by asymmetric information between physician and patient.[274] Patients do not have enough information generally, which leads to fear, anxiety, and reluctance to switch to another version of a medicine.[275] Unwavering loyalty to a particular medicine also induces patients or doctors to stay with the same product.[276] This loyalty makes it difficult not only to leave a familiar product for a new product in the same therapeutic class, but also for a generic version of the same product. Since doctors and patients are accustomed to brand-named products, although available generic substitutes containing exactly the same active ingredients are much cheaper, they remain reluctant to substitute any unknown generic versions for the brand-named drug, even if health authorities guarantee their bioequivalencies.[277] Another contributing factor is that the price changes have a small effect on the quantity of the drug in demand. Some

271 *Temin*, 10 Bell J. Econ. 429, 434-5 (1979) (noting that the customers were changed from patients to doctors who had a peculiar characteristic; "they did not pay for the drugs they ordered. In fact, they did not even know how much these drugs cost."); *Steele*, 5 J. Law Econ. 131, 139-43 (1962) (noting the demand curve for the physicians' were an upward slope, but "the demand curve of the patient is perhaps nearly vertical up to prohibitively high prices if he trusts the judgment of his physician."); *Teece*, 15 Res. Policy 285, 301 (1986) (noting "FDA regulation which had the de facto effect of reducing the elasticity of demand for drug…").

272 *Temin*, 10 Bell J. Econ. 429, 434-35 (1979) (noting that the customers were changed from patients to doctors who had a peculiar characteristic; "they did not pay for the drugs they ordered. In fact, they did not even know how much these drugs cost."); *Steele*, 5 J. Law Econ. 131, 139-43 (1962).

273 *Rai*, Ill. L. Rev. 173, 206 (2001).

274 *Frank*, 2004, 10.

275 *Frank*, 2004, 27-28; *Yu/Gupta*, 2008, 31.

276 *Landes/Posner*, 2003, 190, 313-14; *Grabowski/Vernon*, 35 J. Law Econ. 331, 333-35 (1992).

277 *Landes/Posner*, 2003, 314; *von Hippel*, 1988, 53.

evidence suggests that, even after the expiration of the basic patent term, the price of product covered by the basic patent sometimes does not substantially decrease.[278]

d) Pricing

"*Every day in our lives monopoly takes its toll.*"[279] One may recall the term monopoly from the term patent. Monopoly, however, is a term that relates to a market rather than to any particular good or service sold in that market.[280] While all property rights can be regarded as monopolies, only those that convey effective control over the relevant market can provoke economic inefficiencies associated with monopolies, such as when there are no adequate market alternatives and consumers are consequently willing to pay a monopoly price.[281] In the same vein, patent law does not confer an economic monopoly, but only the right to exclude others from producing products covered by the patent.[282]

Though some scholars argue that there is no competition where patented drugs are concerned,[283] the reality is different. Firstly, the prices of prescription drugs are largely regulated.[284] As Landes and Posner noted, "The evidence is consistent with government regulation that limits the ability of

278 *Grabowski/Vernon*, 35 J. Law Econ. 331, 374 (1992); Even there were evidences that branded-drug prices raised after the patent expiry and generic's entrance; *Berndt*, 16 J. Econ. Perspect. 45, 63 (2002); *Davis/Murphy/Topel*, 2001, 2.

279 *Kefauver*, 1966, 3.

280 *Kieff*, 2008, 21; *Dam,* 23 J. Legal Stud. 247, 249-50 (1994) (noting "it is readily apparent that the right to exclude an-other from "manufacture, use, and sale" may give no significant market power, even when the patent covers a product that is sold in the market. Also "leading companies may obtain 1,000 or more patents in a single year, and yet many such firms are unlikely ever to obtain even a single monopoly in the market"); *Illinois Tool Works Inc. v. Independent Ink, Inc.,* 547 U.S. 28, 46 (2006) ("Congress, the antitrust enforcement agencies, and most economists have all reached the conclusion that a patent does not necessarily confer market power upon the patentee.").

281 *Kieff*, 2008, 21; *Hovenkamp, et al*, 2010, § 4.2.

282 *Hovenkamp, et al*, 2010, § 4.2.

283 *See e.g., Steele*, 5 J. Law Econ. 131, 147 (1962).

284 *Vernon*, Regulation, 22, 22 (2002-2003, Winter) (for example, direct price control, profit control, reference pricing, approval delays, procedural barriers, and reimbursement).

drug manufacturers to charge monopoly prices to certain segments of the population."[285] According to a report about pharmaceutical price controls in Organisation for Economic Co-operation and Development ("OECD") countries, almost all governments rely on some sort of price controls[286] to limit spending on pharmaceuticals, to prevent pharmaceutical companies from charging a market/based price for their products, and to require that they be transparent about the rationale for prices or reimbursement amounts.[287]

The most direct method is to set the sale price and to make sales at any other price illegal, which generally results in lowering prices below what they would have been in a free market.[288] Another method used is to set the reimbursement price of a new drug at levels well below the free market price.[289] Even in Germany, where pharmaceutical companies could have decided the drug price, rendering Germany one of the highest drug price countries in Europe along with the Netherlands and Sweden, new laws took effect in January of 2011, which forced a company to negotiate new drug prices with health insurers after determining whether the new medication had an additional benefit.[290]

Furthermore, getting a better price and reimbursement is no longer enough, and manufacturers must further prove the effectiveness of products in the real world and provide a pharmacoeconomic analysis that includes cost-effectiveness.[291] Thus, it is more difficult to charge high prices. Sec-

---

285 *Landes/Posner*, 2003, 315.

286 *U.S. Department of Commerce International Trade Administration*, 2004, vii-viii; *see also Vernon*, Regulation, 22, 22 (2002-2003, Winter); *see also*, *UK Office of Fair Trading*, 2007, 1-2 (UK had broadly two components; *profit controls* which set a maximum level for the profits which a company could earn from the supply from branded drugs to the NHS and *price controls* which provided companies with freedom to set the initial price of new active substances but impose restrictions on subsequent price increase or *cut the price* at the time of scheme renegotiations); In the US, there are no government price controls over private sector purchases, but the government relies on a strong generic pharmaceutical industry to create added competitive pressures. *See*, *Ellery/Hansen*, 2012, 14.

287 *Ellery/Hansen*, 2012, 12-16; *U.S. Department of Commerce International Trade Administration*, 2004, viii.

288 *U.S. Department of Commerce International Trade Administration*, 2004, ix.

289 *U.S. Department of Commerce International Trade Administration*, 2004, ix.

290 *Bohsem*, Süddeutsche Zeitung, January 23, 2012.

291 *Ellery/Hansen*, 2012, 13-14 (noting a drug company used to only need to prove safety, efficacy, and quality to obtain approval and to market a product.).

ondly, therapeutic competition is more common. Once an innovative drug comes onto the market, the market becomes more competitive, since more than one company may be developing compounds with similar mechanisms of action, even though the compounds themselves are different and can be patent protected.[292] Indeed, there are practically always alternative medications on the market for products treating the same disorders, such as headaches,[293] unless the drug is the first in its class, regardless of whether the alternatives are protected by the patent. Thus, a patent in the pharmaceutical industry does not provide protection that will permit a complete or almost complete market.[294]

On the other hand, it is true that patent rights can confer some power in the market, and the anticipation of a price above the marginal cost creates the incentive to engage in research in the first place.[295] In addition, considering the fact that the manufacturing cost of medications is usually low, the public may have to pay higher prices even for a limited amount of time, which is inherent in the patent system. This can be particularly problematic in this industry, given that the product is a medication, which can improve health condition and save lives.[296]

3. Specificities of the patent protection for pharmaceuticals

a) Patent protection for industrial technologies

There is a strong assumption that patents have played and are playing a crucial role in promoting innovation and the growth of industries.[297] However, it is also clear that, in many areas of technology, their role has

---

292 *Dickson/Gagnon*, 3 Nat. Rev. Drug Discov. 417, 421-422 (2004); see also subsection II.D.2.

293 *Landes/Posner*, 2003, 314 (noting the manufacturers of differentiated drugs are competing with each other in a market).

294 *Domeij*, 2000, 174.

295 *Hovenkamp, et al*, 2010, § 4.2.

296 *Rai*, Ill. L. Rev. 173, 187-88 (2001).

297 *Luski/Wettstein*, 1 Probl. Perspect. Manage. 31, 31 (2004); *Ann*, 2009, 361; *Crouch*, 16 Geo. Mason L. Rev. 141, 141 (2008); *Graham v. John Deere Co.*, 383 U.S. 1, 9 (1966) ("The patent monopoly was not designed to secure to the inventor his natural right in his discoveries. Rather, it was a reward, an inducement, to bring forth new knowledge."); *Crouch*, 39 Seton Hall L. Rev. 1125, 1134 (2009).

changed.[298] Arguably, patent protection did not seem to be crucial in most industries except the drug industry,[299] where exploitation of the lead time, moving rapidly along the learning curve, use of complementary sales, service capabilities and secrecy are more emphasized than patent exclusivity.[300] For example, the computer software industry can rely on trade secrecy and copyright protection as alternative intellectual property protection to patents.[301] In the semiconductor industry, since semiconductor chips are covered by many different patents[302] and many companies are pursuing the same faster and smaller chips, they can file applications for similar inventions with overlapping claims and face a greater likelihood of infringing others' patents. Thus, patents can be used actively albeit rather defensively to prevent companies from being sued.[303] Along with these two industries, the computer industry has been among the most innovative in recent years in spite of relatively weak patent protections and rapid imitations, partly because these innovations are both very sequential and complementary.[304] In the end, the usual result in these industries is cross-licensing with a modest royalty fee.[305]

---

298 *Kash/Kingston*, 28 Sci. & Pub. Pol'y 11, 11 (2001).

299 *Mansfield/Schwartz/Wagner*, 91 Econ. J. 907, 915 (1981); *Levin et al.*, 1987 Brookings Paper on Econ. Activity, 783, 802 (1987) (noting "the three industries in which product patents were viewed as most effective [were] organic chemicals, pesticides, and drugs."); *Cohen/Nelson/Walsh*, 2000, 1-2, 9, 14; *Cadot/Lippman*, 1995, 4 (noting "[a]fter patents, the most important isolating mechanism emanates from lead times or lags."); *Teece*, 15 Res. Policy 285, 287 (1986) (noting "although [patent] do afford considerable protection on new chemical products"). Some survey results have found that large majority of innovations are not patented in certain sectors. *See Arundel/Kabla*, 27 Res. Policy, 127, 138 (1998) (providing examples of such sectors, such as food, tobacco, petroleum refining, basic metals, automobiles, and other transport equipment); *Bessen/Meurer,* 2008, 89.

300 *Bessen/Meurer,* 2008, 89 ; *Levin et al.*, 1987 Brookings Paper on Econ. Activity, 783, 783-84, 816 (1987); *Cohen/Nelson/Walsh*, 2000, 1.

301 *Landes/Posner*, 2003, 313; *Burk/Lemley*, 89 Va. L. Rev. 1575, 1628 (2003).

302 Such as circuit designs, materials, packaging, manufacturing process, and the like.

303 *Burk/Lemley*, 89 Va. L. Rev. 1575, 1628 (2003).

304 *Bessen/Maskin*, 1999, 2-3 ("complementary" was meant that each potential innovator takes a different research line and thereby enhances the overall probability that a particular goal is reached within a given time.); *Bessen/Maskin*, 1999, 11-13 (also noting that distinctive pattern of cross-licensing in these industries).

305 *von Hippel*, 1988, 53.

Companies not only have different reasons to patent across technologies,[306] but also different controlling power over the products.[307] An individual patent that can protect a whole product or a process is rare.[308] For example, in "complex technology", such as technologies involved in electronic products comprised of a large number of patentable elements, where a new commercializable product or process is comprised of numerous patentable elements,[309] firms rarely have proprietary control over all of the essential components of the products that they are developing.[310] It is difficult to have sole controlling power over products where standard-essential patents have to be exploited. Consequently, in these industries, patents are used as trading currencies.[311] By contrast, in "discrete technology" fields, such as drugs or chemicals, which are comprised of relatively few patentable elements,[312] firms often have full power to control their products and, as a result, patent exclusivity provides significant benefits.[313]

b) Patent protection in the pharmaceutical industry

The pharmaceutical industry has been famously dependent upon patent protection to recover its R&D costs.[314] The profit power of innovative drugs overwhelmingly hinges upon the extent to which the patent rights cover the

---

306 *Cohen/Nelson/Walsh*, 2000, 30.

307 *Cohen/Nelson/Walsh*, 2000, 19; *Kash/Kingston*, 28 Sci. & Pub. Pol'y 11 (2001).

308 *Scherer/Ross*, 1990, 624.

309 *Kash/Kingston*, 28 Sci. & Pub. Pol'y 11 (2001); *Cohen/Nelson/Walsh*, 2000, 19.

310 *Cohen/Nelson/Walsh*, 2000, 19.

311 *Kash/Kingston*, 28 Sci. & Pub. Pol'y 11, 16 (2001.).

312 *Cohen/Nelson/Walsh*, 2000, 19; *Merges/Nelson*, 90 Colum. L. Rev. 839, 911 (1990) (noting invention in chemical industry has discrete and cumulative features).

313 *von Hippel*, 1988, 53.

314 *Eisenberg*, 5 Yale J. Health Pol'y L. & Ethics 717, 721 (2005); *See also Weissman*, 25 U. Pa. J. Int'l Econ. L. 1079, 1085-94 (2004) (noting that pharmaceutical industry keep insisting stronger patent protection); *Kash/Kingston*, 28 Sci. & Pub. Pol'y 11, 21 (2001) (asserting the need of change the emphasis of patent system on serving large firms in simple technologies); *Mansfield/Schwartz/Wagner*, 91 Econ. J. 907, 913-915 (1981); *Jaffe/Lerner*, 2004, 39-41; *Cadot/Lippman*, 1995, 3; *Levin et al.*, 1987 Brookings Paper on Econ. Activity, 783, 824 (1987) (noting pharmaceutical industry is one of the few in which patents really do seem to matter); *Harhoff*, 2009, 32 (noting "impact of patent protection is particularly pronounced in the field of pharmaceuticals"); *Abramowicz/Duffy*, 120 Yale L.J. 1590, 1615 (2011); *contra*, *Boldrin/Levine*, 2010, 212 *et seqq*.

product.[315] The existence of this relationship can be seen in the fact that the pharmaceutical industry and the chemical industry are not influenced by increases in the cost of patenting.[316] The expectation of patent protection plays a more important role.[317] It has been empirically shown that when more patent protection is provided, greater R&D productivity occurs in pharmaceuticals and biotechnology.[318] Even a leading patent-sceptic economist, Nelson, mentions the need for patents to protect the product.[319]

The importance of the patent system matches well with the specificities of the pharmaceutical industry. To begin with, although pharmaceutical companies have very high fixed R&D costs, their marginal costs are very low, which means that they cannot help counting upon their patent and patent-protected revenues to recover their R&D expenditure.[320] As Landes and Posner properly point out, the greater the fixed costs of research and development, the greater the degree of patent protection required to create adequate incentives to invest in developing the invention in the first place.[321] Secondly, enormous uncertainties lining the path to the approval of a new drug and the resulting high failure rate seem to justify the importance of patents in this industry. [322] This means that patent protection allows pharmaceutical firms to capture much of the value of successful trials, even

315 *Kash/Kingston*, 28 Sci. & Pub. Pol'y 11, 14 (2001); *Cohen/Nelson/Walsh*, 2000, 23; *Bessen/Meurer,* 2008, 88-89 (noting pharmaceutical industry is atypically dependent on the patents, which is different from most other industries); *Glasgow*, 41 IDEA 227, 231 (2001).

316 *Lanjouw/Schankerman*, 114 Econ. J. 441, 454-55 (2004); *cf.* *Cohen/Nelson/Walsh*, 2000 (noting one of the reasons that people less use patent system is the costs of obtaining and enforcing patents).

317 *Scherer*, 2007, 1.

318 *Arora/Ceccagnoli/Cohen*, 26 Int. J. Ind. Organ. 1153, 1170-73 (2008) (further noting that it leads much less additional innovations in other industries such as electronics and semiconductors.).

319 *Mazzoleni/Nelson*, 27 Res. Policy, 273, 276 (1998) (noting "[t]he collection of small and medium sized firms in the American biotechnology industry is, of course, a striking example of enterprises that would not have come into existence without the prospect of a patent, and which depend on patent protection to make their profits, and to attract capital […].").

320 *Landes/Posner*, 2003, 313.

321 *Landes/Posner*, 2003, 295, 300; *Roin*, 87 Tex. L. Rev. 503, 537 (2009). It is in the same vein that the conventional rationale for granting patent exclusivity is the difficulty that a manufacturer may encounter while trying to recoup the investment in his R&D when the invention is readily copiable without protection.

322 *Scherer*, 2007, 33.

though it does not recover the cost of failed trials.[323] Thirdly, the fact that a pharmaceutical compound may be information rich can be one of the reasons why patent protection is provided in the form of a license for exclusivity on information.[324] Kitch notes that "the patent owner has an incentive to make investments to maximize the value of the patent without fear that the fruits of the investment will produce unpatentable information appropriable by competitors."[325] Even though the majority of information, the generation of which consumes time and money and from which generic producers are exempted, is usually produced after the patent filing and cannot be protected with patents,[326] nonetheless, patent exclusivity functions for innovators to recoup investment in the production of information. Fourthly, the ratio of the cost of innovation to the cost of copying makes patent protection a prerequisite to encouraging firms to invest in their R&D programs.[327] As Arrow argued, there would be little or no incentive for innovators to carry out innovation if the imitation cost is substantially lower than the cost of innovation.[328] Fifthly, the necessity of patent protection is clearly adducible from the fact that partners in the industry of the inventors in universities or government institutions are not willing to fund the development of drugs unless they are patent protected.[329]

B. Challenges and overcoming efforts

> "Conventional wisdom has long held that drug companies are a safe haven for capital during times of economic turbulence. People don't stop getting sick, the argument goes, so companies who make medicines should be insulated from all but the worst economic weather."[330]

---

323 *Eisenberg*, 5 Yale J. Health Pol'y L. & Ethics 717,721 (2005).

324 *Nordhaus*, 1969, 70.

325 *Kitch*, 20 J. Law Econ. 265, 276 (1977).

326 *Eisenberg*, 5 Yale J. Health Pol'y L. & Ethics 717, 721 (2005); *Roin*, 87 Tex. L. Rev. 503, 511 (2009).

327 *See e.g., Mansfield*, 32 Manage. Sci. 173, 174-75 (1986) (reporting the survey results showing that 65% of new pharmaceutical would not have been introduced without patent protection).

328 *Arrow*, 1962.

329 *Owen-Smith/Powell*, 26 J. Technol. Transfer 99, 108 (2001); *Mazzoleni/Nelson*, 27 Res. Policy, 273, 276 (1998) (noting the patent protection has contributed for the small and medium sized firms to have survived and thrived).

330 *Holmes*, 379 Lancet 1863, 1863 (2012).

In addition to the above-cited conventional wisdom, pharmaceutical companies that are investor-owned and publicly traded entities, perform their duties very well, which are to provide shareholders with an optimal return on their investments.[331] Is the pharmaceutical industry still profitable, or is conventional wisdom these days being put to the test? Since 2000, the pharmaceutical industry has collectively destroyed shareholder value and showed a decline in R&D productivity.[332] Some investors have expressed doubts about receiving returns from drug developments, drug companies have been forced to reduce their R&D investments, and it has been reported that big pharmaceutical companies are struggling to gain returns on investments.[333] According to one report on R&D spending, the net present value and the number of new drug approvals showed that with the single exception of Novartis, the situation was not promising.[334] There have been several reports on cost-reduction plans by many companies that include reducing the number of employees and closing plants or research centers.[335] This aggressive reduction in jobs has been blamed in part on frugal insurers, generic competition, and a dearth of new medicines. [336] The estimates for top-line

331 *Avorn*, 309 Science 669, 669 (2005).

332 *Lindgardt/Reeves/Wallenstein*, 26 In Vivo: Bus. Med. Rep. 1, 1 (2008); *O'Hagan/Farkas,* Bain Insights [online] 1 (2009); *Paul, et al.*, 9 Nat. Rev. Drug Discov. 203, 203 (2010).

333 *Jack*, Fin. Times, page 20, October 17, 2011.

334 *Jack*, Fin. Times, page 20, October 17, 2011 (reporting Company, R&D spending, Net present value of new drug approvals, and number of new drug approvals, respectively as follows: Roche, $35.1bn, $6.0bn, 2; Sanofi, $28.7bn, $10.2bn, 5; Novartis, $28.7bn, $37.7bn, 15; GSK, $28.3bn, 19.6bn, 16; AstraZeneca, $22.5bn, $7.1bn, 3; and Bayer, $10.6bn, $6.6bn, 3).

335 The world's largest pharmaceutical company, Pfizer, is continuing a cost-reduction plan including firing 19,000 employees, closing 8 plants and shutting 6 research centers. And even before this plan was enacted, Pfizer eliminated about 40,000 jobs during the 6 years till 2009, *see Randall*, Bloomberg, February 1, 2011; Soon after its anti-cholesterolemic pill Lipitor began facing generic versions, Pfizer has pledged to trim $1 billion from operations in 2012, *see Armstrong*, Bloomberg, April 12, 2012; U.K. drug maker AstraZeneca also announced to eliminate another 7,300 jobs, resulting its total job cuts over the last five years to almost 30,000, *see Whalen/Stovall*, the Wall Street Journal, February 2, 2012; In addition, AstraZeneca further announced it would cut 8,000 jobs worldwide in 2010; and GSK announced that 12,000 positions will be eliminated by 2014. *See Ellery/Hansen*, 2012, 26.

336 *Whalen/Stovall*, the Wall Street Journal, February 2, 2012.

growth for the leading pharmaceutical companies from 2013-2014 is not promising either.[337]

1. Decreased R&D productivity

There has been increasing concern about whether the pharmaceutical industry is facing an R&D productivity crisis. R&D productivity is the relationship between the value created by a new medicine and the investments required to generate that medicine.[338] In reality, however, it is not easy to measure either the value or the size of an investment. Thus, proxies are used to measure it.

R&D productivity can be gauged by outputs, such as patents, but this can be problematic, because the definition of patents has changed and certain industries can obtain patents more easily than others.[339] In 2012, Thomson Reuters provided a list of the top 100 global innovators based on their patenting activities.[340] The report was not based on all kinds of patents, but mainly on the companies' activities on "innovative" patents, which, according to its definition, means "the first publication in a patent document of a new technology, drug, business process, etc., [which] could also be called 'basic' patents."[341] As in 2011,[342] the pharmaceutical industry was ranked last.[343] While distinguishing the pharmaceutical industry as "molecule-focused" as compared to other industries that are "technology-focused", the report added that the pharmaceutical industry is nevertheless innovative.[344]

Ultimately, the targeted output of R&D of pharmaceutical companies are the available medications. Cockburn insists that the number of NMEs may

---

337 *Ellery/Hansen*, 2012, 26 (Top 10 pharma sales growth forecast: Pfizer, -1.7% growth; Novartis, 2.9% growth; GSK, 6.2%; Merck & Co., -0.6%; Roche, 1.9%; Sanofi, 2.5%; AstraZeneca, 1.4%; Johnson & Johnson, -0.5%; Abbott, -3.1%; Eli Lilly, -9.4%).

338 *Paul, et al.*, 9 Nat. Rev. Drug Discov. 203, 204 (2010).

339 *Hunt*, 1999, 39.

340 *Thomson Reuters*, 2012.

341 *Thomson Reuters*, 2012, 4.

342 *Thomson Reuters*, 2011, 13.

343 *Thomson Reuters*, 2012, 12. Other industries ranked at the last were Agriculture & Forestry, Healthcare, Media/Internet, Petroleum, and Primary Metals.

344 *Thomson Reuters*, 2012, 18.

not be the proper proxy for the R&D program's true output for comparing low R&D productivity with high R&D expenditure.[345] However, he did not counterargue that the number of NMEs is a major measurement of productivity; he simply argued that a more accurate measure of R&D productivity in the pharmaceutical industry must include more factors than the number of NMEs.[346] Other factors that he insists be considered[347] prove only that the industry was working more on second generation inventions and products than on basic breakthrough inventions. He also notes that the declining counts of new drug approvals are "worrisome."[348] Furthermore, many analysts have carefully distinguished between the approval of NMEs and that of minor chemical modifications of existing drugs. The number of NMEs is one of the most representative indicators of pharmaceutical R&D activity, and NME development, as a whole, is therapeutically and economically significant.[349] Lastly, although patents and/or new chemical entities are not the best measures of R&D activity, much evidence on productivity is concentrated on these two measures.[350]

---

345 *Cockburn*, 2006, 4-11.

346 *Cockburn*, 2006, 4-11 (pointing out, from the input side, the value adjustment of inflation; from the output side, the much larger volume of approvals of minor chemical modifications, ii) significant variance of drugs value, iii) complete ignorance of incremental innovation and iv) time lag between the investment period and the time of market approval).

347 *Cockburn*, 2006, 5-10 (such as i) consideration of the much larger volume of approvals of minor chemical modifications of existing drugs, new formulations, dosage strengths, new combinations of already approved drugs, or new indication other than NMEs ii) significant variance of drugs in their scientific significance, health impact, and economic value while comparing breakthrough innovation and the "me-too" products; iii) complete ignorance of incremental innovation because of only focus on NMEs; and the like).

348 *Cockburn*, 2006, 25.

349 *DiMasi/Hansen/Grabowski*, 10 J. Health. Econ. 107, 108 (1991); *See also Paul, et al.*, 9 Nat. Rev. Drug Discov. 203, 204 (2010); *Higgins/Graham*, 326 Science 370, 370 (2009) (noting "[i]mprovements in pharmaceutical research and development (R&D) depend on product innovation. But the number of new compounds approved annually by the U.S. Food and Drug Administration(FDA) has fallen from an average of 35 in 1996-2001 to 20 in 2002-2007.").

350 *Grabowski/Kyle*, 2008, 273.

2. Dearth of new medical entities

a) Significance of NMEs

> "Statistical studies show an historical correlation since the 1950s between the number of new drugs introduced and declines in mortality and other health indicators across a wide range of diseases and health problems."[351]

NMEs are medications containing an active ingredient that has not been previously approved for marketing in any form.[352] The role of NMEs is vital to the morbidity and mortality of human beings. Further, newer drugs are significantly better than their predecessors in terms of greater efficacy, fewer side effects, and easier dosing.[353] Although the "drug-offset effect" - whether the use of a new drug reduces total health system costs - is arguable,[354] the development of new medication certainly provides net benefits to society.[355]

b) Decreased number of NMEs

Pharmaceutical companies invest vastly in R&D in the hope that this investment will produce new medications. However, it does not always turned out that way. The number of approvals of NMEs by the FDA provides a telling example. Although it concerns the number of approvals in only one country, since in the pharmaceutical industry globally the United States is its largest market, the figures are indicative of overall trends.[356] Although investment in pharmaceutical R&D has increased tremendously,[357] the num-

351 *Cockburn*, 2006, 2-3, *Lichtenberg*, 5 Int. J. Health Care Fi. 47, 70 (2005) (reporting that launches of New Chemical Entities (NCEs) had a strong positive impact on the probability of survival, based on the relationship between the launches of new drugs and the longevity based on the data from 52 countries).

352 *See* subsection II.D.1.

353 *Cockburn*, 2006, 7.

354 *Lichtenberg*, 20 Health Affair. 241, 250 (2001) (arguing huge "drug-offset effect" meaning the use of certain new and effective drugs may reduce total health system costs; the savings can more than offset the increase in drug costs; therefore there might be net cost savings to society); *cf. Zhang/Soumerai*, 26 Health Affair. 880 (2007) (insisting the said drug-offset effect was not proven).

355 *Zhang/Soumerai*, 26 Health Affair. 880, 884 (2007).

356 *Paul, et al.*, 9 Nat. Rev. Drug Discov. 203, 204 (2010).

357 See subsection III.A.1.b).

ber of new drugs approved by the FDA has remained consistently low over the last sixty years.[358] In particular, over the last decade, the cost of R&D has increased by around 70% with a reduction for the first time in 2009, while the output of NMEs on the market has seen a reduction of around 40%, despite a slight increase in 2009.[359] (See Figure 4) Even if one treats NME output as stable, taking the increased R&D expenditure and the scientific progress of technology into account[360] reveals the number of potential NMEs has incontestably fallen. Additional statistics show that only some newly marketed medications are breakthrough drugs,[361] the first in their class,[362]

358 *Munos*, 8 Nat. Rev. Drug Discov. 959, 959 (2009) (further noting until 1980, the trend line is basically flat; for the next 15 years, the slope gently upwards; and since 1996, approvals have dropped to their historical range.); *See also Pisano*, 2006, 118 (noting this phenomenon suggests "we are spending more but getting less."); see as another example, *Carmichael*, News Wk. May 15, 2010 (noting from 1996 to 1999, the U.S. FDA approved 157 new drugs, while during the comparable period, from 2006 to 2009, only 74 drugs were approved). There was a peak in 1996, which was speculated to be caused by the FDA processing a backlog of application on drugs awaiting approval; *Scherer*, 2007, 4-5.

359 *See also, Ellery/Hansen*, 2012, 4-5 (noting "the FDA approved half as many NMEs as in the period of 1996 - 2010").

360 *Cockburn*, 2006, 17; For example, estimated number of "druggable targets" in the human body has risen from around 500 (*Drews*, 1999, 77) to over 3,000 after the human genome project. *See Hopkins/Groom*, Nature Rev. Drug Discov. 727, 728 (2002); *Russ/Lampel*, 10 Drug Discov Today. 1607, 1607 (2005) (suggesting the count is up to 3,000).

361 *Morgan, et al.*, 331 Brit. Med. J. 815, 815 (2005) (reporting in Canada between 1990 and 2003, only 6% of new drugs met the "breakthrough drugs" criteria, and 88% of new drugs did not provide a "substantial improvement" over existing drug products.); *Patented Medicine Prices Review Board*, 2005, 11 (defining the breakthrough drugs as "the first drug to treat effectively a particular illness or which provides a substantial improvement over existing drug products" while distinguishing from other medicines).

362 *Paul, et al.*, 9 Nat. Rev. Drug Discov. 203, 203 (2010) (reporting out of 21 and 24 new drugs approved by the FDA in 2008 and 2009, only 29% and 17% could have been considered first-in-class.); cf. *FDA*, 2011, 4, 13-17 (reporting approval of 35 NMEs in 2011 including two new treatments for hepatitis C (boceprevir and teleprevir), the first new drug to treat Hodgkin's lymphoma in 30 years (brentuximab vedotin), and the first new drug to treat lupus in 50 years(belimumab)).

or treated disorders in a novel way.[363] These statistics indicate that the number of truly innovative new medicines approved by the regulatory bodies around the globe is decreasing.[364]

Figure 4: Global R&D expenditure, development times, global pharmaceutical sales and new molecular entity output in 2000-2010.[365]

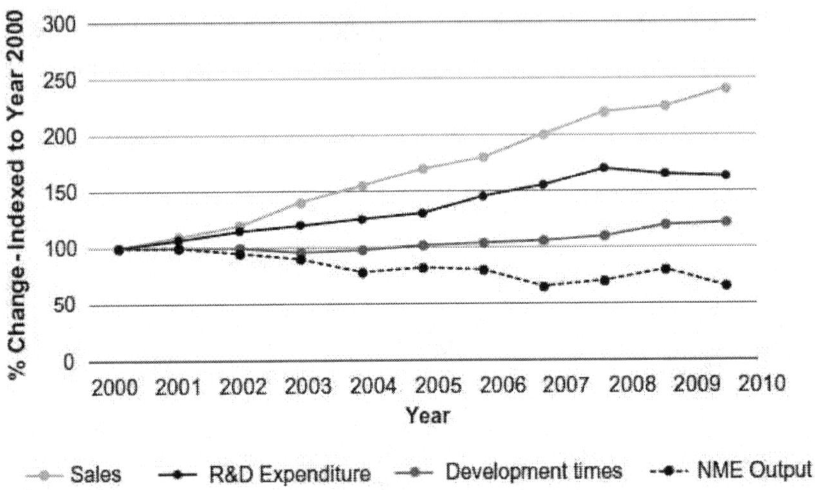

In particular, chronic disorders such as diabetes, obesity, Alzheimer's disease, Parkinson's disorder, and schizophrenia still do not have efficient and tolerable medications, and no new broad-spectrum antibiotics have been marketed in almost 40 years.[366]

363 *NIHCM*, 2002, 3 (Only around 35% of FDA newly approved drugs between 1989 and 2000 were based on new molecular entities that treats diseases in novel ways and most of approvals contained marketed active ingredients, and remaining 65% contained marketed active ingredients. Of these 65%, 54% of approval (incrementally modified drugs: IMDs) were only differed from the marketed product in dosage form, route of administration, or were combined with another active ingredient, and 11% of approvals were identical to products already available on the U.S. market.).

364 *Paul, et al.*, 9 Nat. Rev. Drug Discov. 203, 203 (2010).

365 *Arrowsmith/Harrison*, 2012, 11 (originally reproduced from *CMR International 2011 Pharmaceutical FactBook* and the widening gap between the global sales and R&D curves may be attributable to the rise in generic drug sales).

366 *Cockburn*, 2006, 3.

c) Potential reasons for the decrease

In addition to the uncertainties discussed in above chapter A.1.c), the following reasons may explain the decrease.

(1) Decrease in solvable scientific problems

Since there are still many diseases that are not well understood, researchers must depend to a large extent on serendipity.[367] Despite the sky-rocketing incidence and severity of antimicrobial resistances, which seriously impact the management of infections such as malaria, tuberculosis, pneumonia, and AIDS, pipelines for anti-infective agents have also been dry, and pharmaceutical companies have been halting their research in this area.[368] The less costly scientific problems were resolved in previous decades, leaving the industry with only the complex and systemic problems, such as Alzheimer's.[369] The shift in focus to more complex disorders, such as Alzheimer's, strokes, obesity, diabetes, and arteriosclerosis, where there is a high degree of unmet medical need, has confronted the industry with huge challenges.[370] The challenge to find efficient treatment paradigms is enormous, since the biochemistry and the disease pathology underlying complex disorders are much more difficult and expensive to investigate, which has naturally resulted in the design of highly sophisticated clinical study protocols to show both efficacy and safety in humans.[371]

---

367 *Dutfield*, 2009, 296.

368 *Talbot, et al.*, 42 Clin. Infect. Dis. 657, 665-666 (2006) (reporting some causes, such as relatively small size of market and unpredictability); *Norrby/Nord/Finch*, 5 Lancet Infect. Dis. 115, 116-117 (2005) (pointing out more rapid emergence of resistance of antimicrobials having higher sales figures as one of the reasons why the companies are leaving this field).

369 *Cockburn*, 2006, 14.

370 *Federsel*, 18 Bioorgan. Med. Chemistry 5775, 5777 (2010); *Cockburn*, 2006, 14-15.

371 *Federsel*, 18 Bioorgan. Med. Chemistry 5775, 5777 (2010); *Cockburn*, 2006, 14.

(2) Stringent safety regulations

More stringent safety regulations are among the best explanations for the decrease.[372] While tough regulations are indisputably appropriate, they make it more likely that several drugs which could have provided substantial benefits for patients despite their side effects have been weeded out. In fact, if current safety standards had been applied, even Aspirin® and Tylenol® might well have not been approved.[373] However, this is not to imply that relaxing safety regulations would be a desirable solution.

(3) Problem of over-disclosure

In the field of pharmaceuticals, there is a tendency to early and over disclosure, owing not only to the way in which research is published and the norms of academic publication, but particularly with respect to patenting practice in the industry. Firstly, researchers in universities rush to disclose their results by publishing them in well-known scientific journals, which reward them more, before trying to secure patent rights over them.[374] Secondly, on the one hand, it is relatively easy to show the structure of something being invented in the field of chemistry without actually having done it. A skilled person in the art can easily draw a chemical structure and make quite an accurate assumption about its physicochemical properties.[375] On the other hand, this disclosure can be more than sufficient to destroy the novelty of a compound which may show a promising effect and can be developed further. Thirdly, while a Markush type claim is an extremely helpful tool when claiming a large number of compounds,[376] using them can theoretically disclose and ruin the futures of millions of potential medications.

Last but not least, pharmaceutical companies file patent applications at very early stages in the R&D process, sometimes when they are still selecting a lead compound from numerous candidates. Thus, the patent applications may disclose a group of compounds as broadly as possible, while the appli-

---

372 See subsection III.A.1.a); *Dutfield*, 2009, 295-96; *Federsel*, 18 Bioorgan. Med. Chem. 5775, 5777 (2010).

373 *Dutfield*, 2009, 295-96.

374 *Roin*, 87 Tex. L. Rev. 503, 527 (2009).

375 *See e.g., Szabo,* IIC 1995, 457, 484-85.

376 See *supra* 104 -109 and accompanying texts.

cants have not decided yet which one they will develop. When its relevant properties are either disclosed prematurely or reasonably predictable at the time of invention, it is unpatentable regardless of whether its efficacy has already been proven, which might mean society would not have access to the potential medications.[377] Consequently, since such potential medications would no longer represent opportunities for investment, not only the medications themselves but also the second generation products therefrom would be unlikely to appear on the market.

(4) Early and numerous abandonments of potential candidates

The over-disclosure problem becomes more serious in conjunction with scrutinized go/no-go decisions.[378] This decision making process is a regular practice, and from the outset of R&D activities, pharmaceutical companies start to screen the patentability of their drugs.[379] As a result, the ones with weak or no patent protection or the ones which may infringe others' patents will be eliminated from the candidate list and will seldom be developed for medical use.[380] Companies eliminate the candidates as early as possible, because the cost of terminating the project at an early stage is obviously less.[381]

The real problem here is that an NME that may succeed in reaching the market is one of the thousands of compounds in the patent claim, and the rest may not be developed further. For the patent holder, the clock on their patent terms has started to run long before, and they expect that the window of potential market exclusivity is too diminished to recover their investments. Other potential investors have little incentive to invest in them either because of concerns about patent infringement or because they doubt their potential to recoup the investment even without patent exclusivities.

---

377 *Roin*, 87 Tex. L. Rev. 503, 517-545 (2009).

378 See *supra* 249 and accompanying texts; *Roin*, 87 Tex. L. Rev. 503, 569 (2009).

379 *deStevens*, 1990, 266 ("Needless to say, the lead structure series must be patentable."). After this initial screening of patentability, the candidates would go through at least twice more screening before clinical trials, such as before the filing of patent applications and before the first clinical trials. The last audit is regarded as a "gate-keeping event" before the commencement of clinical trials.

380 *Roin*, 87 Tex. L. Rev. 503, 507 (2009).

381 *Pisano*, 2006, 145; *Dickson/Gagnon*, 3 Nat. Rev. Drug Discov. 417, 419-420 (2004) (noting the late stage failures are extremely costly).

3. Patent cliffs of blockbuster medications

One distinguishing feature of the field in the mid 1980s and 90s was the generation of high revenues from the sale of blockbuster drugs which were protected by patents. However, these blockbuster drugs came up against the so-called patent cliff, which refers to the sharp fall in profits caused by competition from generic versions of medications after expiration of the patents on those drugs, and is one of the most widely publicized challenges that big drug companies face.[382] In the U.S., this phenomenon was triggered by the introduction of a key legislative change, the Drug Price Competition and Patent Term Restoration Act 1984 ("Hatch-Waxman Act") with the Bolar exception, which allowed generic manufacturers to enter the market merely by proving bioequivalency.[383] Generic competition has increased in several respects, which are typically observed after the blockbuster drugs' patents expire.[384] For example, sales in the United States of the world's best-selling drug, Lipitor®, dropped by around 40% in the last three months of 2011 compared with the same period a year earlier, despite measures taken to maintain its sales.[385] The fate of Pfizer's Lipitor® ($5.3 billion in the 2010 in U.S. American market) was followed by Eli Lilly's antipsychotic drug Zyprexa® ($2.5 billion), Johnson & Johnson's antibiotic Levaquinin® ($1.3 billion), among others.[386]

4. Frequent merger and acquisitions (M&As) and in-licensing

The pharmaceutical industry has been characterized by both significant consolidation of large pharmaceutical firms and the vertical disintegration of the R&D process. A study has shown that eight of the top ten ranked phar-

382 *Holmes*, 379 Lancet 1863, 1863 (2012); *Whalen/Stovall*, the Wall Street Journal, February 2, 2012.

383 *See* subsection V.C.1.b).

384 *Grabowski/Kyle*, 28 Manage. Decis. Econ. 491, 496, 501 (2007).

385 *Holmes*, 379 Lancet 1863, 1863 (2012).

386 *Alazraki*, Daily Finance February 27, 2011 (further reporting Bristol-Myers Squibb and Sanofi-Aventis' anti-platelet drug Plavix (6.1 billion$), AstraZeneca's antipsychotic drug Seroquel (3.7 billion$), Merck's anti-asthmatic drug Singulair (3.2 billion$), Takeda's anti-diabetes drug Actos (3.4 billion$), and Amgen's anti-arthritis drug Enbrel (3.3 billion$) would lose their patent protection in 2012.); *see also Wilson*, The New York Times, March 6, 2011.

maceutical companies in 2004 had completed major *mergers* with other pharmaceutical companies, with two notable exceptions, Merck and Johnson & Johnson.[387] Traditional economic motives for mergers, such as increasing market share and marketing power to gain competitive advantage, have not been major issues in large pharmaceutical mergers.[388] Various researchers have pointed out that companies in economic distress with pipeline gaps, ageing portfolios of marketed drugs, and expired patents for major products are more likely to engage in mergers and acquisitions.[389] Along with these factors,[390] higher R&D costs have been also cited as one of the main factors underlying the trend toward more mergers and industry consolidation.[391] Although some companies have contended that these mergers were intended to pursue R&D efficiencies, the benefits from increased size and diversity were reported as less than expected,[392] and there is still little evidence that the mergers have increased long-term R&D performance or outcomes.[393]

Along with M&As, there has been a significant shift toward *license-in* technology from biotechnological companies and small and medium enterprises ("SMEs") to reduce R&D costs and effort. [394] While facing and preparing for the eventual patent expiry of their own best sellers and the resulting revenue loss, innovative companies, such as Pfizer, which saw its Lipitor patent expired in 2011, and Bristol-Myers, which saw its Plavix patent expired in 2012, have focused on acquiring small biotech compa-

387 *Grabowski/Kyle*, 2008, 263-64 (other eight companies: Pfizer, GlaxoSmithKline, Sanofi-Aventis, Novartis, AstraZeneca, Roche, BMS, and Wyeth).

388 *Grabowski/Kyle*, 2008, 270.

389 *Higgins/Rodriguez*, 80 J. Financ. Econ. 351 (2006); *Danzon/Epstein/Nicholson*, 28 Manage. Decis. Econ. 307, 307 (2007); *Burgess/Terblanche*, 3 Open Access J. Clin. Trials 45, 45 (2011) (noting M&As are attempts to retain profitability). One report estimated sales at risk from patent expiration would be over 183 billion USD in 2011/14 (*EvaluatePharma*, 2009, 6); *Munos*, 8 Nat. Rev. Drug Discov. 959, 965-66 (2009) (noting revenue losses caused by the expiration of patents on key blockbuster drugs with continuing the current business model may result in a reduction of 5~10% in sales and 20~30% in new income in 2012-2015.).

390 *Grabowski/Kyle*, 2008, 262.

391 *DiMasi/Hansen/Grabowski,* 22 J. Health Econ. 151, 152 (2003).

392 *Henderson/Cockburn*, 27 RAND J. Econ. 32, 53 (1996).

393 *Grabowski/Kyle*, 2008, 283; *Munos*, 8 Nat. Rev. Drug Discov. 959, 965 (2009) (noting "[f]or now, the evidence suggests that M&A can help small companies, but are not an effective means to boost NME output among larger companies.").

394 *Holmes*, 379 Lancet 1863, 1863-64 (2012).

nies.[395] These kinds of alliances or in-licensing can also function as previous measures before the mergers and acquisitions in the pharmaceutical area.[396] Many research-based pharmaceutical companies are also quite active in the *generic business* directly, through affiliate companies, or mergers with generic companies.[397] These activities, such as M&As, in-licensing, or engagement of generic business can be understood as ways of investing money in other businesses which are less risky and less costly.

5. Drastic increase of second generation inventions

> "Because it gets more and more difficult and expensive to find and develop new drugs, more effort is being put into finding ways of delivering existing drugs more effectively."[398]

395 *Thomas*, The New York Times, May 1, 2012.

396 *Higgins/Rodriguez*, 80 J. Financ. Econ. 351, 352-53 (2006).

397 For example, a Japanese pharmaceutical company, Daiichi-Sankyo took 35% stake in an Indian generic drug maker, Ranbaxy. *See Anonymous*, New York Times, June 11, 2008; Pfizer announced it had entered into major licensing agreement with three India-based pharmaceutical companies, such as Aurobindo Pharma Ltd., Claris Lifesciences Ltd. and Strides Arcolab, thereby adding new non-Pfizer products to its portfolio, see *Pfizer*, Annual Review 2009, 27; Also while announcing "[g]enerics are an increasingly important part of Sanofi-aventis' plans to become a diversified global healthcare company", Sanofi-Aventis announces it has created the third largest generic company in the European market by unifying the Group's generic activities under the name of Zentiva. *See Zentiva*, Zentiva Press Release, Apr. 4, 2011; Most representatively, Novartis grouped together the generic sections under the name of Sandoz in 2003; subsequently acquired BASF Generics, Lec, Hexal, and Eon; an reached the second biggest generic company in the world after Israeli company, Teva. *See Ellery/Hansen*, 2012, 27; Also the generic companies buy innovative companies. For example Teva not only acquire the generic companies, such as US company - Barr pharmaceuticals or German one - Ratiopham; but also it completed its acquisition of US biopharmaceutical company, Cephalon in 2011. *See Teva*, Teva News Release, Oct. 14, 2011.).

398 *Grubb/Thomsen*, 2010, 258.

a) Life cycle management or evergreening

The incentive to maximize the monopoly period of brand name drugs is huge.[399] Different strategies are pursued by pharmaceutical firms to maximize the exclusivity of their particularly successful drugs,[400] which are collectively known as "evergreening" or "life cycle management."[401] Others refer to these strategies as "line extensions" or "product reformulation." Whatever the term used, through these methods pharmaceutical firms increase R&D costs on second generation inventions, heighten barriers to market entry that may become excessive, and thereby restrict competition beyond the 20-year patent term.[402] Some refer to this as building "patent walls" in the attempt to broaden the scope of the basic patent.[403] This phenomenon is well recognized as important by the industry[404] and markedly noticeable when the companies are heavily dependent on a small number of highly profitable products;[405] or when the product is a so-called "blockbuster", just as generic competition is directed at products achieving larger markets. Angell argues that the pharmaceutical industry has been "ingenious in finding ways to extend patents on its bestselling drugs."[406] Firms can move the high pricing potential of NMEs to second generation products by effectively modifying older products in order to make them attractive.[407] When

399 *Dutfield/Suthersanen*, 8 Intell. Prop. Q. 379, 389 (2004); *Glasgow*, 41 IDEA 227, 232 (2001).

400 *Dutfield/Suthersanen*, 8 Intell. Prop. Q. 379, 389 (2004); *Glasgow*, 41 IDEA 227, 233-254 (2001).

401 See e.g. *GSK*, 2011, 1 (noting "'[e]vergreening' is an inherently pejorative term.").

402 *Gaudry*, 29 Nature Biotech. 876, 876 (2011); *Dutfield/Suthersanen*, 8 Intell. Prop. Q. 379, 389 (2004); *Shadowen/Leffler/Lukens*, IIC 2011, 698, 699; *Rathod*, 7 J. Generic Medicines 227, 227 (2010) (defining "evergreening is a strategy by which technology producers, using serial secondary patents and other mechanisms, keep their product sales protected for longer periods of time than would *normally* be permissible under the law.").

403 *Hopenhayn/Mitchell*, 32 RAND J. Econ. 152, 163 (2001).

404 *Ellery/Hansen*, 2012, 3-4 (a series of interviews with pharmaceutical industry executives in a survey conducted on pharmaceutical lifecycle management in 2004 reported that the executives felt that LCM had been important, and 90% predicted that its importance would growing during 5 years following the report publication (2006-2010), while 60% expecting it to become much more important.).

405 *Dutfield/Suthersanen*, 8 Intell. Prop. Q. 379, 389 (2004).

406 *Angell*, 342 New Eng. J. Med. 1902 (2000); cf. *Holmer*, 343 New Eng. J. Med. 1415 (2000).

407 *NIHCM*, 2002, 4.

the line extension is positioned and designed properly, it can improve the value proposition and the whole status of the previous NME,[408] thereby driving revenue growth. In the 1990s, when the evergreening practice first appeared, second generation inventions were polymorphs, metabolites, enantiomers, change in strength/dosage and the like. Since then, however, the list of second generation patents has lengthened to include patents on a much larger number of characteristics, such as impurities/substantially pure compounds, new methods of use, additional process, new dosing route, packaging/patient instructions, pharmacokinetic/pharmacodynamic parameters regarding drug delivery system, combination with other drugs, segmented patient populations, and the like.[409]

In addition to the companies who hold patents for original active ingredients, other companies will seek to obtain patents on second generation inventions.[410] Indeed, an empirical study conducted in Australia has found that there are substantial patenting activities undertaken by companies other than originators of high-cost drugs, including generic companies.[411] Numerous forces have joined to encourage manufacturers to modify drugs that are already on the market. Firstly, pharmaceutical firms may expect it to be vastly less time-consuming, expensive and risky to invest in the R&D of second generation medicine containing an active ingredient whose safety and efficacy have already been established.[412] The development of one or even many line extensions can be much easier than that of an NME. Secondly, if the original manufacturers are the developers of next generation drugs, they can benefit from the experience already gained from the basic substance.[413] Furthermore, since they already have real market experience, the companies already know the potential concerns.[414] Thirdly, other frame-

408 *Ellery/Hansen*, 2012, 15, but it would be difficult to get a premium price over the original.

409 *See e.g., Rathod*, 7 J. Generic Medicines 227, 229 (2010); *Dutfield/Suthersanen*, 8 Intell. Prop. Q. 379, 389 (2004), *Parthasarathy/Goddar*, IIC 2009, 38, 41 (noting secondary inventions including new versions of the active compound such as enantiomers, salts, esters, or polymorphs, or new uses of a drug, the metabolite of a prodrug, and the like).

410 *Dutfield/Suthersanen*, 8 Intell. Prop. Q. 379, 389-90 (2004) (the other firms will be willing to license their patents to the original patent holders.).

411 *Christie, et al*, 8 PLoS Med 1, 6 (2013).

412 *NIHCM*, 2002, 4.

413 *Landes/Posner*, 2003, 330.

414 *Ellery/Hansen*, 2012, 15.

works of protection, especially market exclusivity by regulatory regimes, rewards manufacturers for making even modest changes to their products by providing three years of market exclusivity for the new version of the product, the new use, new dosage form, new route of administration, or combinations of older drugs, and the like.[415] Fourthly, as some scholars have affirmed, this phenomenon has bolstered the at-risk revenues by the generics' challenges to their basic patent. [416] Lastly, there are other driving forces, such as remarkable advances in the drug delivery system and separation technology of a single component, regulatory promotion for the IMDs,[417] an effective mechanism to prevent generic entry by acquiring patents on IMDs (+ 30 months' automatic stay[418] in the United States) and the like.[419]

b) Drastic increase of this activity supported by the number of second generation patents

One study analyzing drugs that were associated with at least one patent and approved by the FDA from 2000 to 2010 reported that drug companies frequently explored the evergreening strategy.[420] It was further reported that the phenomenon of acquiring additional patents, whose validity or applicability are often dubious, have increased.[421] It was estimated that about 30% of R&D spending is devoted to bringing "line extensions" to market.[422] A report of the European Commission on the pharmaceutical sector[423] further identified the following trends: i) A markedly sharp increase in the number of patent applications in pharmaceutical inventions was observed during the period of 2000 to 2007;[424] ii) 93% of the pending applications were classified

---

415 *NIHCM*, 2002, 4, 15-18; Title 21 United States Code - Food and Drugs ("21 U.S.C.") § 355; Council Directive 2001/83/EC, Art. 10.

416 *Higgins/Graham*, 326 Science 370, 370 (2009).

417 e.g. 505(b) way of the 21 U.S.C.

418 *See infra* 1221 and accompanying texts.

419 *NIHCM*, 2002, 15-18.

420 *Gaudry*, 29 Nature Biotech. 876, 876 (2011).

421 *Engelberg/Kesselheim/Avorn*, 361 New Eng. J. Med. 1917 (2009); *Hemphill/Sampat*, 31 J. Health Econ. 327, 327 (2012).

422 Cited in *Frank*, 22 J. Health Econ. 325, 327 (2003).

423 See DG competition, 2009.

424 This statistics was based on the IPC (International Patent Classification) A61K with some exceptions (e.g.: preparations for dentistry(A61K6) and so on), which can be regarded as the closest proxy for pharmaceutical applications.

as selection inventions;[425] and iii) 84% of the granted patents were categorized as selection inventions. Clearly, the number of patents for selection inventions had soared.

Figure 5: Patent portfolio life cycles as a function of claim types for the top 20 INNs by total sales (2000 –2007).[426]

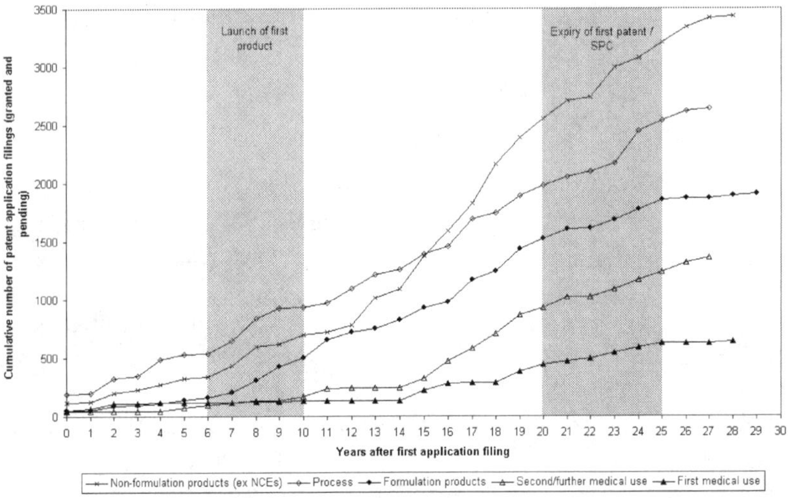

The uppermost line in Figure 5, which shows the cumulative number of patent applications for non-formulation products (such as salts, particles, polymorphic forms, and so on, except NCEs), provides evidence of the trend toward patent filings for selection inventions which are the focus of this paper. Even though it represents the cumulative number of patent filings, this line indicates a marked preference for second generation invention re-

425 The terminology in the pharmaceutical Sector Inquiry is "secondary patent (application) " which is an application not related to the first the patent (application) for the active molecules for which the contrary category of "primary patent (application)" is used.

426 *DG competition*, 2009, 179.

lated claims.[427] It is clear that life cycle management strategies have brought the industry to a more complex and confusing patent landscape for nearly all drug patents.[428]

C. Summary

The pharmaceutical industry is one in which the economic rationale for patents works to protect inventors from imitations and provides incentives to bear the cost of innovation.[429] The patent system is therefore highly effective, and its protection is essential.[430] However, even though the patent system as it has existed for some time, the number of real medicines has not changed, which challenges the theory that patent protection provides incentives for real medicines and promotes progressive technological development in this field. As has been argued in this chapter, this industry is facing challenges, such as a decline in performance so that fewer products are reaching the market, with concomitant losses of billions of dollars in revenue as some of the blockbuster medications go off patent, the cost of developing new drugs and conducting clinical studies spirals, more stringent regulatory requirements are imposed, and healthcare systems become increasingly cost-constrained.[431]

> "Perhaps the industry has finally reached bottom, and it recognises the enormous need to look for a new business model."[432]

Thus, it has become increasingly important to have strategies to protect and to take full advantage of existing patents, or to invest assets in less risky and costly areas. A possible consequence of this is that the pharmaceutical in-

---

427 *DG competition*, 2009, 179, the report was arguing there is clear trend for companies to file patent applications as the expiry date of the primary patent approaches. However, patents are only granted to the novel inventions, and there are many competitors in the same field of research. Thus, even if the companies want to file them as late as possible, the later they file applications, the more risks they will face to get a patent. Thus, above argument is not persuasive.

428 *Howard*, 4 J. Generic Med 231, 236 (2007).

429 *Bessen/Maskin*, 40 RAND J. Econ. 611 (2009).

430 *Roin*, 87 Tex. L. Rev. 503, 513-15 (2009); *Bessen/Meurer,* 2008, 88-89.

431 *See e.g., Federsel*, 18 Bioorgan. Med. Chem. 5775, 5775 (2010); *Paul, et al.*, 9 Nat. Rev. Drug Discov. 203, 203 (2010).

432 *Holmes*, 379 Lancet 1863, 1863 (2012).

dustry is led in a direction that might be lucrative but not well aligned with public health requirements.[433]

On the one hand, the number of NMEs is decreasing because of the over-disclosure problem in relation to the novelty requirement, more stringent safety regulations,[434] and for various scientific reasons, including the existence of diseases which are poorly understood,[435] and the shift of focus to more complex disorders, such as Alzheimer's, strokes, obesity, diabetes, and arteriosclerosis, where there is a high degree of unmet medical need.[436] On the other hand, the number of second generation patents is drastically increasing. One may argue that at least there are more patents and/or product inventions, which one hopes have been practically improved. However, one must consider whether more patents mean more and better innovations.[437] Moreover, companies other than the basic patentee are also seeking to acquire more patents for the second generation inventions and are becoming more dependent on those patents for cost reduction and product improvements, because they lack the first mover's advantages or the learn-by-doing knowledge of the basic patentees.[438] In this regard, Avorn argues that patent law guarantees a patent to manufacturers who make trivial changes in existing active ingredients, even if the "new" drug has the same clinical effect.[439] This can also allow companies to extend the life of a blockbuster product by making a virtually identical drug and shifting use to the new drug.[440]

Therefore, the dearth of NMEs is sensitive to a wide range of factors, which have been discussed at length in this chapter, and the increased number of second generation patents is influenced by several factors. The next chapter will analyze the role that patent law and the patent system have played in the changing landscape of pharmaceutical innovation.

---

433 *Avorn*, 309 Science 669, 669 (2005).

434 *See* subsection III.B.2.c)(1).

435 *Dutfield*, 2009, 296.

436 *Federsel*, 18 Bioorgan. Med. Chemistry 5775, 5777 (2010) (noting this led to the design of highly sophisticated clinical study protocols to show both efficacy in man and safety); *Cockburn*, 2006, 14-15.

437 *Landes/Posner*, 2003, 325.

438 *Landes/Posner*, 2003, 330.

439 *Avorn*, 309 Science 669, 669 (2005).

440 *Angell*, 2004, 76.

IV. STANDARDS OF PATENTABILITY FOR PHARMACEUTICAL SELECTION INVENTIONS

So far we have explored specificities and recent developments in the field of pharmaceuticals. As noted, patent protection is crucial for pharmaceutical innovation. Based on these observations, such as high regulation in the industry, the characteristics of the technology, market factors, as well as the norms that dictate the behaviour of researchers in universities or institutes, we have seen a trend towards second generation inventions, products and patents. In this chapter, we explore the patentability of these second generation inventions.

In order to obtain a patent, patent law requires a claimed invention to be new, to involve an inventive step (non-obviousness), to be susceptible to industrial application (utility), and to be sufficiently supported by a description (sufficiency of disclosure), although these elements are expressed slightly differently from jurisdiction to jurisdiction.[441] It is difficult to interpret these requirements of patentability and the requirements are judicially determined, administered by the patent offices, and litigated in courts.[442] To determine whether there is any correlation between the drastic increase of second generation inventions and patentability standards, this chapter examines the basic test for patentability requirements as they are applied to selection inventions. It will also analyze whether or how the present requirements in Europe and in the United States have been lowered by comparing the former requirements in those jurisdictions with those of Korea, respectively.

---

441 It was noted that these requirements as a series of doors through which an applicant should pass in order to acquire a patent right. *See e.g. In re Bergy*, 596 F.2d 952, 960 (C.C.P.A. 1979). One thing to note is, no Patent law, in fact, provides the definition of invention, although some provide what shall not be regarded as an invention. *E.g.* EPC Art. 53.

442 *Luski/Wettstein*, 1 Probl. Perspect. Manage. 31, 42-43 (2004) (further noting that there were no fixed set of rules to judge patents in the court, but the decisions are rather very discretionary in nature.); *Scotchmer/Green*, 21 RAND J. Econ. 131, 131-32 (1990).

A. Novelty and anticipation

1. Introduction

The novelty requirement is not controversial.[443] It is a concept that is fundamental to patentability[444] and "a separate examination" step from other requirements when examining patentability.[445] There are several concepts of novelty that have been applied to inventions in different jurisdictions, such as absolute novelty,[446] local novelty,[447] or mixed novelty.[448] Novelty of an invention is required to avoid double patenting,[449] to prevent patenting in-

---

443 *Duffy*, 71 U. Chi. L. Rev. 439, 502 (2004).

444 *Jacob*, IIC 1996, 170, 170; *Chou/Haller*, 1995, 1 (noting along with "inventive step," novelty is the most important patentability criteria).

445 *BGH/Olanzapine, IIC 2009,* 596, 599 (noting "with regard to the purpose of the (separate) examination of novelty").

446 *Anten*, 54 J. Pat. Off. Soc'y 75, 76 (1972) (noting absolute novelty means "the invention cannot have been made known by prior publication or prior use anywhere in the world."); *Dessemontet*, 1976, 195 (noting "absolute novelty means the novelty that exists in relation to the world state of the technique, without limit in time or space, and by relative novelty is understood that situation which exists within a given country, or within a specific period of time"); *Green Lane Products Ltd v. PMS International Group Plc & Ors* [2008] EWCA Civ 358, para 20.

447 "Local novelty" means the rule that a prior publication or use have to occur within the country in order to destroy the novelty of invention. *Grubb/Thomsen*, 2010, 62 (providing example of this system, which is the early days of patents in England, when patents were frequently granted for inventions, that, although it was known abroad, were brought into the kingdom for the first time by the patentee to U.K.).

448 *Grubb/Thomsen*, 2010, 63-64; *See also Anten*, 54 J. Pat. Off. Soc'y 75, 76 (1972) (noting "mixed novelty" system have been applied in some countries, like USA, that a later patent application is rendered invalid by written publication anywhere in the world, but by oral publication or use of the invention only in USA.).

449 *Tilmann*, IIC 2010, 149, 151-152 (noting "[o]utdated, because, according to Art. 54(2) EPC, not only a patented invention may destroy novelty but any kind of prior art information. And even if there is a prior patented (or applied for, Art. 54(3) EPC) invention, "avoiding double patenting" (as the alleged aim of the novelty requirement) is not restricted to mean, that the claims of that patented invention are the same as the claims of the invention under examination; the disclosure may also be given by the description or by the drawings of the first patented invention."). Double patenting is not acknowledged under the EPC.

formation that already exists in the public domain by a first disclosure,[450] and thus to assure that information remains in the public domain for the free use of the public.[451] An invention is generally considered new if it does not form part of the state of the art.[452] If the concept of an invention is completely disclosed within a single piece of prior art, [453] it lacks novelty, regardless of whether it was independently developed from the earlier invention.[454] "Anticipation" is a conclusion as to the failure of the invention to meet the novelty requirement.[455] A claim is said to be "anticipated" by a prior art that identically discloses the claimed invention,[456] when the prior disclosure en-

450 *Bayer/Diastereomer*, T 12/81 OJ EPO 1982, 296, 301 (noting "[t]he purpose of Article 54(1) EPC is to prevent the state of the art being patented again."); *Dupont/Copolymer*, T 124/87, OJ EPO 1989, 491, 495; *Tilmann*, IIC 2010, 149, 151-152; *Seymore*, 60 Duke L. J., 919, 919, 931 (2011) (noting "novelty serves to safeguard the public's right to enjoy what it already possesses."); *Jacob*, IIC 1996, 170, 170 (noting this concept was described as a "golden thread" running through patent jurisprudence).

451 *Aronson v. Quick Point Pencil Co.*, 440 U.S. 257, 262 (1979); *Bonito Boats, Inc. v. Thunder Craft Boats, Inc.*, 489 U.S. 141, 148 (1989) (holding "[s]ections 102(a) and (b) operate in tandem to exclude from consideration for patent protection knowledge that is already available to the public.").

452 *See, e.g.*, EPC 54 (1); 35 U.S.C. § 102.

453 *Spenner*, 90 J. Pat. & Trademark Off. Soc'y, 477, 510 (2008). Prior arts cannot be combined to show the elements of the claimed invention.

454 *Mauer/Scotchmer*, 69 Economica 535, 535 (2002) (noting "patents differ from other forms of intellectual property in that independent invention is not a defense to infringement."); *cf. Diener/Shear*, T305/87, OJ EPO 1991, 419, 429 (holding it was not permissible to combine separate items belonging to different embodiments described in one and the same document (which was a catalogue) merely because they were disclosed in that one document, unless of course such combination had been specifically suggested there.).

455 *Chisum*, 15 AIPLA Q. J. 57, 58 (1987).

456 *Chisum*, 15 AIPLA Q. J. 57, 58 (1987).

ables the entire claimed invention in addition to disclosing each and every element of the invention.[457]

2. Examination of novelty

Assessing the novelty requirement may on the face of it appear fairly straightforward.[458] The sole test of novelty is the comparison between the invention and the whole knowledge from the prior art, and the invention will be determined as novel if there is a difference from the prior art.[459] However, the determination of novelty is not as simple as it sounds. Firstly, the determination involves multiple factors and is dominated by standards that apply to various elements as with the determination of other patentability requirements.[460] For example, to determine whether an invention is anticipated in an enabling manner, we should judge the level of ordinary skill of a person skilled in the art and the degree of experiments which would be regarded as "undue,"[461] In addition, to determine what is "undue," several factors must

457 *Kieff/Schwartz/Newman*, 2011, 490-91; *See. e.g., Elan Pharmaceuticals., Inc. v. Mayo Foundation*, 346 F.3d 1051, 1054 (Fed. Cir. 2003) (holding a reference is enabled when its disclosures are sufficient to allow one of skill in the art to make and use the claimed invention, quoting *Bristol-Myers Squibb Co. v. Ben Venue Labs., Inc.*, 246 F.3d 1368, 1374 (Fed. Cir. 2001)); *See also Atlas Powder Co. v. Ireco, Inc.,* 190 F.3d 1342, 1346 (Fed. Cir. 1999) (holding that in order to anticipate a claim, a prior art reference must disclose every limitation of the claimed invention, either explicitly or inherently, quoting *In re* Schreiber, 128 F.3d 1473 (Fed. Cir. 1997)); *RCA Corp. v. Applied Digital Data Systems, Inc.,* 730 F.2d 1440, 1444 (Fed. Cir. 1984) (noting "[a]nticipation is established only when a single prior art reference discloses, expressly or under principles of inherency, each and every element of a claimed invention."); *Synthon BV v. SmithKline Beecham plc* [2005] UKHL 59, para 14 (noting if an earlier published document discloses the claimed invention and a person skilled in the art can perform the claimed invention when he tries to do so by using the matter disclosed in the earlier document and-or his common knowledge, the claim is anticipated by the earlier document.).

458 *Kieff*, 45 B. C. L. Rev., 55, 86-87 (2003); *Grubb/Thomsen*, 2010, 67.

459 *Dessemontet*, 1976, 195.

460 *Duffy*, 51 Wm. & Mary L. Rev. 609, 638-639 (2009).

461 *Duffy*, 51 Wm. & Mary L. Rev. 609, 638 (2009); *see also* Advanced Display Sys., Inc. v. Kent State Univ., 212 F.3d 1272, 1282 (Fed. Cir. 2000) (holding that anticipation requires describing every element of the claimed invention, either expressly or inherently, such that a person of ordinary skill in the art could practice the invention without undue experimentation).

be determined.[462] To judge "inherent anticipation" – "[the invention] is inherently disclosed only if it is the natural result flowing from the explicit disclosure of the prior art" –[463] it should first be decided what is to be regarded as a "natural result."[464] Secondly, the determination of novelty also depends on the developmental status of inventions. The novelty requirement is usually easier to achieve for fundamental inventions (e.g. basic patents) than for improvement inventions[465] taking into consideration the accumulated amount of prior arts over time. Thirdly, the complexity of determining novelty varies according to the field of technology. Determining novelty is more straightforward in relatively predictable fields, like electrical or mechanical engineering; however, it is more difficult for chemical, biotechnological, or pharmaceutical inventions, which lie in unpredictable fields.[466] Considering these complexities, one may be surprised to learn that anticipation is a finding of fact "with which an appellate court should be reluctant to interfere."[467] Last but not least, the novelty requirement, including the level of enablement, depends on the jurisdiction and on the developmental status of law, as will be discussed in chapter IV.A.4.

---

462 *See e.g.* MPEP§ 2164.01(a) (providing exemplary multi-factors to determine "undue" experiments as follows: (A) The breadth of the claims; (B) The nature of the invention; (C) The state of the prior art; (D) The level of one of ordinary skill; (E) The level of predictability in the art; (F) The amount of direction provided by the inventor; (G) The existence of working examples; and (H) The quantity of experimentation needed to make or use the invention based on the content of the disclosure, quoting *In re* Wands, 858 F.2d 731, 737 (Fed. Cir. 1988)).

463 *For details,* see subsection IV.A.3.

464 *Duffy*, 51 Wm. & Mary L. Rev. 609, 638 (2009); *See also Schering Co. v. Geneva Pharmaceuticals*, 339 F.3d 1373, 1379 (Fed. Cir. 2003) (holding "a limitation or the entire invention is inherent and in the public domain if it is the "natural result flowing from'' the explicit disclosure of the prior art.").

465 *See also Van Dijk*, 44 J. Ind. Econ. 151, 152-153 (1996); see the differences and difficulties in pharmaceutical art in subsection VI.E.2.b).

466 *Seymore*, 60 Duke L. J., 919, 933-936 (2011).

467 *Synthon BV v. SmithKline Beecham plc* [2005] UKHL 59, para 38; *Merck v. Teva Pharmaceuticals USA*, 347 F.3d 1367, 1369 (Fed. Cir. 2003) ("Anticipation is a question of fact, and after a bench trial is reviewed under the clearly erroneous standard"); *Eli Lilly and Company v. Zenith Goldline Pharmaceuticals. Inc.*, 471 F.3d 1369, 1375 (Fed. Cir. 2006) (anticipation is a question of fact, including whether or not an element is inherent in the prior art and the prior art reference must disclose each and every feature of the claimed invention, either explicitly or inherently).

The construction of the concept and the assessment of novelty differ among patent offices. In Europe, an invention is considered new if it does not form part of the state of the art,[468] which comprises everything made available to the public before the critical date of patent filings.[469] To test this novelty, ***EPO***, representatively, uses a strict definition of the disclosure of a prior art, the so-called "*photographic novelty approach,*" as in T 12/81 through "*purposive selection*" as in T 198/84, which is contrary to "arbitrary selection."[470] Consider a range selection as an example: Although a range of value falls within the scope of a previously disclosed range, it could be found novel when the selected interval i) is narrower; ii) is sufficiently far removed from the preferred alternatives in the prior art; and iii) is not an arbitrary choice from the prior art but results in a better effect ("purposive selection").[471] This "non-arbitrary" but "purposive selection" can be found when only the selected range has some better properties, not over the whole known range, which in turn makes the selection a new invention.[472] The novelty will be denied only when a skilled artisan could have seriously contemplated the claimed invention by applying the technical teaching of the prior art in the overlapping range.[473] According to this approach, an implicit disclosure of an invention in the prior art may not be sufficient to deny the novelty thereof, which can allow some pieces of existing knowledge to be patented.[474] Some scholars have even warned that this kind of novelty requirement could be met just by cleverly drafting a patent application.[475]

Until the *Olanzapine* decision, the greatest discrepancy between the EPO's and the ***German*** interpretation of novelty was the one between this "photographic" theory and the "list" theory.[476] Germany had a typical interpretation for assessing the novelty of a selection invention - the so-called

468 EPC Art. 54(1); German Patent Act 2011 ("GPA") Section 3(1); UK Patents Act 1977 (as amended 2011, "UK Patents Act 1977"), Section 2(1).

469 EPC Art. 54(1); GPA Section 3(2); UK Patents Act 1977, Section 2(2).

470 *Weaver/Perakis/Riolo*, 15 World Pat. Info. 81, 83 (1993).

471 *Hoechst/Thiochloroformates*, T198/84, OJ EPO 1985, 209, 209; *see also Texaco/Novelty*, T279/89 (1991), point 4.1.

472 *Hoechst/Thiochloroformates*, T198/84, OJ EPO 1985, 209, 214, point 7.

473 *Unilever/Washing Composition,* T 666/89, OJ EPO 1993, 495, 503; *see also Toshiba/Thickness of Magnetic Layers*, T 26/85, OJ EPO 1990, 22, 22.

474 World Bank, 2003, 180.

475 *See e.g., Correa*, 2006, 3.

476 *Singer/Lunzer*, 1995, 54.15B.

"*Bruchhausen doctrine*".[477] The BGH held that, in the absence of any other indication, patent claims would lead a person skilled in the art to expect that the desired result can be achieved in all values within the specified range.[478] It further held that this was because, according to the rules of arithmetic, the indication of a quantitative range, e.g. 0.1-50 ppm, was a simplified representation of all conceivable intermediate values within the range.[479] In the *Inkrustierungsinhibitoren* case, where the disclosure of prior art was questioned, while explicitly disagreeing with the EPO's jurisprudence, the BGH confirmed that, since the indication of a quantitative range was a simplified representation of the continuous intermediate value, all intermediate values were as a rule to be regarded as disclosed.[480] The range of disclosure according to these two theories can be well understood by the following diagram, and the same principle was applied to selection inventions:

Figure 6: The scope of disclosure of "0.1-50 ppm" according to both theories[481]

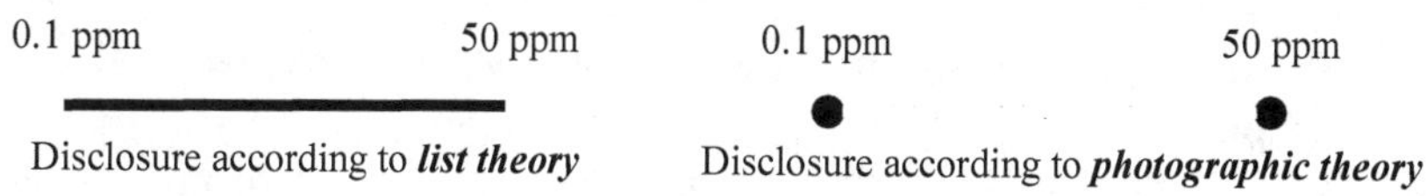

The ***British*** novelty test, which is referred to as the "*clear and unmistakable direction test*", is set out in the *General Tire v. Firestone* case[482] as follows: A claim is regarded as anticipated either if the prior art included a clear disclosure to do something that would infringe the patentee's claim, or if following the direction provided by the prior art would result inevitably in something that would fall within the patentee's claim.[483] Lord Hoffman affirmed that when a prior art disclosing the subject matter that would unavoidably have infringed the patent if it performed after granting the patent,

477 *Singer/Lunzer*, 1995, 54.15B.

478 *BGH/Crackkatalysator (Cracking catalyst)*, GRUR 1990, 510, 512.

479 *BGH/Crackkatalysator (Cracking catalyst)*, GRUR 1990, 510, 512.

480 *BGH/Inkrustierungsinhibitoren (Incrustration inhibitors)*, GRUR 2000, 591, 593-94.

481 This figure is prepared by the author on the basis of *Hansen/Hirsch*, 1997, 141.

482 *General Tire v. Firestone* [1972] RPC 457.

483 *General Tire v. Firestone* [1972] RPC 457, 485-86.

this prior art anticipated the later claimed invention.[484] Further, since whether a person is working or not an invention is an objective fact, the person's awareness of what he is doing does not matter.[485] However, as the House of Lords acknowledged, there is one exception to this test, i.e. an act performed secretly or without knowledge of the relevant facts, even if it would amount to infringements afterwards, will not anticipate the invention before.[486]

In the ***United States***, even though the law regarding novelty is more complicated,[487] basically, novelty is destroyed by a previous disclosure, a prior use, or other forms of public communication. As Learned Hand J stated, "a prior art patent or other publication to be an anticipation must bear within its four corners adequate directions for the practice of the patent invalidated." [488] In ***Korea***, the invention should be considered as novel, unless it is (i) an invention publicly known or worked in the Republic of Korea or a foreign country or (ii) an invention described in a publication distributed in the Republic of Korea or a foreign country, or iii) an invention publicly available through certain telecommunication lines before the filing date of the patent application.[489]

In the case of a compound invention, the ability to produce the compound in question is the common basic requirement in many jurisdictions, i.e., the novelty-destroying prior art must enable the compound. However, if all elements of the claimed invention are disclosed in a single reference, other references as common knowledge might be used to show that the claimed

---

484 *Synthon BV v. SmithKline Beecham plc* [2005] UKHL 59, paras 22-24.

485 *Synthon BV v. SmithKline Beecham plc* [2005] UKHL 59, para 22.

486 *Merrell Dow Pharmaceuticals Inc v. HN Norton & Co Ltd* [1995] UKHL 14, para 29 (noting there is a gap between the tests for infringement and anticipation after the 1977 Act.).

487 35 U.S.C. (2007) § 102 and 35 U.S.C. (2011) § 102.

488 *Dewey & Almy Chemical Co v. Mimex Co.*, 124 F.2d 986, 989 (2nd Cir. 1942) (further holding "[i]f the earlier disclosure offers no more than a starting point for further experiments, if its teaching will sometimes succeed and sometimes fail, if it does not inform the art without more how to practice the new invention, it has not correspondingly enriched the store of common knowledge, and it is not an anticipation.").

489 Korean Patent Act, Art. 29 (1).

invention is enabled.[490] In any event, it is unclear what is common knowledge and what is simply another publication.[491]

3. Inherent anticipation and enablement

> "It would certainly not be absurd to say that no one can obtain a claim that literally covers an item described in a prior art reference even if a method of making the described item was not disclosed or known in the art. In such a situation, it can be argued that a person who later invents a method of making that item is entitled to no more than that - a process claim to the method of making. Nevertheless, the contrary view that a prior art publication or a patent must be enabling in order to constitute an anticipation is the prevailing one today."[492]

The basic novelty question is whether the public already "possesses" the invention,[493] and the question of possession matters more when inherent anticipation is to be determined, which is more diverse from one jurisdiction to another. To constitute an anticipation of an invention, a description in a prior art must be sufficient to place the invention in the possession of the public, i.e. it must be *enabling*.[494] Namely, a prior art disclosure must enable the invention either explicitly or inherently, such that the person skilled in the art could practice the invention without undue experimentation.[495] The House of Lords reformulated the novelty test in the *General Tire* case with-

---

490 *See e.g. In re Donohue*, 766 F.2d 531, 533 (Fed. Cir. 1985) (noting "even if the claimed invention is disclosed in a printed publication, that disclosure will not suffice as prior art if it was not enabling. [...]It is not, however, necessary that an invention disclosed in a publication shall have actually been made in order to satisfy the enablement requirement.); *See also, In re Wiggins*, 488 F.2d 538, 543 (C.C.P.A. 1973) (noting "[e]very patent application and reference relies to some extent upon knowledge of persons skilled in the art to complement that disclosed in order that it be "enabling" within the meaning of § 112 and to satisfy the requirements of a reference under § 102. [...] In closer cases, where it might be reasonably doubted that a reference or patent application satisfies § 102 or § 112, other references can be cited as evidence of the level of skill in the art.").

491 *Grubb/Thomsen*, 2010, 67.

492 *Chisum*, 15 AIPLA Q. J. 57, 59-59 (1987).

493 *Seymore*, 60 Duke L. J., 919, 929 (2011).

494 *Holbrook*, 59 SMU L. Rev. 123, 151 (2006); *Chisum*, 15 AIPLA Q. J. 57, 61 (1987).

495 *See Kieff/Schwartz/Newman*, 2011, 174-75, 182-83; *see also Smithkline Beecham Corporation v. Apotex Corp.,* 403 F.3d 1328, 1329-30 (Fed. Cir. 2005); *see* also *In re* Brown, 329 F.2d 1006, 1011 (C.C.P.A. 1964).

out significant change, and confirmed that anticipation had two requirements, prior disclosure and enablement,[496] and that the requirement of each was distinct from the other.[497] Similarly, in the United States, this enablement requirement in the context of anticipation has been consistently affirmed.[498]

Under ***EPO*** practice, assessing novelty requires determining not what may have been "inherent" in what was made available, but what was "made available" to the public, for example, by a written description or by a prior use.[499] A hidden or secret use is not a ground for rejection.[500] Since these secret prior uses do not make the invention available to the public, it seems that there is no such thing as an inherent lack of novelty[501] before the EPO. This approach was followed by the House of the Lord in a metabolite case, i.e. *Merrell Dow Pharmaceuticals v. HN Norton.*[502] ***In the United Kingdom***, since an invention is a piece of information and making it available to the public requires the communication of information, for an invention to be anticipated by prior use, the use must have made the necessary information available.[503] Thus, acts performed secretly or without the knowledge of the relevant facts, even if they would amount to infringements, will not anticipate the invention.[504] On the other hand, if the procedure in the prior art that inevitably produces the substance is part of the prior art, so is the substance made by the procedure.[505]

---

496 *Synthon BV v. SmithKline Beecham plc* [2005] UKHL 59, para 19.

497 *Synthon BV v. SmithKline Beecham plc* [2005] UKHL 59, paras 28-33.

498 *Sanofi-Synthelabo v. Apotex, Inc.*, 550 F.3d 1075, 1083-85 (Fed. Cir. 2008).

499 *Mobil Oil/Friction Reducing Additives, G2/88,* OJ EPO 1990, 93, 111.

500 *Mobil Oil/Friction Reducing Additives, G2/88,* OJ EPO 1990, 93, 111; *Bayer/Plant growth regulating agent*, G 6/88, OJ EPO 1990, 114, 123.

501 *Grubb/Thomsen*, 2010, 248; *CPC/Flavour concentrates*, T 303/86 (1988), para 2.1. (Once the technical Board of Appeal held it was sufficient to destroy the novelty of the claimed process, when the claimed process and the process in the prior art were identical with respect to starting materials and reaction conditions, since processes identical in these features must inevitably yield identical products.).

502 *Merrell Dow Pharmaceuticals Inc v. HN Norton & Co Ltd* [1995] UKHL 14.

503 *Merrell Dow Pharmaceuticals Inc v. HN Norton & Co Ltd* [1995] UKHL 14, para 28.

504 *Merrell Dow Pharmaceuticals Inc v. HN Norton & Co Ltd* [1995] UKHL 14, para 29.

505 *Merrell Dow Pharmaceuticals Inc v. HN Norton & Co Ltd* [1995] UKHL 14, para 44.

In the United States, a prior art may be anticipating despite being silent about a feature of the claimed invention when that missing descriptive matter was necessarily present or inherent in the single prior art.[506] A prior art includes the inherent feature when it is the "natural result" flowing from the explicit disclosure of that prior art.[507] This inherent feature of a prior art reference does not need to be perceived as such by a person skilled in the art at the time of invention.[508] A secret or confidential use of an invention could give rise to the public use bar.[509] For instance, a product constitutes prior art although the knowledge needed to produce the product was not publicly available. Such a product is called a "non-informing" product.[510] In the *Metallizing Engineering* case, the patentee used a secret process to recondition worn metal parts for its customers before the critical date of the relevant patent application, and this fact rendered the patent invalid.[511] The principle underlying this doctrine of inherent anticipation is to ensure that the public remains free to exploit the invention, regardless of whether they understand its makeup sufficiently to allow them to operate.[512] The Federal Circuit in *Atlas Powder v. Ireco* held as follows:

> "Anticipation of a patent claim requires a finding that the claim at issue 'reads on' a prior art reference. In other words, if granting patent protection on the disputed claim would allow the patentee to exclude the public from practicing the prior art, then that claim is anticipated, regardless of whether it also covers subject matter not in the prior art."[513]

---

506 *Continental Can Co. USA, Inc. v. Monsanto Co.*, 948 F.2d 1264, 1268 (Fed. Cir. 1991).

507 *In re Kratz*, 592 F.2d 1169, 1174 (C.C.P.A. 1979); *Eli Lilly & Co. v. Barr Labs.*, 251 F.3d 955, 970 (Fed. Cir. 2001).

508 *Atlas Powder Co. v. Ireco, Inc.*, 190 F.3d 1342, 1348-49 (Fed. Cir. 1999); *Schering Co. v. Geneva Pharmaceuticals*, 339 F.3d 1373, 1378 (Fed. Cir. 2003); *Toro Co. v. Deere & Co.*, 355 F.3d 1313, 1321 (Fed. Cir. 2004) (holding "the fact that a characteristic is a necessary feature or result of a prior-art embodiment [...] is enough for inherent anticipation, even if that fact was unknown at the time of the prior invention").

509 35 U.S.C. § 102(b); *see, e.g., Metallizing Engineering Co. v. Kenyon Bearing & Auto Parts Co.*, 153 F.2d 516 (2nd Cir, 1946).

510 *Merges/Duffy*, 2011, 395-96.

511 *Metallizing Engineering Co. v. Kenyon Bearing & Auto Parts Co.*, 153 F.2d 516 (2nd Cir, 1946).

512 *Atlas Powder Co. v. Ireco, Inc.*, 190 F.3d 1342, 1348 (Fed. Cir. 1999).

513 *Atlas Powder Co. v. Ireco, Inc.*, 190 F.3d 1342, 1346 (Fed. Cir. 1999).

In Korea, anticipation is not a concept which appears in the determination of novelty of inventions.

4. Novelty of selection inventions

"Selection" is an act of selecting or rejecting one or more things. In other words, the selected item has already existed before, or at least at the time of selection. This initiates the whole discussion on the novelty of selection inventions.

a) Species selection inventions

A single prior art disclosing a species within a patent's claimed genus reads on the generic claim; thus, the species prior art anticipates the genus claim.[514] Therefore, to acquire a patent, an applicant must limit the claim to an extent which does not overlap with the prior art disclosure of species. A genus prior art, however, does not stop the applicant from filing a selection patent to claim species with certain useful properties.[515] As long as no member of the narrow subgroup is *specifically* disclosed in the publication, the compounds in the subgroup are considered novel, though they may have been described in general terms.[516] Therefore, although the species invention was disclosed in the prior genus invention, a patent on the species invention

---

514 *Atlas Powder Co. v. Ireco, Inc.,* 190 F.3d 1342, 1346 (Fed. Cir. 1999) (holding it is also true for the range selection inventions); *see also Titanium Metals Corp. v. Banner*, 778 F.2d 775, 783, 782 (Fed. Cir. 1985) (holding "a claim covers several compositions, the claim is 'anticipated' if one of them is in the prior art.").

515 *Integra Lifesciences I, Ltd. v. Merck KGaA*, 331 F.3d 860 (Fed. Cir. 2003), *cert. granted*, 545 U.S. 193 (2005).

516 *Robinson*, IIC 1972, 139, 143 (noting "[t]he selected group is regarded as novel because the disclosure, by generalization from a few specific investigated products, of a general class, comprising hundreds or thousands or even millions of members, cannot be considered a disclosure specifically of each member of that class."); *Grubb/Thomsen*, 2010, 64; *Chisum*, 2012, § 3.02[2][b]; *Metabolite Laboratories, Inc. v. Laboratory Corporation of America Holdings*, 370 F.3d 1354, 1367-68 (Fed. Cir. 2004) (holding that a prior art reference that discloses a genus still does not inherently disclose all species within that broad category); *See also Meier-Beck*, GRUR 2009, 893, 895.

can be granted. Thus, there can be overlapping scope of patents between a prior genus patent and a species patent. See Figure 7.

Figure 7: Genus v. species invention[517]

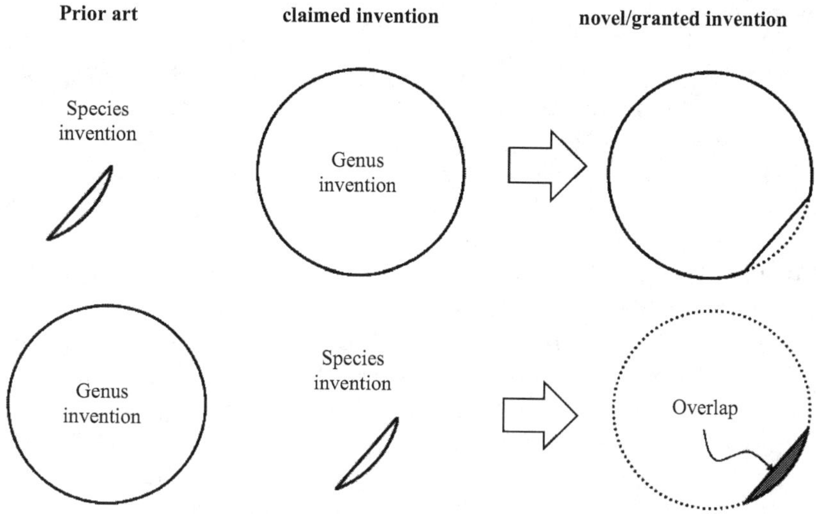

In the EPO

The teaching of a prior art is not confined to the detailed information given in the examples of how the invention is carried out, but embraces any information in the claims and description enabling a person skilled in the art to carry out the invention.[518] However, a generic disclosure does not generally deprive specific compounds of novelty.

The BOA distinguished between the following two situations; (i) if the subject matter of a claimed invention is a second family of compounds that

517 This figure is prepared by the author.

518 *Bayer/Diastereomer*, T 12/81 OJ EPO 1982, 296, 301 (holding the disclosure of the starting substance and the reaction process is always prejudicial to novelty because those data inevitably establish the end product, however, if two classes of starting substances are required to prepare the end products and examples of individual entities in each class are given in two lists of some length, then the resultant from the reaction of a specific pair from the two lists can nevertheless be regarded as new.).

partially covered the first class in the prior art, the invention is not new;[519] and (ii) if the subject matter is a defined compound, whereas the prior art discloses a family of compound defined only by a general formula covering the defined compound but not describing it explicitly, the invention must be considered novel.[520]

The former is the case where the invention was not found novel when a major part of the previously disclosed class was claimed. In T 133/92, the prior art was a product patent where part of the structural formula was an alkyl between 1 and 20 carbon atoms, and preferably the alkyl group was alkyls with between 6 and 15 carbon atoms (*C_6-C_{15} alkyl group*).[521] The application in suit claimed alkyl groups with between 6 and 10 carbon atoms (*C_6-C_{10} alkyl group*), which totally fell within the scope of the earlier patent, but no part of the compounds had been explicitly disclosed in the earlier patent. Though the Board noted an improved effect within the selected area, since the selection comprised almost half of the generic disclosure, the selection lacked novelty.[522] The Board further found that the selection of the alkyl groups between 6 and 8 carbon atoms (*C_6-C_8 alkyl group*) was not novel, but the selection of five specific examples (*n-hexyl, n-octyl, 2-ethylhexyl, 3,5,5-trimethylhexyl or n-decyl group*) was narrow enough and novel.[523] The Board reiterated the EPO's position as follows:

> "[A] distinction must be drawn between the novelty of a group of compounds defined by a general formula, and the novelty of particular individual compounds, because of the concept of individualisation which only applies to the structural definition of a single compound […]."[524]

It is not clear from this decision, however, if the five compounds had been defined in a general formula, whether the same selection would have been found to lack novelty. This would barely be reasonable. Meanwhile, it is assumed that in the case where the selection was made from relatively small numbers of a group disclosed in the prior art, it would be more problematic

---

519 *Dupont/Copolymer*, T 124/87, OJ EPO 1989. 491, 497.

520 *Draco/Xanthines*, T 7/86, OJ EPO 1988, 381, 385 (holding the novelty was in question in the case a prior document disclosed a class of compounds and the claimed invention was concerned with the selection of a class of compounds, not the specific individual compounds).

521 *AKZO/Bleaching activators*, T 133/92, 1994, point 4.2.2.

522 *AKZO/Bleaching activators*, T 133/92, 1994, point 2.1.3.

523 *AKZO/Bleaching activators*, T 133/92, 1994, point 2.1.3.

524 *AKZO/Bleaching activators*, T 133/92, 1994, point 4.2.2.

to establish the novelty thereof; thus, the general disclosure might be regarded as the disclosure of each member.[525]

Other than the relative size of the selection, the distinction between the disclosure of a generic formula and that of individual substances in prior art seems to be a separate criteria and to have taken root within the EPO case law to assess novelty.[526] In T181/82, it was held that, when the products of the reaction of specific compounds with a '$C_{1\text{-}4}$ alkyl bromide' was disclosed, a product as a result of the reaction with C_1 alkyl bromide is the only lack of novelty. This was because, among eight alkyl bromides,[527] only methyl bromide was disclosed, since C_1 was mentioned as the lower end of the range and was only the methyl.[528] This decision was interpreted in the later decision[529] as holding that only methyl bromide was disclosed in an individualized form, and that no special alkyl group with more than two carbon atoms was disclosed, and that the four individual groups comprised in the upper basic value (C_4) were disclosed only as a generic term.[530]

In Germany

The patentability of a "selection invention" was widely debated in Germany, especially right after the prohibition against product protection was repealed

525 *Grubb/Thomsen*, 2010, 234; cf. *Vivian*, IIC 1989, 303, 306 (noting the size of genus itself is normally not decisive as to the question of anticipation regardless of whether the selection was one from a class of 10 million or one from a class of two.).

526 *see also* EPO Examination Guidelines G-VII, Annex 3.1.(iv) (noting that if the selected group has not been specifically disclosed in the prior art, it would have been the question of lacking of novelty rather than obviousness.).

527 C1-C4 alkyls are 8 alkyls as follows: C1 alkyl is methyl; C2 alkyl is ethyl; two C3 alkyls are n-propyl and isopropyl; and four C4 alkyls are n-butyl, isobutyl, *sec*-butyl, and *tert*-butyl.

528 *Ciba-Geigy/Spiro compounds,* T 181/82, OJ EPO 401 (1984).

529 *Hoechst/Enantiomers*, T296/87, OJ EPO 1990, 195, 206.

530 *Hoechst/Enantiomers*, T296/87, OJ EPO 1990, 195, 206; *see also PFIZER/Penem Derivatives*, T 1048/92, point 2.1.

as of January 1, 1968.[531] In the *Fluoran* decision, the BGH held that a Markush claim disclosure in the prior art would be enough to be a novelty-destroying reference of a selection invention and to be regarded as disclosing an individual species, when a person skilled in the art was able to implement the invention on the basis of the indications given regarding the contested compound of the prior art publication.[532] It further held that "[t]he fact that a chemical compound falls within a previously published formula says nothing about the question of novelty [...]. The only decisive factor is whether the information contained in a previous publication alone enables a person skilled in the art to make the invention relating to this chemical compound, i.e. to produce the substance in question."[533] Thus, the compounds were not novel, because a person skilled in the art could have worked the invention. After this decision, it was very difficult to get patents for selection inventions until the *Olanzapine* decision in late 2008.

In the *Olanzapine* case, the BGH held that all compounds embraced by a generic formula would not automatically be regarded as individually disclosed.[534] Lilly's patent in suit[535] was on a single chemical compound "olanzapine."[536] One of the most relevant prior arts was a patent document that was also filed by Lilly and that was acknowledged in the very patent specification.[537] This patent document disclosed a general formula covering theoretically millions of individual compounds, identified around 100 com-

---

531 *Katzenberger*, IIC 1972, 357, 364-365 (providing arguments against granting selection patent such as, i) anticipatory prior art effect of the patent covering that group of compounds and ii) prohibition against double patenting; and arguments for selection patent such as, discovery of a new and valuable compound from a group of compounds valued as much as discovering a new group of compounds.); *see also Schmied-Kowarzik*, IIC 1970, 190, 196 (arguing selection inventions must be able to obtain an absolute product protection); *see also Nastelski*, IIC 1972, 267, 291-294 (especially arguing selection patent shouldn't be deemed to be novel, even if the products have not been individually designated, "if the producibility of an appropriate variety and number of individual representatives of the group is experimentally proven so that in accordance with the decision the manufacture or existence of the remaining products belonging to the group has also been substantiated for the skilled artisan"); *see also Vossius*, GRUR 1976, 165, 171.

532 *BGH/Fluoran*, GRUR 1988, 447.

533 *BGH/Fluoran*, GRUR 1988, 447, 449.

534 *BGH/Olanzapine*, IIC 2009, 596.

535 EP 0,454,436, US 5,229,382.

536 a widely prescribed anti-psychotic agent used for the treatment of schizophrenia.

537 GB 1,533,235.

pounds by name, but did not disclose olanzapine specifically. Another prior art ("Chakrabarti" article)[538] document disclosed the Structure-Activity-Relationship[539] observations of a group of compounds and several compounds closely structured to olanzapine, but did not disclose olanzapine. The questions at issue were the effect of a particular kind of disclosure, namely, a "Markush" formula, the consideration of structural similarity of compounds, and whether a person skilled in the art could have modified or supplemented the prior art's teaching to determine the disclosure of prior art.

The Federal Patent Court of Germany ("BPatG") held that, since a skilled person would be able to obtain all necessary information[540] to manufacture olanzapine from *Chakrabarti* prior art, it was a novelty-destroying disclosure of olanzapine.[541] In contrast to this ruling, the BGH held that it was not necessary to determine in what form a person skilled in the art could perform a certain general teaching, using his technical knowledge, or how he can modify this teaching, if necessary.[542] The important point was exclusively what a person skilled in the art derived from the prior publication as the content of the specific (general) teaching.[543] The BGH went on to say that the decisive question was rather what can be "*directly and unambiguously*" derived from a document, from the point of view of a person skilled in the art, which was in line with the jurisprudence of the BOA of the EPO.[544]

538 *Chakrabarti, et al.*, 28 J. Med. Chem. 874 (1980).

539 This is the relationship between the chemical 2D or 3D structure of a molecule and its biological activity. This analysis enables to determine the chemical groups responsible for a target biological effect. This in turn makes modification of the effect or potency of the medication by changing its chemical structure. The chemists uses this relations ship to insert or delete some chemical groups into/from the compound and test the modification, and finally modify its biological effect.

540 The court illustrated this information as follows: lead structure of formula I, a group of only 12 compounds, 3 specific compounds immediately "neighboring" olanzapine, neuroleptic activity of compounds which is useful for treating diseases such as schizophrenia.

541 *Barth/Zimmer*, 27 Biotechnol. Law Rep. 532, 532-533 (2008).

542 *BGH/Olanzapine*, IIC 2009, 596, 599.

543 *BGH/Olanzapine,* IIC 2009, 596, 599.

544 *BGH/Olanzapine,* IIC 2009, 596, 599; The Federal Court of Justice cited the relevant BOA decision as follows: *Bayer/Diastereomer*, OJ EPO 1982, 296; *Ciba-Geigy/Spiro compounds,* T 181/82, OJ EPO 1984, 401, 411; *Draco/Xanthines*, T 7/86, OJ EPO 1988, 381, 38; *Hoechst/Enantiomers*, T296/87, OJ EPO 1990, 195, 206-207; *Hoechst/Diastereomers of 3-cephem-4-carboxylic acid-1-(isopropoxycarbonyloxy) ethyl ester*, T 940/98 (2003); *See also Meier-Beck*, GRUR 893, 895 (2009); *Grubb/Thomsen*, 2010, 64.

The BGH held that the determination of what was not explicitly mentioned in the characteristics of the claim, and in the text of the specification, but was obvious for a person skilled in the art to implement the teaching being protected and therefore did not require any special disclosure, was not aimed at supplementing the disclosure with the technical knowledge.[545] The purpose was not different from determining the meaning of a claim, i.e. the technical information that a person skilled in the art derives from the source with the background of his technical knowledge.[546] Citing the *Elektrische Steckverbindung* decision,[547] the BGH held that modifications would be allowable only if the modifications were so obvious to a person skilled in the art in the entire content of the document that they were easily evident when reading the document attentively, paying attention less to the words than to their meaning, so that he essentially "*reads them along*" in his thoughts.[548]

The BGH then applied this principle to the chemical compound invention as follows: "The decisive factor is whether the concrete compound is disclosed or not, and for this purpose, information that easily enables a person skilled in the art to specifically implement the invention relating to this chemical compound, i.e. to obtain the specific substance, is required."[549] The BGH clarified its position against the *Fluoran* decision by explaining that the *Fluoran* case was decided under the Patent Act of 1968 and that the Court did not adhere to this decision for the current law. The BGH held further that an individual compound that was not explicitly disclosed could only be considered to have been disclosed if a person skilled in the art "read it along" in the sense of the *Elektrische Steckverbindung* decision, for example, because it was familiar to him as the usual implementation of the stated general formula and therefore occurred to him as also having been meant when he read the general formula.[550] Otherwise, the disclosure of the individual compound was necessary to destroy novelty.[551]

545 *BGH/Olanzapine,* IIC 2009, 596, 599.
546 *BGH/Olanzapine,* IIC 2009, 596, 599.
547 *BGH/Elektrische Steckverbindung (Electronic Plug-in connection)*, GRUR 1995, 330.
548 *BGH/Olanzapine,* IIC 2009, 596, 599.
549 *BGH/Olanzapine,* IIC 2009, 596, 600.
550 *BGH/Olanzapine,* IIC 2009, 596, 600.
551 *BGH/Olanzapine,* IIC 2009, 596, 600.

In the United Kingdom

Species selection inventions have been patentable for many decades following a specific rule for these kinds of inventions established by Maugham J in the *I.G. Farbenindustrie's A.G.'s Patent* case ("*IG Rule*").[552] The *IG Rule* stated the following three traditional requirements: i) a selection patent to be valid must be based on some substantial advantage to be secured by the use of the selected members (the phrase will be understood to include the case of a substantial disadvantage to be thereby avoided); ii) the whole of the selected members must possess the advantage in question; and iii) the selection must be in respect of a quality of a special character that can fairly be said to be peculiar to the selected group.[553] Although the second requirement was criticized as impractical, it was well followed in the United Kingdom in other cases, without distinguishing between novelty and inventive step.[554]

Jacob LJ declared the end of the IG Rule's life in the *Olanzapine* decision.[555] In his opinion, Jacob LJ firmly rejected the argument that "every chemical class disclosure discloses each and every member of the class" for two reasons: i) being an *a priori* consideration and ii) not being consistent with the jurisprudence of the BOA of the EPO, particularly the *Hoechst/ Enantiomers* decision.[556] He reiterated that "an anticipation is an 'individualized description' of the later claimed compound or class of compounds."[557] With respect to the *a priori* consideration, he argued as follows:

> "An old question and answer runs as a[sic] follows: 'Where does a wise man hide a leaf? In a forest.' It is, at least faintly, ridiculous to say that a particular leaf has been made available to you by telling you that it is in Sherwood Forest.

---

552 *I.G. Farbenindustrie's AG's Patent* 47 R.P.C. 289, 322-3 (1930); *see also Blanco White,* 1983, 105-106.

553 *I.G. Farbenindustrie's AG's Patent* 47 R.P.C. 289, 322-3 (1930); *see also Blanco White,* 1983, 105-106.

554 *Dr Reddy's Laboratories Ltd v. Eli Lilly & Company Ltd*, [2009] EWCA Civ 1362, paras 36-39.

555 *Dr Reddy's Laboratories Ltd v. Eli Lilly & Company Ltd*, [2009] EWCA Civ 1362, para 37 (holding that the IG rule was just "a part of legal history," but not part of the living law (post-1977 law)); *See also* Manual of Patent Practice - UK Patents Act 1977, paragraph 3.89-3.90 (October 2012).

556 *Hoechst/ Enantiomers,* T296/87, OJ EPO 1990, 195.

557 *Dr Reddy's Laboratories Ltd v. Eli Lilly & Company Ltd*, [2009] EWCA Civ 1362, para 30.

> Once identified, you can of course see it. But if not identified you know only the generality: that Sherwood Forest has millions of leaves."[558]

Jacob LJ noted that the "selection invention" rule of *I.G. Farbenindustrie's Patent* was developed to avoid a finding of anticipation, it did not draw a distinction between lack of novelty and obviousness, and it was too strict, because it is difficult to show that a group (compound) has a "substantial advantage" over the whole prior class without an enormous range of experiments.[559] Lord Neuberger noted that this issue was "not dissimilar from the enantiomer/racemate issue"[560] and recognized the difficulty in the application of the *IG Rule*, where the prior class of compounds was very large.[561] Consequently, when the invention can be found novel in the first place, there is no longer any need to consider whether it is a valid selection invention according to the *IG Rule*.[562]

In the United States

Unlike other jurisdictions, the U.S. American ("American") patent law does not use the term "selection inventions" as a category of invention. Instead, the terms "genus" and "species" are often used in practice, though not as a statutory category, and a significant body of case law has evolved.

In *In re Petering*,[563] the Court held that a prior art reference disclosing a limited genus of twenty compounds rendered every species within the genus unpatentable. The Court pointed out that the significance was not in the mere

---

558 *Dr Reddy's Laboratories Ltd v. Eli Lilly & Company Ltd*, [2009] EWCA Civ 1362, paras 25-30. This argument was in line with the separate judgment of Neuberger L. *see* para 108.

559 *Dr Reddy's Laboratories Ltd v. Eli Lilly & Company Ltd*, [2009] EWCA Civ 1362, paras 36-39.

560 *Generics Ltd. v. Lundbeck* [2009] UKHL 12.

561 *Generics Ltd. v. Lundbeck* [2009] UKHL 12, paras 103-104.

562 *See e.g., Fitt*, 20 Biotechnol. Law Rep. 17, 18 (2010).

563 *In re* Petering, 301 F.2d 681 (C.C.P.A. 1962).

number of compounds in the prior document,[564] but in the total circumstances, including the limited number of variations for R, only two alternatives for Y and Z, and a large unchanging patent structural nucleus.[565] The Court further held that, on reading the prior publication, a person skilled in the art would "envisage each member of" the genus and that "it is no moment that each compound is not specifically named or shown by structural formula in that publication."[566] In *In re Schaumann*, in which the prior art disclosure taught only fourteen possible compounds,[567] the Court held that, when a prior art disclosure embraced "a very limited number of compounds," it would inevitably be concluded that "the reference provides a description of those compounds just as surely as if they were identified in the reference by name." [568] In *Bristol-Myers Squibb v. Ben Venue Laboratories*, the Federal Circuit also noted that "the disclosure of a small genus may anticipate the species of that genus even if the species are not themselves recited."[569] Thus, when the genus embraces a limited number of compounds, the individual

---

564 U.S. Patent No. 2,155,555 (April 25, 1939, under the title of "Iso-alloxazine derivatives and process for the manufacture of same"), and the generic formula was as follows:

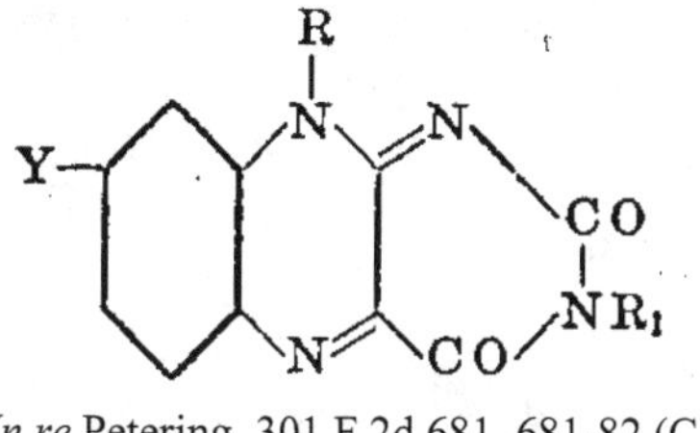

565 *In re* Petering, 301 F.2d 681, 681-82 (C.C.P.A. 1962).

566 *In re* Petering, 301 F.2d 681, 682 (C.C.P.A. 1962).

567 *In re* Schaumann, 572 F.2d 312, 314 (C.C.P.A.1987); the prior patent was U.S. Patent No. 2,344,356 (March 14, 1944, under the title of "Chemical compounds beta-(meta-hydroxyphenol)-isopropylamines") and the disclosed generic formula with single variable (R) was read as:

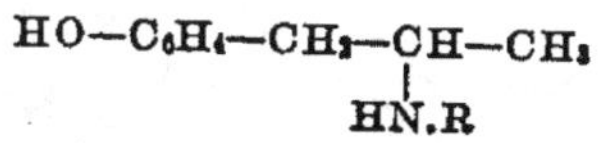

568 *In re* Schaumann, 572 F.2d 312, 316-17 (C.C.P.A.1987).

569 *Bristol-Myers Squibb Co. v. Ben Venue Labs., Inc.*, 246 F.3d 1368, 1380 (Fed. Cir. 2001).

description does not seem to be necessary to destroy the novelty of a species invention.[570]

In the *Olanzapine* decision, the defendants argued that the Chakrabarti article anticipated the patent in view of the holdings in *In re Petering* and *In re Schaumann*. However, in his opinion, Rader J distinguished the *Olanzapine* case, where the Chakrabarti article disclosed millions of compounds, from these two cases, because limited numbers of specific preferences, namely "some 20 compounds," or "14 compounds" were disclosed, respectively. He reiterated that, "[t]o anticipate, a prior art reference must place the inventive compound or composition in the possession of the public. Thus, the prior art reference must disclose each and every feature of the claimed invention, either explicitly or inherently."[571] He then noted that the Chakrabarti patent document had not "expressly spelled out a definite and limited class of compounds that enabled a person of ordinary skill in the art to at once envisage each member of this limited class."[572] Rader J also stated that "one would have to depart from the teaching of the article and recombine the components of the specific illustrative compounds *with hindsight*" to make the olanzapine starting from another prior art disclosing structure and activity relationship.[573]

In Korea

As it is reiterated by the Korean Patent Court in the Olanzapine case,[574] it is established case law that, to deny the novelty of selection invention, the prior art document should specifically disclose the concept of a selection invention, and it could also be that a person skilled in the art could directly learn the existence of the selection invention from the prior document based on

---

570 *Corning Glass Works v. Sumitomo Elec. U.S.A., Inc.*, 868 F.2d 1251, 1262 (Fed. Cir. 1989) (rejecting once the argument "a claim to a genus would inherently disclose all species" as wholly meritless).

571 *Eli Lilly and Company v. Zenith Goldline Pharmaceuticals. Inc.*, 471 F.3d 1369, 1375 (Fed. Cir. 2006).

572 *Eli Lilly and Company v. Zenith Goldline Pharmaceuticals. Inc.*, 471 F.3d 1369, 1376 (Fed. Cir. 2006). In fact, this was the first decision among four jurisdictions which upheld the validity of Olanzapine patent.

573 *Eli Lilly and Company v. Zenith Goldline Pharmaceuticals. Inc.*, 471 F.3d 1369, 1377 (Fed. Cir. 2006).

574 *Korean Patent Court/Olanzapine*, 2010Heo371, Nov. 11, 2010.

the disclosure thereof and on common knowledge at the time of application.[575]

In this case, the Korean Patent Court held the novelty of selection invention was not denied, since (i) olanzapine was not specifically disclosed in the prior art references, (ii) though olanzapine was included in the preferred compound groups, the number of compounds comprised in the preferred compound groups was too large for a skilled person to directly learn the existence of Olanzapine, and (iii) there was no indication in the prior art for a skilled person to directly recognize olanzapine.[576]

b) Optical isomers

It seems that the narrower the selection is made with regard to the generic term, the more likely the selection can be deemed novel. What, then, if one is selected out of two? Indeed, the optically active form of a racemate can be considered an extreme example of selection inventions, and it has been arg ued that this invention cannot be novel if the racemate is known, since the racemate can be considered an equimolar mixture of each enantiomer.[577] More generally, the enantiomer invention is about a substantially or totally pure compound that is not contaminated by other possible stereoisomers.[578]

In the EPO

In the early decision on the novelty of optical isomers, the Board stated that "[a] substance selection can come about in various ways, e.g. if an unmentioned compound or group of compounds having formula covered by the state of the art is found, in the absence of any information as to the starting substance or substances."[579] Namely, a specific compound covered by a generic formula of the prior art will be novel if the prior art does not provide any specific information, given in the examples of how the invention was carried out, but embraces any information in the claims and the description

575 *Korean Patent Court/Olanzapine*, 2010Heo371, Nov. 11, 2010, para 3.Ka.
576 *Korean Patent Court/Olanzapine*, 2010Heo371, Nov. 11, 2010, para 3.Na.2).
577 *Grubb/Thomsen*, 2010, 236.
578 *Eli Lilly/Enantiomer*, T 600/95 (1996), point 3.2.
579 *Bayer/Diastereomer*, T 12/81 OJ EPO 1982, 296, 303.

enabling a person skilled in the art to carry out the invention.[580] Afterwards, it was often confirmed by the Boards that the conceptual disclosure of two possible configurations without any pointer to the individual member was insufficient for the novelty to be denied.[581]

In T 296/87, in which the claimed invention was a mixture containing 80% of D-enantiomer, and the prior art made no mention of enantiomers and indicated only a chemical substance with an asymmetric carbon atom, i.e. the racemate, the Board presented the "photographic approach" to test the novelty in the enantiomer invention and held as follows:

> "The novelty of the D- and L-enantiomers is therefore not destroyed by the description of racemates. The situation is different if the state of the art includes enantiomers – however designated (D, d, L, l or + or -) – which are specifically named and can be produced. [...] the only technical teachings prejudicial to novelty are those which disclose a substance as the inevitable result of a prescribed method or in specific, i.e. individualized, form."[582]

This decision demonstrates that novelty was already established when a choice between two possibilities was made. The Board further held that the configuration of one enantiomer was different from the racemate, and the fact that the prior art disclosed only racemates in detail did not disclose the enantiomer's specific configurations. [583] However, it is the context of basic organic chemistry, and once a person skilled in the art sees the chemical structure having chiral carbons, he will automatically know the special configuration of each enantiomers.

In addition, before the EPO, it seems that, even though a skilled person could have successfully separated the racemate into the enantiomers with the help of general knowledge, the claimed enantiomer would be regarded as novel over the previously disclosed racemate. This can be seen in the following paragraph of the decision:

> "In taking this view the Board is aware that the two enantiomers, far from falling merely intellectually within the definition of the structure in question, actually

580 *Bayer/Diastereomer*, T 12/81 OJ EPO 1982, 296, 303 (The Board, however, did not acknowledge the novelty of a compound because it would have been inevitably produced according to the disclosed method and the starting materials).

581 *Pfizer/Penem Derivatives,* T1048/92 (1994), point 2.5; *see also ZENECA/Enantiomer*, T1046/97 (1999), point 2.1.1.6. (held optically-active form in the prior art provides no information about any specific stereochemical form(s) of the chemical compound.).

582 *Hoechst/Enantiomers*, T296/87, OJ EPO 1990, 195, 206-207.

583 *Hoechst/Enantiomers*, T296/87, OJ EPO 1990,195, 195.

> exist unseparated in the racemate. Generally, the latter can also be separated by converting the enantiomers into a mixture of diastereomers, e.g. using optically active substances, then resolving the mixture and recovering the enantiomers from the resulting products. These considerations are immaterial to the question of novelty, however, and will be more usefully applied to the examination as to inventive step."[584]

Furthermore, an enantiomer was found novel despite the prior patent holder's attempt to include all individual isomers and all mixtures. [585] Namely, even a disclosure conveying the previous patentee's desire to cover all possible isomers does not destroy the novelty of a later selection of an isomer, if the previous patent did not disclose the specific isomers.

To sum up, it is EPO's consistent jurisprudence that, unless the prior art contains both an individualized disclosure and a particular method and starting materials that will inevitably lead to the claimed compound, this kind of a chemical selection will be found novel over the racemate disclosed in the prior art.[586]

In Germany

In its early decision, where the patentability of an epimer[587] over the prior art description of the presence of an asymmetric carbon atom of the compound was issued, the BGH held that "[a] chemical compound is no longer novel if it is identified in a previous publication as a chemical individual and a skilled person was able to produce [it]. It is insignificant whether the compound had actually already been manufactured."[588]

A case was decided in 2007, in which the patent in issue claimed an enantiomer of atorvastatin[589] over the prior patent disclosing structure of atorvastatin with the wedges and dashes.[590] Referring to *Elektrische Steckver-*

---

584 *Hoechst/Enantiomers*, T296/87, OJ EPO 1990,195, 207.

585 *Pfizer/Penem Derivatives,* T1048/92 (1994), points 2.3-2.5. (holding "as will be appreciated, various optically active isomers of the new compounds are possible. ***The present invention embraces such optically active isomers and mixtures thereof.***"[Emphasis added]).

586 *E.g., Eli Lilly/Enantiomer*, T 600/95 (1996) (holding one isomer is not novel over the prior art description of the very isomer and of the method to obtain it).

587 See *supra* 115 .

588 *BGH/ α-aminobenzylpenicillin,* GRUR 1978, 696, 698.

589 Atorvastatin is the active ingredient of an anti-cholesterol drug sold under the brand name Lipitor® which was the best selling drug in the world.

590 *BPatG/Atorvastatin*, Beck-Rechtsprechung ("BeckRS") 2007, 18183.

bindung and *Schmierfettzusammensetzung*,[591] the BPatG held that, according to the jurisprudence of the BGH, the disclosure of a document belonging to the prior art was not limited to the literal description, but encompassed everything that the skilled person supplemented self-evidently or nearly essentially, or that he recognized directly with his careful study of the document and read along in thoughts.[592] The Court further held that

> "These principles which refer to the disclosure content of a prior publication in the field of mechanics are applicable in the field of chemistry, provided that a chemical compound is viewed as prejudicial to novelty, when a prior publication or a document with earlier priority date conveys to the skilled person a concrete indication to the compound in question, that is that a skilled person easily reads this compound in his thoughts and because of this indication he is directly put in the position of laying his hands on the compound in question. It is not necessary to that the compound has actually already been prepared. The mere possibility of its preparation and, thus thereby being made available suffices (referring α-Aminobenzylpenicillin, Fluoran, and Herbicid wirksames Enantiomer)."[593]

The Court further held that the novelty of stereoisomer (epimer, enantiomer, diastereomer) was thus already to be denied, when the stereoisomer was recognizably described to the skilled reader in the form of a mixture of its stereoisomers, and was accessible to him without difficulties by means of conventional separation methods from this mixture.[594] The Court also properly stated that "an indication or an explicit naming of the stereoisomer in question is as little necessary as a specification or description of method to its isolation."

However, the BGH confirmed its new position on this issue in the *Escitalopram* decision, the first decision on the patentability of an enantiomer after its *Olanzapine* decision.[595] The main issue for debate was again whether the prior patent disclosure of racemate, Citalopram,[596] allowing a person skilled in the art clearly to recognize two enantiomers, i.e. (S)- and (R)-

591 *BGH/Schmierfettzusammensetzung(Grease composition)*, GRUR 2000, 296.

592 *BPatG/Atorvastatin*, BeckRS 2007, 18183, point II.1.a).

593 *BPatG/Atorvastatin*, BeckRS 2007, 18183, point II.1.a).

594 BPatG/*Atorvastatin*, BeckRS 2007, 18183, point II.1.a).

595 *Zu Waldeck und Pyrmont*, Gewerblicher Rechtsschutz und Urheberrecht, Praxis im Immaterial- und Wettbewerbsrecht ("GRUR-Prax"), 2010, 13 (stating that the Escitalopram decision seems to show that the Court continues its new line regarding the concept of disclosure stated in its Olanzapine decision.).

596 Citalopram is a selective serotonin reuptake inhibitor anti-depressant.

enantiomers, was enough to destroy the novelty of a patent on the (S)-enantiomer, ES-Citalopram. [597]

In this case, the BPatG held that the patent was invalid for lack of novelty for the similar reasons that a chemical compound having one chiral atom was no longer novel when claimed in the form of an enantiomer, if specific indication of the enantiomer in a prior publication had been given, and if a skilled person was able to produce the compound on the basis of this indication and his general knowledge.[598] The Court found that the person skilled in the art would easily have been able to separate the Escitalopram from the racemic mixture disclosed in the prior art patent specification in a way that was commonly used before the priority date of the Escitalopram patent.[599]

While admitting that the person skilled in the art on the basis of his general knowledge was able to recognize that citalopram having a chiral carbon had two different structures, the BGH stated nevertheless that this fact did not lead to a disclosure that was detrimental to novelty.[600] Citing the *Olanzapine* decision, the Court said that, to "make them [the individual enantiomers] available to the skilled person for the purpose of novelty examination, further information was as a rule required, in particular with regard to their individualization."[601] The Court concluded that, since the prior document did not directly and unambiguously disclose the individual enantiomers to the person skilled in the art, and since he had to find a way to resolve the racemate, the prior patent was not detrimental to novelty.[602]

In the United Kingdom

The *Ranbaxy v. Warner-Lambert* case concerned two patents owned by Warner-Lambert, one of which covered a class of compounds including

597 EP 0,347,006, U.S. RE34, 712.
598 *BPatG/Escitalopram*, BeckRS 2007, 14624, para II, especially II b).
599 *BPatG/Escitalopram,* BeckRS 2007, 14624, para II, especially II b).
600 *BGH/Escitalopram*, GRUR 2010, 123, 125.
601 *BGH/Escitalopram,* GRUR 2010, 123, 126.
602 *BGH/Escitalopram*, GRUR 2010, 123, 126.

atorvastatin[603] and the other covered a single enantiomer of atorvastatin (Lipitor®).[604] Ranbaxy appealed against the decision refusing a declaration of non-infringement of the previous patent with respect to its particular compound, enantiomeric atorvastatin calcium salt, and Warner-Lambert cross-appealed the decision ruling that the enantiomer patent was invalid for lack of novelty and obviousness.[605] The Court of Appeal held that the patent claiming an enantiomer was anticipated by the prior art, which did not disclose the salt of the pure enantiomer, but clearly taught that one of the things that could be made was the single enantiomer, and the way of carrying out the teaching of the earlier patent application would necessarily infringe the later claim of an enantiomer.[606] This case was slightly different from other cases, because the general formula of the earlier patent on the compounds showed a three dimensional arrangement. [607]

In *Lundbeck v. Generics*, while citing *Synthon BV v. Smithkline Beecham Plc,*[608] Lord Hoffmann restated that, to anticipate a patent, the prior art must have disclosed the claimed invention and enabled a ordinary skilled person to perform it. He also stated that it was settled jurisprudence in the EPO[609] that disclosure of a racemate did not in itself amount to disclosure of each of its enantiomers.[610] Regarding the plaintiff's argument that claim 1 was

603 EP No. 0247633 (January 30, 1991, under the title of "Trans-6-(2-(3- or 4-carboxamido-substituted pyrrol-1-yl)-alkyl)-4-hydroxypyran-2-one inhibitors of cholesterol synthesis"), claim 1: A compound of structural formula

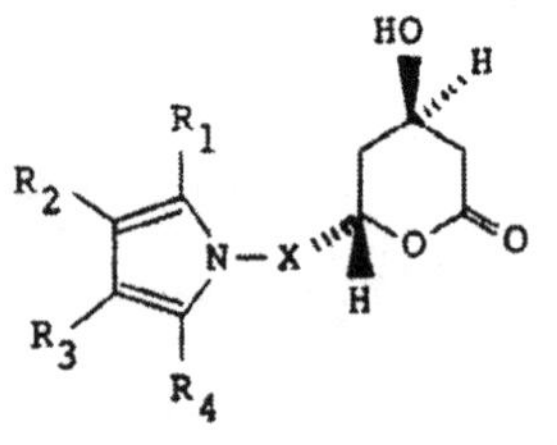

(I)

I

[…].

604 *Ranbaxy (UK) v. Warner-Lambert*, [2006] EWCA Civ 876.

605 *Ranbaxy (UK) v. Warner-Lambert*, [2006] EWCA Civ 876, para 1.

606 *Ranbaxy (UK) v. Warner-Lambert*, [2006] EWCA Civ 876, paras 36-40.

607 See subsection II.C.1.b).

608 *Synthon BV v. SmithKline Beecham plc*, 20 October 2005, [2005] UKHL 59.

609 *Lundbeck v. Generics Ltd.* [2008] EWCA Civ 311 (citing the decisions T 296/87 (OJ EPO 1990, 19, point 6.2), T 1048/92 and T 1046/97).

610 *Lundbeck v. Generics Ltd.* [2008] EWCA Civ 311, para 9.

not only directed to the isolated enantiomer, namely that claim 1 could include the racemate, thus, to that extent the claim was anticipated by the prior art, Lord Hoffmann noted that the claim did not include an unresolved part of the racemate, based on the title of the patent ("new enantiomers and their isolation"), and the knowledge of a person skilled in the art.[611] Jacob LJ stated further that this was a pure question of construction, namely whether claim 1 covered the (+) enantiomer when in the racemate, and he held that claim 1 obviously did not – the patentee was plainly not intending to cover the racemate, thus, how much more than 50% of the (+) enantiomer must have been present for a product to fall within the claim was simply a moot point as far as the case was concerned.[612]

After this decision, the Court in *Generics (UK) v. Daiichi Pharmaceutical* reaffirmed, since the prior patent on a racemate (ofloxacin, an anti-microbial agent) neither taught nor suggested the resolution of racemate into enantiomers, and the prior art disclosing ofloxacin did not anticipate one enantiomer, i.e. levofloxacin.[613]

In the United States

Unlike other jurisdictions, challenges to the patentability of chiral molecules based on novelty and non-obviousness have been asserted since as early as 1948, and have been met with a rule favorable to pharmaceutical companies.[614] In *In re Williams,* while quoting the famous Aspirin® case, the Court held that "the existence of a compound as an ingredient of another substance does not negative novelty in a claim to the pure compound, although it may, of course, render the claim unpatentable for lack of invention."[615] Apart from the Aspirin® case, which was decided in 1910, among the three countries where patents for aspirin were granted, the American patent was the only

611 *Lundbeck v. Generics*, [2008] EWCA Civ 311, paras 10-13.

612 *Lundbeck v. Generics Ltd.* [2008] EWCA Civ 311, para 50; Since the challenge based on lack of novelty had failed in both courts below, it was not renewed before the House of Lords. *See Generics Ltd. v. Lundbeck* [2009] UKHL 12, paras 11, 43, 65 (also noting that the patentee would not have intended to cover racemate).

613 *Generics (UK) v. Daiichi Pharmaceutical* [2008] EWHC 2413 (Pat), para 317-18.

614 *In re Williams*, 171 F.2d 319 (C.C.P.A. 1948); *Darrow*, 2 Stan. Tech. L. Rev. 1, para 13 (2007).

615 *In re Williams*, 171 F.2d 319, 320 (C.C.P.A. 1948).

one that survived.[616] Furthermore, in *In re May* in 1978, the Court held that the novelty of an optical isomer was not negated by the prior art disclosure of its racemate;[617] and, in *Brenner v. Ladd* in 1965, the Court held it did not matter even that a racemate may dissociate in the solution.[618]

In *Sanofi-Synthelabo v. Apotex, Inc.*, the prior art patent disclosed clopidogrel,[619] in which there was one chiral center and which consisted of two enantiomers, and claimed that the invention related both to each enantiomer and their mixture.[620] Like the BOA,[621] the Federal Circuit, while mentioning the difficulty of separating enantiomers and the unpredictability of their properties, held that a reference that did not enable the separation of those enantiomers, would not have enabled a person skilled in the art to obtain clopidogrel substantially separated from the l-enantiomer.[622]

In *Forest Labs., Inc. v. Ivax Pharms., Inc.*, the District Court found that the alleged prior art did not disclose "substantially pure" *Escitalopram* and did not enable the person skilled in the art to obtain the product, since the separation technique at the time of the invention was relatively new and unpredictable, and the inventor himself failed to separate the enantiomer several times.[623] The Federal Circuit did not find errors in the District Court's

---

616 *Kuehmsted v. Farbenfabriken of Elberfeld Co.*, 179 F. 701 (7th Cir. 1910) (holding that a pure compound might be patentable, under certain conditions, over the same compound in an impure form.); *cf. infra* 1335 -1338 and accompanying texts; Among three patent applications claiming Aspirin in US, UK, and Germany, those patents in UK and Germany were invalidated on the ground of lack of novelty.

617 *In re May*, 574 F.2d 1082, 1090 (C.C.P.A. 1978); *see also Pfizer Inc. v. Ranbaxy Laboratories Ltd.*, 405 F.Supp.2d 495, 519 (D.Del. 2005), remanded in a different ground (holding "a prior art disclosure of a racemate does not anticipate the individual isomers of the racemate or render the individual isomers of the racemate obvious.").

618 *Brenner v. Ladd*, 247 F.Supp. 51, 56 (D.D.C. 1965) (holding enantiomer should not be considered to be anticipated by the solution of racemate disclosed in the prior art, even though a racemate may dissociate in solution).

619 Clopidogrel is an antiplatelet agent used to inhibit blood clots, and this antiplatelet agent is used to inhibit blood clots in coronary artery disease, peripheral vascular disease, and cerebrovascular disease.

620 U.S. Patent No., 4,529,596 (July 16, 1985, under the title of "Thieno [3,2-c] pyridine derivatives and their therapeutic application"), column 1, lines 39-41.("These compounds having an asymmetrical carbon may exist in the form of two enantiomers. The invention relates both to each enantiomer and their mixture.").

621 *See Pfizer/Penem Derivatives,* T1048/92 (1994), points 2.3-2.5.

622 *Sanofi-Synthelabo v. Apotex, Inc.*, 550 F.3d 1075, 1085 (Fed. Cir. 2008).

623 *Forest Labs., Inc. v. Ivax Pharms., Inc.*, 501 F.3d 1263, 1265 (Fed. Cir. 2007).

conclusions.[624] The Federal Circuit affirmed that, since the prior art, which in effect did state Escitalopram, did not enable the person skilled in the art to prepare the enantiomer and did not anticipate the claimed invention.[625]

In any case, this rule of novelty of enantiomers over their racemates seems to have been consistently applied for over a century. The difficulty of separation with the technology in the early 20th century is understandable and the novelty should be decided from case to case. However, one may doubt whether it is still as difficult as it was a hundred years ago to separate one ingredient from another.

In Korea

In the *Clopidogrel* case, [626] a patent on d-enantiomer[627] of clopidogrel was challenged,[628] with the same relevant facts as *Sanofi-Synthelabo v. Apotex, Inc.* in the United States.[629] The Supreme Court of Korea reiterated that to deny the novelty of selection invention, the prior document should specifically disclose the concept of a selection invention, and it could also be that a person skilled in the art could directly learn the existence of the selection invention from the prior document based on the disclosure thereof and on common knowledge at the time of application.[630] Based on the same disclosure,[631] however, the Court stated that the prior document disclosed the claimed d-enantiomer of clopidogrel, because the prior document i) disclosed clopidogrel itself, and ii) noted that the invention related both to each enantiomer and their mixture and the each enantiomer of clopidogrel was d- and l-enantiomer, respectively.[632] Further, the Court held that the use of

---

624 *Forest Labs., Inc. v. Ivax Pharms., Inc.*, 501 F.3d 1263, 1267 (Fed. Cir. 2007).

625 *Forest Labs., Inc. v. Ivax Pharms., Inc.*, 501 F.3d 1263, 1268-69 (Fed. Cir. 2007).

626 *Korean Supreme Court/Clopidogrel*, 2008Hu736 & 2008Hu743, Oct. 15, 2009.

627 "Dextro-rotatory" and "levo-rotatory" is another way of indicating the chirality of each enantiomer. However, there is no fixed relation to the (R)- or (S)- enantiomer. For example, an *(R)* isomer can be either dextro-rotatory or levo-rotatory.

628 The prior patent disclosed especially "[…] is an asymmetric carbon atom. In fact, this formula represents both the dextro-rotatory molecule claimed as well as its levo-rotatory enantiomer.".

629 See *supra* 619 -622 and accompanying texts.

630 *Korean Supreme Court/Clopidogrel* , 2008Hu736 & 2008Hu743, Oct. 15, 2009, para 1.Ka.

631 See *supra* 622 ; both enantiomer and mixture.

632 *Korean Supreme Court/Clopidogrel*, 2008Hu736 & 2008Hu743, Oct. 15, 2009, para 1.Na.

clopidogrel also lacked novelty, since the prior art already disclosed clopidogrel and its use.[633] The Court finally held that, since it was specifically disclosed and the person skilled in the art would have acknowledged the racemate, its d-enantiomer, and l-enantiomer as separate compounds, *it was not necessary* that the method of separation or possibility of separation of enantiomers from racemates to obtain enantiomers be disclosed *unless the invention is directed to the method of separating d-enantiomer.*[634]

In *Warner Lambert v. CJ et al.*,[635] the issue was the same as the BPatG/Atorvastatin in Germany.[636] While citing the *Clopidogrel* case,[637] the Supreme Court held that, even though only the racemate of R-trans-heptanoic acid and S-trans-heptanoic acid was disclosed, considering that a carboxamide compound of formula I was acknowledged as separate 4 enantiomers and not as a mixture, a person skilled in the art could have acknowledged formula I's open-ring form, namely, R-trans-heptanoic acid and S-trans-heptanoic acid, as separate enantiomers, too, and, thus, the prior art disclosed the R-trans-heptanoic acid.[638] The Court restated that the selection invention was recognized as separate enantiomers, not as a mixture in the prior document, and that it was not necessary to disclose the method of separation or the possibility of separation of the enantiomer from racemates unless the invention was directed to the method of separating the dextrorotatory enantiomer.

However, most patent offices consider the optical isomer of known racemates as novel per se as long as the individual enantiomers have not been explicitly disclosed or separated.[639]

---

633 *Korean Supreme Court/Clopidogrel*, 2008Hu736 & 2008Hu743, Oct. 15, 2009, para 1.Na. (describing the use as "a therapeutic composition having blood-platelet aggregation inhibiting activities and antithrombotic activities containing the above compound and a pharmaceutically acceptable carrier.").

634 *Korean Supreme Court/Clopidogrel*, 2008Hu736 & 2008Hu743, Oct. 15, 2009, para 1.Na.

635 *Korean Supreme Court/Atorvastatin*, 2008Hu3469, Mar. 25, 2010.

636 See *supra* 590 .

637 *Korean Supreme Court/Clopidogrel.*, *supra* 626 .

638 *Korean Supreme Court/Atorvastatin*, *supra* 635 , at para 1.Na.

639 *Hoechst/Enantiomers*, T296/87, OJ EPO 1990, 195, 206-207; *In re May*, 574 F.2d 1082, 1090 (C.C.P.A. 1978) (holding "the novelty of an optical isomer is not negated by the prior art disclosure of its racemate.").

c) Crystalline forms

In the EPO

The Board held that a chemical substance was new once it differed from a known substance in a reliable parameter.[640] Since the physicochemical properties of the polymorphs are different from each other, which can be represented by reliable parameters, as long as the applicants can prove the differences, it would be held novel.

In *SmithKline Beecham/Paroxetine methanesulfonate*, the parameters indicating the polymorph in the prior art and those of the claimed invention were not identical.[641] The Board, however, held that this difference did not mean that the two crystalline forms are different because the list of peaks was not limiting; the claimed invention had no further distinctive technical features other than the parameters;[642]and the claimed form was sufficient to be produced by a skilled person.[643]

The prior document for the crystal forms, of course, must enable the invention in question. The Board held that, even if the prior art unambiguously taught that finasterid existed in two polymorphic differentiations, since there was no indication of how the polymorph form I might be prepared, the prior art was not an enabling disclosure and was not a novelty-destroying disclosure for the claimed invention.[644] While noting that the submission was not supported by any evidence, the Board did not accept the examining division's submission that the crystal forms were accessible by means of any known crystallisation method and that a skilled person would not have had

---

640 *Hoechst/Enantiomers*, T296/87, OJ EPO 1990, 196, headnote (this case was about the patentability of an enantiomer).

641 The Claim 1 of granted patent EP-B-0 970 955: "1. Paroxetine methane sulfonate in crystalline form having inter alia the following characteristic IR peaks:1603, 1513, 1194, 1045, 946, 830, 776, 601, 554, and 539 4 cm–1; and/or the following characteristic XRD peaks [...] .".
The disclosure of prior art: Preparation of crystalline paroxetine mesylate, which was characterized by the following list of IR peaks:3023, 2900, 2869, 2577, 1615, 1515, 1500, 1469, 1208, 1169, 1100, 1038, 962, 931, 838, 777, 546, and 531 cm–1 (and no XPRD spectrum).

642 *Smithkline Beecham/Paroxetine methanesulfonate,* T 0885/02 (2004), points 3.4.10-3.1.13.

643 *Smithkline Beecham/Paroxetine methanesulfonate,* T 0885/02 (2004), points 3.6 and 3.7.

644 *Merck/Finasteride,* T605/02 (2005), point 3.2.1.

any difficulty in finding out under which crystallisation conditions either of two polymorphic forms could have been obtained.[645] Thus, even if the prior art discloses the claimed invention, if it does not enable the invention, it is not novelty destroying. In the case where the novelty of the crystalline forms of *Famotidine* was issued, the Board held that the product prepared according to the process disclosed in a prior art was the same as the claimed polymorph, thus the polymorph was not novel.[646]

In Germany

In the *Kristallformen,* the BPatG held that a compound, in the sense of patent law, was every individual chemical that could be reliably differentiated from another, if they provide sufficient and appropriate parameters.[647] This case involved two polymorphic forms of an already known antibiotic, Cefaloridin, which showed non-hygroscopicity. The Court further ruled that compounds having the same chemical composition were basically identical, did not apply for special forms of compounds, if these forms could not have been produced.[648]

In the United Kingdom

Smith Kline & French Laboratories v. Evans Medical involved a polymorph of the first H2-blocker Cimetidine (Tagamet®).[649] After some years of filing of the basic patent application covering cimetidine, the patentee claimed one polymorphic form of the same compound.[650] The Court dismissed the case noting that this patent was anticipated over its basic patent because the claimed form A of cimetidine was inevitably obtained by following the process disclosed in the prior art.[651]

Similar to the BOA's decision,[652] in the case on a crystal form of *Paroxetine methansulphonate,* the House of Lords held that the incorrect data indicating that the claimed invention was different from the subject disclosed

---

645 *Merck/Finasteride,* T605/02 (2005), point 3.2.1.

646 *Richter Gedeon/Famotidine,* T 226/98, OJ EPO 2002, 498, 509-514.

647 *BPatG/Kristallformen(Crystal forms),* Entscheidungen des Bundespatentgerichts ("BPatGE") 20, 6, 6.

648 *BPatG/Kristallformen,* BPatGE 20, 6.

649 *Smith Kline & French Laboratories v. Evans Medical* [1989] F.S.R. 561.

650 *Smith Kline & French Laboratories v. Evans Medical* [1989] F.S.R. 561, 561.

651 *Smith Kline & French Laboratories v. Evans Medical* [1989] F.S.R. 561, 579.

652 *SmithKline Beecham/Paroxetine methanesulfonate,* T 0885/02 (2004).

in the prior art were irrelevant because the evidence showed that the claimed invention would have inevitably resulted from the prior art and that the prior art was enabling, because the person skilled in the art would have tried a different solvent if the solvent in the main example was not suitable for crystallization.[653]

In *Laboratories Servier v. Apotex,* while noting that "the individual peaks of the table should not have too much significance attached to them – it is the overall set that matters," Jacob LJ held that the claimed polymorph was not novel when it would inevitably be obtained by carrying out the process disclosed in the earlier patent for the basic substance.[654] While pointing out that the exclusivity based on this crystalline form could have extended to 2020, Jacob LJ remarked that "[i]t is the sort of patent which can give the patent system a bad name."[655]

In the United States

In *Abbott Laboratories v. Geneva Pharmaceuticals*, the novelty of an anhydrous crystalline form IV of Terazosine hydrochloride ("THC")[656] over sales of a product containing this form of THC without the parties' knowledge was in issue.[657] The Federal Circuit held that the third party's sales of the anhydrous crystalline form of THC before the patent filing date rendered the patent on that particular anhydrous crystalline form of THC invalid, even though the parties to those sales did not know that they were dealing with the particular form claimed in the patent.[658] The Court further clarified that if a product offered for sale inherently possesses each of the limitations of the claims, then the invention was on sale, whether or not the parties to the

653 *Synthon BV v. SmithKline Beecham plc* [2005] UKHL 59, paras 34-38.

654 *Laboratoires Servier v. Apotex* [2008] EWCA Civ 445, paras 21-38 (a case about the novelty of one crystal form of the t-butylamine salt of perindopril).

655 *Laboratoires Servier v. Apotex*, [2008] EWHC Civ 445, para 9.

656 Terazosin is a medication for the treatment of hypertension and benign prostatic hyperplasia.

657 *Abbott Laboratories v. Geneva Pharmaceuticals, Inc.*, 182 F.3d 1315 (Fed. Cir. 1999).

658 *Abbott Laboratories v. Geneva Pharmaceuticals, Inc.*, 182 F.3d 1315, 1315 (Fed. Cir. 1999).

transaction recognized that the product possessed the claimed characteristics.[659]

In *SmithKline Beecham v. Apotex*, Apotex, which was seeking to practice the invention in the prior art, was found to have infringed the patent, based on which, logically, the prior art should have anticipated the claim before the patent filing date.[660] The Federal Circuit held that the patent covering crystalline Proxetine Hydrochloride ("PHC") *hemihydrate*[661] was invalid, because it was inherently anticipated based on the fact that the process of making PHC *anhydrate* in the prior art, which did not discuss PHC *hemihydrate*, inherently resulted in the production of at least trace amounts of the hemihydrates.[662]

There is no equivalent case law regarding novelty of crystalline form in Korea.

d) Metabolite

In the United Kingdom

Merrell Dow was a patentee of an anti-histamine called terfenadine (Teldane®). The subsequent research on the product showed that the anti-histaminic effect was due to a specific metabolite. After the determination of the structure of the metabolite, called Fexofenadine (Allegra®), Merrell Dow filed a new patent application. After the basic patent for the terfenadine expired in 1992, the patent holder for the metabolite, Merrell Dow, sued a generic company selling Terfenadine for infringing not the basic patent but the metabolite patent, which would not expire until 2000.[663] Merrell Dow argued that the supply of terfenadine provided the essential means for making the patent protected metabolite, and thus for puting the patented inven-

---

659 *Abbott Laboratories v. Geneva Pharmaceuticals, Inc.*, 182 F.3d 1315, 1319 (Fed. Cir. 1999) (further noting "The question is not whether the sale, even a third party sale, 'discloses' the invention at the time of the sale, but whether the sale relates to a device that *embodies* the invention.").

660 *SmithKline Beecham Corp. v. Apotex Corp.*, 403 F.3d 1331, 1341 (Fed. Cir. 2005).

661 See *supra* 140 .

662 *SmithKline Beecham Corp. v. Apotex Corp.*, 403 F.3d 1331, 1342-46 (Fed. Cir. 2005).

663 *Merrell Dow Pharmaceuticals Inc v. HN Norton & Co Ltd* [1995] UKHL 14, paras 7-8.

tion into effect.[664] The House of Lords found that the acid metabolite of the anti-allergic drug terfenadine lacked novelty. It held that the metabolite was not novel, not because of its previous use but because of the previous disclosure of "a part of the chemical reaction in the human body produced by the ingestion of terfenadine and having an anti-histamine effect," which contained sufficient information and enabled the public to work the invention to make metabolites in their livers by taking the medication.[665] The Lords rejected the argument that the metabolite was made available to the public by the clinical trials of terfenadine, because they did not make the necessary information of its metabolite available, i.e. they did not enable anyone to perform the metabolite invention.[666] The Lords seemed to accept that the metabolite could be patented provided that the claim was limited to the metabolite produced by methods other than metabolism in the body.[667]

In Germany

The same case that was litigated in the United Kingdom[668] was appealed to the Munich Higher Regional Court in 1992, which held that the patent of metabolite was not infringed, since it was not manufactured, sold, or kept for filing by the defendants.[669] Because of the bifurcated system in Germany, the Court could not rule on the validity of the patent in issue.

In the United States

After first construing the word "compound" in the patent on metabolite, the District Court limited the patent scope only to the synthetically produced version of acid metabolite of terfenadine.[670] However, the Court did not question the patentability of the metabolite patent in this case. In *In re Bu-*

664 *Merrell Dow Pharmaceuticals Inc v. HN Norton & Co Ltd* [1995] UKHL 14, para 8.

665 *Merrell Dow Pharmaceuticals Inc v. HN Norton & Co Ltd* [1995] UKHL 14, paras 22-48.

666 *Merrell Dow Pharmaceuticals Inc v. HN Norton & Co Ltd* [1995] UKHL 14, paras 22-48; *Jacob*, IIC 1997, 880, 880-81.

667 *Merrell Dow Pharmaceuticals Inc v. HN Norton & Co Ltd* [1995] UKHL 14, para 15; *Jacob*, IIC 1997, 880, 881.

668 *Merrell Dow Pharmaceuticals Inc v. HN Norton & Co Ltd* [1995] UKHL 14.

669 *OLG München/Terfenadine*, GRUR, 1994, 746.

670 *Marion Merrell Dow Inc. v. Baker Norton Pharmaceuticals, Inc.*, 948 F.Supp. 1050, 1055-56 (S.D.Fla.,1996), appeal dismissed, 152 F.3d 941 (Fed. Cir. 1998).

spirone Patent Litigation, the District Court held that the fact that the use of the parent drug was described in a package insert of the parent drug and that it was prescribed more than one year prior to the filing date of metabolite patent application alone were sufficient to decide the issue of invalidity.[671]

In *Schering Co. v. Geneva Pharmaceuticals*, the Federal Circuit held that a metabolite of Loratadine was anticipated over the prior art, which disclosed the administration of loratadine to a patient, since it "necessarily and inevitably" resulted in the formation of the metabolite.[672] The Federal Circuit further held that inherent anticipation required neither the recognition of the person skilled in the art, nor the actual creation or reduction to practice of prior art subject matter before the priority date, i.e. the actual administration of the patent drug to any patients, but required only enabling disclosure.[673] Unlike the House of Lords, the Federal Circuit also restated that "that which would literally infringe if later in time anticipates if earlier."[674] Interestingly, Rader J noted that these metabolites might not receive protection via bare compound claims, which were defined by structure only, since the scope of these claims could include the compounds in any surroundings, including those with the body as metabolites of a drug. However, he stated that it could be claimed in its pure and isolated form,[675] since the prior art would not provide an enabling disclosure to anticipate such claims.[676] Thus, in the United States, as in the United Kingdom, a metabolite may be patentable if it is claimed in its pure and isolated form.[677]

Novelty of metabolites has not been issued in Korea.

---

671 *In re Buspirone Patent Litigation*, 185 F. Supp. 2d 340, 360 (S.D.N.Y., 2002).

672 *Schering Co. v. Geneva Pharmaceuticals*, 339 F.3d 1373, 1378 (Fed. Cir. 2003).

673 *Schering Co. v. Geneva Pharmaceuticals*, 339 F.3d 1373, 1378-80 (Fed. Cir. 2003), quoting *In re Donohue*, 766 F.2d 531, 533 (Fed. Cir. 1985).

674 *Schering Co. v. Geneva Pharmaceuticals*, 339 F.3d 1373, 1379 (Fed. Cir. 2003), quoting *Bristol-Myers Squibb Co. v. Ben Venue Labs., Inc.*, 246 F.3d 1368, 1378 (Fed. Cir. 2001).

675 Examples were a pharmaceutical composition, a method of administering the metabolite or the corresponding pharmaceutical composition.

676 *Schering Co. v. Geneva Pharmaceuticals*, 339 F.3d 1373, 1381 (Fed. Cir. 2003).

677 *Schering Co. v. Geneva Pharmaceuticals*, 339 F.3d 1373, 1381 (Fed. Cir. 2003).

5. Analysis and conclusion

For species selection inventions, the EPO has the most extreme approach, i.e. to destroy the novelty of a species selection invention, the prior art must disclose the same, as it is the photograph of a later invention.[678] Germany and the United Kingdom relaxed their previous stringency in this regard to allow assessment of the novelty of species selection inventions, and it was declared by the courts that the *Fluoran* decision or the *IG Rule* exist only in history; therefore, the novelty requirement is much lowered. The United States, where the decision on Olanzapine was first held, appears to consider the size of the genus from which the selection was made. Although there are some differences from jurisdiction to jurisdiction, a species selection invention will be found novel unless it is individually spelled out in the prior art. This seems to be based on the difficulty of identifying and envisaging a specific species selection invention with effects that distinguish it from the millions of others as per Jacob J's *a priori* consideration.[679]

This lowered novelty requirement applied to the optical isomers inventions, although differently. The novelty of an optical isomer is already established over the racemic mixture, if its structure is clearly disclosed and it is acknowledged by the person skilled in the art that one or the other would exert its pharmacological effect, unless purification of that isomer from the racemate is not disclosed and is difficult. For example, while referring to the *Olanzapine* decision, the BGH held that an enantiomer was not available to the public, since the prior document did not directly and unambiguously disclose an enantiomer because the person skilled in the art should find the way to resolve the racemate. This is also because anticipation requires the *enablement* of the invention.

For the crystalline forms, the issue of novelty arose mainly because the claimed crystalline forms were inevitably produced according to the process disclosed in the prior art, and novelty was generally not found. If a new crystalline form were shown, it would have no difficulty being found novel.

The reasoning on novelty of metabolites in the United Kingdom and the United States shows an interesting contrast. In the United States, where a *secret or confidential use* of an invention could give rise to the public use bar, so that "non-informing" prior art can be the prior art, the Federal Circuit

---

678 This extreme approach could make novelty test be subject to the skill of drafting person.

679 See *supra* 558 .

found that it was not-novel based on its rule that "that which would literally infringe if later in time, anticipated if earlier." However, the House of Lords held that the metabolite was available not by the previous use of its parent drug, but by a disclosure which was common knowledge.[680] This is because, in the United Kingdom, to make something available to the public, the communication of information is required,[681] but the use of the parent drug does not present any information about the metabolite. Thus it could not be a prior art. Through this effort, it seems that the House of Lords invoked the "golden thread" that a patent cannot stop someone from doing something that was old,[682] which is the basis of the novelty requirement. Since the non-enabling/communicating use – the ingestion of the parent drug - does not constitute the prior art, if the Court could not have found another way, the metabolite patent could ultimately have prevented the public from practicing the parent drug. Thus, the Court held that the metabolite lacked novelty based on the prior disclosure, which merely described the same non-enabling use, while the use would inevitably produce the metabolite. Indeed the patent on the metabolite precisely patents the state of the art again, insofar as it precludes the use of the parent drug as an anti-histamine treatment.[683]

B. *Inventive step / Non-obviousness*[684]

> "We are like dwarfs on the shoulders of giants, so that we can see more than they, and things at a greater distance, not by virtue of any sharpness on sight on our part, or any physical distinction, but because we are carried high and raised up by their giant size."[685]

No invention occurs in a vacuum, and every invention is built upon previous inventions. The inventive step requirement in patenting ensure that patented invention is qualitatively distinguished from previous invention.

680 See *supra* 665 -666 and accompanying texts.

681 See *supra* 666 and accompanying text; *see also Jacob*, IIC 1996, 170, 171 (arguing the disclosure of a process made available to the public, for the purposes of that process, everything that inevitably took place as part of the process, whether appreciated or not.).

682 *Jacob*, IIC 1997, 880, 880.

683 *Jacob*, IIC 1996, 170, 171.

684 "Inventive step" and "non-obviousness" are used in this thesis without distinction.

685 *Bernard of Chartres*, 1130 AD.

1. Inventive step in patentability requirements

The novelty requirement is not controversial, and utility will be found on a relatively trivial showing.[686] The two other requirements are arguably relatively "mild"[687] compared to the rigor of the inventive step requirement. The inventive step requirement is considered the "final gatekeeper of the patent system"[688] and the "ultimate condition of patentability."[689] In other words, even if relatively trivial changes to the prior art could survive these two requirements, inventive step functions as the ultimate requirement and filters the patentable from the unpatentable.[690]

The inventive step requirement has been traditionally justified as a corollary to the "reward theory" of patent law.[691] The purpose of having this requirement is to encourage invention, while not over-rewarding it.[692] The inventive step asks whether a development is a significant enough technical advance to merit the award of a patent.[693] Without this requirement, the possibility of using the variations of prior art from everyday practice would be jeopardized.[694] The requirement guarantees that the information inherent in the claimed invention has a minimum threshold quantum of value in exchange for a patent.[695] As Lord Hoffman noted, "[t]he question was whether, in accordance with this policy, the patent in suit disclosed something sufficiently inventive to deserve the grant of a monopoly."[696] This requirement is also to ensure that the patent system rewards those inventions that would

686 *Duffy*, 71 U. Chi. L. Rev. 439, 502-03 (2004).
687 *Merges/Duffy*, 2011, 619.
688 *Merges/Duffy*, 2011, 619-20 (also noting "nonobviousness can accurately be described as a 'non-triviality' requirement in patent law.").
689 *Witherspoon*, 1980.
690 *Merges/Duffy*, 2011, 620.
691 *Duffy*, 71 U. Chi. L. Rev. 439, 503 (2004) (noting "[n]ew and useful creations that are also relatively obvious do not deserve the reward of a patent because the social benefits of the invention are outweighed by the social costs of the patent monopoly.").
692 *Merges*, 7 High Tech. L. J. 1, 3 (1992).
693 *Merges/Duffy*, 2011, 620.
694 *Kraßer*, 2009, 301-02; *Grubb/Thomsen*, 2010, 68.
695 *Merges*, 7 High Tech. L. J. 1, 18-19 (1992).
696 *Societe Technique de Pulverisation Step v. Emson Europe Ltd. and others* [1993] R.P.C. 513.

not have been created without the inducement of a patent.[697] Thus, the inherent problem was to develop some means of selecting out those inventions.[698]

One cannot claim a patent right on a subject matter that, though it is not fully anticipated, would nevertheless be obvious to a person skilled in the art at the applicant's date of invention or of filing.[699] Thus, the inventive step assures that, although the invention may be novel in some technical sense, it is not merely a straightforward extension, a simple application of some familiar invention,[700] or an incremental development of technology.[701]

2. Examination of inventive step

An invention may be obvious to the person skilled in the art over more than one piece of prior arts.[702] In other words, if a subject matter is obvious to the person skilled in the art over the entire state of the prior art, a patent will not be granted. This judgment of whether an invention involves an inventive step is one that is intrinsically much more difficult than that of novelty, since to some extent judgement of the inventive step is rather subjective.[703] Thus, the assessment of the inventive step raises largest single cause of uncertainty

697 *Graham v. John Deere Co.*, 383 U.S. 1, 11-17 (1966); *Kitch*, 1966 Sup. Ct. Rev. 293, 301 (1966) (noting if an invention would not have been developed absent the prospect of a patent, it should be granted); *Gilfillan*, 31 J. Pat. & Trademark Off. Soc'y 611, 611 (1949) ("A patent is helpful and proper when it rewards sufficiently useful creative work *which might not have been done without* that prospective reward.").

698 *Graham v. John Deere Co.*, 383 U.S. 1, 11 (196) (holding "[t]he inherent problem was to develop some means of weeding out those inventions which would not be disclosed or devised but for the inducement of a patent.").

699 *Chisum*, 15 AIPLA Q. J. 57, 58 (1987).

700 *Grady/Alexander*, 78 Va. L. Rev. 305, 340 (1992).

701 *Holbrook*, 59 SMU L. Rev. 123, 170 (2006).

702 *Spenner*, 90 J. Pat. & Trademark Off. Soc'y, 477, 510 (2008); EPO Examination Guidelines-G-VII, 6; Examination Guidelines for Patent and Utility Model in Korea ("Korean Examination Guidelines"), January 2011, Ch 5.1.

703 *Grubb/Thomsen*, 2010, 67.

about the validity of patents, and has thereby resulted in a rich jurisprudence.[704]

In the EPO

An invention shall be considered as involving an inventive step if, having regard to the state of the art, it is not obvious to a person skilled in the art.[705] Even though the BOA held that this approach was no more than one possible route to assessing inventiveness,[706] the practice in the EPO basically applies the "problem-and-solution approach" to assessing the inventive step. This can be divided into three main stages:

"(i)Determining the 'closest prior art'

(ii) Establishing the 'objective technical problem' to be solved; and

(iii)Considering whether or not the claimed invention, starting from the closest prior art and the objective technical problem, would have been obvious to the skilled person."[707]

This approach is based on the principle that every invention is a solution to a technical problem. "The objective technical problem" in the second step concerns the aim and the task of modifying or adapting the closest prior art to provide the technical effects of the invention over the closest prior art, which may be different from what is presented as "the problem" in the patent application, and this in turn could require the reformulation.[708] While noting that the "reformulation" involved the court artificially, creating a problem that was supposed to be solved by the invention, Jacob LJ pointed out that

---

704 *Cornish/Llewelyn/Aplin*, 2010, 210 (noting "[t]he evaluative issue that this introduces is the largest single cause of uncertainty about the validity of patents and hence a frequent inflator of the scale and length of patent disputes.").

705 EPC Art. 56, first sentence; GPA Section 4, first sentence; UK Patents Act 1977, Section 3.

706 *Alcan/Aluminium alloys*, T 465/92, OJ EPO 1996, 32, 50 (holding that "[T]he problem and solution approach ought to be considered as one amongst other possible approaches, each of which has its own advantages and drawbacks.").

707 EPO Examination Guidelines-G-VII, 5.; *See e.g.*, *Bayer/Carbonless copying paper*, T 1/80, OJ EPO 1981, 206; EPC Rule 42(1)(c) (The description shall disclose the invention, as claimed, in such terms that the technical problem, even if not expressly stated as such, and its solution can be understood, and state any advantageous effects of the invention with reference to the background art.).

708 EPO Examination Guidelines-G-VII, 5.2 (further noting this could be specially the case when "the prior art cited in the search report may put the invention in an entirely different perspective from that apparent from reading the application only.").

this reformulation might be the weakest part of the problem-and-solution approach.[709] To answer the question in the third step, the word, "would" must be defined. The point here is not whether the skilled person could have arrived at the invention, i.e. that it was within their technical ability, but whether he would have done so because the prior art motivated him to do so while wishing to solve the objective technical problem or expecting some improvement or advantages.[710] It is not sufficient that the person skilled in the art *could* have arrived at the invention from the prior art; it must be shown that he *would* have done so.[711] This last step is similar to the TSM test in the United States.[712]

Some secondary considerations are relevant to the last step again, especially in determining whether the person skilled in the art "would" have made the claimed modifications to the closest prior art to solve the objective technical problem, and include unexpected or synergistic technical effects, long-felt need or commercial success.[713] However, commercial success is not to be regarded as a sole criterion and needs to be coupled with evidence of long-felt need.[714]

In the United Kingdom

An invention shall be considered as involving an inventive step if, having regard to the state of the art, it is not obvious to a person skilled in the art.[715] The British Court's approach to assessing the inventive step was set out in *Pozzoli v. BDMO*, which provided four steps:

"1. a) Identify the notional "person skilled in the art"
    b) Identify the relevant common general knowledge of that person;
2. Identify the inventive concept of the claim in question or if that cannot readily be done, construe it;

---

709 *Actavis UK Ltd v. Novartis AG* [2010] EWCA Civ 82, paras 30-34; *see also Ranbaxy UK & Anor v. Warner-Lambert* [2005] EWHC 2142, para 71 (noting this kind reformulation of the problem could provide a substantial risk that would lead to a finding of non-obviousness based on the after-discovered advantages.).

710 EPO Examination Guidelines-G-VII, 5.3.

711 *Actavis UK Ltd v. Novartis AG* [2010] EWCA Civ 82, para 46 (further commenting this seemed, however, to be self-evident).

712 See *infra* 732 -733 and accompanying texts.

713 EPO Examination Guidelines-G-VII, 10.

714 EPO Examination Guidelines-G-VII, 10.3.

715 UK Patents Act 1977, Section 3.

3. Identify what, if any, differences exist between the matter cited as forming part of the "state of the art" and the inventive concept of the claim or the claim as construed;
4. Viewed without any knowledge of the alleged invention as claimed, do those differences constitute steps which would have been obvious to the person skilled in the art or do they require any degree of invention?"[716]

Jacob LJ explained that (i) the only thing that mattered for step 2 was what was claimed, and (ii) the meaning of "obvious" for the purpose of step 4, which is the key statutory step, was technically rather than commercially obvious.[717]

In the United Kingdom, obviousness is a multifactorial question. Namely, the Court makes a full multifactorial assessment of all relevant facts of each case, which may include commercial success, a long-felt want, a motive to find a solution to the problem, the number and extent of the possible avenues of research, the effort involved in pursuing them, and the expectation of success.[718] Unexpected results can only fail to defend against an obviousness attack, when there is a real motivation to use the idea apart from that advantage, since only then will the person skilled in the art more or less inevitably bump into the unexpected advantage.[719]

In Germany

An invention shall be considered as involving an inventive step if, having regard to the state of the art, it is not obvious to a person skilled in the art.[720] In *Betrieb einer Sicherheitseinrichtung,* the BGH placed the focus on whether the person skilled in the art had motivation to develop the prior art further in the direction of the claimed subject matter. [721] The BGH held that seeing the use of an approach that deviated from previous approaches as not only possible but as obvious to the skilled person required additional im-

---

716 *Pozzoli v. BDMO* [2007] EWCA Civ 588, para 122 (reviewing the English Court's approach in the earlier case, *Windsurfing v. Tabur Marine* [1985] RPC 59.).

717 *Actavis UK Ltd v. Novartis AG* [2010] EWCA Civ 82, paras 18-21.

718 *Actavis UK Ltd v. Novartis AG* [2010] EWCA Civ 82, paras 26, 41 (citing *Conor Medsystems Inc v. Angiotech Pharmaceuticals Inc & Ors* [2008] UKHL 49, para 42).

719 *Napp Pharmaceuticals v. Ratiopharm* [2009] EWCA Civ 252, para 115.

720 GPA Section 4, first sentence.

721 *BGH/ Betrieb einer Sicherheitseinrichtung (Operating a Safety Device)*, GRUR 2009, 746.

pulses, stimuli, suggestions or other motives going beyond discernability of a technical problem to prompt the skilled person to solve the technical problem by inventive means.[722] However, there seems to be no formal approach to assessing the inventive step.

The secondary indications cannot establish or replace the inventive step. Further, they may only be the occasion in exceptional cases for a particularly critical review of the solutions known in the state of the art to determine whether they provide sufficient indications for the obviousness of the subject matter of the claimed invention against the background of general technical knowledge and whether they merely appear to contain a suggestion leading to the invention from a post-hoc point of view.[723] Secondary considerations often applied are economic success based on the invention, overcoming difficulties, satisfaction of a long lasting need, evidence of others' failures, unexpected technical progress, overcoming prejudices, and unexpected results.[724]

In the United States

A patent may not be obtained if the differences between the subject matter sought to be patented and the prior art are such that the subject matter as a whole would have been obvious at the time the invention was made to a person having ordinary skill in the art to which the subject matter pertains.[725]

Under the *Graham* decision,[726] which established a basic framework for judging non-obviousness, courts must identify (1) the scope and content of the prior art, (2) the differences between the prior art and the claimed invention, and (3) the level of ordinary skill in the art. Then, they must determine whether the subject matter of the claimed invention is obvious.[727] These are referred to as the "Graham factors." The Graham Court further held that secondary considerations, which are subsequently called the fourth

722 *BGH/ Betrieb einer Sicherheitseinrichtung (Operating a Safety Device)*, GRUR 2009, 746, 748.

723 *BGH/Dreinahtschlauchfolienbeutel (Three-Seam Tubular Sachet)*, GRUR 2010, 44, 46-47.

724 *Pagenberg*, GRUR Int 1986, 83 *et seqq.*

725 35 U.S.C. § 103(a).

726 *Graham v. John Deere Co.*, 383 U.S. 1 (1966).

727 *Merges/Duffy*, 2011, 670.

Graham factors,[728] such as commercial success, long felt but unsolved needs, failure of others, etc., might be utilized to determine obviousness.[729] However, the *Graham* decision does not specify precisely how a court is to make this ultimate determination.[730] The imaginary person, typically referred to in the United States as a PHOSITA (a person having ordinary skill in the art), is the yardstick by which the bar to obtaining patent protection can be adjusted to specific technological fields.[731]

Soon after its creation, the Federal Circuit articulated what would become its exclusive test for deciding obviousness, which was known as the "Teaching, Suggestion or Motivation" or the so-called TSM test.[732] The Federal Circuit held that "[o]bviousness cannot be established by combining the teachings of the prior art to produce the claimed invention, absent some teaching or suggestion supporting the combination."[733] However, this test came under increasing scrutiny, and the Supreme Court granted certiorari on the question whether the Federal Circuit had erred in holding that a claimed invention could be deemed "obvious" by applying the TSM test too rigidly.[734]

---

728 *Transocean Offshore Deepwater Drilling, Inc. v. Maersk Drilling USA, Inc.*, 699 F.3d 1340, 1348-49 (Fed. Cir. 2012).

729 *Graham v. John Deere Co.*, 383 U.S. 1, 17-18 (1966); *cf. Newell Companies, Inc. v. Kenney Mfg. Co.*, 864 F.2d 757, 768 (Fed. Cir. 1988) (holding although secondary considerations must be considered, they do not necessarily control the obviousness conclusion); *cf. Pfizer, Inc. v. Apotex, Inc.,* 480 F.3d 1348, 1372 (Fed. Cir. 2007), *reh'g denied, cert. denied.*

730 *Merges/Duffy*, 2011, 670.

731 *Strandburg*, 1 UC Irvine L.R.,265, 267 (2011); For the PHOSITA, see MPEP § 2141.03, citing *In re GPAC*, 57 F.3d 1573, 1579 (Fed. Cir. 1995); *Custom Accessories, Inc. v. Jeffrey Allan Industries, Inc.*, 807 F.2d 955, 962-63, (Fed. Cir. 1986); *Environmental Designs, Ltd. V. Union Oil Co.*, 713 F.2d 693, 696 (Fed. Cir. 1983) (noting "the factors that may be considered in determining the level of ordinary skill in the art may include: (A) type of problems encountered in the art; (B) prior art solutions to those problems; (C) rapidity with which innovations are made; (D) sophistication of the technology; and (E) educational level of active workers in the field. And in a given case, every factor may not be present, and one or more factors may predominate.").

732 *Merges/Duffy*, 2011, 672.

733 *ACS Hosp. Systems, Inc. v. Montefiore Hosp.,* 732 F.2d 1572, 1577 (Fed. Cir. 1984) (further noting "[u]nder section 103, teachings of references can be combined only if there is some suggestion or incentive to do so.").

734 *KSR Intern. Co. v. Teleflex Inc.,* 548 U.S. 902 (Mem) (2006).

In *KSR v. Teleflex*, the Supreme Court held that "[i]f a person of ordinary skill can implement a predictable variation, § 103 likely bars its patentability." The Court rejected the Federal Circuit's "rigid approach" to obviousness in favour of a more "expansive and flexible" approach.[735] The Court held that "any need or problem known in the field of endeavour at the time of invention and addressed by the patent can provide a reason for combining the elements in the manner claimed."[736] The Court added an "obvious to try" test: "When there is a design need or market pressure to solve a problem; and there are a finite number of identified predictable solutions; then a person of ordinary skill has good reason to pursue the known options, and this leads to the anticipated success."[737]

When evaluating obviousness, the American patent system further uses a procedural device called the "*prima facie* case of obviousness," which differs from obviousness and was established to shift the burden of proof to the applicant.[738] The *prima facie* case of obviousness is initially established by an examiner based on the application of the first three Graham factors and maintained unless and until the applicant provides sufficient evidence to demonstrate non-obviousness, such as "secondary considerations."[739] To establish *prima facie* obviousness in the field of chemistry, size of the genus, structural similarities, and reasonable expectation of success can be used. To rebut the *prima facie* obviousness in the field, in addition to the factors presented in *Graham*, industry acclaim, unexpected results, prior art teaching away from the invention,[740] industry praise, copying, industry scepticism, and licensing are secondary considerations. [741] Regarding a "teaching away," a court found that a prior art reference "taught away" from combining references could alone defeat an obviousness claim.[742] For commercial suc-

735 *KSR Intern. Co. v. Teleflex Inc.*, 550 U.S. 398, 401, 415 (2007).

736 *KSR Intern. Co. v. Teleflex Inc.*, 550 U.S. 398, 401, 420 (2007).

737 *KSR Intern. Co. v. Teleflex Inc.*, 550 U.S. 398, 401, 421 (2007).

738 *In re Piasecki*, 745 F.2d 1468, 1471-72 (Fed. Cir. 1984).

739 MPEP § 2142; *In re Dillon*, 919 F.2d 688, 692-93 (Fed. Cir. 1990) (noting the applicants can prevail this prima facie obviousness if they overcome it by providing evidences).

740 *Eli Lilly and Company v. Zenith Goldline Pharmaceuticals. Inc.*, 471 F.3d 1369, 1380 (Fed. Cir. 2006); In re Sullivan, 498 F.3d 1345, 1351 (Fed. Cir. 2007).

741 *Transocean Offshore Deepwater Drilling, Inc. v. Maersk Drilling USA, Inc.*, 699 F.3d 1340 (Fed. Cir. 2012).

742 *Alza Corp. v. Mylan Labs. Inc.*, 388 F. Supp. 2d 717, 738 (N.D. W. Va. 2005), *aff'd*, 464 F.3d 1286 (Fed. Cir. 2006).

cess, the Federal Circuit declared that the presence of certain secondary considerations of non-obviousness were not sufficient as a matter of law to overcome its conclusion that the evidence supported only a legal conclusion that claims would have been obvious.[743]

Recently, however, while referring to *Stratoflex, Inc. v. Aeroquip Corp*,[744] the Federal Circuit further held that the evidence of secondary considerations must have been "considered as part of all the evidence, not just when the decision maker remains in doubt after reviewing the art. Thus, in order to determine obviousness, the decision maker must be able to consider all four *Graham* factors." [745]

In Korea

If a person with ordinary skill in the art to which the invention pertains would have easily been able to perceive the invention based on the prior art, the patent shall not be granted for such an invention.[746] To assess the inventive step, one shall consider the overall state of the art, the purpose, technical structure, and advantageous effects of the invention, while paying attention to the opinion of the applicant, in consideration of its specific purpose and effectiveness, and the difficulty of the technical structure of the claimed invention. [747] The main factors to be considered are: (a) whether the prior art provides any motivation to a person skilled in the art to reach the claimed invention; (b) whether the difference between the prior art and the claimed invention is considered as an exercise of ordinary creativity; and (c) whether the claimed invention has any advantageous effects over the prior art. [748] Regarding the motivation to reach the claimed invention, the Korean Patent Court held that to say the claimed invention could have been easily conceived by the combination of the cited references, there should be a suggestion of combination in the cited references.[749]

---

743 *DyStar Textilfarben GmbH & Co. Deutschland KG v. C.H. Patrick Co.*, 464 F.3d 1356, 1371 (Fed. Cir. 2006).

744 *Stratoflex, Inc. v. Aeroquip Corp.*, 713 F.2d 1530, 1538-39 (Fed. Cir. 1983).

745 *Transocean Offshore Deepwater Drilling, Inc. v. Maersk Drilling USA, Inc.*, 699 F.3d 1340, 1349 (Fed. Cir. 2012).

746 Korean Patent Act, 2012, Art. 29(2).

747 Examination Guidelines for Patent and Utility Model in Korea ("Korean Examination Guidelines"), January 2011, Ch3. 5.

748 Korean Examination Guidelines, January 2011, Ch3. 5.

749 *Korean Patent Court/Kimchi fridge*, 2002Heo8424, Sept. 04, 2003, para 2.Na.(3) (Ba).

Secondary considerations, such as teach away, long-felt but unmet need, and commercial success, can be considered to assess the inventive step.[750] However, while commercial success alone is not enough, it can be considered as indicative of the inventive step when the applicant proves that the success was derived from the technical features of the invention.[751] Based on overwhelming commercial success, the Korean Patent Court found the invention nonobvious once, because, in contrast to the prior inventions, which failed to be commercialized or were withdrawn right after being on the market, the product based on the claimed invention achieved commercial success owing to the significant effects derived from the claimed invention.[752] For the long-felt but unmet need, the Korean Patent Court held that the claimed invention could not have been easily conceived from the cited invention considering the fact that the claimed invention had not emerged over eight years.[753]

3. Inventive step requirement for selection inventions

a) Species selection invention

In the EPO

The EPO Examination Guidelines provides an exemplary case when the selections from the Markush formula are found to be obvious (a) if they are neither described as having nor shown to possess any advantageous properties not possessed by the prior art examples; or (b) if they are described as possessing advantageous properties compared with the compounds specifically referred to in the prior art, but these properties are ones which the person skilled in the art would expect such compounds to possess, so that he is likely to be led to make this selection.[754] Once the selection of compounds is regarded as novel, then the compounds must show either the advantageous properties over those *not* possessed by the prior art examples or unexpected advantageous properties that were possessed by the prior art examples.

---

750 Korean Examination Guidelines, January 2011, Ch3. 8.
751 Korean Examination Guidelines, January 2011, Ch3. 8 (2).
752 *Korean Patent Court/Kimchi fridge*, 2002Heo8424, Sept. 04, 2003, para 2.Na.(3) (Ba).
753 *Korean Patent Court/A combining method*, 98Heo8397, Apr. 23, 1999, para 3.Na.
754 EPO Examination Guidelines G-VII Annex 3.1.(iv.).

In Germany

In *Olanzapine* decision, the BGH held that the claimed compound was not obvious to the person skilled in the art over either the "Chakrabarti" document or other prior art in any other manner.[755] In this case, the BGH made it clear that its position was not in line with the EPO's way of determining obviousness, in "only" applying the so-called "problem-solution approach,"[756] which started from its fundamental step in identifying the "closest prior art." While disagreeing with the BPatG's assumption that a person skilled in the art would have chosen the Chakrabarti document first, the Court stated that there was no such higher ranking of the "closest prior art" and that only from a retrospective view did it become clear which prior publication came closest to the invention and how an inventor could have approached the problem to arrive at the solution according to the invention.[757] It appears that the BGH was concerned about the risk of hindsight if, as a starting point for the determination of an inventive step, one selected the closet prior art. The Court also stated that the selection of the starting point therefore required the justification that generally lay in the efforts of a person skilled in the art to find a better solution for a specific purpose than the known state of the art makes available.[758]

While elaborating the structure and activity relationship of the disclosed compounds, the Court held that, since the "Chakrabarti" document taught away or did not provide a skilled person the information, according to which the further research appeared to be interesting or promising, it was not obvious.[759]

In the United Kingdom

In the Patent Court of olanzapine case,[760] Floyd J employed the structured approach of the obviousness test developed in the *Windsurfing v. Tabur*

755 *BGH/Olanzapine,* IIC 2009, 596, 601.
756 See *supra* 707 and accompanying texts.
757 *BGH/Olanzapine,* IIC 2009, 596, 601.
758 *BGH/Olanzapine,* IIC 2009, 596, 601-602.
759 *BGH/Olanzapine*, GRUR 2009, 382, 387.
760 *Dr Reddy's Laboratories (UK) Ltd v. Eli Lilly & Company Ltd* [2008] EWHC 2345.

Marine case.[761] He found the "skilled addressee" to be a team of scientists with a particular interest in finding anti-psychotics led by a medicinal chemist having access to other disciplines such as pharmacology and toxicology,[762] found "common general knowledge," such as medicinal chemistry, including structure-activity-relationships, psychological disorders and associated side effects,[763] and held the patent was not obvious over all prior arts argued.[764] Considering that the determination of what a person skilled in the art perceived at the filing date was crucial to judging obviousness,[765] this Court seems to start from the very basic element. In addition, he found that "commercial success" is not helpful in deciding obviousness, since that fact alone did not support obviousness if olanzapine was technically obvious.[766] He emphasized that the commercial success was not because the third parties had not appreciated the advantages of olanzapine, but because the basic patent covering olanzapine had prevented the manufacture and sale of olanzapine.[767]

On appeal, Jacob LJ stated that the objection of obviousness could be made where there was "no real technical advance" in the art, since the patent monopoly could be justified by the technical contribution to the art.[768] While endorsing Jacob LJ's position on this issue, Lord Neuberger noted that it

---

761 *Windsurfing International Inc. v. Tabur Marine (GB) Ltd.* R.P.C. 59 (1985). (4 step tests to the obviousness: (1) (a) Identify the notional "person skilled in the art" (b) Identify the relevant common general knowledge of that person; (2) Identify the inventive concept of the claim in question or if that cannot readily be done, construe it; (3) Identify what, if any, differences exist between the matter cited as forming part of the "state of the art" and the inventive concept of the claim or the claim as construed; (4) Viewed without any knowledge of the alleged invention as claimed, do those differences constitute steps which would have been obvious to the person skilled in the art or do they require any degree of invention?").

762 *Dr Reddy's Laboratories (UK) Ltd v. Eli Lilly & Company Ltd* [2008] EWHC 2345, para 140.

763 *Dr Reddy's Laboratories (UK) Ltd v. Eli Lilly & Company Ltd* [2008] EWHC 2345, paras 141-148.

764 *Dr Reddy's Laboratories (UK) Ltd v. Eli Lilly & Company Ltd* [2008] EWHC 2345, paras 149-184.

765 *Spenner*, 90 J. Pat. & Trademark Off. Soc'y, 477, 477 (2008).

766 *Dr Reddy's Laboratories (UK) Ltd v. Eli Lilly & Company Ltd* [2008] EWHC 2345, para 185.

767 *Dr Reddy's Laboratories (UK) Ltd v. Eli Lilly & Company Ltd* [2008] EWHC 2345, para 186.

768 *Dr Reddy's Laboratories Ltd v. Eli Lilly & Company Ltd*, [2009] EWCA Civ 1362, paras 40-52.

should be asked whether the selection was arbitrary or whether the teaching of prior art established that the selection achieved "a particular technical result."[769] If there was no technical advance, it was just an arbitrary selection that was obvious. However, since olanzapine provided its superior therapeutic effect to the prior art, and selection from almost millions of compounds could not be regarded as random,[770] it was nonobvious over the prior art.

In the United States

In the *Olanzapine* case, the Federal Circuit held that several prior art references, in fact, taught away from exploring the compounds that did not possess an electron-withdrawing group in one benzene ring, because olanzapine has exactly one hydrogen atom, which was an electron-withdrawing group.[771] While the Court recognized the structural similarity with a compound that has an ethyl group ("ethyl-olanzapine") instead of a "methyl" group of olanzapine, the Court noted that patentability for a chemical compound did not depend only on structural similarity, but also accounted for the unexpected beneficial significant properties that might render the invention nonobvious.[772] After Rader J noted the similarity with the case of *Yamanouchi Pharm. Co., Ltd. v. Danbury Pharmacal, Inc.*,[773] he stated that the defendants did not sufficiently show the motivation for a person skilled in the art to select the above "ethyl-olanzapine" as a lead compound that did not contain an electron-withdrawing group.[774] This analogy is interesting, since, in *Yamanouchi*, an entire complex combination was required, selecting and combining separate parts of two embodiments followed by further

769 *Dr Reddy's Laboratories Ltd v. Eli Lilly & Company Ltd*, [2009] EWCA Civ 1362, para 109.

770 *Dr Reddy's Laboratories Ltd v. Eli Lilly & Company Ltd*, [2009] EWCA Civ 1362, paras 54-57, 98-101, 109-115.

771 *Eli Lilly and Company v. Zenith Goldline Pharmaceuticals. Inc.*, 471 F.3d 1369, 1378 (Fed. Cir. 2006).

772 *Eli Lilly and Company v. Zenith Goldline Pharmaceuticals. Inc.*, 471 F.3d 1369, 1378-80 (Fed. Cir. 2006).

773 *Yamanouchi Pharm. Co., Ltd. v. Danbury Pharmacal, Inc.*, 231 F.3d 1339, 1344 (Fed. Cir. 2000) (holding that [The ANDA filer] did not show sufficient motivation for person skilled in the art at the time of invention to take any necessary steps to reach the patented invention from the prior arts).

774 *Eli Lilly and Company v. Zenith Goldline Pharmaceuticals. Inc.*, 471 F.3d 1369, 1378-79 (Fed. Cir. 2006).

chemical reactions to produce the patented compound. However, there was only a single difference between the compounds in the prior art (ethyl group) and that in the patent at issue (methyl group) in the *Olanzapine* case. While citing *Yamanouchi* again, he stated that to make obvious the combination as a whole was not the mere identification in the prior art of each component, but rather a motivation to select the reference and to combine them in the particular claimed manner to reach the claimed invention.[775] The Court held that it was not obvious based on the above "teaching away" and extensive "secondary considerations of non-obviousness" such as (i) a long-felt and unmet need; (ii) failure of others; (iii) industry acclaim; and (iv) unexpected results.

The size of the genus has special impacts on the finite obvious to try case; where there is a finite number of possibilities from which to start, a technique that is within the grasp of the person skilled in the art is used to modify the prior art to arrive at the claimed invention, and the results are not unexpected, then the invention is obvious.[776] In *Pfizer v. Apotex*, a prior patent claimed amlodipine and its pharmaceutically acceptable salts, disclosed maleate as the best salts, but did not explicitly disclose besylate.[777] A later patent application claiming amlodipine besylate salt was rejected on the basis of a reasonable expectation of success over the above prior patent in combination with the *Berge* reference that disclosed fifty-three FDA-approved, commercially marketed anions that were useful for making pharmaceutically-acceptable salts and included besylate.[778] The Court found the fact that there were a limited number of choices to start from, and a reasonable probability

---

775 *Eli Lilly and Company v. Zenith Goldline Pharmaceuticals. Inc.*, 471 F.3d 1369, 1379 (Fed. Cir. 2006).

776 *See Spenner*, 90 J. Pat. & Trademark Off. Soc'y, 477, 510 (2008).

777 *Pfizer, Inc. v. Apotex, Inc*, 480 F.3d 1348, 1353 (Fed. Cir. 2007), *reh'g denied*, 488 F.3d 1377 (Fed. Cir. 2007), *cert. denied* 552 U.S. 941 (2007).

778 *Pfizer, Inc. v. Apotex, Inc.*, 480 F.3d 1348, 1355 (Fed. Cir. 2007) *reh'g denied*, 488 F.3d 1377, 1383-84 (Fed. Cir. 2007) (This denial of rehearing *en banc* decision was not unanimous, i.e., Judges Newman, Lourie, and Rader wrote their own dissents. Regarding the "obvious to try" analysis, Judge Rader stated that since a salt selection was unpredictable, there would not have been a reasonable expectation of success.).

of success to make the salt, prevented its unexpected results from rebutting the *prima facie* obviousness.[779]

In Korea

In August, 2012, the Korean Supreme Court upheld the validity of Eli Lilly's patent on olanzapine.[780] The Supreme Court reiterated that for the inventive step of a selection invention not to be denied, all specific concepts in the selection invention must exhibit *qualitatively different or qualitatively the same but quantitatively superior effects* over the prior invention, and that these effects should be clearly disclosed in the specification of the selection invention patent by either a description of qualitative differences or data supporting any quantitative advantages.[781] The Supreme Court did not acknowledge the therapeutic superiority of olanzapine over prior art, since the superiority of parameters comparing the therapeutic effects thereof were not consistent.[782] Based on the description of the patent specification regarding the avoidance of side effects,[783] however, the Supreme Court held that such effects were qualitatively different, since these were not disclosed in the prior art, and a person skilled in the art could not anticipate from the prior art that olanzapine would have such effects.[784] Further, the Supreme Court noted that where a selection invention had multiple effects, the selection invention could be recognized as showing qualitatively different effects compared to a prior art, even if only a part of the effects of the selection invention, not all of the effects, was recognized as being qualitatively different or quantitatively remarkable compared to the prior art.[785]

---

779 *Pfizer, Inc. v. Apotex, Inc.*, 480 F.3d 1348, 1372 (Fed. Cir. 2007) *reh'g denied, cert. denied* (holding "even if Pfizer showed that amlodipine besylate exhibits unexpectedly superior results, this secondary consideration does not overcome the strong showing of obviousness in this case.").

780 *Korean Supreme Court/Olanzapine*, 2010Hu3424, Aug. 23, 2012 (this was the first case to upheld the validity of a selection invention).

781 *Korean Supreme Court/Olanzapine*, 2010Hu3424, Aug. 23, 2012, para 1.

782 *Korean Supreme Court/Olanzapine*, 2010Hu3424, Aug. 23, 2012, para 2.Na.

783 Korean Patent No. 195566, 11-3 (noting "[i]n dog toxicity studies with a closely analogous compound (ethyl olanzapine), at a dosage of 8 mg/kg, it was observed that four out of eight dogs showed a significant rise in cholesterol levels, whereas the compound of the present invention (olanzapine) did not show any rise in cholesterol levels.").

784 *Korean Supreme Court/Olanzapine*, 2010Hu3424, Aug. 23, 2012, para 2.Da.

785 *Korean Supreme Court/Olanzapine*, 2010Hu3424, Aug. 23, 2012, para 2.Ra.

b) Optical isomers

Considering that the novelty of the optical isomer is not negated by the earlier disclosure of disclosed racemate, the patentability of this invention would more likely hinge on the question of the inventive step. To establish the inventive step, the inventor should show that the optical isomer has surprisingly superior properties in comparison with the known racemate.[786] One may recall that the existence of the chiral center means the existence of optically active forms, and it is generally recognized that one optical isomer normally has higher activity than the others.[787]

In the EPO

Initially BOA found the invention of a mixture containing at least 80% of one of two enantiomers novel over the prior art disclosing a mixture of two enantiomers containing 50% of each. However, BOA found it lacking an inventive step.[788] The Board noted that test of different ratios of mixture to analyze their effects was a routine procedure.[789]

> "Long before the contested patent´s priority date, it was generally known to specialists that, *in physiologically active substances* (e.g. herbicides, fungicides, insecticides and growth regulators, but also pharmaceuticals and foodstuffs) with an asymmetrical carbon atom enabling them to occur in the form of a racemate or one of two enantiomers, *one of the latter frequently has a quantitatively greater effect than the other or than the racemate.* If – as here - the aim is therefore to develop agents with increased physiological activity from a physiologically active racemate the obvious first step - before any thought is given, say, to synthesizing structurally modified products - is to produce the two enantiomers in isolation and test whether one or the other is more active than the racemate. *Such tests are routine.* Under established Board case law, *an enhanced effect cannot be adduced as evidence of inventive step if it emerges from obvious tests.* Since, in the present case, tests with the enantiomers were obvious in view of the task at hand, discovery of the claimed effect of the D-enantiomers

---

786 *Grubb/Thomsen*, 2010, 236.

787 *See e.g., Forest Labs., Inc. v. Ivax Pharms., Inc.,* 501 F.3d 1263, 1269 (Fed. Cir. 2007) (Forest's argument: "the general expectation in the art that one enantiomer would be more potent than the other provided reason for a person of ordinary skill in the art to isolate the enantiomers").

788 *Hoechst/Enantiomers*, T296/87, OJ EPO 1990, 195, 206, 209.

789 *Hoechst/Enantiomers*, T296/87, OJ EPO 1990, 195, 206, 209.

compared with corresponding racemates does not involve an inventive step."[790] [Emphasis added]

Ten years later in T 229/97,[791] however, the Board held that a patent on hemicalcium salt of R-enantiomer of atorvastatin (Lipitor®)[792] involved an inventive step over the prior patent claiming sodium salt of the racemate of atorvastatin.[793] Based on the experimental evidence of favourable handling properties of a claimed invention submitted just one month before the appeal hearing, the Board held that i) the problem to solve was providing a hypocholesterolemic compound having improved handling properties, i.e. improved hygroscopicity and solubility, and that ii) the closest prior art gave no hint of how to solve the problem nor any incentive to modify those salts of the racemates in the hemicalcium salt of the particular R-enantiomer. Thus, the claimed invention involved the inventive step.[794] However, the original patent specification as filed did not mention either the problem of handling the substance nor the solution thereof, i.e. the evidence showed a radically different problem and solution disclosed by the original patent specification. As Pumfrey J noted, this reformulation of the problem i.e. the better handleability of calcium salt of atorvastatin over the sodium salt, could provide a substantial risk that would lead to a finding of non-obviousness based on the later discovered advantages.[795]

In Germany

In the *Atorvastatin* decision in 2007, after holding that claims 1 to 3 directed to product invention were not novel,[796] the BPatG held that claim 4 directed to the process to produce atorvastatin did not involve the inventive step, since a person skilled in the art would have been able to manufacture it according to the method described in the prior art.[797]

---

790 *Hoechst/Enantiomers*, T296/87, OJ EPO 1990, 195, 206, 209.

791 *Warner-Lambert/Atorvastatin,* T 0229/97 (2000).

792 EP No. 0,409,281 (October 31, 2001, under the title of "(R-(R*R*))-2-(4-fluorophenyl)-beta,delta-dihydroxy-5-(1-methylethyl-3-phenyl-4((phenylamino)-carbonyl)-1H-pyrrole-1-heptanoic acid, its lactone form and salts thereof").

793 U.S. Patent No. 4,681,893 (July 21, 1987, under the title of "Trans-6-[2-(3- or 4-carboxamido-substituted pyrrol-1-yl)alkyl]-4-hydroxypyran-2-one inhibitors of cholesterol synthesis").

794 *Warner-Lambert/Atorvastatin*, T229/97 (2000), paras 4.2.-4.7.

795 *Ranbaxy UK & Anor v. Warner-Lambert* [2005] EWHC 2142, para 71.

796 See *supra* 589 -594 and accompanying texts.

797 *BPatG/Atorvastatin*, BeckRS 2007, 18183, para II.4.

In the *Escitalopram* decision, the BPatG held that it was obvious to resort to the method of chiral chromatography to separate the enantiomers.[798] The BGH agreed with the BPatG in that a person skilled in the art had reason as of the date of priority to attempt to produce or isolate the citalopram's enantiomers, since it was known that one enantiomer can have a better effect and another might have the opposite or a side effect.[799] However, based on the fact that there was no obvious way to obtain the escitalopram as of the date of priority, that it was not certain which way would provide an industrially useful scale production, that there was not enough motivation to choose the method, that there was uncertain expectation of success, and that there were many failures to separate it, the Court held that the invention was not obvious.[800] All of the reasoning was directed to the *difficulty of the method* in separating escitalopram, and it was the precisely reason for finding that the escitalopram was "novel."

In the United Kingdom

The differences from the EPO approach were drawn into sharp focus in the *Ranbaxy v. Warner-Lambert* case. In this case, the Patent Court found that a patent relating to the hemi-calcium salt of atorvastatin (Lipitor®) was invalid for the lack of obviousness.[801] This contrasted markedly with an earlier decision of the EPO's Technical Board (T 229/97), in which the same patent was found to involve an inventive step over an equivalent piece of prior art.[802] The Court noted the following: i) by 1989 resolution of racemates with pharmaceutical activity was well established; ii) for the family of statins, the skilled person would have known that the activity would reside in a specific enantiomer; iii) the salts would likely be more soluble than the free acid; and iv) testing the properties of salts was standard practice.[803] The Court also held that the difference between the claimed invention and the prior art was most certainly obvious, since the resolution of the racemate was common general knowledge, and the seven salts were specifically described including calcium.[804] The Court further explained that, according to

798 *BPatG/Escitalopram,* BeckRS 2007, 14624, para II.1.b).
799 *BGH/Escitalopram*, GRUR 2010, 123, 126.
800 *BGH/Escitalopram*, GRUR 2010, 123, 127-130.
801 *Ranbaxy UK & Anor v. Warner-Lambert* [2005] EWHC 2142.
802 See *supra* 791 -794 and accompanying texts.
803 *Ranbaxy (UK) v. Warner-Lambert* [2006] EWCA Civ 876, paras 55-57.
804 *Ranbaxy (UK) v. Warner-Lambert* [2006] EWCA Civ 876, para 62.

the *IG Farbenindustrie AG's Patents* case, although the selection of a single element having advantageous properties from a class was possible, the prior disclosure had to be a disclosure of a class rather than a disclosure of the individual members of that class.[805] In the appeal, the Court noted that it was unnecessary to consider the obviousness point.[806]

However, in *Lundbeck v. Generics Ltd.*, a patent for an enantiomer (escitalopram) of the known drug citalopram was held valid. Before the Court of Appeal, whether the so-called amino diol route for resolving the racemate would have been obvious was an issue.[807] Lord Hoffmann stated that the Court might reverse the trial judge's finding when the error of principle occurred, because the judge failed to consider whether it was obvious for the skilled person to try the reaction to see if it worked, as in the *Biogen*[808] case.[809] While stating that Kitchin J applied the state of the law correctly to the facts of this case, Lord Hoffmann rejected the obviousness argument. Jacob LJ rejected the plaintiff's argument that a person skilled in the art could have come to the invention by doing a short and simple experiment, stating that, by itself, it was insufficient, as one could say that "with hindsight" of many inventions, and as it was not enough motivation for a skilled person to carry it out. Therefore, the invention was not obvious.

On appeal, the obviousness was not a major issue before the House of Lords, since the attack based on obviousness failed in both courts below. On the other hand, Lord Neuberger summarized basic knowledge that had long been known about enantiomers as follows: i) Two enantiomers could have different properties from each other; ii) a racemate's therapeutic effect might be mainly dependent on one enantiomer; iii) the other enantiomer might have toxic or side effects; iv) the only way to tell which one had which effect was to separate one from another and to compare; v) however, that was not possible to predict yet.[810] He continued that the notion to obtain a pure therapeutic form from a racemate was obvious, but to obtain a pure form was not obvious, and it was particularly difficult to separate (S)-citalopram from the

805 *Ranbaxy (UK) v. Warner-Lambert* [2006] EWCA Civ 876, para 63.
806 *Ranbaxy (UK) v. Warner-Lambert* [2006] EWCA Civ 876, para 32.
807 *Lundbeck v. Generics Ltd.* [2008] EWCA Civ 311, para 14.
808 *Biogen Inc v. Medeva Plc* [1996] UKHL 18.
809 *Lundbeck v. Generics Ltd.* [2008] EWCA Civ 311, para 23.
810 *Generics Ltd. v Lundbeck* [2009] UKHL 12, para 61.

racemate.[811] The difficulty of separating the racemates again seemed to be weighted to determine obviousness.

After this *Escitalopram* case, the Court of Appeal again held that an enantiomer of ofloxacin, i.e. *Levofloxacin,* was not obvious over a prior art disclosing the method of producing other compounds having the same core structure as ofloxacin.[812] Specifically, Jacob LJ held:

> "I am not sorry to reach this conclusion. Daiichi's work led to a better medicine than ofloxacin. Levofloxacin is not just twice as active as ofloxacin (which might have been expected) but is a lot more soluble and less toxic than was predictable. It can be used in higher dosages than might have been expected with corresponding medical benefit."[813]

In the United States

Unlike the *Levofloxacin* case in the United Kingdom where the equivalent prior art was found not to provide enough motivation to resolve the levofloxacin, the *Ortho-McNeil* Court found that the prior art provided ample motivation to separate optical isomers of the racemate in question.[814] However, the Court held that, even though the prior art enabled the production of enantiomer and provided enough motivation, the patent was not invalid, since there was no evidence showing that the improved result was reasonably expected in light of secondary considerations.[815] Simply put, the *prima facie* obviousness that was established by enabling the difficult way of production was rebutted based on its unexpected effect.[816]

The *Atorvastatin* case in the United States was somewhat simpler. In *Pfizer, Inc. v. Ranbaxy,* the Federal Circuit held that one claim at issue over *Atorvastatin* was invalid for failure to satisfy 35 U.S.C. § 112 and remanded

---

811 *Generics Ltd. v Lundbeck* [2009] UKHL 12, paras 61-65.

812 *Generics (UK) Ltd v. Daiichi Pharmaceutical* [2009] EWCA Civ 646, paras 30-44.

813 *Generics (UK) Ltd v. Daiichi Pharmaceutical* [2009] EWCA Civ 646, para 45.

814 *Ortho-McNeil Pharm., Inc. v. Mylan Labs., Inc.*, 348 F. Supp. 2d 713, 752 (N.D.W.Va. 2004), *aff'd,* 161 Fed.Appx. 944 (quoting a part of the book "[W]ith the development of synthesis methods via stereoselection and improvement in the analytical methods of optical isomers in the recent years, many came to believe that only one of the enantiomers is the important substance and that the other one is, if bluntly said, almost an impure substance.").

815 *Ortho-McNeil Pharm., Inc. v. Mylan Labs., Inc.*, 348 F. Supp. 2d 713, 752-62 (N.D.W.Va. 2004), *aff'd,* 161 Fed.Appx. 944.

816 *Ortho-McNeil Pharm., Inc. v. Mylan Labs., Inc.*, 348 F. Supp. 2d 713, 754 (N.D.W.Va. 2004), *aff'd,* 161 Fed.Appx. 944 (noting "levofloxacin is pharmaceutically superior to ofloxacin in virtually every relevant aspect").

the case to the District Court.[817] However, since Pfizer sought to reissue the patent at issue to correct the above error and provided Ranbaxy with a convenant not to sue Ranbaxy on all remaining claims of the original patent,[818] and since the patent was unenforceable, the District Court dismissed this allegation.[819]

In *Forest Labs. v. Ivax Pharms.*, the District Court found that the alleged prior art did not provide a reasonable expectation of success of obtaining the enantiomer (escitalopram) for similar reasons to those that supported a finding of enablement regarding the same prior art.[820] The Court further found that one of ordinary skill in the art at the time of the invention would generally have been motivated to develop new compounds rather than undertake the difficult and unpredictable task of resolving a known racemate.[821] In the appeal, the Federal Circuit noted that Ivax emphasized only the evidence that was favorable to its desired outcome without addressing the evidence favorable to Forest, such as the failure of the inventors to resolve citalopram without undue experiments, and so on,[822] and concluded that it was not obvious to the person skilled in the art. Considering that this decision was rendered several months after *KSR*, the decision is interesting, because the Federal Circuit did not consider more than the ordinary view regarding obviousness while relying on the District Court's finding based on *Graham v. John Deere Co*.

One week after the *Escitalopram* decision, the Federal Circuit answered the same question, i.e. whether the one stereoisomer of Ramipril with five chiral centers, 5(S) Ramipril was obvious over its prior racemate. [823] While quoting the *KSR* decision, the Federal Circuit reasoned that requiring an explicit teaching to purify the 5(S) stereoisomer was precisely the sort of rigid application of the TSM test that was criticized in *KSR*.[824] The Federal

---

817 *Pfizer, Inc. v. Ranbaxy Laboratories Ltd.*, 457 F.3d 1284, 1291-92 (Fed. Cir. 2006).

818 *Pfizer, Inc. v. Ranbaxy Laboratories, Ltd.*, 525 F.Supp.2d 680, 684 (D.Del.,2007).

819 *Pfizer, Inc. v. Ranbaxy Laboratories, Ltd.*, 525 F.Supp.2d 680, 685 (D.Del.,2007).

820 *Forest Labs., Inc. v. Ivax Pharms., Inc.*, 501 F.3d 1263, 1267 (Fed. Cir. 2007).

821 *Forest Labs., Inc. v. Ivax Pharms., Inc.*, 501 F.3d 1263, 1267 (Fed. Cir. 2007); *contra BGH/Escitalopram*, GRUR 2010, 123, 126; *contra Darrow*, 2 Stan. Tech. L. Rev. 1 paras 21 and 39 (2007).

822 *Forest Labs., Inc. v. Ivax Pharms., Inc.*, 501 F.3d 1263, 1268 (Fed. Cir. 2007).

823 *Aventis Pharma Deutschland GmbH v. Lupin, Ltd.*, 499 F.3d 1293, 1300 (Fed. Cir. 2007).

824 *Aventis Pharma Deutschland GmbH v. Lupin, Ltd.*, 499 F.3d 1293, 1301 (Fed. Cir. 2007).

Circuit found that the prior art motivated a person skilled in the art to isolate 5(S) Ramipril and taught how to do so, based on the facts (i) that one therapeutically active racemate contained only two enantiomers, namely SSSSS and SSSSR,[825] (ii) that the person skilled in the art would have reasons to believe that the mixture derived properties from particular components of the compound,[826] and (iii) that the prior art taught that the stereoisomers of ramipril "can be separated by conventional chromatographic or fractional crystallization methods."[827] The Federal Circuit also held that there was no evidence that separating 5(S) Ramipril from the above therapeutically active racemate was beyond the capability of a person skilled in the art and the patentee failed to prove unexpected results over the above mixture, since the potency of an isomer precisely varied with the absolute amount of the isomer in the racemate.[828]

In *Sanofi-Synthelabo v. Apotex, Inc.*, experts testified about the degree and kind of stereoselectivity of a selected enantiomer, i.e. a situation where one enantiomer having biological activity and the other having toxicity was rare and could not have been predicted, since usually if one enantiomer has better biological activity than the other, that activity also includes the adverse as well as the beneficial properties.[829] The Federal Circuit held that these unexpected and unpredictable properties of *Clopidogrel* would not be what one would have expected in the *Ramipril* case.[830] In response to the argument that potential regulatory pressure for the separation of enantiomers would have motivated to resolve the racemate, the Court found that the resolution was undertaken not because of the potential regulation but because of the purpose to study the adverse neurological effects.[831]

---

825 This seems to be similar to the situation one enantiomer was selected from a racemate with one chiral center.

826 Prior art provided the molecules with close structural relationship to Ramipril, such as enalapril or captopril were more active in the (S) form.

827 *Aventis Pharma Deutschland GmbH v. Lupin, Ltd.*, 499 F.3d 1293, 1302 (Fed. Cir. 2007).

828 *Aventis Pharma Deutschland GmbH v. Lupin, Ltd.*, 499 F.3d 1293, 1302 (Fed. Cir. 2007).

829 *Sanofi-Synthelabo v. Apotex, Inc.*, 550 F.3d 1075, 1081 (Fed. Cir. 2008).

830 *Sanofi-Synthelabo v. Apotex, Inc.*, 550 F.3d 1075, 1089 (Fed. Cir. 2008); *see Aventis Pharma Deutschland GmbH v. Lupin, Ltd.*, 499 F.3d 1293, 1302 (Fed. Cir. 2007) (holding that the ramipril isomer's potency was "precisely what one would expect, as compared to a mixture containing other, inert or near-inert stereoisomers.'').

831 *Sanofi-Synthelabo v. Apotex, Inc.*, 550 F.3d 1075, 1089-90 (Fed. Cir. 2008).

Even though the motivation to resolve the racemate could be found and the separation method in general may be known, particular enantiomers may not be obvious, since various factors, including the obviousness of the resolution method, may play a role in determining obviousness.[832]

In Korea

With regard to obviousness in the *Clopidogrel* decision, [833] the Supreme Court held that, for the inventive step not to be denied, all specific concepts in the selection invention must show effects that are *qualitatively different or qualitatively same but quantitatively superior* to those of the prior invention,[834] and these effects should be clearly disclosed in the specification of the selection invention by either a description of qualitative differences or data supporting any quantitative advantages.[835] The Court further noted that a two-fold superiority in platelet aggregation inhibition or around 1.6-fold superiority in acute toxicity to the racemate in the prior art could not be regarded as superior considering that the administration of one enantiomer yielded approximately 2-fold better effects than that of a racemate, which is a 50:50 mixture of enantiomers.[836]

In the Atorvastatin decision, the Supreme Court determined that the enantiomer invention was also obvious, since, even under the consideration of hygroscopicity or solubility, which were argued by the patentee, there was no special disclosure in the specification which could show any qualitatively different or qualitatively identical but quantitatively superior effects.[837]

c) Crystalline forms

The systematic investigation of a compound to determine whether it is prone to polymorphism as well as the nature of polymorphism is routine practice

832 *Spenner*, 90 J. Pat. & Trademark Off. Soc'y, 477, 487-88 (2008).

833 *Korean Supreme Court/Clopidogrel*, 2008Hu736 & 2008Hu743, Oct. 15, 2009.

834 This requirement seems to be similar to those of *I.G. Rule* in U.K.

835 *Korean Supreme Court/Clopidogrel*, 2008Hu736 & 2008Hu743, Oct. 15, 2009, Headnote 2.

836 *Korean Supreme Court/Clopidogrel*, 2008Hu736 & 2008Hu743, Oct. 15, 2009, para 2.Na.

837 *Korean Supreme Court/Atorvastatin*, 2008Hu3469, Mar. 25, 2010, para 2. Na.

in pharmaceutical pre-formulation studies.[838] This understanding forms the part of the common general knowledge in the art.

In the EPO

In T 51/97, where an issue was whether one crystalline form of a compound established its inventive step over another modified form of the same compound, the Board held that it was obvious over the combination of the closest prior art which was acknowledged in the specification of the patent in suit and another prior art which indicated the incentives and a concrete hint as to how to solve the dispersion instability at high temperatures.[839] The Board further held that it was not necessary to establish that the success of a solution of a technical problem was predictable with certainty; it was sufficient to establish that the skilled person would have done so with a reasonable expectation of success. [840]

One recent Technical BOA decision that attracted considerable attention in the pharmaceutical industry was T 777/08, where crystal forms II and IV of atorvastatin were claimed, and two closest prior arts each disclosing amorphous forms of atorvastatin were identified.[841] After explaining the common knowledge at the priority date of the patent in suit [in 1995],[842] the Board held that, in the absence of any technical prejudice, the mere provision of a crystalline form of a known pharmaceutically active compound could not be regarded as involving an inventive step.[843] The Board further held as follows:

> "[I]n view of his general knowledge, as reflected in this excerpt from [another prior art], the skilled person, starting from the amorphous form of a pharmaceutically active compound as closest prior art, would have a clear expectation that a crystalline form thereof would provide a solution to the problem [to pro-

---

838 *Caira*, 1998, 165.

839 *Nippon/Crystalline dye,* T 0051/97 (2000), points 2.6. and 2.7.

840 *Nippon/Crystalline dye,* T 0051/97 (2000), point 2.7.3.

841 *Warner-Lambert/Atorvastatin polymorphs,* T 0777/08 (2011).

842 *Warner-Lambert/Atorvastatin polymorphs,* T 0777/08 (2011), Headnote 1 ("At the priority date of the patent in suit, the skilled person in the field of pharmaceutical drug development would have been aware of the fact that instances of polymorphism were commonplace in molecules of interest to the pharmaceutical industry, and have known it to be advisable to screen for polymorphs early on in the drug development process. Moreover, he would be familiar with routine methods of screening.").

843 *Warner-Lambert/Atorvastatin polymorphs,* T 0777/08 (2011), point 5.2.

> vide atorvastatin in a form having improved filterability and drying characteristic]. Although this might not be true of every crystalline form obtained [examples], it was nevertheless obvious to try this avenue with a reasonable expectation of success without involving any inventive ingenuity. [...] [A]n arbitrary selection from a group of equally suitable candidates cannot be viewed as involving an inventive step."[844]

Thus, it must be expected that the inventiveness of a new polymorph can be acknowledged only if it is associated with an unexpected pharmaceutical activity, while improved physical and/or physicochemical properties will not be sufficient. As the Board also noted, one should not overlook the fact that it is not always the case that every single polymorph provides improved characteristics. As *McCrone* famously noted in 1965, "[...] every compound has different polymorphic forms and that, in general, the number of forms known for a given compound is proportional to the time and money spent in research on that compound."[845]

In the United Kingdom

In the case on a crystal form of *Paroxetine methansulphonate,* obviousness was not the issue.[846] In another case on a crystal form of *t-butylamine salt of perindopril*, the Court of Appeal held that the claim on the process to produce the crystal form, i.e. a solution "is heated at reflux and is then cooled gradually until crystallisation is complete," which differed from the prior art procedure only in the qualification "gradually," was obvious over the prior art.[847]

In *Leo Pharma v. Sandoz*, where a single crystalline form of *Calcipotriol*[848] monohydrate which was said to have superior stability and technical properties useful in the manufacture of suspension formulations, the inventive step of claimed crystalline form over the prior art disclosed anhydrous form of crystalline calcipotriol was one of the issues in the appeal.[849] The Court found this case unusual, since Sandoz argues that the skilled person

844 *Warner-Lambert/Atorvastatin polymorphs,* T 0777/08 (2011), point 5.2.

845 Cited in *Bernstein*, 2002, 9; indeed there are a good number of companies who are specialized in polymorph screening, such as Analytics-Pharm, Poly Crystal Line, Crystal Pharmatech, Avantium and the like.

846 *Synthon BV v. SmithKline Beecham plc* [2005] UKHL 59.

847 *Laboratoires Servier v. Apotex* [2008] EWCA Civ 445, paras 13-20 (a case about the novelty of one crystal form of the t-butylamine salt of perindopril).

848 Calcipotriol is a Vitamin D3 analogue.

849 *Leo Pharma v. Sandoz Ltd* [2009] EWCA Civ 1188.

would, using his technical knowledge, have come across the invention (namely the hydrate and its beneficial technical properties) without any expectation of successfully finding a better product.[850] Sandoz argues that, given the instructions disclosed in the prior art for an aqueous suspension cream containing calcipotriol, it was obvious to find and use calcipotriol monohydrate. The Court of Appeal considered the four different approaches argued by Sandoz against the finding of non-obviousness,[851] but held in each case that the lower court's conclusion could not be faulted. The Court further held that it was not universal practice to conduct a polymorph screen and that a skilled team would not regard such a screen as mandatory.[852] The Court held that the demand of the regulatory authorities could not be equated to knowledge of the person skilled in the art.[853] The Court held that it was not obvious to use the screen and so to find the hydrate as a part of a routine check in the course of stability studies or in anticipation of a regulatory requires, since it was not proven that the above investigation would reveal the hydrate.[854] The Court of Appeal further held that, although the wet-milling[855] was accepted at first instance to be an obvious variant to dry milling, as the hydrate would have been produced only 50% of the time, the lower court was correct to conclude that it did not make the hydrate obvious.[856] The Court of Appeal also rejected the argument that routine crystallisation experiments would have produced the hydrate, since the nature

850 *Leo Pharma v. Sandoz Ltd* [2009] EWCA Civ 1188, para 9.

851 *Leo Pharma v. Sandoz Ltd* [2009] EWCA Civ 1188, para 11 ((i) obviousness over the acne use patent because it was obvious to conduct a full polymorph screen, during which the monohydrate and its properties would have been discovered; (ii) obviousness over the acne use patent because a product screen would have revealed the monohydrate and its technical properties; (iii) obviousness over the acne use patent because wet milling instead of dry milling would have produced the monohydrate and its technical properties would have then been revealed; (iv) obviousness in the light of common general knowledge alone because experiments into crystallisation would have revealed the monohydrate and its technical properties.).

852 *Leo Pharma v. Sandoz Ltd* [2009] EWCA Civ 1188, paras 51-63; *contra Warner-Lambert/Atorvastatin polymorphs,* T 0777/08 (2011), point 5.2. (noting it was the routine tasks of the skilled person involved in the field of drug development to screen for solid-state forms of a drug substance); *contra McCrone*, cited in *Bernstein*, 2002, 9.

853 *Leo Pharma v. Sandoz Ltd* [2009] EWCA Civ 1188, para 54.

854 *Leo Pharma v. Sandoz Ltd* [2009] EWCA Civ 1188, paras 64-68.

855 Milling is one of the most efficient methods of producing small particle size. And wet milling is a process in which the substance is steeped in water.

856 *Leo Pharma v. Sandoz Ltd* [2009] EWCA Civ 1188, paras 69-71.

of the experimental programme was neither established nor sufficiently defined to enable a conclusion as to what it would have uncovered.[857]

The problem with each approach outlined by Sandoz was that the skilled person would not have necessarily had any expectation of finding calcipotriol monohydrate. On the one hand, all approaches pursued by Sandoz were essentially plausible; on the other hand, a non-obviousness challenge based on "obvious to try" must have a fair expectation of success for the skilled person. The British courts seem to require a relatively high standard for a non-obviousness case based on "obvious to try."

In Germany

Unlike the British case, where it was mainly argued that the way to make monohydrates was part of the common knowledge of a skilled person, the same prior arts disclosing three other Vt. D3 monohydrates were used as main references to challenge the inventive step of the claimed crystalline form of calcipotriol mononhydrate. Figure 8 presents the respective structures of three other Vt D3 analogues and Calcipotriol.

Figure 8: The structures of Vt D3 analogues and Calcipotriol

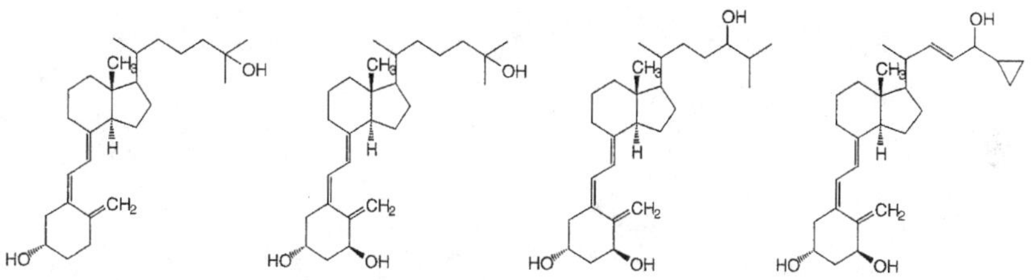

25-Hydroxy-Cholecalciferol 1α,25-Dihydroxy-Cholecalciferol 1α,24-Dihydroxy-Cholecalciferol Calcipotriol

The BGH held that, in the assessment of inventive step, the question of whether the skilled person had an incentive to adopt the measurement described in the prior art and to apply a known scheme to a known subject matter grew in importance depending on whether the skilled person could reasonably expect to succeed this way in solving the technical problem.[858] The BGH further held that these requirements were fulfilled in this case,

857 *Leo Pharma v. Sandoz Ltd* [2009] EWCA Civ 1188, paras 73-76.
858 *BGH/Calcipotriol-Monohydrat*, GRUR 2012, 803, 807.

since, based on those three prior arts, the skilled person had the incentive to adopt the described measurement – solution of the solid in organic solvent with the addition of water – and to apply it to the Calcipotriol; consequently, he could have obtained the calcipotriol monohydrate.[859] The implementation of these measurements would have been with a view to the structurally related Vt. D analogues in the prior art and a possible similar reaction of calcipotriol coupled to the reasonable expectation of success; moreover, the effort to be introduced – use of organic solvents and water – in relation to an expected result was to be proportionate.[860]

In the United States

Obviousness was not the issue in either *Abbott Laboratories v. Geneva Pharmaceuticals*[861] or *SmithKlein Beecham v. Apotex*.[862]

In Korea

The Supreme Court reiterated the inventive step requirement for crystalline form as follows:

> "It is well-known in the field of pharmaceutical compounds that the same compounds may have various crystalline forms and that the pharmaceutical properties thereof, such as solubility, stability, etc., may vary. Thus, prior to designing a preparation method of a compound, it is common to first confirm the existence of polymorphism of the compound. Accordingly, an invention for a compound having a specific crystalline form, which is different from a compound disclosed in the prior art only in terms of the crystalline form, namely, an invention relating to a crystalline form, is recognized as having an inventive step only if the effect thereof is qualitatively different from a compound disclosed in the prior art or is quantitatively very different, but not necessarily qualitatively different, from a compound disclosed in the prior art. Although not absolutely required to provide comparative experimental data with the prior art, the specification of the invention relating to a crystalline form must clearly describe the above effect, in order for the effect to be considered when determining the inventive step of the invention. If the effect is questionable, the applicant or the patentee must specifically demonstrate the effect through reliable comparative experimental data after the filing date of the application."[863]

---

859 *BGH/Calcipotriol-Monohydrat*, GRUR 2012, 803, 807.
860 *BGH/Calcipotriol-Monohydrat*, GRUR 2012, 803, 807.
861 *Abbott Laboratories v. Geneva Pharmaceuticals, Inc.*, 182 F.3d 1315 (Fed. Cir. 1999).
862 *SmithKline Beecham Corp. v. Apotex Corp.*, 403 F.3d 1331 (Fed. Cir. 2005).
863 *Korean Supreme Court/Lercanidipine*, 2010Hu2872, Jul. 14, 2011, para 1.

In this case, the Supreme Court acknowledged that the results of experiments regarding the bioavailability, solubility, and reduced batch-to-batch variability were clearly described in the patent specification.[864] Since the bioavailability disclosed in the patent specification was based on the blood concentration of the claimed racemate of Lercanidipine hydrochloride, the submitted result of bioavailability on the prior art was based on the blood concentration of S-enantiomer of Lercanidipine hydrochloride, and, even though each condition of the experiment could not be acknowledged by the submitted document, the Court held that the superior bioavailability of claimed crystalline form over the prior art could not be recognized.[865] In addition, for argument that the solubility of the claimed crystalline form was improved, the Court noted that according to the submitted experimental data, it was not confirmed whether the crystalline form compared to those of prior art was also non-hydrate as those disclosed in the prior art, and it was already known at the time of patent filing that 5~10 times of improved solubility could be obtained by the change of crystalline form.[866] The Court further held that, since it was not recognized what kind of *specific pharmaceutical effect* was achieved by the 5 times improved solubility of claimed crystalline form, the 5 times improved solubility could not be regarded as a superior effect.[867] The reduced batch-to-batch variability in mono-crystalline form was a logical result, since less variability would have been derived from the mixture ratio of different crystalline forms.[868] Accordingly, the Court held that, since the claimed crystalline form was not recognized as having a different or quantitatively remarkable effect in comparison to the compound disclosed in the prior art, the invention lacked an inventive step.[869]

In *Ibandronate* case, the Supreme Court noted that the patent specification disclosed the stability of the crystalline form under certain conditions and the particle size distribution of the claimed crystalline form. However, the experimental data submitted by the plaintiff included only the results of testing the stability of the claimed crystalline form without providing comparative experimental results with the compound disclosed in the prior

864 *Korean Supreme Court/Lercanidipine*, 2010Hu2872, Jul. 14, 2011, para 2.
865 *Korean Supreme Court/Lercanidipine*, 2010Hu2872, Jul. 14, 2011, para 2.
866 *Korean Supreme Court/Lercanidipine*, 2010Hu2872, Jul. 14, 2011, para 2.
867 *Korean Supreme Court/Lercanidipine*, 2010Hu2872, Jul. 14, 2011, para 2.
868 *Korean Supreme Court/Lercanidipine*, 2010Hu2872, Jul. 14, 2011, para 2.
869 *Korean Supreme Court/Lercanidipine*, 2010Hu2872, Jul. 14, 2011, para 3.

art.[870] Thus, the Supreme Court held that, since the degree of improvement of the claimed invention over the prior art could not be confirmed and *the pharmaceutical effect* achieved by the improved stability of particle size distribution of the claimed crystalline form could not be confirmed, the claimed crystalline form was not recognized as having a different or quantitatively remarkable effect in comparison to the compound disclosed in the prior art. Thus, the invention lacked an inventive step.[871]

d) Metabolites

The case laws on the patentability of metabolites have focused mainly on the novelty of inventions, and inventive step thereof has not been the issue.

4. Analysis and conclusion

For species selection inventions, the courts in each jurisdiction acknowledged the advantageous effects over the prior art, i.e. the technical advance in the art through the selection; subsequently, the selection was regarded as non-arbitrary. The size of the genus from which the selection invention is made is important in establishing an inventive step. However, because of the lowered inventive step requirement, the advantageous effects do not need to be shown over the whole scope of the prior art.

For the optical isomers, the much lower inventive step requirements are distinctly observed. Unlike the early rulings that the stereochemistry and the different effect of one enantiomer from another were known, and that the production of an enantiomer and the testing of the activity thereof were routine, meaning even the advanced effects could not be the evidence of inventive step,[872] the BOA held an enantiomer invention established an inventive step based on the radically different problem and solution from those disclosed in the patent specification as filed.[873] In addition, in Germany, after the Olanzapine decision, the BGH held an enantiomer invention established its inventive step simply based on the difficulty of separating the racemate.

---

870 *Korean Supreme Court/Ibandronate*, 2010Hu3554, Sept. 8, 2011, para 2.

871 *Korean Supreme Court/Ibandronate*, 2010Hu3554, Sept. 8, 2011, para 2.

872 See *supra* 790 and accompanying texts.

873 See *supra* 791 -794 and accompanying texts.

The same seems to be true in the United Kingdom. In contrast to the decision holding that the enantiomer was obvious because the resolution of the racemate was common general knowledge,[874] even if these facts regarding the enantiomer invention were known, there was either not enough motivation to resolve the racemate or the separation was not predictable, such that the inventive step of racemate was established.[875] In the United States, acknowledging that there was ample motivation to separate an enantiomer, based on the difficulty of separation, or even based on the expectation that the person skilled in the art would have worked on the new compounds rather than try to resolve the racemate, the enantiomer inventions were held to be non-obvious. At best, a two-fold increase in activity could be expected,[876] and this modest increase in activity would be offset by the difficulty and complexity of resolving the racemates.[877]

The decisions on the inventive step of enantiomer of clopidogrel in the United States and Korea showed quite stark differences. The Federal Circuit acknowledged the inventive step of one enantiomer, because the fact that one enantiomer was responsible for the biological activity and the other one was responsible for the side effect was not predictable. However the Korean Supreme Court held that it was obvious because a two-fold superiority in the therapeutic effects and around 1.6-fold superiority in acute toxicity to the racemate could not be regarded as better than that of the racemate considering that the administration of one enantiomer gave around 2-fold better effects than that of a racemate which is a 1:1 mixture of enantiomers.[878]

For the crystalline forms, the inventive step of one crystalline form was denied either because it was sufficient to establish that the person skilled in the art could have done so with a reasonable expectation of success, or because it was a clear expectation that a crystalline form would provide a solution to the performance of substance. The Korean Supreme Court held that the properties of crystalline forms were well known, and it was a common practice to confirm the existence of polymorphism of a substance.[879] The

874 See *supra* 803 -804 and accompanying texts.

875 See *supra* 809 -811 and accompanying texts.

876 *Ortho-McNeil Pharm., Inc. v. Mylan Labs., Inc.*, 348 F. Supp. 2d 713, 747 (N.D.W.Va. 2004), *aff'd*, 161 Fed.Appx. 944 (stating "a difference in [activity] of two, a two-fold difference ordinarily would not be considered to be a substantial difference.").

877 *Pfizer Inc. v. Ranbaxy Laboratories Ltd.*, 405 F.Supp.2d, 495, 517 (D.Del. 2005).

878 See *supra* 836 and accompanying texts.

879 See *supra* 863 and accompanying texts.

Supreme Court specifically held that it could not acknowledge the improved "*pharmaceutical effect*" achieved by the improved physical characteristics of a crystalline form,[880] and it further noted that the reduced batch-to-batch variability in mono-crystalline form was just a logical consequence.[881]

For the metabolite inventions, the novelty was the central issue, and the inventive step was not.

The tendency to a lowered inventive step requirement is also observable from the fact that even if there is clear motivation leading to the invention, the unexpected effects from the obvious test was well adapted to defend the non-obviousness attack. In other words, unexpected or enhanced results could fail to establish the inventive step when there is a real motivation to use the idea, i.e. the effects emerged from obvious tests.[882] Of course, no recipe to obtain separation of enantiomers[883] or crystalline forms is infallible, and the separation can be a paradigm of trial and error.[884] However, decisions to develop either a single enantiomer or racemates as a drug substance are already a key milestone in the drug R&D process.[885] There is also the regulatory pressure to require separation of enantiomers from its racemic mixture.[886] The situation is similar in crystalline form identification and development.[887] However, either the courts do not acknowledge these as motivation,[888] or the motivation is countervailed by unexpected results.

The case law could develop and change, but the current direction of the changes seems to be going against or at least not considering the development of scientific technology.

---

880 See *supra* 867 and accompanying texts.

881 See *supra* 868 and accompanying texts.

882 *Napp Pharmaceuticals v. Ratiopharm* [2009] EWCA Civ 252, para 115; *Hoechst/Enantiomers*, T296/87, OJ EPO 1990, 195, 206, 209.

883 *Sanofi-Synthelabo v. Apotex, Inc.*, 550 F.3d 1075, 1088 (Fed. Cir. 2008).

884 *Sanofi-Synthelabo v. Apotex Inc.*, 492 F.Supp.2d 353, 370 (S.D.N.Y.,2007).

885 *Beary*, 339 Lancet 495 (1992); *Caldwell*, 16 Hum. Psychopharm. S67, S69 (2001); *Mansfield/Henry/Tonkin*, 43 Clin. Pharmacokinet. 287, 287 (2004).

886 *Sanofi-Synthelabo v. Apotex, Inc.*, 550 F.3d 1075, 1089-90 (Fed. Cir. 2008).

887 *Korean Supreme Court/Lercanidipine*, 2010Hu2872, Jul. 14, 2011, para 1.

888 *Sanofi-Synthelabo v. Apotex, Inc.*, 550 F.3d 1075, 1089-90 (Fed. Cir. 2008).

C. Disclosure requirement

The concept of "possession" or "occupancy" is one of the most fundamental concepts in property,[889] which provides the boundaries of what is mine or another's. Due to the nature of intellectual property, the object that someone possesses, such as an invention, is intangible. This is the fundamental reason why patent law sets out the disclosure requirement, which is divided into a written description and the enablement.[890] In general, the written description requirement helps to define the boundary of possession of the invention, and the enablement requirement works to prove that the inventor did not just describe the invention but really possessed the invention at the time of filing. As evidence of possession, either the embodiment that was physically created and existed or the disclosure that enabled others to do so without many difficulties will usually be provided.

The purposes of this disclosure requirement are i) to permit others to make use of a patented invention once the patent expires, thereby ensuring that the invention will ultimately enter the public domain, and ii) to enable others to improve on the patented technology, either by designing around the patent, or by developing improved versions.[891] Thus, this disclosure requirement is

---

889 *See generally, Rose*, 52 U. Chi. L. Rev. 73 (1985).

890 EPC Art. 84, the second sentence ("[The claims] shall be clear and concise and be supported by the description) and EPC Art. 83 ("The European patent application shall disclose the invention in a manner sufficiently clear and complete for it to be carried out by a person skilled in the art."); 35 U.S.C. § 112 ("The specification shall contain (i) a written description of the invention, (ii) and of the manner and process of making and using it, in such full, clear, concise, and exact terms as to enable any person skilled in the art to which it pertains, or with which it is most nearly connected, to make and use the same, (iii) and shall set forth the best mode contemplated by the inventor of carrying out his invention."); the best mode requirement of U.S. patent law would not be discussed in this dissertation; *Chisum*, 15 AIPLA Q. J. 57, 58 (1987); *Synthon BV v. SmithKline Beecham plc* [2005] UKHL 59, para 19 (stating two requirements for anticipation is prior disclosure and enablement).

891 *Burk/Lemley*, 17 Berkeley Tech. L.J. 1155, 1161 (2002).

the *quid pro quo* for granting patent exclusivity.[892] This requirement for the chemical invention, however, has seldom been the subject of decisions at the highest legal level, and most of the litigation has been fought in the areas of novelty and the inventive step.[893] Thus, the disclosure requirement will be only briefly discussed.

1. Written description requirement

As a result of disclosure, later inventors can build on their own inventions based on the information disclosed, and the overall knowledge of society increases. Thus, courts have regarded disclosure as a crucial standard for the patent system.[894] As Newman J stated, this requirement sets forth what was invented and sets boundaries for what can be claimed.[895] This requirement limits the claims to the extent that they are adequately disclosed in the specification.[896] To the question of whether the claims constitute a description, the *Gardner* Court once answered that the claim, which was an original

---

892 *Enzo Biochem, Inc. v. Gen-Probe Inc.*, 323 F.3d 956, 971 (Fed. Cir. 2002), *reh'g denied,* (Lourie, J., concurring) ("The statute states that the invention must be described. That is basic patent law, the *quid pro quo* for the grant of a patent; the public must receive meaningful disclosure in exchange for being excluded from practicing the invention for a limited period of time."); *Capon v. Eshhar*, 418 F.3d 1349, 1357 (Fed. Cir. 2005) (noting "[t]he written description requirement thus satisfies the policy premises of the law, whereby the inventor's technical/scientific advance is added to the body of knowledge, as consideration for the grant of patent exclusivity."); *J.E.M. AG Supply, Inc. v. Pioneer Hi-Bred Intern., Inc.*, 534 U.S. 124, 142 (2001) ("The disclosure required by the Patent Act is 'the quid pro quo of the right to exclude.'"); *Ariad Pharmaceuticals, Inc. v. Eli Lilly and Co.*, 598 F.3d 1336, 1361 (Fed. Cir. 2010); *Beecham Group v. Bristol Laboratories S.A.* [1978] RPC 521, 579 ("The quid pro quo for the monopoly granted to the inventor is the public disclosure by him in his specification of the special advantages that the selected members of the class possess.").

893 *Hansen/Hirsch*, 1997, 51 (further noting recently this got to play a role at the area of biotechnology, such as the inventions involving gene technology).

894 *Anonymous*, 118 Harv. L. Rev. 2007, 2011 (2005) (noting courts had embraced the disclosure rationale as a centerpiece of patent policy. However, the author has a contrary opinion.).

895 *Enzo Biochem, Inc. v. Gen-Probe Inc.*, 323 F.3d 956, 975 (Fed. Cir. 2002) , *reh'g denied,* (Newman, J., concurring) (noting "[t]he description of invention has always been the foundation of the patent specification. It sets forth what has been invented and sets boundaries of what can be claimed.").

896 *Tronzo v. Biomet, Inc.*, 156 F.3d 1154, 1158 (Fed. Cir. 1998).

claim, in itself constituted a description in the original disclosure equivalent in scope and identical in language to the total subject matter being claimed, and nothing more was necessary to comply with the description requirement.[897]

The written description requirement traditionally played a role in limited circumstances: i) When determining whether the claims were entitled to the application's filing date after claims were amended or newly-added, ii) when assessing whether a patentee was entitled to the benefit of the filing date of an earlier application claiming a priority date, and iii) when an interference mattered.[898] More recently, the requirement has been invoked against claims that were not originally filed as part of the written description, although commentators have heavily criticized this as a heightened written description requirement. [899]

In Europe, separately from the enablement requirement embodied in Art. 83 EPC, the written description requirement is set out in Art. 84 EPC, which requires that the claim be clear and concise and be supported by the

897 *In re Gardner*, 475 F.2d 1389, 1391 (C.C.P.A., 1973), *reh'g denied* 480 F.2d 879, 879-80 (holding that the original claim in itself adequate written description of the claimed invention, and whether the descriptive part of the specification should be amended to include the language of the claim in suit was more of an administrative matter.).

898 *Janis*, 2 Wash. U. J. L. & Pol'y 55, 57, 59-60 (2000); *Rai*, 34 Wake Forest L. Rev. 827, 830 (1999); *In re Wright*, 866 F.2d 422, 424 (Fed. Cir. 1989) (holding the essence of written description requirement is to judge whether the newly claimed subject matter was described in the patent application as filed, in the case that the scope of a claim has been amended and directed to a different invention than the original claim.).

899 *Sampson*, 15 Berkley Tech. L.J. 1233, 1262 (2000) (The primary argument against the Federal Circuit's heightened written description requirement for biotechnological invention is that … it also 'reduces incentives to invest in innovation by depriving potential patentees of the opportunity to fully benefit from their research.'"); *Rai*, 34 Wake Forest L. Rev. 827, 834-35 (1999) ("the Lilly court used the written description requirement as a type of elevated enablement requirement." "[T]he CAFC's is based on its view that DNA-based technology is simply a subset of chemical technology generally."); *Mueller*, 13 Berkeley Tech. L.J. 615, 617 (1998) ("The *Lilly* decision establishes uniquely rigorous rules for the description of biotechnological subject matter that significantly contort written description doctrine away from its historic origins and policy grounding. The *Lilly* court's elevation of written description to an effective 'super enablement' standard of uncertain scope and applicability […]"); *Moba, B.V. v. Diamond Automation, Inc.*, 325 F.3d 1306, 1326 (Fed. Cir. 2003).

description. The BOA explained that a principle purpose of this requirement in Art. 84 is to ensure that the monopoly given by a patent normally corresponded to the invention described in the application, and that the claim is not drafted so broadly that it dominates activities that do not depend upon the invention described in the application.[900] The Board further made clear that the term "supported" applies to a claim in a generalized form.[901] In the *Exxon* case, the Board noted that "a claim might be well supported by the description in the sense that it corresponded to it, but still encompassed subject-matter that was not sufficiently disclosed within the meaning of Art. 83 EPC, as it cannot be performed without undue burden, or vice versa." [902]

In the United States, a written description was not a separate requirement from the enablement requirement before 1967. That year, however, the Court in *In re Ruschig*[903] created a new written description doctrine for the sole purpose of enforcing priority issues.[904] It could have been based on the historical rationale derived from the Supreme Court's interpretation of a predecessor to § 112 in *Evans v. Eaton*, which was decided when American patent law had not required to contain claims.[905] In *Evans v. Eaton*, the Supreme Court held that a patent specification had two objects: (i) To enable artisans to make and use the invention, and (ii) to put the public in possession of what the party claimed as his own invention.[906] Some scholars argued that the distinction between the written description and the enablement requirement was arbitrary and redundant.[907] However, the Federal Circuit recently reaffirmed the distinction between these two requirements in the *Ariad v. Lilly* case.[908]

---

900 *Xerox/Amendments*, T 133/85, OJ EPO 1988, 441, 448.

901 *Xerox/Amendments*, T 133/85, OJ EPO 1988, 441, 448. .

902 *Exxon/Fuel oils*, T 409/91, OJ EPO 1994, 653, 662; *see also Mycogen/Modifying plant cells*, T 694/92, OJ EPO, 1997, 408, 414-15 (noting "it follows that, despite being supported by the description from a purely formal point of view, claims may not be considered allowable if they encompass subject-matter which in the light of the disclosure provided by the description can be performed only with undue burden or with application of inventive skill.").

903 *In re Ruschig*, 379 F.2d 990, 995-96 (C.C.P.A. 1967).

904 *See, Moba, B.V. v. Diamond Automation, Inc.*, 325 F.3d 1306, 1323 (Fed. Cir. 2003); cf. *Janis*, 2 Wash. U. J. L. & Pol'y 55, 57, 62-69 (2000) (arguing this distinction between the written requirement and enablement requirement is artificial.).

905 *Vas-Cath Inc. v. Mahurkar*, 935 F.2d 1555, 1561 (Fed. Cir. 1991).

906 *Evans v. Eaton*, 20 U.S. 356, 433-34 (1822).

907 *See e.g., Janis*, 2 Wash. U. J. L. & Pol'y 55, 80-88 (2000).

908 *Ariad Pharmaceuticals, Inc. v. Eli Lilly and Co.*, 598 F.3d 1336 (Fed. Cir. 2010).

In Korea, the written description is set out in the Korean Patent Act, Art. 43(4), which requires the claim to be supported by the description and to define the invention clearly and concisely. The enablement requirement is set out in Art. 42(3) which requires the detailed description of an invention states the invention clearly and fully in a manner that allows a person skilled in the art to carry out the invention easily.

2. Enablement requirement

a) Enablement requirement

The enablement requirement requires that patent applicants disclose the description of the invention sufficiently to enable the person skilled in the art to make and use it.[909] This disclosure, which is a trade off between the patentees and the public, is one of the fundamental functions of patent law.[910] This can be read in the U.S. Supreme Court's language: "[T]o obtain a utility patent, a [patentee] must describe the [invention] with sufficient specificity to enable others to 'make and use' the invention after the patent term expires."[911]

This requirement ensures that the invention is available to be taught to the public once it is published and to enable others to practice the invention once the patent term expires.[912] This is the proper way to answer the question of "possession" of an invention by the inventor, [913] and, at the same time, guar-

---

909 *See e.g.*, EPC Art. 83, 35 U.S.C. § 112.

910 *Kewanee Oil Co. v. Bicron Corp.*, 416 U.S. 470, 489 (1974); *Burk/Lemley*, 17 Berkeley Tech. L.J. 1155, 1161 (2002).

911 *J.E.M. AG Supply, Inc. v. Pioneer Hi-Bred Intern., Inc.*, 534 U.S. 124, 142 (2001).

912 *United States v. Dubilier Condenser Corp.*, 289 U.S. 178, 186-87 (1933) (" An exclusive enjoyment is guaranteed him for seventeen years, but, upon the expiration of that period, the knowledge of the invention inures to the people, who are thus enabled without restriction to practice it and profit by its use."); *J.E.M. AG Supply, Inc. v. Pioneer Hi-Bred Intern., Inc.*, 534 U.S. 124, 142 (2001).

913 *Enzo Biochem, Inc. v. Gen-Probe Inc.*, 323 F.3d 956, 988 (Fed. Cir. 2002) , *reh'g denied,* (Linn, J., dissenting) ("The question presented by 35 U.S.C. § 112, paragraph 1, is not, 'Does the written description disclose what the invention is, or does it merely describe what it does?' The question is, 'Does the written description describe the invention recited and described in the claims-themselves part of the specification-in terms that are sufficient to enable one of skill in the art to make and use the claimed invention?'").

antees that the public will be in possession of the invention.[914] In other words, this requirement seeks to ensure that the inventor actually has conceptual possession of the invention at the time of filing.[915]

To meet the enablement requirement, the specification, which is part of the application for a patent, must describe not only the invention but also the manner of making and using the invention in sufficiently full terms as to enable a person skilled in the art to make and use the invention without resort to "undue" experimentation.[916] The patent specification does not need to disclose all of the ways to enable the invention. For example, even if only one way of performing the invention is disclosed, it can be sufficient as long as it allows the person skilled in the art to perform the invention in the whole range that is claimed.[917] Accordingly, the scope of enablement inversely varies with the degree of unpredictability of the factors and the arts involved.[918] The patentee is entitled only to a scope that is commensurate with the scope of his innovation, which is represented by the disclosure in the

914 *Janis*, 2 Wash. U. J. L. & Pol'y 55, 63 (2000); *See generally, Holbrook*, 59 SMU L. Rev. 123 (2006) (noting this teaching function of patent disclosure was rather limited, however, functioned more to demonstrate the inventor's possession of the invention.).

915 *Burk/Lemley*, 89 Va. L. Rev. 1575, 1653 (2003) (further explaining that after the written description requirement was served by the claim in the United States, this requirement had evolved to serve a new purpose, i.e. enablement); *Tronzo v. Biomet, Inc.*, 156 F.3d 1154, 1158 (Fed. Cir. 1998).

916 *Chisum*, 15 AIPLA Q. J. 57, 58 (1987); *see also Synthon BV v. SmithKline Beecham plc* [2005] UKHL 59, paras 28-33; *Martek Biosciences Corp. v. Nutrinova, Inc.*, 579 F.3d 1363, 1378 (Fed. Cir. 2009) (noting "the specification of a patent must teach those skilled in the art how to make and use the full scope of the claimed invention without undue experimentation.", quoting *In re Wright*, 999 F.2d 1557, 1561 (Fed. Cir. 1993)); *In re* Wands, 858 F.2d 731, 736-37 (Fed. Cir. 1988); *see also* subsection IV.A.3.

917 *BGH/Textilgarn*, GRUR 1959, 125, 125; *Exxon/Fuel oils*, T 409/91, OJ EPO 653, 662-63 (1994) point 3.5.(further noting the disclosure of the invention was sufficient if it enabled the skilled person to obtain substantially all embodiments falling within the ambit of the claims.).

918 *Brandi-Dohrn*, GRUR Int 1995, 541.

patent specification.[919] Thus, this demarcation is especially important in the field of unpredictable arts. Given that it is harder to predict the technical result in chemical reactions, and especially physiological responses, than to predict those in other fields, the level of enablement in pharmaceutical art seems to be naturally higher than those in other fields. Conducting a large number of tests to monitor the results of a minor structural change would be of little value. However, the extent to which the invention should be enabled is not certain and must be determined in each case.[920]

The effort to be expected of the person skilled in the art is the total sum of the experimental effort necessary to advance successfully step-by-step toward the desired final goal, even though each individual experimental step can be considered feasible with a certain amount of trial and error.[921] "Without undue experimentation" therefore means that it allows certain sensible degree of trial and error. In Europe, this experimentation must lead to the desired result with "an acceptable statistical expectation rate" in case of random experiments.[922] In the United States, the relevant factors to determine this include "the quantity of experimentation that was actually needed, the amount of guidance provided in the reference, the presence or absence of actual examples of the experimental procedure, the state of the knowledge already available concerning the subject matter at issue, and the predictability or unpredictability in the specific area of science or technology."[923] The determination of "undueness" is "not a single, simple factual determination,

---

919 *See e.g., Chiron Corp. v. Genentech, Inc.*, 363 F.3d 1247, 1263 (Fed. Cir. 2004) (Bryson, J., concurring) (noting the proper approach is "to address cases of new technology by construing claims, where possible, as they would have been understood by one of skill in the art at the time of the invention, and not construing them to reach the as-yet-undeveloped technology that the applicant did not enable. That approach preserves the benefits of patent protection for the invention that the applicant has actually conceived and enabled, without extending those benefits for an invention that the applicant may not have conceived and certainly has not enabled.").

920 In the pharmaceutical field where there is narrower room for the person skilled in the art could have known the inventor's possession of the invention, the broader variants need to be shown to be enabled.

921 *MIT/Biopolymers*, T639/95 (1998), point 15; *Molecular Biosystems/Oligonucleotide therapeutic agent*, T 994/95 (1999), point 9.

922 *Unilever/Stable bleaches*, T 0226/85, OJ EPO 1988, 336, 340.

923 *Sanofi-Synthelabo v. Apotex, Inc.*, 550 F.3d 1075, 1085 (Fed. Cir. 2008).

but rather a conclusion reached by weighing many factual considerations."[924]

However, the enabling disclosure of the specification must be correlated with the scope of the claim under consideration.[925] A specification may only enable part of a claim. For example, the chemical embodiments in the specification might not include the whole number of the generic class of compounds. Similarly, a specification might enable a broader scope than the claim. For example, a claim may be narrowed down by adding a limitation, but the specification fails to provide sufficient information as to the limited scope of the claim. These limitations are imposed, because a patent should not control inventions that it does not enable.[926] In the *Exxon/Fuel Oils* case, the application was refused, because, while it claimed fuel oils containing certain crystals with an average particle size of "less than 4000 nm," it provided only an example thereof with a crystal particle size of 1200 nm and gave no further teaching regarding the production of smaller particles.[927] The Board held that, to fulfil the requirement of Art. 83 EPC, the application as filed should have contained sufficient information to allow a person skilled in the art, using his common general knowledge, to carry out the invention within the whole area that was claimed.[928]

As the BGH held, "claims for chemical compounds, in which generic formulae characterise the claimed compounds, may not cover compounds which it is established were not available to the skilled person at the time of the patent application."[929] In traditional chemistry, however, since the information in the patent application has made it feasible to manufacture the compounds with generally available starting materials and standardized reactions, the more valuable information concerns the use of the compounds,

924 *Martek Biosciences Corp. v. Nutrinova, Inc.*, 579 F.3d 1363, 1378 (Fed. Cir. 2009) (quoting *In re Wands*, 858 F.2d 731, 737 (Fed. Cir. 1988)).

925 *Chisum*, 15 AIPLA Q. J. 57, 61 (1987); *National Recovery Technologies, Inc. v. Magnetic Separation Systems, Inc.*, 166 F.3d 1190, 1195-96 (Fed. Cir. 1999) (noting "[t]he enablement requirement ensures that the public knowledge is enriched by the patent specification to a degree at least commensurate with the scope of the claims."); MPEP § 2164.08 ("All questions of enablement are evaluated against the claimed subject matter. The focus of the examination inquiry is whether everything within the scope of the claim is enabled.").

926 *Merges/Nelson*, 25 J. Econ. Behav. Organ. 1, 18 (1994).

927 *Exxon/Fuel oils*, T 409/91, OJ EPO 653, 657 (1994) point 2.

928 *Exxon/Fuel oils*, T 409/91, OJ EPO 653, 657 (1994) point 2.

929 *BGH/7-Chlor-6-demethyltetracyclin*, GRUR 1978, 162, 165.

not the way to manufacture them.[930] Self-evidently, each invention should lead to the described results as well, when one applies the relevant technical teaching.[931]

b) Enablement requirements in the patent law

Although there was a case requiring enablement in the context of obviousness rejection, [932] enablement requirements are generally found in the disclosure requirement and in the novelty requirement.

(1) Enablement as a requirement for anticipation

As discussed in chapter IV.A.3, an enabling disclosure is required in addition to the disclosure requirement for anticipation of the invention in main jurisdictions. For example, the BGH held in the *Olanzapine* decision that the concept of disclosure was exclusively what a person skilled in the art directly and unambiguously derived from the prior art as the content of teaching, thereby enabling him specifically to carry out the invention.[933] The House of Lords explained that there is a difference in the role of the person skilled in the art for the two requirements of anticipation. For the disclosure requirement, the person skilled in the art is taken to be trying to understand what the author of the prior art meant, and, once the meanings of the prior disclosure are determined, the author has no further part to play.[934] For the purpose of the enablement requirement, however, the question is no longer what the skilled person would think the disclosure meant, but whether he would have been able to work the invention.[935] Enablement has played a key

930 *Domeij*, 2000, 45.
931 *Hansen/Hirsch*, 1997, 56.
932 *In re* Payne, 606 F.2d 303, 314 (C.C.P.A. 1979) ("References relied upon to support a rejection under 35 USC 103 must provide an enabling disclosure, i. e., they must place the claimed invention in the possession of the public.").
933 *BGH/Olanzapine*, IIC 2009, 596, 599.
934 *Synthon BV v. SmithKline Beecham plc* [2005] UKHL 59, para 32.
935 *Synthon BV v. SmithKline Beecham plc* [2005] UKHL 59, para 32.

role in the context of anticipation; however, it has rarely been discussed.[936]

(2) Basic similarity of the two enablement requirements

The BOA held that any prior art cited under the novelty provisions must contain an enabling disclosure to destroy novelty and that this enabling requirement was identical to that under Art. 83 EPC. Thus, the cited document must have disclosed the invention in a manner sufficiently clear and complete for it to be carried out by a person skilled in the art.[937] In other words, the same degree of clarity and practical usefulness is required regarding the possibility of using the invention, which is part of the state of the art, and that of using the invention in the application filed.[938] *Tilman* also noted that the prior art document must have clarity, such as a patent claim would have, and that this requirement comes close to the wording of Arts. 83 and 84 EPC. Thus it was correct to require that the information in a prior art disclosed "directly and unambiguously" the subject matter of a claim to avoid double patenting.[939] Lord Hoffman mentioned that he could think of no reason why there should be any difference between the test of enablement of a prior disclosure for the purpose of anticipation and the test of enablement of the patent itself for the purpose of sufficiency.[940] He held that the authorities on section 72(1)(c) regarding the grounds for the revocation of a patent were equally applicable to enablement for the purpose of sections 2(2) and (3) regarding novelty.[941] Thus, the tests of enablements may seem to have no difference.

---

936 *Seymore*, 60 Duke L. J., 919, 925 (2011); *see also, e.g., Chester v. Miller*, 906 F. 2d 1574, 1576 n.2 (Fed. Cir. 1990) (noting that for being prior art under section 102(b), the reference must place the anticipating subject matter at issue into the possession of the public through an enabling disclosure).

937 *See e.g., ICI/Herbicides*, T 206/83, OJ EPO 1987, 5, 9; *Collaborative/Preprorennin*, T81/87, OJ EPO 1990, 250, 257.

938 *Domeij*, 2000, 136.

939 See *Tilmann*, IIC 2010, 149, 152.

940 *Synthon BV v. SmithKline Beecham plc* [2005] UKHL 59, para 27 (noting "[i]n the present case the Court of Appeal was reluctant to say that the test of enablement of a prior disclosure for the purpose of anticipation was the same as the test of enablement of the patent itself for the purpose of sufficiency. But I can think of no reason why there should be any difference […].").

941 *Synthon BV v. SmithKline Beecham plc* [2005] UKHL 59, para 27.

(3) Differences between the two enablement requirements

The differences between enablement as a requirement for anticipation and as a requirement for sufficiency of disclosure can be summarized as follows. The first distinction depends on whether the requirement is introduced by legislation or by judicial bodies. The statutes clearly state the enablement requirement (sufficiency of disclosure) for obtaining a patent.[942] However, the enablement requirement for anticipation is specified neither in Art. 54 EPC, nor 35 U.S.C. § 102, nor anywhere else in the patent statutes. This requirement for anticipation was established by the courts.[943]

The second difference depends on whether the utility of the invention is to be enabled as well. The Federal Circuit in *Novo Nordisk Pharms., Inc. v. Bio-Tech. Gen. Corp.*[944] confirmed that the standard for enablement of a prior art reference for purposes of anticipation under § 102 differed from the enablement standard under 35 U.S.C. § 112; namely, the specification should enable a person skilled in the art to "use" the invention to meet the requirement under § 112, but the specification need not do so to meet the requirement under § 102.[945]

The third difference is whether the scope of the invention has to be enabled when the prior art reference is a patent (application) itself. To meet the enablement requirement for the "patent-obtaining purpose" under Art. 83 EPC

---

942 EPC Art. 83 (2010); 35 U.S.C. § 112 ¶1 (2006); Korean Patent Act Art. 42(3).

943 *Mueller/Chisum*, 45 Hous. L. Rev. 1101, 1137-38 (2008) (stating "the courts have read the enablement requirement into anticipation under § 102(b)."); *see also In re LeGrice*, 301 F.2d 929, 939 (C.C.P.A. 1962) (holding that anticipation under § 102(b) "requires that the description of the invention in the printed publication must be an 'enabling' description").

944 *Novo Nordisk Pharms., Inc. v. Bio-Tech. Gen. Corp.*, 424 F.3d 1347, 1355 (Fed. Cir. 2005); *Rasmusson v. SmithKline Beecham Corp.*, 413 F.3d 1318, 1325 (Fed. Cir. 2005).

945 *Novo Nordisk Pharms., Inc. v. Bio-Tech. Gen. Corp.*, 424 F.3d 1347, 1355 (Fed. Cir. 2005) (citing *In re Hafner*, 410 F.2d 1403, 1405 (C.C.P.A.1969) stating "section 102 makes no such requirement as to an anticipatory disclosure."); *see also In re Schoenwald*, 964 F.2d 1122, 1124 (Fed. Cir. 1992) (citing *In re Donohue*, 632 F.2d 123, 126 (C.C.P.A. 1980) ("proof of utility is not a prerequisite to availability of a prior art reference under 35 U.S.C. § 102(b)"); *see also Bristol-Myers Squibb Co. v. Ben Venue Labs., Inc.*, 246 F.3d 1368, 1379 (Fed. Cir. 2001)) (holding that "anticipation does not require actual performance of suggestions in a disclosure. Rather, anticipation only requires that those suggestions be enabled to one of skill in the art."). This can be viewed differently in different jurisdictions.); *Rasmusson v. SmithKline Beecham Corp.*, 413 F.3d 1318, 1325 (Fed. Cir. 2005).

or 35 U.S.C. § 112, the specification must enable the whole scope of the claimed invention. In contrast, to meet the enablement requirement for the "patent-defeating purpose", it is enough to enable the scope of the invention at issue.[946] Thus, the description of a single embodiment for a broad claim in an earlier patent (application) can enable the invention for anticipation purposes, but the same embodiment alone may not be enough to provide a sufficient description for the earlier patent (application) itself.[947] However, even in this case, the single embodiment of the prior art reference (earlier patent) could have enabled a narrower claim scope in the earlier patent covering at least the embodiment itself.

3. Disclosure requirement of selection inventions

Unlike novelty or inventive step requirements, the disclosure requirement for the chemical invention has seldom been the subject of decisions at the highest legal levels.[948] Thus, only a few relevant cases are discussed under this title.

a) Species selection invention

In *Dr Reddy's Laboratories v. Eli Lilly* in the United Kingdom, the lack of sufficiency was challenged by Dr. Reddy's Laboratories. The main ground raised before the Patent Court was that the patent specification did not disclose alleged superior advantages to other members of preferred classes in the prior art,[949] which was required to meet a selection invention. In other words, this insufficiency attack was based on the premise that the patent could be upheld over the prior disclosure only if it was a valid selection patent. However, since the Patent Court found that the patent was valid without relying on the selection principles, the insufficiency attack lost its

946 *Vas-Cath Inc. v. Mahurkar*, 935 F.2d 1555, 1562 (Fed. Cir. 1991); *see also Kieff/Schwartz/Newman*, 2011, 207-211.

947 *In re Lukach*, 442 F.2d 967, 970 (C.C.P.A. 1971) (noting the difference of the enablement requirement for the patent obtaining purposes from that for the patent defeating purposes).

948 *Hansen/Hirsch*, 1997, 51.

949 *Dr Reddy's Laboratories (UK) Ltd v. Eli Lilly & Company Ltd* [2008] EWHC 2345, para 188.

ground.[950] Jacob LJ on appeal restated that, since Lilly had not complied with the 'old selection rules', it was unnecessary to discuss this issue.[951]

b) Optical isomers

In the first instance of the *Escitalopram* decision in the United Kingdom, while citing the *Biogen* decision,[952] Kitchin J held that the claims were not sufficient, basically because the scope of protection was broader than the invention's technical contribution. He restated that enantiomer's inventive idea is only one way to make it, neither on the discovery of the enantiomer nor on its medicinal effect.[953] He further stated that, since the claim in issue was to a monopoly of that enantiomer but the specification provided only one way to make it, the patentee was not entitled to a monopoly of every way of making it i.e. a product *per se* claim. Consequently, the claim was not sufficient.[954]

While distinguishing a product-by-process claim, as in the *Biogen* case, from an ordinary product claim, Lord Hoffmann[955] held that, "since the product itself is the invention, it is sufficiently enabled if the specification and common general knowledge enables the skilled person to make it and one method is enough."[956] The difference between this case and *Biogen* was whether the product made by the inventive procedure was available before the invention. While agreeing with the EPO's decision on the *Exxon* case,[957] Lord Hoffmann concluded that, "if the patentee had found a non-obvious way of making the product, he was entitled to a product claim, with

950 *Dr Reddy's Laboratories (UK) Ltd v. Eli Lilly & Company Ltd* [2008] EWHC 2345, para 189.
951 *Dr Reddy's Laboratories Ltd v. Eli Lilly & Company Ltd*, EWCA Civ 1362, paras 75-76.
952 *Biogen Inc v. Medeva Plc* [1996] UKHL 18, para 75.
953 *Lundbeck v. Generics Ltd.* [2008] EWCA Civ 311, para 26.
954 *Lundbeck v. Generics Ltd.* [2008] EWCA Civ 311, para 26.
955 Lord Hoffmann the very who gave *Biogen* decision specially stepped down an instance and sat on the Court of Appeal where he had served more than ten years ago.
956 *Lundbeck v. Generics Ltd.* [2008] EWCA Civ 311, para 27.
957 *Lundbeck v. Generics Ltd.* [2008] EWCA Civ 311, para 59 (citing the Technical Board of Appeal said in Exxon/ Fuel Oils T409/91 as "The extent of the patent monopoly, as defined by the claims, should correspond to the technical contribution to the art in order for it to be supported or justified.").

the full monopoly of the product which that conferred."[958] Jacob LJ noted that the product claim actually provides a broader monopoly[959] and concluded that the fact that the patentee should not have more than he deserved did not form part of the statutory test for sufficiency.[960]

The House of Lords' reasoning was very much in line with Lord Hoffmann's. Lord Walker noted the discussion before the House of whether "inventive concept" meant the same as "technical contribution to the art." He stated that they are certainly connected, but that "inventive concept" was concerned with the identification of the core of the invention, while the invention's "technical contribution to the art" was concerned with the evaluation of its inventive concept.[961] Lord Neuberger stated that based on the fact that the patentee's "technical contribution" was to make the invention available for the first time, the patentee was entitled to claim the enantiomer. This decision brought the British patent courts into line with EPO jurisprudence and with a more patentee friendly disposition.

c) Crystalline forms

In T1066/03, where a process for the preparation of amorphous atorvastatin (Lipitor ®) and hydrates was claimed, the Board revoked the patent based on the lack of sufficiency, since the patent did not enable the skilled person to produce without undue burden the crystalline form I of atorvastatin, i.e. the starting material (seed crystal) to be used in the claimed process.[962]

D. Conclusion

The patentability requirements on selection inventions have been explored and analyzed. Regarding species selection invention, the novelty requirement has been lowered in Germany and the United Kingdom, where the courts declared that their established patentability requirements for the species selection invention were no longer valid. To establish novelty re-

958 *Lundbeck v. Generics Ltd.* [2008] EWCA Civ 311, para 37.
959 *Lundbeck v. Generics Ltd.* [2008] EWCA Civ 311, para 54.
960 *Lundbeck v. Generics Ltd.* [2008] EWCA Civ 311, para 57.
961 *Generics Ltd. v. Lundbeck* [2009] UKHL 12, para 30.
962 *Warner-Lambert/Polymorphic Atorvastatin*, T 1066/03 (2006), para 2.6.

quires overcoming the difficulty of identifying and isolating a specific member from the genus disclosure. The inventive step of a species selection invention was mainly established based on its advantageous effects.

The novelty of optical isomers was based on the difficulty of separation, regardless of the extent to which the structures were clearly disclosed in the prior art and regardless of whether it was well-known to a person skilled in the art that one or the other would exert its pharmacological effect. The difficulty of resolution was key in assessing novelty, because for an invention to be anticipated by a prior art, it must not only disclose the element of invention but also enable the invention. The much relaxed inventive step requirement on optical isomers was glaring. For example, the routine test became the non-routine test after ten years. In many jurisdictions except Korea, unlike their earlier rulings, it was held that the inventive step was re-established based on the difficulty of separation or on the fact that the separation could not have been achieved with reasonable expectation thereof, even though there was ample motivation to do so.

For crystalline forms, the issue of novelty was mainly about the extent to which the claimed crystalline forms were inevitably produced according to the process disclosed in the prior art, and novelty was generally not found. In addition, the inventive step for crystalline forms was denied either because there was a reasonable expectation of success or because the argued better effects were expected. The Korean Supreme Court noted that the improved pharmaceutical effect achieved by the altered physical characteristics of a crystalline form was not acknowledged.

Even though the reasoning behind the novelty of metabolite inventions in the British and American decisions was different, it was very clear that the courts acknowledged that the new exclusivity could have prevented the public from continuing to do something that was done before. If the metabolite had been found to be novel, the patent would have been granted on it, and the scope of the metabolite patent could have covered the metabolite generated by the body, thereby leading to an absurd result.

In addition, by granting these patents with lowered patentability requirements, the patent system could have influenced manufacturers to do the research on it separately or laterally. For example, the inventive step for optical isomers was identified because of the difficulty of resolution or the unpredictability of which isomer among the racemic mixture would exert the pharmacological effect of the racemate and which isomer would exert the side effects thereof. If this is so, should the manufacturers not be encouraged to do so from the very beginning, not after the research on the racemates is done? This would be tantamount to exposing the public to drugs containing risky components.[963]

The low quality of pharmaceutical patents can also be seen in the report by the American Federal Trade Commission ("FTC"). The FTC report presented data from the litigation that resulted from paragraph IV challenges from 1992 to 2000, in which 73% of the para. IV filers prevailed.[964] Although winning a suit not only invalidates the challenged patent or leads to abandonment by the reference drug company, it also means non-infringement of the generic version. The high number is enough to imply that the quality of these patents is poor. The Pharma Sector Inquiry further confirmed that the opposition rate before the EPO was consistently higher for the pharmaceutical sector (about 8%) than it is in the organic chemistry sector (about 4%) and across all sectors (overall EPO average was about 5%).[965] The Pharma Sector Inquiry further reported that generic companies exclusively opposed second generation patents and prevailed in approximately 60% of the final decisions rendered by the EPO (including the BOA) in the period 2000 to 2007, and that the scope of the originator patent was restricted in another 15% of cases.[966] Furthermore, an empirical study on completed patent litigation on all drugs that first became eligible for challenges between 2000 and 2008 (covering 277 patents and 147 drugs) reported i) that for the patents at issue in settled litigation, 89% were secondary patents,[967] and ii) that for the patents litigated to completion (not settled), the brand name companies nearly always won a suit asserting an NMEs (92%), however, they usually lost suits asserting secondary patents (32% wins).[968]

Patentability requirements are assessed by a person skilled in the art. Thus, these lowered patentability requirements could well mean that a person skilled in the art has even fewer skills in the most scientifically developed era. Further, the much relaxed patentability requirements made both the newer version of products and the older versions concurrently available in

---

963 *Daniels/Nestman/Kerr*, 31 Drug Inf. J. 639, 643 (1997) (noting regulatory bodies would be more interested with the toxicological aspects of the stereochemistry issues, and they would expect full toxicological evaluation of each enantiomer if the toxicity had been detected.).

964 *FTC*, 2002, 20.

965 *DG Competition*, 2009, 239-253.

966 *DG Competition*, 2009, 239-253.

967 *Hemphill/Sampat, Bhaven N.*, 339 Science 1386, 1387 (2013).

968 *Hemphill/Sampat, Bhaven N.*, 339 Science 1386, 1387 (2013).

the market.[969] Although the case law may develop and change, the direction of the changes seems to be running counter to or at least not to be taking into consideration the development of scientific technology.

969 *Hutt/Valentová*, 50 Acta Facultatis Pharmaceuticae Universitatis Comenianae 7, 8 (2003).

V. IMPLICATIONS OF THE PATENTABILITY REQUIREMENTS ON INNOVATION AND COMPETITION IN THE PHARMACEUTICAL INDUSTRY

The patent system grants the right to exclude others from practicing the claimed invention. However, it does not convey the freedom to operate the invention.[970] The question of the freedom to operate mainly concerns whether one can practice in a certain area without infringing a patent held by another party.[971] It is quite possible for overlapping patents to be held by different parties leaving no single party with the freedom to operate.[972] If practicing the invention infringes another's patent, one patentee may consider avoiding another's patent, while trying to obtain a license from him, or invalidating his patent.[973] Sometimes designing-around the other patent is originally impossible, such as in the case of practicing a combination of active ingredients, one ingredient of which is covered by a valid patent; or in the case where it is very hard to separate one polymorph, since it is easily included even in trace amounts in the process of manufacturing the basic substance.

Chapter IV argued that there is a gradual relaxation of patentability requirement for selection invention in EPO practices and the case laws of Germany, the U.S., the U.K., and Korea. The lowered thresholds of patentability have a significant impact on competition. In particular, as the scope and length of patents defines what competitors may do, this chapter will examine the scope and length of second generation patents in this context.

970 *Miller/Evans*, 2010, 2-5; *See e.g.* 35 United States Code ("35 U.S.C.") § 154 (2010) "the right to exclude others from making, using, offering for sale, or selling […] or importing the invention".

971 *Miller/Evans*, 2010, 6.

972 *Miller/Evans*, 2010, 6.

973 *Miller/Evans*, 2010, 4.

A. Concerns about lowered patentability

Firstly, patent offices are gate keepers of patent quality. Once the patent offices fail to fulfil their duties, the quality of patents issued deteriorates. One result of low quality patents is patent litigation war that is waged by the companies that can afford the cost of litigation and that try to obtain patent-based property rights on existing technologies.[974]

1. General concerns about lowered patentability

a) Superfluous second generation patents

The radical increase in patent applications and patents on second generation inventions was discussed in chapter III.B.5. To explain some impacts of these increases, the lesson from the "wild card patent term extension" is noted here. It was the key recommendation of a white paper prepared by the Infectious Diseases Society of America (IDSA) to incentivize the pharmaceutical companies to research into anti-infectious agents as supplementary intellectual property protection.[975] The IDSA recommended a balance between the special efforts needed to bring more medications to patients and the concerns about the social costs of those efforts.

A so-called, "wild card" patent term extension is a kind of transferable patent term extension concept. A company which successfully develops and acquires marketing approval for a certain antibiotic could extend the market exclusivity period of "another" FDA-approved drug for 2 years.[976] As is clear from the term "wild card" itself, the company may choose any other approved drug in its portfolio for which to apply for patent term extension. A study reported that this kind of patent extension as the compensation for treating multi-drug-resistant *pseudomonas aeruginosa* would be cost-neutral for 10 years after approval of the new antibiotics and would save society around $4.6 billion for 20 years after approval.[977]

974 *Jaffe/Lerner*, 2004, 74.
975 *IDSA*, 2004, 24.
976 *IDSA*, 2004, 24.
977 *Spellberg, et al.*, 35 Infection 167, 170 (2007).

However, this proposal has been highly controversial and its proposed inclusion in the Project Bioshield II Act of 2005[978] was ultimately rejected. One of the bases for rejection was that this kind of newly created patent right would not only be inefficient, but would also create tens of billions of dollars in annual patent taxes[979] on other common diseases.[980] Critics also argued that this is very unfair for those patients who must pay an extra patent tax on the particular drug which is chosen for extension.[981] This is mainly because the patent term extension on the blockbuster drug would provide a tremendous income by transferring the cost to the patients, which would in turn be an extra burden to the health insurers. This would also be anticompetitive, because only the companies that already have a patent whose extension was exceptionally lucrative would contend for the reward[982] and because the generic companies would have to wait another two years to launch their products onto the market.

Similar conditions can be observed in the thriving area of second generation patents. By obtaining second generation inventions, the move of market exclusivity to these types of patents[983] could work like a patent term extension. Namely, the patients would have to pay an extra patent tax, which means higher exclusivity prices on the product covered by the selection patents; this would be a burden on society and on health insurers. The generic company would have to wait years longer, and the selection patents would follow the lucrative patents. More important, unlike the wild card patent term extension, society would not acquire something such as new antibiotics in the case of second generation patents. There is hardly any reason not to grant a patent to an invention that meets patentability requirements, but the social costs should be taken into consideration. If this is a consequence of lowering patentability requirements, the patent system could help to fix the problem.[984]

---

978 Project Bioshield II Act of 2005. S. 975, 109th Congress (2005–2006).

979 Patent tax means the pharmaceutical patent rent appropriation upon consumers and insurers through higher prices during the period of marketing exclusivity.

980 *Outterson/Samora/Keller-Cuda*, 7 Lancet Infect. Dis. 559, 561-62 (2007).

981 *Power*, 12 Clin. Microbiol. Infec. 25, 32 (1998); *Nathan/Goldberg*, 4 Nat. Rev. Drug Discov. 887, 888-89 (2005); *Outterson/Samora/Keller-Cuda*, 7 Lancet Infect. Dis. 559, 562 (2007).

982 *Nathan/Goldberg*, 4 Nat. Rev. Drug Discov. 887, 889 (2005).

983 See subsection V.D.3.c).

984 See subsection VI.E.

b) Increased patent exclusivities and amplified uncertainties thereof

Along with the lowered novelty requirement, the lenient obviousness requirement more than any other has resulted in increased number of marginal patents, which could constrain the freedom to operate basic inventions.[985] The relaxed enablement requirement[986] would bring broader patent scopes.[987] Thus, the lower the patentability requirement becomes, the more patent applications (with a broader scope of patents) would be filed, the less attention would be paid to patent examinations considering the limited amount of resources and time in the patent offices, which would in turn lead to poorer quality of patents.[988] Lemley argues, regarding the low standard of patent examination ("Rational Ignorance"), that it would be socially efficient to ignore the low standard itself, since i) the majority of patents would have small economic importance and cost little to grant despite being invalid, and ii) only a fraction of all patents carrying heavy importance would be dealt with in the judicial system, which is expensive but still more efficient because of the small numbers that would be litigated.[989]

However, since it would be easier to obtain patents thanks to lower patentability requirements, the incentives to file marginal patent applications would increase and would complete this vicious circle.[990] For example, a single search for the keyword "esomeprazole" in the patent database of EPO as of December 20, 2013, showed 347 patent applications filed by many applicants, including AstraZeneca.[991] If the patent applications mentioning different terms of esomeprazole, such as its chemical name, are also taken into account, the number increases. In addition, this number includes only the second generation patent applications for esomeprazole, not those for

985 *Thomas*, 52 Am. U. L. Rev. 771, 773 (2003) ("A lenient view of nonobviousness is ordinarily seen as inventor-friendly and propatent. But this trend allows the patenting of marginal inventions, increasing the possibility that primary inventors will have to share the rewards of their pioneering inventions with follow-on inventors of improvements.").

986 This was not observed in the selection patents.

987 *Burk/Lemley*, 89 Va. L. Rev. 1575, 1953-54 (2003) (This is because if the invention is not enabled by the patent specification, the permissible breadth of a patent would be narrowed.).

988 *Friebel et al.,* 2006, 36; *Jaffe/Lerner*, 2004, 175-76.

989 *Lemley*, 95 Nw. U. L. Rev. 1495 (2001).

990 *Jaffe/Lerner*, 2004, 174-76.

991 Espacenet, available at: http://worldwide.espacenet.com. (Last accessed on December 20, 2013).

omeprazole. Moreover, the difficulty of appealing to a court should not be overlooked simply because of the cost of litigation, which pre-empts opportunities for many people to obtain judicial review. In other words, Lemley's rational ignorance argument can be applied to the case when most applicants can afford the costs of litigation. Furthermore, the poor quality of issued patents would result in overly broad patent claims and patent thickets.[992] These all, in turn, would force society to pay the increased exclusivity tax.[993]

Even the companies that could afford the litigation costs would still face the difficulty of accessing their positions because of rationally ignored low patentability standards. Using omeprazole as an example, in Europe, in 1994, AstraZeneca filed a patent application for a salt of an enantiomer, Nexium®, which the EPO granted a patent in 2000, with the following claim 1:

> "The magnesium salt of [S-enantiomer of omeprazole, i.e. Nexium®]."[994]

Following opposition by Ratiopharm in 2001, the EPO finally revoked the patent for this enantiomer in 2007.[995] But the story did not end there. AstraZeneca thereafter filed a divisional application of the patent application in 2000,[996] for which the EPO granted a patent in 2009 with the following claim 1:

> "The use of a <u>magnesium salt of [S-enantiomer of omeprazole, i.e. Nexium ®]</u> with an optical purity of ≥ 99.8% enantiomeric excess (e.e.) for the manufacture of a medicament for the inhibition of gastric acid secretion."[997] [Underline added]

However, oppositions was filed first by Hexal AG and then by others, and the patent was revoked in August 2011. [998] AstraZeneca immediately ap-

992 *Ann*, 2009, 363.
993 *Kefauver*, 1966, 3 (noting "[e]very day in our lives monopoly takes its toll").
994 European Patent No EP0652872B1.
995 European Patent Register of European Patent No EP0652872 B1, available at: https://register.epo.org/ espacenet/regviewer (Last accessed on December 20, 2013).
996 This is one of the reasons the EPO limited the duration during when an applicant can file divisional applications under Rule 36.
997 European Patent No EP1020461B1, available at: https://register.epo.org/espacenet/regviewer (Last accessed on December 20, 2013).
998 European Patent Register of European Patent No EP1020461B1, with the record of 33 notices of oppositions.

pealed to the decision based on the suspicion of partiality, but it was rejected in November 2012.[999]

The situation in the United States is somewhat different. AstraZeneca settled with the first Paragraph IV[1000] filer Ranbaxy Pharmaceuticals in 2008, with Teva Pharmaceuticals in 2010, with Dr. Reddy's Laboratories in 2011 [1001], with Sandoz and Sun Pharm in 2011, and with Lupin Limited in 2012. [1002] While the ANDA filers conceded that all patents at issue were valid and enforceable, AstraZeneca granted licenses to these ANDA filers to allow them to enter the US American market in 2014.[1003] Meanwhile, AstraZeneca has either received a Paragraph IV notice letter from, or commenced a patent infringement action against four other companies.[1004]

Nexium® was launched in the European market in 2000 and in the American market in 2010,[1005] although the generic version of Nexium® will be available in some European countries when the 10-year data exclusivity has run out[1006] and in the American market in 2014 after the expiration of the patent. One may wonder why the long settlement history is enumerated here. Three reasons: Firstly, neither the validity of the omeprazole, nor the validity of the enantiomer of omeprazole (esomeprazole), nor even the validity of the magnesium salt of the esomeprazole, but the validity of certain purity of the same salt in esomeprazole entailed this long history. Secondly, even without resorting to harsh arguments and reports on the dubious effective-

---

999 *AstraZeneca/Hexal et al.*, T 1760/11 (2012).

1000 Code of Federal Regulations Title 21, § 314.94(a)(12)(i)(A)(4): "[...]the applicant shall provide the patent number and certify, in its opinion and to the best of its knowledge, [...]that the patent is invalid, unenforceable, or will not be infringed by the manufacture, use, or sale of the drug product for which the abbreviated application is submitted. The applicant shall entitle such a certification 'Paragraph IV Certification.'".

1001 *AstraZeneca*, AstraZeneca Annual Report 2010, 186.

1002 *AstraZeneca*, AstraZeneca Annual Report 2011, 185.

1003 *AstraZeneca*, AstraZeneca Annual Report 2010, 186; *AstraZeneca*, AstraZeneca Annual Report 2011, 185.

1004 *AstraZeneca*, AstraZeneca Annual Report 2011, 185.

1005 *AstraZeneca*, AstraZeneca Annual Review 2000, 7.

1006 For example, http://www.shop-apotheke.com/arzneimittel/6456801/esomeprazol-ratiopharm-40mg-hartkapseln.htm?know=search%3Aesomeprazole~. (Last accessed on December 20, 2013).

ness of S-omeprazole over omeprazole,[1007] both the results of revocation for the patent covering a magnesium salt of esomeprazole in Europe and the tedious list of settlement with generic manufacturers in the United States, have established little if any improved effect of esomeprazole over omeprazole. Last but not least, even if the patent were ultimately invalidated, AstraZeneca have successfully delayed the launch of generic versions by competitors for many years.

The practice of granting a patent mistakenly or easily to a less significantly advanced invention, in turn, would cause substantial expense for society, because a technology that was already in the public domain could become private property.[1008] More important, the uncertainties created by overlapping patent claims and the uncertainties about the validity of patents due to the poor quality of examination would be major problems for players in the industry.[1009]

c) Encouraged waste of resources

Furthermore, the expensive process of obtaining a patent results in the waste of resources and money. In addition, almost every single step incurs cost. Consequently, the increased number of patents and of patent applications themselves threatens industry as well as society. Firstly, search costs should be mentioned. A large number of second generation patents must be searched and analyzed to determine whether there is room for further research or whether a generic version will infringe any of them. In addition to the innovative companies that secured the basic patents, other competitors, both other innovative companies and generic manufacturers, have actively filed patent applications surrounding the basic invention, either to gain a better position in licensing or to secure more tactical means after the expiration of the basic patent. Indeed, an empirical study found three-quarters of patents connected to high-cost drugs were owned by companies other than the drug's

1007 *E.g., Angell*, 2004, 78-79 (reporting trials which compared not likely equivalent doses but higher doses of Nexium® with Prilosec®, and two of the four trials showed Nexium® had marginal improvement); *Harris*, The Wall Street Journal, June 6, 2002.

1008 *Merges*, 76 Cal. L. R. 803, 876 (1988).

1009 *Jaffe/Lerner*, 2004, 174-76.

originator.[1010] The study further reported that non-original companies are investing substantial resources in second generation inventions related to blockbuster drugs.[1011] Even in the U.S., where the Orange book, a list of patents that covers a launched medicine, is available, simply looking at the list is insufficient,[1012] and those who wish to launch their own products without risk or with reduced risks need to spend a great deal of time and effort in conducting their own analyses. This response by the companies to the high number and low quality of patent application filings makes the situation worse for the industry, simply by adding more confusion, uncertainty and cost to the development process.[1013]

There are also costs involved in obtaining a patent, after filing a patent application. In the U.S., as long ago as 2001, it was reported to cost about $10,000 to $30,000 in filing fees, attorneys' fees, and other expenses to prepare a patent application.[1014] The increased number of patent rights on trivial improvements owing to lowered patentability requirements would result in blocking patent technology or increasing transaction costs without offsetting advantages in innovation.[1015] Considering the territoriality principle of patent protection,[1016] cost would be multiplied by the number of countries in which an applicant would seek a patent.

This problem is compounded by the fact that pharmaceutical companies will resort to creative litigation tactics, especially in securing evergreening patents.[1017] Based on these secured patents, companies not only try to bring the reformulated drugs to the market through regulatory approvals, but also turn to litigation to stifle competition based on those patent rights. Naturally, this adds to the cost incurred by generic companies in challenging or circumventing low-quality improvement patents.[1018] It is always easier and less costly to prevent patent applications from being patented than it is to invalidate the patents. Increasing numbers of challenges have been brought against patents covering products with revenues below $100 million as well

1010 *Christie, et al*, 8 PLoS Med 1, 4 (2013) (further reporting that a multitude of players seek monopoly control over innovations to blockbuster drugs).
1011 *Christie, et al*, 8 PLoS Med 1, 4-6 (2013).
1012 *Christie, et al*, 8 PLoS Med 1, 4 (2013).
1013 *Howard*, 4 J. Generic Med 231, 235-36 (2007).
1014 *Lemley*, 95 Nw. U. L. Rev. 1495, 1498 (2001).
1015 *Landes/Posner*, 2003, 319.
1016 *Doi*, 26 Fordham Int'l L.J. 377 (2002).
1017 *Eisenberg*, 13 Mich. Telecomm. Tech. L. Rev. 345, 348-49 (2007).
1018 *Howard*, 4 J. Generic Med 231, 235-36 (2007).

as those covering the blockbusters with annual sales in excess of $1 billion.[1019] Long and tedious battles over dozens of patents on one drug force not only patent holders but also challengers to waste valuable resources.[1020] Yet, once again, this cost applies only to those who can afford to carry on the costly litigation procedure. The situation is worse in the United States than in other countries, since defending against patent infringement suits is particularly expensive there.[1021] In addition, the American civil procedure makes it easy for claimants to sue, basically because attorneys can charge contingency fees, and because there is no duty to reimburse the attorney fees of the winning party. Thus, right holders incur little financial risk at the time of filing a patent infringement suit.[1022]

d) Hindrance of pharmaceutical innovation

At the end of the day, all of the activities discussed above certainly distract the pharmaceutical companies from their genuine task of "providing the society with new medicines."[1023] Considering that when the number of NMEs increases, mortality and health problems decline, [1024] the problems caused by lowered patentability could hinder real pharmaceutical innovation and threaten our health. Some scholars have even argued that more than 90% of the "countering" drugs to recent challenges were likely to be reformulations or second generation products, at best marginal improvements over present-day pharmaceuticals, as compared with all other product introduction. [1025] Launch of these new forms of (older) drugs does not help to increase human longevity.[1026] Indeed, second generation patents have little to do with the drugs' medical use. Rai also argued that there were drugs that provided little or even no therapeutic advantage over existing drugs as follows:

1019 *Grabowski/Kyle*, 28 Manage. Decis. Econ. 491, 495-496 (2007).
1020 See subsection V.A.1.c).
1021 *Jaffe/Lerner*, 2004, 68.
1022 *Ann*, 2009, 363-64.
1023 *Herper*, Forbes, February 5, 2002.
1024 *Cockburn*, 2006, 2-3.
1025 *Higgins/Graham*, 326 Science 370, 370 (2009).
1026 *Lichtenberg*, 5 Int. J. Health Care Fi. 47, 70 (2005) ("Launches of (older) drugs that are not NCEs - any of which may already have been on the market -do not increase longevity. [...] increasing the ratio of non-NCE to NCE launches reduces the fraction of people consuming NCEs, which in turn reduces longevity.).

> "The cost-effectiveness of me-too drugs, particularly in the [well established categories], is questionable. Although the me-too drug may prove more effective than the innovator drug for a certain population of patients, this marginal benefit is likely to be small."[1027]

Here, she meant "me-too drugs"[1028] as drugs addressing the same illness while managing to do so without infringing innovator patents,[1029] such as cimetidine (Tagamet®), ranitidine (Zantac®), or famotidine in the category of H2-receptor antagonist.[1030] These me-too drugs, however, at least can play some roles in curbing prices through limitation of the scope of exclusivity enjoyed by any given patented drug[1031] can function to generate another patient population which can be better treated by them,[1032] or can provide the patients with more choices. Contrary even to these me-too drugs, the therapeutic advantage would be harder to expect from the products (e.g. Esomeprazole) covered by second generation patents (e.g. S-enantiomer of omeprazole), which arguably contains the same active ingredient as Omeprazole. New versions (e.g. isomer) of basic drugs can often eliminate or mitigate their side effects, which were present in the old version of the drugs.[1033] However, it is debatable whether these incremental therapeutic advantages, can justify these new monopoly costs to the patients.[1034]

Apart from the effectiveness of second generation products, basic patentees greatly increased the spending attributable to line extensions as set out above, short-term priorities encouraged marginal inventions that provided more reliable returns on investment at the expense of major changes,[1035] and the market became flooded with products that did not provide significant clinical improvement over older medications.[1036] These factors result in more imitative research and fewer actual breakthroughs and drugs.[1037] This

1027 *Rai*, Ill. L. Rev. 173, 205-06 (2001).
1028 See subsection II.D.2.
1029 *Rai*, Ill. L. Rev. 173, 201 (2001).
1030 H2-receptor antagonists are used in the treatment of dyspepsia or peptic ulcer disease.
1031 *Rai*, Ill. L. Rev. 173, 206 (2001).
1032 For example, the prototypical H2-blocker, Cimetidine has serious drug interactions with other drugs, but famotidine does not have serious interactions, which allows the patients to be less careful to take multiple medications.
1033 *Glasgow*, 41 IDEA 227, 251 (2001).
1034 *Glasgow*, 41 IDEA 227, 251 (2001).
1035 *Munos*, 8 Nat. Rev. Drug Discov. 959, 966 (2009).
1036 *NIHCM*, 2002, 18-19.
1037 *Munos*, 8 Nat. Rev. Drug Discov. 959, 966 (2009).

becomes a greater problem in conjunction with the lowered patentability of second generation patents. Merges and Nelson note that where incentives for improvement are increased, incentives for innovative inventions are decreased.[1038] Hunt also contends that, if protection were extended to more obvious inventions, there would be an additional social cost of monopolies and also additional losses, if firms redirect their research toward less risky projects.[1039] In addition, crucially, the uncertainty created by overlapping patent claims and the questionable validity of patents due to the poorer quality of examination with the increased number of patent applications will undermine incentives to invest even in new technology and will stifle innovation.[1040] Consequently, considering the limited resources of most companies and the effort required for second generation inventions, granting selection inventions may siphon off resources that can be exploited to research the new medical entities that society has found in short supply. Some scholars have also warned that there will be a clear risk of diverting a significant proportion of investment from more innovative research and from areas particularly in need of therapeutic breakthroughs.[1041] Therefore, the lowered patentability criteria on second generation inventions can actually hamper meaningful innovation in the pharmaceutical industry. Most importantly, the inordinate delay for marginal benefits disadvantages patients in need of new medicines.[1042]

2. Concerns about the novelty requirements

The problem faced by selection inventions concerns the most fundamental patentability requirement, novelty.

a) Language dependent prior art disclosure problem

As discussed in chapter IV.A.4., the amount of disclosure is more dependent upon the language of the claim than upon the disclosure perceived by the

---

1038 *Merges/Nelson*, 90 Colum. L. Rev. 839, 873-78 (1990).
1039 *Hunt*, 1999, 11.
1040 *Jaffe/Lerner*, 2004, 174-76.
1041 *Pifferi/Perucca*, 20 Eur. J. Drug Metab. Ph. 15, 24 (1995).
1042 *Beary*, 339 Lancet 495 (1992).

person skilled in the art. In particular, the distinction between the disclosure of generic formulae and that of individual substances in prior art seems to have taken root within EPO case law in assessing novelty.[1043] In T181/82, the BOA stressed that there was a strict distinction between the "purely intellectual content" of the definitions and their "information content in the sense of a specific teaching with regard to technical action."[1044] In other words, the novelty of the selection invention was judged differently when the prior art disclosed the invention in a generic term rather than an individualized form.

However, it is very difficult to understand the absurd conclusion that the same expressions in scientific language, such as "C_{1-4} alkyl" and "alkyl with less than five carbon atoms" disclose different radicals in legal language.[1045] According to the BOA, "C_{1-4} alkyl" discloses only C_1 alkyl i.e. methyl, while the latter phrase discloses nothing, because this expression does not disclose any individual alkyl group. This method of interpretation does not appear to be performed through the eyes of a person skilled in the art, who cannot differentiate between these expressions. In addition, the assessment of novelty becomes dependent on the draft of the claim. For example, the applicant would need to draft depending upon whether he wants to destroy all prior art or whether he wants to leave room for another application to other parties or even to himself. For an applicant to achieve a "defensive patent application" or a "defensive publication," he must disclose every possible element other than the efficiency of disclosure. For example, according to the BOA, to disclose "C_{1-4} alkyl," one must disclose methyl as a C_1 alkyl; ethyl as a C_2 alkyl; n-propyl and isopropyl as C_3 alkyls; and n-butyl, isobutyl, *sec*-butyl, and *tert*-butyl as C_4 alkyls. But if he wants to keep some for further application, the applicant would disclose only "C_{1-4} alkyl" or even "alkyl with less than five carbon atoms." He would still be able to enforce the patent against the third party if he used it, since the claim would cover all eight alkyls in any case. The situation would be different if a third party patented it. This photographic approach to assessing novelty is problematic.

1043 *See* EPO Examination Guidelines G-VII, Annex 3.1.(iv) (noting that if the selected group has not been specifically disclosed in the prior art, it would have been the question of lacking of novelty rather than obviousness.).

1044 *Ciba-Geigy/Spiro compounds,* T 181/82, OJ EPO 1984, 401, 411.

1045 *Grubb/Thomsen*, 2010, 235.

b) Rendering inventive step requirement meaningless

Novelty examination is a separate test to determine patentability[1046] and is not the first step in examining obviousness. However, by lowering the bar for novelty, the courts appear to fail to sufficiently distinguish between the test of novelty from that of obviousness. In particular, the *Escitalopram* Courts in major jurisdictions made significant efforts to evaluate "the difficulty of the separation of citalopram" in order to assess novelty, after admitting that it was apparent that a racemate of a chemical compound like citalopram had equal amounts of two enantiomers. In the end, the courts found that difficult separation did not lead to Escitalopram being anticipated. This could be interpreted as rendering novelty dependent on the "difficulty" or amount of effort and time involved in obtaining a claimed compound, whose structure was described in the prior art based on the common knowledge of a person skilled in the art.

The level of enablement of the prior art reference is determined to assess novelty. [1047] This could be one of the reasons why the determination of novelty has become more relative and, to some extent, similar to that of obviousness. In the United States, for example, *prima facie* obviousness established based on the prior art disclosure of racemates and *de facto* disclosure of the enantiomer itself was rebutted based on no reasonable expectation of success and the difficulty of separation.[1048] It is indeed difficult to differentiate how difficult it will be for a skilled person to obtain the claimed invention within the context of anticipation depending on whether there was any expectation of success in separating within the context of non-obviousness. Once it is determined that the claimed invention was not easy to obtain from the prior art disclosure, the inventive step of the invention could also be established to some extent. This in turn suggests that the courts may not clearly distinguish between the novelty and the non-obviousness requirements, which is contrary to what the BGH has postulated in Germany.[1049]

Indeed, the BOA addressed a distinction between novelty and the inventive step of selection inventions to the arguments that deciding selection

1046 *BGH/Olanzapine*, IIC 2009, 596, 599.

1047 *See* subsection IV.A.3.

1048 *See Sweet*, 24 Berkeley Tech. L.J. 129, 142 (2009); *See also Forest Labs., Inc. v. Ivax Pharms., Inc.*, 501 F.3d, 1263, 1269 (Fed. Cir. 2007); See subsection IV.B. 3.b).

1049 *BGH/Olanzapine,* IIC 2009, 596, 599.

novelty was identical or closely similar to that used to determine obviousness as follows:[1050]

> "[T]he Respondent sought to convince the Board that the legally correct approach for deciding selection novelty was identical or closely similar to that employed in determining obviousness. In particular, he put forward the proposition that in cases of overlapping ranges of compounds, a claim to a narrower range as compared with a broader prior art range was always selectively novel if it could be demonstrated that the narrow range was inventive over the broader range. [...] Whereas it is undoubtedly true that there can be no selection novelty in a range of overlap where the choice of moving into that overlapping range from the prior art one is obvious, it doesn't either as a matter of law or as a matter of logic follow that the converse is true, namely that if a choice of a narrower range is inventive, then there must of necessity be selective novelty in it. For the above reasons, the Respondent's argument in this respect cannot be accepted."[1051]

Simply put, the Board admitted that if the selection from the prior art is obvious, then there is no novelty in the selection thereof. As the Board further noted, it is not always true; if the selection is inventive, then there is the novelty of selection. However, and importantly, the contrapositive of the first sentence is also undoubtedly true.[1052] If there is novelty in the selection in a range of overlap, then the choice of moving into the overlapping range from the prior art one is not obvious. Therefore, even borrowing the Board's own words, the same test is repeated in both steps, or both steps are determined by a single test for the assessment of patentability. In the end, can it be said that the test for novelty is placed in the broader context of the test for "inventive step"?[1053]

Furthermore, to assess inventiveness, more information is often required in addition to the teaching from the prior art disclosure. Given that that information seems to be close enough, such as the difficulty of separation, the additional information could already be used to destroy novelty. Thus, again it appears that, to some extent, the examination of patentability is *de facto* reduced to the examination of novelty, thereby making the test of obviousness redundant.

1050 *AKZO/Bleaching activators*, T 133/92, 1994.

1051 *AKZO/Bleaching activators*, T 133/92, 1994, point 2.1.4.

1052 *Peterson*, 1974, 9-10 (explaining when a statement is true, a contrapositive of the sentence is also true).

1053 *See e.g., Tilmann*, IIC 2010, 149, 158-59.

c) Potential concerns of "direct and unambiguous" disclosure requirement

According to the case law in selection inventions, the courts require that the prior art disclose the selection inventions "directly and unambiguously."[1054] However, there are further areas in which the rules for disclosure play a role. Firstly, the disclosure of priority application(s) matters to the validity of priority claiming compared with the disclosure of application claiming the priority. Secondly, the content of the application, in terms of the disclosure of patent specification matters to the sufficiency of the disclosure regarding the scope of the claim. Thirdly, the disclosure of the originally filed content of the patent application matters in whether it supports the amended claims. It is especially important that the species is not disclosed by the genus patent but falls within the scope of the same genus patent. Fourthly, when a patentee limits the scope of the patent, the disclosure of the granted patent specification matters to the scope of the limited patent.

Therefore, it will be interesting to see whether the courts will uniformly apply this concept of disclosure in terms of novelty to other areas of disclosure, and, if not, to what extent they will do so individually.

B. Implications considering the breadth of selection patents

A selection invention is generally chosen from the available broader prior art and directed to a specific species or a subgroup thereof which falls within the scope of the prior wider genus. As the other side of the coin, this kind of invention can be an overlap invention, as the result of which the later selection patent invention can be practiced only by licenses from the prior patentee, since the patent claiming general class will protect each member of the class, even though it is not considered a disclosure of those specific members.[1055] This is one of the cases where such claims may reach beyond the

1054 *See e.g. Tilmann*, IIC 2010, 149, 159; *See also Bublak/Coehn,* GRUR 2009, 382, 389.

1055 *Robinson*, IIC 1972, 139, 143; *Nastelski*, IIC 1972, 267, 293-94 (describing "product protection is simultaneously granted for every individual member of this group irrespective of whether or not such member has been specially designated in the group formula.").

scope that even the patentee had in fact invented in three circumstances.[1056] Needless to say, this phenomenon will often be observed according to the increased number of second generation inventions based on the lowered patentability requirements thereof. For this reason, the scope of second generation patents will be analyzed first, after which the impact of lowered patentability will be examined.

1. Scope of the protection

Even though the breadth of a patent is a more abstract concept than its length, the allowable breadth of claims is determined by examiners and upheld by the judiciary,[1057] and the "doctrine of equivalents" and "reverse doctrine of equivalents" are adopted by the courts.[1058]

The scope of the claim is a matter of quantity, and the clarity of the claim is a matter of quality. The claims are interpreted with the help of description and drawings.[1059] If there is another definition in the description, this definition is decisive in determining the scope of the patent.[1060] Thus, it is the function of the claims to define clearly and with precision the monopoly claimed, so that others may acknowledge the exact boundaries of the area within which they will be trespassers.[1061] In the EPO, the extent to which the breadth of the claims should be allowed is considered under Art. 83 EPC and Art. 84 EPC second sentence. Although Art. 83 EPC is directed to the

---

1056 *Lemley*, 75 Tex. L. Rev. 989 (1997) (The other two cases are the case where the doctrine of equivalents can be applied; and the case when patent claims may reach new and unanticipated inventions made after the patent issues, but which fall within the literal language of the claims.).

1057 *Scotchmer*, 5 J. Econ. Perspect. 29, 30 (1991).

1058 *Friebel et al.*, 2006, 22.

1059 *See e.g.*, EPC Art. 69 and the Protocol on the Interpretation of Article 69 EPC, 35 U.S.C. § 113.

1060 *See e.g., BGH/Bierklärmittel (Beer Fining Agent)*, GRUR 1984, 425, 426 (holding that if the definitions used in the patent specification differed from those in the literature in the field, the definitions in the specification prevailed for the interpretation of the patent); *see also, Electric & Musical Industries Ltd v. Lissen Ltd* [1939] R.P.C. 23, 57 (holding "[i]f the claims have a plain meaning in themselves, then advantage cannot be taken of the language used in the body of the specification to make them mean something different.").

1061 *Electric & Musical Industries Ltd v. Lissen Ltd* [1939] R.P.C. 23, 39; *See* e.g., EPC Art. 84, 35 U.S.C. § 112, second sentence.

disclosure of the invention, the underlying purpose thereof is the same as Art. 84 EPC, namely, to secure the grant of the proper breadth of patent exclusivity that can be justified by the technical contribution to the art.[1062] This reflects quite well the so-called "reward theory" of the patent system, which could be the most common justification. Regarding the claim construction, in the *Catnic* case, the British court tempered its previous way of interpreting claims, the "literal approach"[1063] to the "purposive construction."[1064] And the scope of patent is not generally limited to the version that the inventor invented, but could cover the subsequently modified versions as long as each falls within the scope.[1065]

Beyond the literal scope of claims, courts may consider an equivalent of certain elements in the claims, the so-called doctrine of equivalents. The application of the doctrine of equivalents in each jurisdiction is quite diverse. Notably, it is argued that there is no general doctrine of equivalents in ***British*** courts,[1066] which instead have used the so-called "pith and marrow" approach that is a similar principle.[1067] This means that the use of the pith and marrow of the invention, i.e. its important parts, is an infringement even though there are insubstantial differences between the allegedly infringing embodiment and the patent claim. There was a case in which the court applied its pith and marrow doctrine to the product claim.[1068] Similar to the terfenadine cases below, the issue was whether the prodrug infringed the metabolite patent. An acetone adduct (Hetacillin) of another medication (Ampicillin) was immediately hydrolyzed in the body to the medication (Ampicillin), and hetacillin in itself did not have an antibiotic effect. The Court held that the accused product infringed the patent, because it was a

1062 *Exxon/Fuel oils*, T 409/91, OJ EPO 653, 661-62 (1994) point 3.5.

1063 *Electric & Musical Industries Ltd v. Lissen Ltd* [1939] R.P.C. 23, 39 (expressly noting that there was nothing like infringement of the equity of a patent).

1064 *Catnic Components Limited and another v. Hill & Smith Limited* [1982] R.P.C. 183, 243 (holding "[a] patent specification should be given a purposive construction rather than a purely literal one […]").

1065 *Kitch*, 20 J. Law Econ. 265, 268-69 (1977) (further noting this feature of the patent system is important to the drug industry, just as a new use invention to a known drug, e.g. secondary therapeutic indications.).

1066 *See e.g.*, *Occlutech GmbH v. AGA Medical Corp* [2010] EWCA Civ 702, paras 23; *see also Kirin-Amgen Inc v. Hoechst Marion Roussel Limited*, [2004] UKHL 46 (Lord Hoffman asserted again there was no doctrine of equivalents in UK).

1067 *Kirin-Amgen Inc v. Hoechst Marion Roussel Limited*, [2004] UKHL 46, paras 36-37.

1068 *Beecham Group v. Bristol Laboratories Ltd.* [1978] RPC 153.

temporarily disguised or altered form of the medication.[1069] A similar line of analysis is found in German jurisprudence, such as whether the allegedly infringing embodiment achieves the same function, or whether a person skilled in the art could replace the changed features while expecting the same effect.[1070]

In Germany, the following conditions must be met to find patent infringement: (i) Whether the modified embodiment solves the problem underlying the invention by means which have objectively the same technical effect, (ii) whether a person skilled in the art by means of his specialist knowledge is able to identify the modified means as having the same effect, (iii) whether the considerations that the person skilled in the art applies are drawn from the technical teaching of the patent claim (so that the person skilled in the art takes the modified embodiment into account as the equivalent solution in question), and (iv) whether the modified embodiment is anticipated or made obvious by the state of the art (the so-called "Formstein objection").[1071] Even though prosecution history estoppel,[1072] which requires an extensive research on the file wrapper, is not accepted, one may raise the Formstein defence that the allegedly infringing embodiment argued to be an equivalent would not be patentable over the prior art, either because it is known from the prior art, or because it is obvious in view of the prior art.[1073] This is obviously because the allegedly infringing product within the scope of the patent is not patentable over the prior art, and the patent claiming

---

1069 *Beecham Group v. Bristol Laboratories Ltd.* [1978] RPC 153, 192 (noting "[t]he mere temporary cloaking or masking of a product does not in general suffice to avoid infringement of letters patent whose specification claims that product.").

1070 *See e.g., BGH/Schneidermesser I (Cutting blade I),* GRUR 2002, 515, 517; *see also Catnic Components Limited and another v. Hill & Smith Limited* [1982] R.P.C. 183, 243; *see also Kirin-Amgen Inc v. Hoechst Marion Roussel Limited,* [2004] UKHL 46, paras 41-42, 75; *cf., Occlutech GmbH v. AGA Medical Corp* [2010] EWCA Civ 702, para 28 (even though the decision is denying general existence of doctrine of equivalents in UK, it found German approach is lacking one question which is applied by the UK court, i.e. "[w]ould the reader skilled in the art nevertheless have understood from the language of the claim that the patentee intended that strict compliance with the primary meaning was an essential requirement of the invention? If yes, the variant is outside the claim").

1071 *BGH/Schneidermesser I (Cutting blade I)*, GRUR 2002, 515, 517; *BGH/Formstein*, GRUR 1986, 803, 805-06.

1072 *See infra* 1077 -1078 and accompanying texts.

1073 *BGH/Formstein*, GRUR 1986, 803, 805-06.

infringement also has a reason for invalidity. In other words, this is to prevent something in the prior art from being taken away from the public.

In the United States, this doctrine originated more than a century ago.[1074] Hand J noted that the purpose of this doctrine was to temper unsparing logic and to prevent an infringer from stealing the benefit of the invention.[1075] This was acknowledged by the Supreme Court in the *Graver Tank* case, where it held that to find the infringement under this doctrine, the alleged embodiment had to perform substantially the same function in substantially the same way to obtain the same result.[1076] In *Warner Jenkinson v. Hilton Davis*, while upholding this doctrine, the Supreme Court also noted that "prosecution history estoppel"[1077] was available as a defence to infringement, unless the amendment's purpose was not related to patentability. [1078] The following additional exceptions to prosecution history estoppel were provided in the *Festo* case: i) The equivalent might have been unforeseeable at the time of the application, ii) the rational underlying the amendment might bear no more than a tangential relation to the equivalent in question, or iii) there might have been other reasons.[1079]

In Korea, the Supreme Court recognized a five-step test of the doctrine of equivalents: When an element of an invention is substituted in an accused device, the substituting element of the accused device is equivalent to the substituted element of the patented invention, if i) the problem solving principles are the same in the patented invention and the accused device, ii) the substituting element of the accused device provides substantially the same operational effects as the substituted element of the patented invention, iii) the substitution is obvious to one having ordinary skill in the art, iv) the

---

1074 *Graver Tank & Mfg. Co. v. Linde Air Products Co.*, 339 U.S. 605, 608 (1950) (noting "[o]riginating almost a century ago in the case of Winans v. Denmead, 15 How. 330, 14 L.Ed. 717, it has been consistently applied by this Court and the lower federal courts, and continues today ready and available for utilization when the proper circumstances for its application arise.").

1075 *Royal Typewriter Co. v. Remington Rand, Inc.*, 168 F.2d 691, 692 (2nd Cir. 1948).

1076 *Graver Tank & Mfg. Co. v. Linde Air Products Co.*, 339 U.S. 605, 608 (1950).

1077 A patentee who had made narrowing amendments to the application in order to meet the patentability requirements, may not invoke the doctrine of equivalent to recapture the scope of his claims which he already surrendered.

1078 *Warner-Jenkinson Co., Inc. v. Hilton Davis Chemical Co.*, 520 U.S. 17, 40-21 (1997).

1079 *Festo Corp. v. Shoketsu Kinzoku Kogyo Kabushiki Co., Ltd.*, 535 U.S. 722, 740-41 (2002).

accused device was not known or could not have been easily conceived from known technologies by a person skilled in the art at the time of filing the application for the patent, and v) there are no special circumstances such as intentional exclusion of the substituting element of the accused device from the claimed scope during the prosecution of the patent.[1080]

2. Scope of selection patents

a) Species selection patents

It is well established that a species selection patent falls within the scope of the previous genus patent,[1081] although there was an exceptional decision in Italy.[1082] In that case, a Markush type claim covered some 10 million compounds, and the active substance in Cimetidine was not explicitly mentioned in the patent specification.[1083] The Supreme Court of Italy held that a pharmacologically active substance, such as Cimetidine, which could be determined from a patented formula only through further complex research and experiments, was not eligible for the protection of the patent, because it was not clearly and completely described in the patent document.[1084] However, this decision was an exception.

b) Optical isomers

In Europe

In *Ranbaxy v. Warner-Lambert*, the issue was whether the claim[1085] was limited only to racemates or also covered enantiomers.[1086] Ranbaxy tried to argue that the claim must be limited to the racemates. It argued that since the patentee would have known that one enantiomer was ineffective, there

1080 *Korean Supreme Court/Bayer Aktiengesellschaft v. Union Quimico Famaceutica*, S.A, 97Hu2200, Jul. 28, 2000, para 2.
1081 *See e.g., Domeij*, 2000, 317.
1082 *Corte di Cassazione/Cimetidin*, GRUR Int 1991, 497.
1083 *Corte di Cassazione/Cimetidin*, GRUR Int 1991, 497.
1084 *Corte di Cassazione/Cimetidin*, GRUR Int 1991, 497, 498-99.
1085 *See supra* 603 .
1086 *Ranbaxy (UK) v. Warner-Lambert*, [2006] EWCA Civ 876.

was no reason to claim this ineffective enantiomer. Thus, he could not have intended to claim the other single enantiomer either.[1087] It further argued that if the patentee wished to, he could have done so easily by claiming one type of enantiomer explicitly. Therefore, the patent covered only the racemate.[1088] However, Jacob LJ reiterated the point in the *Kirin-Amgen* case[1089] regarding the purposive claim construction that the claim construction was an exercise in discerning what the person skilled in the art would have understood the claim to mean, not an exercise in over-meticulous semantic analysis.[1090] Jacob LJ dismissed this argument on the basis that, since the purpose of the claim was to "demarcate" the invention, there was no rational basis for assuming that the patentee would have intended to exclude the pure enantiomer, which he would have known was the substance that really mattered.[1091] Ranbaxy further argued that, according to convention, the structural formula shown in the patent could represent either a particular enantiomer or a racemate, but not both.[1092] This argument also failed, since this convention needed to be proved as a matter of fact, but the judge in the first instance had made no such finding.[1093] Accordingly, in the context of the patents, claim 1 was construed as covering *both* the racemate and either of the enantiomers.

Neuberger LJ further explained why the patent covered the enantiomers. He noted that although the racemate was the racemic mixture which would have been regarded as a different substance from either of the two enantiomers of which it was composed, it was a 50/50 mixture of the two enantiomers.[1094] He further noted as follows:

> "[W]here a racemate is administered as a drug, one enantiomer is likely to have all, or the great majority, of the biological activity, and that activity will be either unaffected or reduced by the presence of the other enantiomer. The fact that the racemate in the present case has the claimed pharmaceutical effect shows that it is no exception. This demonstrates that the sole or mainly effective enantiomer maintains its character and (at least to a substantial extent) its effectiveness,

---

1087 *Ranbaxy (UK) v. Warner-Lambert*, [2006] EWCA Civ 876, para 18.
1088 *Ranbaxy (UK) v. Warner-Lambert*, [2006] EWCA Civ 876, para 18.
1089 *Kirin-Amgen Inc v. Hoechst Marion Roussel Limited*, [2004] UKHL 46, paras 32-35.
1090 *Ranbaxy (UK) v. Warner-Lambert*, [2006] EWCA Civ 876, para 7.
1091 *Ranbaxy (UK) v. Warner-Lambert*, [2006] EWCA Civ 876, para 19.
1092 *Ranbaxy (UK) v. Warner-Lambert*, [2006] EWCA Civ 876, para 23.
1093 *Ranbaxy (UK) v. Warner-Lambert*, [2006] EWCA Civ 876, para 24.
1094 *Ranbaxy (UK) v. Warner-Lambert*, [2006] EWCA Civ 876, paras 44-45.

> notwithstanding that it is administered as part of a racemic mixture. Accordingly, it appears to me that it is wrong to conclude that a racemate, and in particular the racemate in this case, cannot be regarded as a mixture of the two enantiomers. […] "A+B" can be regarded both as a single entity, namely (A +B), and as a mixture of two entities, namely A and B."[1095]

Even though the patent claiming an enantiomer was held invalid because of the lack of novelty based on the fact that the prior art disclosed the method for producing the enantiomer,[1096] this Court clearly noted that one enantiomer was responsible for the efficacy of the racemate thereof, and a racemate was the mixture of two enantiomers. Even though Neuberger LJ noted that this construction was dependent upon the facts and on the context,[1097] a claim on a racemate can be construed so that it also covers the enantiomers.

To the contrary, the scope of a claim over an enantiomer does not extend to the old racemate, as Jacob LJ noted "such would be an absurd construction given the fact that the patent acknowledges that [the racemate] is old, having been disclosed in [the previous patent]."[1098]

In the United States

In *Pfizer v. Ranbaxy*, as it did before the British court, Ranbaxy argued that the structural formula I was limited to racemates.[1099] The specification of patent disclosed as follows: "The compounds of structural formula I above possess two asymmetric carbon centers … [which] gives rise to four possible isomers, two of which are the R-cis- and S-cis-isomers and the other two of which are the R-trans- and S-trans-isomers. This invention contemplates only the trans-form of the compounds of formula I above." Based on this intrinsic evidence, even though the claim 1 presented the formula of racemate, the Federal Circuit held that the patentee disclaimed the R-cis- and S-cis-isomers out of four isomers.[1100] The Federal Circuit further noted that the terms "racemate" or "racemic mixture" did not appear in the patent

---

1095 *Ranbaxy (UK) v. Warner-Lambert*, [2006] EWCA Civ 876, paras 45-46.

1096 See *supra* 605 -606 and accompanying texts.

1097 *Ranbaxy (UK) v. Warner-Lambert*, [2006] EWCA Civ 876, para 47.

1098 *Generics (UK) v. Daiichi Pharmaceutical* [2009] EWCA Civ 646, para6; see also *Generics (UK) v. Daiichi Pharmaceutical* [2008] EWHC 2413 (Pat), para 317.

1099 *Pfizer, Inc. v. Ranbaxy Laboratories Ltd.*, 457 F.3d 1284, 1288-89 (Fed. Cir. 2006).

1100 *Pfizer, Inc. v. Ranbaxy Laboratories Ltd.*, 457 F.3d 1284, 1289 (Fed. Cir. 2006).

specification. Thus, there was no intrinsic evidence that limited claim 1 to trans-racemates, as opposed to an R-trans enantiomer, an S-trans enantiomer or any mixture thereof.[1101] Moreover, against Ranbaxy's contention that the examples did describe reaction sequences that produced racemates, the Federal Circuit held that "restricting claim 1 on this basis would improperly import limitation from the specification into the claims, which should be avoided unless the patentee clearly intends for the claims and the embodiments in the specification to be strictly coextensive."[1102] Accordingly, the Court held that the claim was correctly construed to include enantiomers and that the Ranbaxy's product infringed the patent.

c) Metabolite

In the United Kingdom

Section 64 of UK Patents Act provides a person with a personal right to continue an act if he or she was performing effective and serious preparations to carry out an act that would have been an infringement if the patent were in force, before the priority date.[1103] In *Merrell Dow Pharmaceuticals Inc v. HN Norton & Co Ltd* case, Merrell Dow argued that the existence of Section 62 showed that the Parliament recognized the effect of the new 1977 Act that people might find themselves unable to go on doing what they or someone else had done before. The House of Lords, however, held that this argument may produce results that seem contrary to common sense and, furthermore, that this provision had no application to the case, since no defendants were marketing terfenadine before the priority date of the acid metabolite patent.[1104] On the other hand, the Court solved the difficulty that the exclusivity of the parent drug could have been extended by the metabolite patent by holding that the patent was invalid because of the lack of novelty.[1105]

1101 *Pfizer, Inc. v. Ranbaxy Laboratories Ltd.*, 457 F.3d 1284, 1289 (Fed. Cir. 2006).
1102 *Pfizer, Inc. v. Ranbaxy Laboratories Ltd.*, 457 F.3d 1284, 1290 (Fed. Cir. 2006).
1103 UK Patents Act 1977, Section 64.
1104 *Merrell Dow Pharmaceuticals Inc v. HN Norton & Co Ltd* [1995] UKHL 14, paras 19-20.
1105 See *supra* 663 -666 and accompanying texts.

In Germany

The Munich Higher Regional Court held that the patent of metabolite was not infringed if, according to the expired patent, a pharmaceutically active ingredient could be made and used which was converted in the body to a substance protected under a new patent.[1106] The Court's holding was based on the facts that the defendant did not sell, market, or keep for the file the metabolite and that the terfenadine produced and marketed by the defendant was exactly the same compound protected by the plaintiff's patent that had expired. [1107] The Court held that, if the patent was expired, and the inventor was rewarded enough, the teaching of a patent must have been applicable.[1108] It further stated that, if scientific knowledge (in this case, active metabolite) has suddenly made the manufacturing of the old medication into "a purposive manufacture of medication," this way of interpreting the concept of manufacture was not in line with the patent protection.[1109]

In the United States

In the same terfenadine case, the District Court held that the patent on the metabolite was valid. However, it was not infringed because the scope of the patent to the metabolite was limited to the synthetic version of the metabolite.[1110] This approach seems to be difficult to reconcile with "contributory infringement."[1111]

In other cases, however, the Federal Circuit stated that a person might infringe a claim directed to a metabolite when the parent drug was administered to the person, since it would be metabolized to the claimed inven-

1106 *OLG München/Terfenadine*, GRUR, 1994, 746 (Because of the bifurcate system in Germany, this Court could not nullify the patent).

1107 *Vossius/Vossius/Vossius,* GRUR 1994, 472, 474, 476 (also noting that the defendant did not suggest another use either).

1108 *Vossius/Vossius/Vossius,* GRUR 1994, 472, 476.

1109 *Vossius/Vossius/Vossius,* GRUR 1994, 472, 476.

1110 *Marion Merrell Dow Inc. v. Baker Norton Pharmaceuticals, Inc.*, 948 F.Supp. 1050, 1055-56 (S.D.Fla.,1996), appeal dismissed, 152 F.3d 941 (Fed. Cir. 1998).

1111 *Grubb/Thomsen*, 2010, 253.

tion.[1112] In *Zenith Laboratories, Inc. v. Bristol-Myers Squibb,* however, owing to the absence of evidence, the Federal Circuit reversed the District Court's decision holding that the patent had been infringed,[1113] the Federal Circuit stated that a compound as a form before the ingestion would fall within the scope of a compound claim to the metabolite.[1114] In a later case, Federal Circuit restated that it recognized this possibility of infringement of a patent claim directed to metabolite by taking medication, while holding a claim directed to the "bare" metabolite was anticipated by a prior art which disclosed administration of the parent drug.[1115] In other words, Rader J stated that one might obtain a patent on the synthetic version of something that was already in the public, unless it was an unrestricted product claim.[1116]

d) Polymorphs

The *SmithKlein Beecham v. Apotex* case involved the claim construction of one crystalline form of a known substance. In the late 1970s, a British company, Ferrosan, invented and acquired a patent over a compound known as paroxetine, which was licensed to SmithKline. Ferrosan eventually developed a process to produce the crystalline hydrochloride salt of paroxetine, or paroxetine hydrochloride ("PHC").[1117] In 1985, a chemist at SmithKline discovered a new crystalline form of PHC hemihydrates. These compounds were different from the PHC anhydrate which was Ferrosan's original form, because they comprised of PHC crystals with one bound water molecule for every two PHC molecules so that the compounds were more stable and easily

1112 *Zenith Laboratories, Inc. v. Bristol-Myers Squibb Co.*, 19 F.3d 1418, 1421-22 (Fed. Cir. 1994) (holding infringement may occur if the administered product is converted in vivo into the claimed product); *Hoechst-Roussel Pharmaceuticals, Inc. v. Lehman*, 109 F.3d 756, 759 (Fed. Cir. 1997) ("the right to exclude may arise from the fact that when administered, [parent drug] metabolizes into another product, [metabolite], which [patentee] has claimed).

1113 *Zenith Lab. Inc. v. Bristol-Myers Squibb Co.*, 1992 WL 340761 (D.N.J.1992) (holding the use of a compound which would converted to the metabolite by a patient who took the parent drug was an infringing use).

1114 *Zenith Laboratories, Inc. v. Bristol-Myers Squibb Co.*, 19 F.3d 1418, 1422 (Fed. Cir. 1994).

1115 *Schering Co. v. Geneva Pharmaceuticals*, 339 F.3d 1373, 1380 (Fed. Cir. 2003).

1116 *Schering Co. v. Geneva Pharmaceuticals*, 339 F.3d 1373, 1380-81 (Fed. Cir. 2003).

1117 *SmithKline Beecham Corp. v. Apotex Corp.*, 403 F.3d 1331, 1334 (Fed. Cir. 2005).

packaged.[1118] In this case, while construing claim 1 - "crystalline paroxetine hydrochloride hemihydrates" ("crystalline PHC") - to cover crystalline PHC *without further limitation, i.e. in any amount*, the Federal Circuit held that the Apotex's product would infringe this claim 1, based on the factual finding that Apotex's PHC anhydrate tablets would contain "trace amounts" of PHC hemihydrates.[1119] In this case, the claim was invalidated based on the inherent anticipation doctrine.[1120] The Federal Circuit acknowledged the District Court's concern that the above claim construction could result in "a considerable extension in the effective patent term of paroxetine, because it might become difficult or even impossible to manufacture the pure anhydrous form after the Ferrosan patent expired."[1121]

3. Analysis and conclusion

Genus patents are generally strong, because one can usually apply for a patent not only on the core structure molecules but also their analogues.[1122] Further, the patents are difficult to design around, which can make the patent holders wealthy.[1123] The difficulty of inventing around is not only technological but also a consequence of the product loyalty of both patients and doctors.[1124] This is clear in species invention, i.e. species invention falls within the scope of the genus patent. Thus, if a species selection patent holder is different from the patentee of the basic patent in force, the former cannot exploit his invention without licensing the basic patent (the so-called "blocking effect"). If the species selection patent is owned by the patentee of the basic invention, it could increase the possibility of extension of exclusive rights (the so-called "evergreening effect"). This is notable when one considers that the entire scope of a patent, in general, should be in the public domain once the patent has lapsed.[1125]

1118 *SmithKline Beecham Corp. v. Apotex Corp.*, 403 F.3d 1331, 1334 (Fed. Cir. 2005).

1119 *SmithKline Beecham Corp. v. Apotex Corp.*, 403 F.3d 1331, 1340-42 (Fed. Cir. 2005).

1120 *See supra* 660 -662 and accompanying texts.

1121 *SmithKline Beecham Corp. v. Apotex Corp.*, 403 F.3d 1331, 1342 (Fed. Cir. 2005).

1122 *See supra* 109 and accompanying texts: One single claim can claim millions of different but analogous compounds.

1123 *von Hippel*, 1988, 53; *Landes/Posner*, 2003, 313.

1124 *Landes/Posner*, 2003, 313-14.

1125 *Grubb/Thomsen*, 2010, 335.

For the optical isomers, with the same issue, the British court held that the claim covered both the racemate and the enantiomers, while the American court held that the claim covered only the enantiomers. This case was special because the claim was drafted to show the structure in three dimensions. However, in general, the claim on the racemate would not cover the enantiomer; otherwise the enantiomer would not have been patented, and the scope of the enantiomer, of course, would not extend to the racemate.

In contrast to other jurisdictions, where it was held that selling a parent drug would not infringe the metabolite patent, the United States Federal Circuit repeatedly held that it "would" or "may" infringe the metabolite patent and that, when administered, it could metabolize into the claimed invention. One must wait for the development of case law on metabolites in the United States. Based on the decided cases, however, if a patent on the metabolite is granted, the scope should be restricted to the synthesized version.

The patent on a crystalline form was invalidated in the United States owing to inherent anticipation. However, the Court held that, if the crystalline form was included even in a trace amount, it could have infringed the patent on the crystalline form. One can imagine that, during the course of the production of a basic product, this kind of crystalline form would be co-produced and a patent infringement could be found, at least in the United States.

Of course, the lowered novelty or inventive step requirements have little to do with the scope of these patents. The relaxed sufficiency requirement would result in the broader scope of patent; however, it was not observed in the case law regarding the selection inventions. Nevertheless, the implication could be seen from a different angle, i.e. whether they could affect the entry of generic versions of the product covered by the basic patent, which will be discussed in chapter V.D.2.a).

C. *Implications considering the length of selection patents*

The term of a patent is the maximum period during which it can be maintained and enforced. It is normally expressed in the number of years from the filing date of the patent application, although it can be extended through the patent term extension. The exclusivity can also be prolonged based on the grant of selection patents on the specific characteristics of the basic compounds. This becomes more important if the substance of the selection patents (e.g., enantiomer) can be eligible for the issuance of a patent term extension which provides further exclusivity.[1126]

1. Patent term and patent term extension

The "statutory" patent term is generally 20 years from filing in major jurisdictions.[1127] However, the race to the door of the patent office shortens the real time in which the inventor can enjoy the exclusivity.[1128] The "effective" patent term, which can be defined as the length of the period for which a product is marketed with the benefit of enforceable patent protection, is shorter. The effective patent terms for pharmaceuticals, probably the patent terms after the marketing approval, were reported to average between nine and eleven years,[1129] which is a bitter pill to the drug companies, because their long R&D periods encroach on their time of exclusivity.[1130]

Thus, the patent term extension can be applied for and granted to compensate the term which was subject to the regulatory approvals for the pharmaceuticals and agrochemicals. As a benefit in return for these patent term extensions, for example, the Hatch-Waxman Amendments in the United States insulates generic manufacturers from patent infringement actions during the term of the patent on the reference drug to obtain regulatory approval of their generic versions.[1131] Before the Hatch-Waxman act, it was considered a patent infringement if a generic company began the regulatory approval process before the patent term on the reference drug expired.[1132] A Supplementary Protection Certificate (herein after "SPC") in Europe is a kind of interface between the patent system and the regulatory system, since granting SPC protection relies on holding both a patent and a marketing authorization for a highly regulated product, such as a medication. These

1126 *BGH/Escitalopram,* GRUR 2010, 123, 131.
1127 The U.S. did not adopt this 20 years patent term until 1994, when it amended the patent law to comply with the TRIPS Agreement. *See* 35 U.S.C. § 15 (C)(1).
1128 *Landes/Posner*, 2003, 302.
1129 *Grabowski/Vernon*, 10 Suppl 2 Pharmacoeconomics, 110 (1996).
1130 See subsection III.A.1.b).
1131 *Coggio/Cerrito*, 52 Food & Drug L.J. 345, 346 (1997).
1132 *Eidson*, 82 Wash. U. L. Rev. 1169, 1169 (2004).

provisions are intended to encourage research and accelerate the release of new medications to the public.[1133]

a) In Europe

Different countries in Europe independently introduced corresponding legislation to the Hatch-Waxman Act in the United States in the early 1990s.[1134] Thus, the discrepancy of legislation, especially different extension periods of patent terms, resulted in the promulgation of Regulation 1768/92 in January, 1993. According to the Regulation creating the Supplementary Protection Certificate ("SPC") for pharmaceuticals,[1135] a patent term can be extended for the period equal to the time between the grant of the first marketing authorization in the European Community and the patent filing date, and reduced by five years, up to a maximum duration of five years.[1136] Since SPCs are national rights, a patentee should apply the SPCs in each member state within six months of either the date of the patent grant or the date of the marketing authorization, whichever is later.[1137] The marketing approval may be obtained from the regulatory authority of each country or centrally from the European Medicines Agency. Only one SPC can be granted to one patentee for a single product for the basic patent,[1138] even if the basic patent covers more than one marketed product,[1139] or more than

1133 *Coggio/Cerrito*, 52 Food & Drug L.J. 345, 346 (1997); *contra*, *Engelberg*, 39 IDEA 389, 419-25 (1999) (arguing special extensions of patent terms on pharmaceutical inventions were unnecessary).

1134 *Domeij*, 2000, 267.

1135 Council Regulation (EEC) 1768/92 of 18 June 1992 concerning the Creation of a Supplementary Protection Certificate for Medicinal Products, which was codified under Regulation (EC) No 469/2009 of the European Parliament and of the Council ("Council Regulation 469/2009") that had various amendments but no substantive changes.

1136 Council Regulation 469/2009, Art. 13.

1137 Council Regulation 469/2009, Art. 7.

1138 Case C-181/95, *Biogen v. Smithklein Beecham* [1997] ECR I-357, para 28 (holding if a product was protected by a number of basic patents in force, which might belong to a number of patent holders, each of those patents might be designated for the purpose of the procedure for the grant of a certificate, however, under article 3(c) of the Regulation, only one certificate might be granted for each basic patent).

1139 Council Regulation 469/2009, Art. 3(d).

one substance.[1140] If the patentee has more than one patent on the same product, no more than one certificate may be granted.[1141] The scope of protection extends only to the product covered by the marketing authorization and for the use of the product as a medicinal product that has been authorized before the expiration of the certificate.[1142]

Medicinal products are the category of products which are eligible for the SPC, and the product refers to the active ingredient, which receives the exclusivity right. In other words, the SPC is granted to the active ingredient of the medicinal product. Article 1 of the Council Regulation 469/2009 defines "medicinal product" as "any substance or combination of substances presented for treating or preventing disease in human beings or animals and any substance or combination of substances which may be administered to human beings or animals with a view to making a medical diagnosis or to restoring, correcting or modifying physiological functions in humans or in animals." It defines "product" as "the active ingredient or combination of active ingredients of a medicinal product." However, "the active ingredient" in Art. 1(b) is not defined in the Regulation. In this regard, the BGH stated that, through the definitions of a product and a medicinal product above, "the active ingredient" could be indirectly described as a component of the product, which was presented for treating or preventing human disease.[1143]

b) In the United States

According to the Hatch-Waxman Act, the patent term can be extended for a period corresponding to half of the clinical testing time of an investigative new drug (IND), plus all approval time of the new drug application (NDA), up to a maximum of five years, if the maximum patent term does not exceed 14 years from the NDA approval date and if any such IND or NDA time period to the grant of the patent is not taken into account.[1144] Only one patent can be extended in connection with the first NDA approval, i.e. first per-

---

1140 Council Regulation 469/2009, Art. 3(c).

1141 Regulation (EC) No 1610/96 of the European Parliament and of the Council of 23 July 1996 concerning the Creation of a Supplementary Protection Certificate for Plant Protection products ("Council Regulation 1610/96") Art. 3. Para 2 and Recital 17.

1142 Council Regulation 469/2009, Art. 4; *Brückner/von Czettritz*, 2011, Art. 4 Rdn 32.

1143 *BGH/Doxorubicin-Sulfate*, GRUR 2009, 41, 41.

1144 35 U.S.C. § 156 (c).

mitted commercial marketing or use of the product,[1145] and a patent cannot be extended more than once, though it covers more than one FDA approved products.[1146] This can thus be summarized as "one patent extension per patent, one patent extension per product, and one product per patent extension."[1147] The scope of protection is limited to the "approved product" for any approved use.[1148] Thus, only the scope covering the product is extended.

The product as an objective of the patent term extension means a drug product or any medical device subject to regulation under the FDA Act, and the drug product means the active ingredient of a new drug, including any salt or ester of the active ingredient.[1149]

Under the Hatch-Waxman Act, if the paragraph IV ANDA applicant successfully challenges the patent validity, he is offered 180 days of exclusivity, which prevents other generic makers from entering the market.[1150] The 180 day exclusivity holder will gain a large profit by pricing just below the reference drug without concern about competition from any other generics. However, in Europe, where no such 180 day exclusivity exists, once the first validity challenger is successful, other generics will benefit from the invalidation, and the first challenger will not easily recover the litigation cost.

c) In Korea

The term of the patent concerning drugs can be extended by a period of up to five years, during which the patented invention cannot be practiced, because an approval under other Acts is required to work a patented invention, and it takes an extended period to complete the efficacy or safety tests that are necessary to obtain such approval, and these are prescribed by Presidential Decree.[1151]

1145 35 U.S.C. § 156 (a)(5).

1146 35 U.S.C. § 156 (a)(2); *Merck v. Kessler*, 80 F.3d 1543, 1547 (Fed. Cir. 1996).

1147 *Cardiac Pacemakers, Inc. v. St. Jude Med., Inc.*, No., 96-1718-c H/G, 2001 U.S. Dist. LEXIS 5753, 26 (S.D. Ind. 2001).

1148 35 U.S.C. § 156 (b)(1); *Merck v. Kessler*, 80 F.3d 1543, 1547 (Fed. Cir. 1996) (holding that the restoration period of the patent did not extend to all products protected by the patent but only to the product on which the extension was based).

1149 35 U.S.C. § 156 (f)(2).

1150 21 U.S.C. § 355(j)(5)(B)(iv).

1151 Korean Patent Act Art. 89.

In contrast to the other jurisdictions, more than one patent can be extended for one approval of the product. However, the same patent cannot be extended even if it covers more than one product approved by the regulatory authority. The scope of the patent term extension is also limited solely to the approved product for the approved use.

2. Patent term extension on selection patents

The issue with regard to a patent term extension on a selection patent is whether the subject matter of the patent can be the subject of the patent term extension as a separate product from the products covered by their basic patents.

a) Species selection patents

Although the scope of a species selection patent can be overlapped with that of the genus patent, since the active ingredient covered by the species selection patent will be different from that of the genus patent, the patent term extension will be granted to the species patent. Consequently, if the patentee of the species selection patent is the same as the genus patentee, he can enjoy much longer exclusivity. However, if the basic patentee would have developed the compound covered in the basic patent without securing a species patent, he can enjoy only the 20 years from the filing date of the genus patent.

b) Optical isomers

In Germany

While distinguishing from the *Doxorubicin-sulfate* case, the BGH held that a marketing authorization for a medicinal product containing racemate as an active ingredient did not present a bar to granting an SPC for a medicinal product that contained an enantiomer as an active substance, and that was also the subject matter of both a later marketing authorization and of its own patent.[1152] In the *Doxorubicin-sulfate* case, even if the applicant argued that doxorubicin-sulfate had improved potency, better pharmacological effect and reduced side effects in comparison to doxorubicin-hydrochloride, the BGH dismissed the case and held that a previous SPC granted for doxorubicin-hydrochloride opposed the grant of an SPC of doxorubicin-sulfate, because the active compound was still the same as doxorubicin.[1153]

In the United Kingdom

The Appeal Court in *Generics (UK) v. Daiichi Pharmaceutical* also held that the previously granted SPC on a racemic compound (Ofloxacin) did not hinder granting an SPC for the enantiomer (Levofloxacin). [1154] The Court further held that this was because, while successive SPCs for mere variants of an active substance were not allowed, levofloxacin was not a minor variant but a novel and inventive improvement owing to its own distinctive activity, bioavailability, and toxicity.[1155] In Justice Jacob's words, "[o]nly a curmudgeon would say there was no invention there."[1156]

In the United States

The question whether enantiomers can have "first commercial marketing or use status" for the purpose of patent term extension was answered in *Ortho-McNeil Pharmaceutical v. Lupin Pharms.* [1157] The Federal Circuit upheld the District Court's decision that, regardless of its existence as a component (even the active component) of the previously approved and marketed ofloxacin, levofloxacin was the first permitted commercial marketing or use of this drug.[1158] In this case, the Federal Circuit also affirmed that the FDA and the USPTO practices were in accordance with *Glaxo v. Quigg*, in which the Court held that "product," as used in § 156(a), was "the active ingredient

---

1152 *BGH/Escitalopram,* GRUR 2010, 123, 131; *see also BPatG/Escitalopram II,* 29.03.2011- 3 Ni 22/10 (a dismissed another challenge of nullity action against the granting of SPC based on the argument that escitalopram had no substantially different or improved pharmaceutical effect over the racemate citalopram).

1153 *BGH/Doxorubicin-Sulfate*, GRUR 2009, 41.

1154 *Generics (UK) v. Daiichi Pharmaceutical* [2009] EWCA Civ 646.

1155 *Generics (UK) v. Daiichi Pharmaceutical* [2009] EWCA Civ 646, para 68.

1156 *Generics (UK) v. Daiichi Pharmaceutical* [2009] EWCA Civ 646, para 45.

1157 *Ortho-McNeil Pharmaceutical v. Lupin Pharms.*, 603 F.3d 1377 (Fed. Cir. 2010).

1158 *Ortho-McNeil Pharmaceutical v. Lupin Pharms.*, 603 F.3d 1377, 1381 (Fed. Cir. 2010).

present in the product," not the biologically "active moiety." The Court also extended the term of the patent on a new ester of an acid, even though salts of the same acid had previously been approved.[1159] In order to clarify the availability of a patent term extension, the cases relevant to the salts are discussed.

In *Glaxo v. Quigg*, in which Glaxo sought an extension for its patent covering cefuroxime axetil, an ester of its biologically active moiety, cefuroxime, the Federal Circuit held that the "active ingredient of a new drug" in § 156 meant the "actual active ingredient in the product" as opposed to the "active moiety of the active ingredient", and affirmed the patent term extension on cefuroxime axetil over the previously marketed product including two salts of cefuroxime.[1160] However, about 15 years after the *Glaxo* case, Pfizer, which had a marketing approval for and sold amlodipine besylate salt, sued Dr Reddy's Lab, which sold amlodipine maleate salt, based on a patent whose term was extended.[1161] In *Pfizer Inc. v. Dr. Reddy's Laboratories,* the CAFC held that the patent term extension applied not only to the particular salt of molecule being used in marketing approval but also to all salts and esters of molecule covered by the patent.[1162] While reasoning that the "statute foresaw variation in the salt or ester of an active ingredient, and guarded against the very loophole now urged"[1163], the Federal Circuit held that the "product" was the active moiety, which seems to be different from the ruling in the *Glaxo* case.[1164] In *PhotoCure v. Kappos*, the Federal Circuit distinguished this case from the *Pfizer* case: "The issue in *Pfizer* was whether infringement of an extended patent on the drug amlodipine was avoided by

1159 *Glaxo Operations UK Ltd. v. Quigg*, 894 F.2d 392 (Fed. Cir. 1990).

1160 *Glaxo Operations UK Ltd. v. Quigg*, 894 F.2d 392 (Fed. Cir. 1990).

1161 *Pfizer Inc. v. Dr. Reddy's Laboratories, Ltd.*, 359 F.3d 1361 (Fed. Cir. 2004).

1162 *Pfizer Inc. v. Dr. Reddy's Laboratories, Ltd.*, 359 F.3d 1361, 1365-67 (Fed. Cir. 2004) (quoting also Title 21 Code of Federal Regulation - Food and Drugs ("21 C.F.R.") § 60.3(b)(10): "[h]uman drug product means the active ingredient of a new drug or human biologic product [...], including any salt or ester of the active ingredient, as a single entity or in combination with another active ingredient).

1163 *Pfizer Inc. v. Dr. Reddy's Laboratories, Ltd.*, 359 F.3d 1361, 1366 (Fed. Cir. 2004).

1164 *See also Pfizer Inc. v. Dr. Reddy's Laboratories, Ltd.*, 359 F.3d 1361, 1367 (Fed. Cir. 2004) (In his dissent, however, Meyer Chief J stated the patent term extension should be limited to the specific product which was the subject of FDA approval, since the product which was eligible for a patent term must have been subject to a regulatory review period before its commercial marketing or use, which was neither amlodipine, nor amlodipine maleate, but amlodipine besylate).

changing the salt." [1165] The Federal Circuit further noted that "*Pfizer* did not hold that extension is not available when an existing product is substantively changed in a way that produces a new and separately patentable product having improved properties and requiring full FDA approval."[1166] According to *PhotoCure*, therefore, separate patentability alone could justify finding a drug product distinct from a previously approved product for the purpose of § 156.[1167]

c) Polymorphs

In the case of *Laboratoires Servier v. Apotex*, after the first and basic patent for the active substance (perindopril) expired in 2003 with the effective extension by an SPC, if the second patent on the crystalline form of the active substance is valid, the exclusivity would be extended to 2020.[1168] Thus, the polymorph seems to be regarded as a different active ingredient from the basic product.

d) Metabolite

There seems to be no case law regarding the patent term extension on a metabolite. However, based on the above discussed cases, once the metabolite is patented, it will likely be able to enjoy the patent term extension as well.

3. Analysis and conclusion

For the optical isomers, the BGH distinguished the ofloxacin case from the doxorubicin-sulfate case by holding that, because the active compound of doxorubicin-hydrochloride and the doxorubicin-sulfate were the same as doxorubicin, the previously granted SPC opposed the grant of an SPC for the doxorubicin-sulfate. However, it is difficult to understand the reasoning

---

1165 *PhotoCure v. Kappos*, 603 F.3d 1372, 1376 (Fed. Cir. 2010).
1166 *PhotoCure v. Kappos*, 603 F.3d 1372, 1376 (Fed. Cir. 2010).
1167 *PhotoCure v. Kappos*, 603 F.3d 1372, 1376 (Fed. Cir. 2010).
1168 *Laboratoires Servier v. Apotex*, [2008] EWHC Civ 445, paras 4 and 9.

behind distinguishing the levofloxacin case from the doxorubicin case, because the active ingredient in citalopram is also the one enantiomer, i.e. escitalopram. It is equally hard to understand the reasoning of the ofloxacin case in the British court. The Court held that levofloxacin was patentable, thus, a different SPC should be granted after the SPC on the ofloxacin. Similarly, in the United States, even if the product covered by the second generation invention shares "an active moiety" with the previously approved drug, the applicants could obtain the patent term extensions as long as "the active ingredients" of the products are different.

In general, for other second generation inventions, as long as it could acquire a patent, the SPC would be granted on top of the SPC on the product covered by the basic patent.

Lowered patentability requirements on second generation inventions and the SPC

The scope of the patent extension covers the derivatives, such as salts and esters, which are protected by the basic patent, thereby preventing the third party preparing salts other than the basic patentee's substance and devaluing its SPC protection.[1169] However, if these derivatives are subject to patents specifically covering them, another SPC or patent term extension for derivatives of the substance can be granted.[1170] This could lead the basic patentee to work more on the trivial modifications of an active moiety, which was subject to the authorization of previous products. The phenomenon could be accelerated, because the patentability requirements on the second generation inventions have been lowered, and more derivatives may be patented. Namely, the lowered patentability requirement will allow more patents on the

---

1169 Council Regulation 1610/96, points 13 ("[w]hereas the certificate confers the same rights as those conferred by the basic patent; whereas, consequently, where the basic patent covers an active substance and its various derivatives (salts and esters), the certificate confers the same protection.") and 17 of preamble ("[w]hereas the detailed rules in recitals 12, 13 and 14 and in Articles 3 (2), 4, 8 (1) (c) and 17 (2) of this Regulation are also valid, mutatis mutandis, for the interpretation in particular of recital 9 and Articles 3, 4, 8 (1) (c) and 17 of Council Regulation (EEC) No 1768/92").

1170 Council Regulation 1610/96, points 14 ("[w]hereas the issue of a certificate for a product consisting of an active substance does not prejudice the issue of other certificates for derivatives (salts and esters) of the substance, provided that the derivatives are the subject of patents specifically covering them.") and 17 of preamble; *PhotoCure v. Kappos*, 603 F.3d 1372 (Fed. Cir. 2010).

second generation inventions, which in turn will result not only in longer exclusivity, but also in more incentives to working on second generation inventions than breakthrough innovations.

Patent term extension system and pharmaceutical innovation

The patent term extension system apparently encourages R&D more on the second generation inventions than on the NMEs.[1171] This is especially true for the medications whose safety testing and/or the toxicity testing takes longer than others. For example, for medicines that treat chronic diseases, Alzheimer's disease, or cancers, the maximum cap of five years of extension risk discourages companies from pursuing research in these medicinal fields.[1172] As discussed in chapter III.B.2.c), one of the reasons for the drought of new medications was the movement of focus to complex disorders such as these chronic diseases.

The condition of the SPC in Europe can be more serious, because the calculation system of the SPC is much more favourable to the secondary products than the NMEs. Under the SPC regulation, as seen in Figure 9, the maximum effective patent term protection of the product that succeeded in launching its product from five to ten years after the patent application date is not affected by actual durations. Thus, the medications that need more than ten years to reach the market from the patent filing date can never enjoy fifteen years of effective patent term.[1173]

1171 *See also* subsection VI.D.2.a)(1).

1172 *Domeij*, 2000, 282.

1173 This is different from the Korean patent term extension system which considers the whole period of clinical trials and of regulatory approvals or from the U.S. patent term extension system which considers the 1/2 of clinical trials and whole period of regulatory approvals.

Figure 9: Effective patent term with the compensation of SPC in Europe[1174]

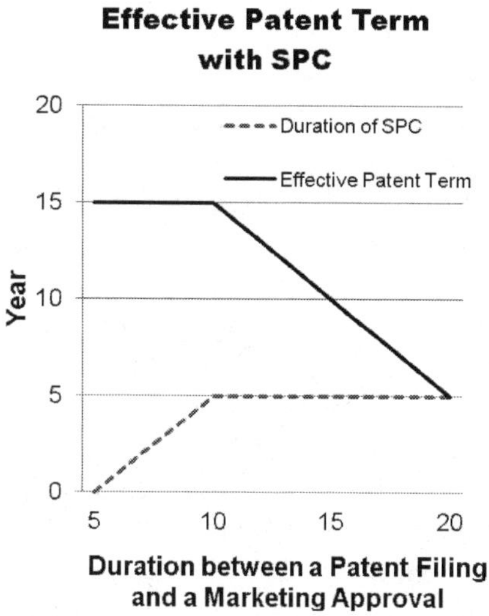

By contrast, the medications that would take between five and ten years from the patent application date to acquire a market approval will enjoy the maximum effective patent term. Obviously, the gap between the patent application date and the market approval date should be much shorter for second generation products and could well be less than ten years. When the basic and second generation patentees are the same, the patentee could even have leeway to control the timing of the market launch up to ten years after the patent application date on the second generation invention. Given that the companies try hard to extend their exclusivities on products protected by their basic patents, this would increase the risk that the patentees who can enjoy the secondary SPC protections may try to use the leeway to bring their products to market later than the moment when society could have earlier access to those products.[1175] These can certainly be among the motivations for the pharmaceutical industries to focus more on second generation patents and products than NMEs.

1174 This figure is prepared by the author.

1175 Of course, this would be the case when they can make no gap from the basic patent's exclusivity.

D. *Implications on the competition in the pharmaceutical industry*

1. Introduction

According to Schumpeter, the existence of monopoly power spurs innovations by allowing the firm with the monopoly to appropriate the surplus generated by such innovations.[1176] He further argues that the old monopoly would eventually be challenged and replaced by the newer one by introducing the concept "Creative Destruction": A process through which the economic structures are revolutionized from within, by opening up new markets that will destroy the old one, and repeating this incessantly.[1177] In addition, as other commentators have noted, the arrival of new knowledge renders the old obsolete,[1178] and an inventor's descendants can actually become the instruments of his destruction.[1179] If there is no competition in the market, however, a patentee who holds an intellectual property right ("IPR") will also have little incentive to reinvest in further innovation,[1180] since this company could already control the market and impose monopoly prices.[1181]

According to Arrow, the incentive to innovate can exist even in perfect competition, and, by charging the royalty to a competitive industry, the inventor can receive a return equal to the monopoly profits. He therefore argues that the incentive of innovation is greater under competitive condition than under monopolistic conditions.[1182] If perfect competition exists in the market, exploitation cannot be confused with the pursuit of profits.[1183] If there is no intellectual property ("IP") protection, however, patentees will be concerned that competitors in the market will easily copy the product.[1184] Ex-

1176 *Schumpeter*, 1942, 134-175 (holding that the firms with monopoly power are the main engines of innovation).

1177 *Schumpeter*, 1942, 137-138 ("[der] Prozess, … der unaufhörflich die Wirtschafts struktur *von innen heraus* revolutioniert, unaufhörflich die alte Struktur zerstört und unaufhörlich eine neue schafft.").

1178 *Belenzon*, 2006, 2.

1179 *Gallini/Scotchmer,* 2002, 65.

1180 *Kamien/Schwartz*, 1982, 190-91 (noting that IPR holders would do so because his reward from innovation is smaller than the total social benefit).

1181 *Drexl*, 2007, 18.

1182 *Arrow*, 1962, 619-22.

1183 *Seißer*, 2008, 2.

1184 *Drexl*, 2007, 18; *Kamien/Schwartz*, 1982, 190 (noting perfect competition corresponds to zero year of patent life, thus there is no reward from innovation, followed by no innovation.).

amples can be easily observed in history. For example, the price of penicillin, which was not patented, and the price of streptomycin, which was licensed on an unrestricted basis, dropped dramatically as the result of the rapid increase in demand during and after World War II and by the competition among many new suppliers.[1185] Therefore, the new "wonder drugs" were found to be unprofitable.[1186] Furthermore, this could make the companies hesitate to or not invest in R&D.[1187]

Competitive pressure could further result in socially wasteful over-investment in R&D or induce defensive investment by those who try to strengthen their bargaining position in the field.[1188] In addition, "more competition" may also involve social costs, such as duplication of entry costs, inefficient production, multiplied investments in the same products, and the like.[1189] In reality, competition is never perfect, and the market can be distorted by many factors, such as government regulation, central planning, monopolistic structures, and so on.[1190] Moreover, considering the limitation of an IPR's life (especially a patent), since the companies cannot enjoy their monopoly position perpetually, companies must reinvest to find another source of income. Furthermore, even if the innovation occurs at a slower pace than is socially optimal, the innovation occurs under monopoly.[1191] During the limited period of their monopoly rights, both IP laws and competition laws should be combined to promote dynamic competition.[1192]

Regarding the situation concerning second generation inventions, Merges and Nelson argue that, since there would be uncertainty, namely, that different technologies would be developed from the common basic innovation by different approaches from different parties, it would be better to let a

1185 *Comanor*, 31 Economia, 372, 373 (1964) (noting "[t]he price of a standard form of penicillin dropped from $20 for 100,000 units in 1943 to 41 cents in 1950."); *Steele*, 5 J. Law Econ. 131, 138, fn24 (1962) (e.g. noting "[f]or the ten-year period 1951-1960 the bulk price of streptomycin dropped from $3.24 to $0.36 for ten grams"); *Temin*, 10 Bell J. Econ. 429, 436 (1979).

1186 *Scherer*, 2007, 11.

1187 *Drexl*, 2007, 18; *Kamien/Schwartz*, 1982, 190 (noting perfect competition corresponds to zero year of patent life, thus there is no reward from innovation, followed by no innovation.).

1188 *Cockburn*, 2006, 21-22, 25.

1189 *Denicolò*, 44 J. Ind. Econ. 249, 263 (1996).

1190 *Seißer*, 2008, 2.

1191 *Kamien/Schwartz*, 1982, 190-91.

1192 *Drexl*, 2007, 18.

variety of minds try.[1193] This provides economic support for improvement patents.[1194] Since, under the monopoly situation, the patent holder or some licensees can be expected to develop only some of the improvements further, many potential improvements might be underdeveloped or even ignored.[1195] Landes and Posner also mention, however, that it might be more efficient to leave the improvements to the original inventors at a slower speed and at a lower cost.[1196] In the end, the answer to the question of whether it would be better to have many improvements, depends on whether and how much these kinds of improvement inventions are needed.

Pharmaceutical companies can face antitrust challenges, because there is a thin line between their aggressive approach in this sector and anti-competitive behaviour.[1197] Some have argued that evergreening tactics and life cycle management based on second generation patents have caused delayed market access not only for the generic companies but also for the patients.[1198] For example, it was reported that the generic entry to the market was delayed, on average, seven months after patent expiration, with the range from zero to more than fifty months.[1199] According to the European Commission, tactics employed to respond to generic entry includes patenting activities of originators; contacts, disputes and litigation between originator and generic companies;opposition procedures and appeals before patent offices; patent settlements and other agreements between originator and generic companies; interventions of originator companies before national authorities deciding on marketing authorization, pricing and reimbursement of generic products; promotional activities; and second generation products.[1200] Other than interventions in national authority decisions, all of these

1193 *Merges/Nelson*, 90 Colum. L. Rev. 839, 873-74 (1990); *see also von Hippel*, 1988, 3-5 (showing generally different sources of innovations according to the field of industries and manufacturer was the sources of innovation in chemical industries, e.g. engineering plastics and plastics additives.).

1194 *Landes/Posner*, 2003, 190, 318-319 (also noting a quasi-Darwinian process, which is “a process almost of trial and error in which the market selects from among diverse approaches whose relative promise cannot be assessed in advance”).

1195 *Merges/Nelson*, 90 Colum. L. Rev. 839, 873-74 (1990).

1196 *Landes/Posner*, 2003, 190, 322.

1197 *Safir*, 50 Food & Drug L. J. 335, 335 (1995).

1198 *See e.g.*, *Rathod*, 7 J. Generic Medicines 227, 227 (2010).

1199 *DG Competition*, 2009, 70-71.

1200 *DG Competition*, 2009, 16.

tactics are deployed in patenting. Even promotional activities can focus on second generation products covered by second generation patents.

On the one hand, the pharmaceutical industry was certainly "ingenious in finding ways to extend patents on its bestselling drugs," such as marketing a new combination of two old drugs.[1201] Gaudry insists that filing as many patents as possible with regard to the product would not only increase the total scope of patent protection but also achieve apparently competing purposes.[1202] On the other hand, it is theoretically possible that the generic companies would practice at least the basic patent once the patent expires. In addition, as EU pharmaceutical law clearly specifies, the development, application, and registration of a generic version are allowed before the expiration of the patent covering the product.[1203] In the following section, therefore, the substantive roles of second generation patents in the competition in generic markets will be analyzed.

2. Quasi-obstacles of generics market entry

a) Scope of second generation patents

There have been concerns that second generation patents could be used to extend the patent protection of basic products unjustifiably.[1204] Some have argued that second generation inventions would significantly impair generic competition but provide modest therapeutic gains for a small subset of the patient population, and thus government intervention must be made to prevent the losses from impaired competition while allowing access to the reformulation for those patients who really value it.[1205] Some also call these strategies "patent walls", which can be built where the innovator acquires patents on the variety of inventions related to the basic invention, but which

---

1201 *Angell*, 342 New Eng. J. Med. 1902 (2000) (providing Vytorin (a combination of Ezetimibe and Simvastatin claimed in U.S. patent No. 5,846,966) as an example); *see also Glasgow*, 41 IDEA 227, 250-51 (2001).

1202 *Gaudry*, 29 Nature Biotech. 876, 877 (2011).

1203 Art. 10. 6 of Council Directive 2001/83/EC of 6 November 2001 on the Community code relating to medicinal products for human use, as amended ("Council Directive 2001/83/EC).

1204 *Grubb/Thomsen*, 2010, 249; *Rathod*, 7 J. Generic Medicines 227, 227 (2010).

1205 *Shadowen/Leffler/Lukens*, IIC 2011, 698, 700.

exist less for the value than to protect the central innovations.[1206] However, second generation patents do not always prevent generics from entering the market, if generic manufacturers want to sell the older version covered by the basic patent after its expiration.

Although a *species selection invention* certainly infringes the basic patent, the exploitation of a basic patent after its expiration will not infringe the selection invention, since the scope of the species patent could not cover the older product. Thus, generic versions of the product covered by the basic patent would be sold soon after its expiration. Although the *Atorvastatin* decision held that the patent covers both racemates and *the enantiomers*,[1207] the decision seemed to be based on a claim drafting issue. More importantly, if the racemate infringes the enantiomer patent, the patent on the enantiomer must be invalidated according to the "infringement test" so that marketing the racemate will not infringe the enantiomer patent. For the *metabolite patent*, as the Munich Higher Regional Court held, exploitation of the parent drug does not infringe the metabolite patent, since the metabolite was not marketed. One may still worry about the contributory or inducement infringement. In addition, the Federal Circuit in the United States has continued to hold that it "would" or "may" infringe the metabolite patent and that, when administered, it could be metabolized into the claimed invention. One may need to await the further development of case law on metabolites in the United States. However, as we have seen from the House of Lords' decision, to find infringement would prevent someone from doing what he had already done before the filing date. Thus, even if a patent claiming a synthesized version of metabolite is granted, its scope should not be extended to the metabolite naturally made by the body.

For a *polymorph*, the concern can be justified. As the Federal Circuit held, if it is difficult or even impossible to manufacture one pure form of polymorph after the basic patent expires – e.g., in the course of manufacturing the basic product, the polymorph form could be synthesized together – a considerable extension in the effective patent term of basic invention will be concerned.[1208] However, if the probability of co-production is high, there

1206 *Hopenhayn/Mitchell*, 32 RAND J. Econ. 152, 163 (2001).
1207 See subsection V.B.2.b).
1208 *SmithKline Beecham Corp. v. Apotex Corp.*, 403 F.3d 1331, 1342 (Fed. Cir. 2005).

will also be higher probabilities that the polymorph patent will be found invalid as inherent anticipation.[1209]

Therefore, there could be real concerns, such as species selection invention or the polymorph. However, contrary to the conventional perception, it could be said that there are fewer cases of the exploitation of a basic patent to be found than those infringing second generation patents.

b) Length of second generation patents

Apart from the patent term extension system's inherent problems,[1210] the patent term of second generation patents matters to the extent that their scope can prevent the generics' entry onto the market.

c) Delayed filing of second generation patent applications

While presenting Figure 10, the European Commission argued that the second generation patents were filed at the very end of a patent term of basic invention.[1211]

1209 *SmithKline Beecham Corp. v. Apotex Corp.*, 403 F.3d 1331, 1342-46 (Fed. Cir. 2005).

1210 See *supra* 1172 -1175 and accompanying texts.

1211 *DG Competition*, 2009, 176-77.

Figure 10: Post-launch patent portfolio for one of the top ten INNs by total sales (2000 – 2007)[1212]

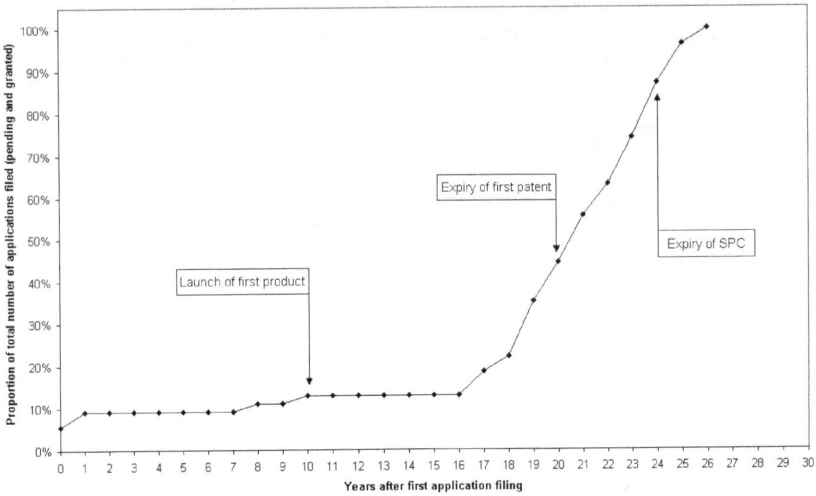

Of course, the timing of second generation patenting is crucial. The later they are filed (but are granted before the primary patent expiration), the longer they can help to extend exclusivity in certain circumstances. However, this argument fails in two crucial respects in this field. First, the later the companies file patent applications, the more likely they will face prior arts and the less likely they will be issued as patents. Secondly, since the innovative companies are not the only ones that can file second generation patent applications, they cannot safely sit and wait to enjoy longer exclusivity with the help of second generation patents. Thus, the patentee of a basic patent cannot wait to file the patent applications until the expiration of the term of the basic patent.

The following issues are more burdensome to the generic manufacturers.

1212 *DG Competition*, 2009, 176-77.

3. Real obstacles to generics' market entry

a) Automatic thirty-month stay and new list up in the Orange Book in the United States

A patent linkage system refers to the practice of linking marketing approval or pricing/reimbursement status of generic drugs to the status of patents on the reference products. The American Orange Book is such a system. A new medication is usually relevant to more than one patent, and each patent listed in the Orange Book will likely have different patent expiration dates. One of the most significant problems with this system is the difficulty of evaluating the validity of patents claimed as being related to the reference products,[1213] because validity can finally be confirmed only by the courts.

When a New Drug Application ("NDA") is filed with the US FDA, the NDA applicant must submit a list of all patents that cover the drug regarding which a claim of infringement could be asserted.[1214] The FDA publishes the list of these patents with their expiration dates in the Orange Book[1215] to give notice to potential ANDA applicants that such patents may hinder them from introducing their generic versions. The generic manufacturers can prepare to launch their products after the analysis of patents listed in the Orange Book. However, the sudden announcement of a new patent grant covering the product will deter and prolong the generics' market entry, as occurred in the *In re Buspiron Patent Litigation* case.

Bristol-Myers obtained a patent for the compound buspirone in 1980, obtained marketing approval in 1986, and sold it on the market.[1216] On November 21, 2000, less than one day before the basic patent was set to expire, Bristol-Myers obtained a patent claiming one of the metabolites of buspirone.[1217] Around eleven hours before the original patent expired, Bris-

1213 *Gaudry*, 29 Nature Biotech. 876, 876 (2011).

1214 21 U.S.C. § 355(b)(1)(G); 21 C.F.R. § 314.53.

1215 Orange Book: Approved Drug Products with Therapeutic Equivalence Evaluations, available at: http://www.accessdata.fda.gov/scripts/cder/ob/default.cfm (Last accessed on December 20, 2013).

1216 *In re Buspirone Patent Litigation*, 185 F. Supp. 2d 340, 345 (S.D.N.Y., 2002). It was sold under the Trademark "Buspar".

1217 U.S. Patent No. 6.150,365 (November 21, 2000, under the title of "Anxiety method", in original claim as filed the use of buspirone as a prodrug of the metabolite was also claimed); *In re Buspirone Patent Litigation*, 185 F.Supp.2d 340, 350 (S.D.N.Y., 2002); *Langreth/Murphy*, Forbes, Apr. 2, 2001.

tol-Myers hand-delivered copies of the metabolite patent to the FDA and applied to have it listed in the Orange Book[1218] as covering buspirone.[1219] The listing with the FDA triggered an automatic forty-five day period during which Bristol-Myers could bring patent infringement suits against generic competitors, who intended to market generic versions.[1220] Bristol-Myers filed suits for patent infringement against competitors within this forty-five day period, which in turn triggered an automatic stay of the FDA's approval of generic versions for up to the earlier of thirty months or until the relevant patent disputes were decided.[1221] One of the generic companies had already manufactured and was ready to ship its product at 12:00 am on November 22, 2000.[1222] The District Court held that the claim of the later patent did not cover uses of buspirone itself.[1223] In a different case, the Supreme Court reversed the Federal Circuit's decision[1224] and found that the patent delisting provision[1225] provided a mechanism for a generic company to challenge the accuracy of the use code in association with an Orange Book listed patent.[1226]

1218 Listing in the Orange Book is important mainly because when the generic company submit an ANDA, it is required to address each patent listed in the Orange Book that claims the drug. According to 21 USC § 355(j)(2)(A)(vii), an ANDA applicant must address for each patent listed i) that such patent has not been filed (paragraph I filing), ii) that such patent has expired (paragraph II filing), iii) the date on which the patent will expire (paragraph III filing), or iv) that such patent is invalid or will not be infringed by manufacture, use, or sale of the new drug for which the application is submitted.

1219 *In re Buspirone Patent Litigation*, 185 F. Supp. 2d 340, 350 (S.D.N.Y., 2002).

1220 *In re Buspirone Patent Litigation*, 185 F. Supp. 2d 340, 343 (S.D.N.Y., 2002).

1221 *In re Buspirone Patent Litigation*, 185 F. Supp. 2d 340, 343 (S.D.N.Y., 2002); 21 U.S.C. § 355(j)(4)(B)(iii).

1222 *Mylan Pharmaceuticals, Inc. v. Thompson*, 268 F.3d 1323, 1327 (Fed. Cir. 2001), *cert denied* (holding neither the patent laws nor the Hatch-Waxman amendments permitted a private right of action to delist a patent from the Orange Book).

1223 *In re Buspirone Patent Litigation*, 185 F. Supp. 2d 340, 363 (S.D.N.Y., 2002).

1224 *Novo Nordisk A/S v. Caraco Pharmaceutical Laboratories, Ltd.*, 601 F.3d 1359 (Fed. Cir. 2010).

1225 21 U.S.C. § 355(j)(5)(C)(ii)(I).

1226 *Caraco Pharmaceutical Laboratories, Ltd. v. Novo Nordisk A/S*, 132 S. Ct. 1670, 1688 (U.S. 2012) (holding "[t]he statutory counterclaim we have considered enables courts to resolve patent disputes so that the FDA can fulfill its statutory duty to approve generic drugs that do not infringe patent rights. The text and context of the provision demonstrate that a generic company can employ the counterclaim to challenge a brand's overbroad use code.").

However, the NDA filers can have *thirty months exclusivity* without having to prove anything to anybody. Thus, the minimum of thirty months' delay in the generic entry certainly harmed not only the generics' businesses but also the public's access to the medication at substantially lower prices. Certainly, such a sudden delay must have damaged the generic companies' legal and economic expectations. Some commentators even argued that a reference drug patent holder could keep filing second generation patents for the same basic drug product with the FDA to receive almost unlimited consecutive thirty month stays, since a generic drug manufacturer had few ways to remove the listing until a Supreme Court decision in 2012.[1227] Second generation patents play pivotal roles in enabling these kinds of activities, and the impact will be expected in other countries[1228] that adopt similar patent linkage systems.

b) Pendency of patent applications: Uncertainty

(1) Pendency of patent applications

"*How on earth can this invention be patented?!*" was the question which the author was asked by a researcher about the Pfizer's patent application on the salts of amlodipine,[1229] which ultimately was invalidated. From her question, one may notice two important points. Firstly, she lacked the legal knowledge required to avoid confusing a patent with a patent application, which is often the case for researchers. Secondly, her scientific instinct was correct; thus, she could not understand how that kind of invention could be patented. However, considering that the application was granted by the USPTO and invalidated by the Federal Circuit, no one could have guaranteed whether the application would be granted or rejected.

1227 *Mahn*, 54 Food & Drug L.J. 245, 250-52 (1999) (noting that the examples of such patents were specially coated tablets, new formulations, crystalline forms of the same active ingredient, and variations on the drug delivery technologies; and that broadening the scope of patents which could be listed in the Orange Book, advantages accrued to NDA holders).

1228 Other examples are PMNOC proceeding in Canada, Administrative Action in Portugal and Mexico, similar system in Singapore, Patent certification processes in Australia, Indonesia, HK, and Italy.

1229 U.S. Patent No. 4,876,303 (November 7, 1989, under the title of "Pharmaceutically Acceptable Salts").

The pendency of a patent application, especially one filed by a major player in the pharmaceutical industry such as Pfizer,[1230] can cause researchers or companies to spend time searching and analyzing before they dive into a new field of research. That is to say, the uncertainty and insecurity about the patent ownership for competitors created by the patent pendency play important roles.[1231] Unlike the United States, where the patent office examines the invention regardless of whether the applicant has requested an examination or not, many other jurisdictions, such as Germany,[1232] the United Kingdom,[1233] and Korea[1234] require the applicant to request the substantive examination to proceed with the patent application. Thus, in these jurisdictions, the pendency of a patent application can be even longer and depend upon the decision each applicant makes. In addition, these uncertainties in the pharmaceutical industry can increase given the already increased number of second generation patents derived from the lowered patentability requirements for second generation inventions.

(2) Filing of divisional applications

The number of pending applications can be effectively increased by the filing of continuation applications in the United States or divisional applications.

Divisional applications

An applicant can file a divisional application with respect to subject-matter that does not extend beyond the content of the earlier application as filed.[1235] The date of filing of a divisional application would be that of the earlier, parent application,[1236] as a result of which the period of protection is the same as the parent's. Typically, a patent applicant files a divisional application after the communication from a patent office that an application

1230 She probably was not that much surprised if the application was filed by a small nameless company.
1231 *Somaya*, 38 J. Manage. 1084, 1100 (2012); *Henkel/Jell*, 2009, 1-2.
1232 GPA, Art. 4.
1233 U.K. Patent Act, Art. 18 (Substantive examination and grant or refusal of patent).
1234 Korean Patent Act, Art. 59 (Request for examination of a patent application).
1235 *See e.g.*, EPC Art. 76 (1).
1236 *See e.g.*, EPC Art. 76 (2).

covers more than a single general inventive concept.[1237] However, a patentee can also file a divisional application without a patent office's requirement. Voluntary divisional applications have been exploited to ward off a rejection, which has increased the incidence of double patenting.[1238] As the European Commission clearly pointed out, voluntary divisional patent application was a legitimate way of splitting an (initial) parent application, and could not extend the content of the original application nor the protection period.[1239]

Arguable abuse of procedural possibility

The possible problem appears to reside in the increase number of pending patent applications. This could also extend the examination period, as the examination of divisional applications continues even after the parent application's withdrawal or revocation, which, under certain conditions, could add to legal uncertainty for generic companies.[1240] This is particularly troublesome, since divisional applications are often filed at a late stage in the parent application, even though the late filing can arise from a change in the applicant's interests to another subject matter disclosed in the parent patent application.[1241]

In *Napp Pharmaceuticals v. Ratiopharm*, where there were "no less than nine divisional stemming from the original application,"[1242] Jacob LJ pointed out that, since each divisional application would stand or fall on its own merits, and each application could enforce its own right, the clutch of divisionals was likely to make it more difficult for the third parties to assess the position.[1243] He even noted that it was questionable whether this voluntary aspect of the divisional system should continue to be permitted.[1244]

Another interesting case involving divisional application was *Ratiopharm v. Pfizer* in Italy in 2012, where Pfizer was sanctioned with a more than 10 million Euro fine for alleged abuses of the patent system in violation of Art. 102 of the Treaty on the Functioning of the European Union

---

1237 *See e.g.*, EPC Art. 82.
1238 *Germinario*, IIC 2011, 387, 387.
1239 *DG Competition*, 2009, 201.
1240 *DG Competition*, 2009, 201.
1241 *Günzel*, GRUR Int 2008, 644, 644-65.
1242 *Napp Pharmaceuticals v. Ratiopharm* [2009] EWCA Civ 252.
1243 *Napp Pharmaceuticals v. Ratiopharm* [2009] EWCA Civ 252, paras 11-12.
1244 *Napp Pharmaceuticals v. Ratiopharm* [2009] EWCA Civ 252, para 12; *cf.* EPC Rule 36(1) (introducing the time limit for voluntary filing a divisional application).

("TFEU"),[1245] which was later annulled.[1246] In this case, Pfizer filed applications in 1997 for SPCs in all European countries except Italy. Thus, it was expected that the patent term would expire in July 2001 for other countries and in September 2009 in Italy.[1247] Pfizer filed a divisional application of the parent patent before the EPO in 2002, which was granted in 2009 and which was translated and validated only in Italy in June 2009,[1248] but was revoked in October 2010.[1249] Based on this divisional application, Pfizer applied for and received an SPC in Italy in July 2011,[1250] although it was also withdrawn according to the revocation of the patent.[1251] The Competition Authority found that Pfizer abused its dominant position by blocking or delaying market access to generics based on these activities. This case was different from the *AstraZeneca* decision of the CJEU, where the conduct in question was the submission of misleading information to the patent offices, not the use of the patent regime as such.[1252] Later, the decision was annulled by the Court, mainly because the Competition Authority failed to prove "a clear exclusionary intent based on a *quid pluris* as opposed to the mere summation of behaviours regarded as legitimate according to the administrative and judicial system."[1253] However, seeking a divisional application can be regarded as an abuse of procedure under certain circumstances, at least by competition authorities.

1245 *Ratiopharm v. Pfizer*, Italian Competition Authority, p23194, Jan 11, 2012.

1246 *Pfizer v. Italian Competition Authority et al.*, Regional Administrative Court for Latium, Case No. 07467/2012, Sept. 3, 2012.

1247 *Ratiopharm v. Pfizer*, Italian Competition Authority, p23194, Jan 11, 2012, para 73.

1248 *Ratiopharm v. Pfizer*, Italian Competition Authority, p23194, Jan 11, 2012, paras 79-81.

1249 *Ratiopharm v. Pfizer*, Italian Competition Authority, p23194, Jan 11, 2012, para 96.

1250 *Ratiopharm v. Pfizer,* Italian Competition Authority, p23194, Jan 11, 2012, para 81.

1251 *Ratiopharm v. Pfizer,* Italian Competition Authority, p23194, Jan 11, 2012, para 96.

1252 Case C-457/10, *AstraZeneca AB v. European Commission,* 2012.

1253 *Pfizer v. Italian Competition Authority et al.*, Regional Administrative Court for Latium, Case N. 07467/2012, Sept. 3, 2012., para 4.1. (appealed to the Italian Council of State (Italy's highest administrative court).

An attempt to adjust this phenomenon by the USPTO

In 2007, the USPTO proposed two regulations that would limit the chances of filing further patent applications. Specifically, an applicant would be permitted to file only two continuation applications and one request for continued examination per application family.[1254] These rules were challenged, and the District Court held that the rules were void because they substantively altered the existing law.[1255] On appeal, the Federal Circuit held that the rules were procedural in nature and within the scope of the USPTO's rulemaking authority.[1256] The challengers filed a petition for rehearing *en banc*, which was granted.[1257] Ultimately, however, the USPTO announced that it would rescind the proposed rules due to vehement opposition from patent applicants, who felt that the rules unduly restricted their capacity to protect their IPs.[1258]

Rule 36 EPC

This problem was also acknowledged by the BOA,[1259] especially in a case where the application under the appeal was the third one in a sequence A1, A2, and A3 of divisional applications, each divided from its predecessor and stemming from a root (originating) application A0.[1260] Based on the Art. 76(1) and Rule 25 of EPC 1973 related to the divisional application, the BOA held that sequences of divisional applications each containing the same broad disclosures of the original patent application with unamended description could be pending for up to twenty years. The BOA could not see any proper reason to impose an additional requirement.[1261] However, the BOA found this practice unsatisfactory and noted that, "It appears that what applicants consider a legitimate exploitation of the procedural possibilities

1254 *Tafas v. Dudas*, 541 F.Supp.2d 805 (E.D.Va.,2008).
1255 *Tafas v. Dudas*, 541 F.Supp.2d 805, 817 (E.D.Va.,2008).
1256 *Tafas v. Doll*, 559 F.3d 1345, 1364-65 (Fed. Cir. 2009).
1257 *Tafas v. Doll*, 328 Fed.Appx. 658 (Fed. Cir. 2009).
1258 USPTO, USPTO Press Release #09-21 (Oct. 8, 2009), available at: http://www.uspto.gov/news/09_21.jsp
(Last accessed on December 20, 2013).
1259 *Astropower/Divisional*, G1/05 (2007); *Seiko/Sequences of Divisionals*, G1/06 (2007) (since similar sets of questions had been referred to the EBA and two proceedings were consolidated, "G1/05" is only referred).
1260 *Seiko/Sequences of Divisionals*, G1/06 (2007).
1261 *Astropower/Divisional*, G1/05 (2007), paras 13.3- 13.5.

afforded by the EPC, others consider an abuse in relation to the law as they think it ought to be rather than as it is."[1262]

The BOA considered this an issue of legal security for third parties, and recommended that the legislator consider this issue while mentioning some administrative measures.[1263] As Teschemacher points out, "the lesson should be clear, i.e. the more speedily examining divisions deal with divisional applications, the less the possibilities for abuse are."[1264] These views seemed to be reflected in Rule 36 of EPC 2000 in shortening the time span for filing a divisional application, namely, all divisionals must be filed within 24 months from either the issuance of the first communication from the examining division or the issuance of a lack of unity objection.[1265] Considering the still increasing numbers of divisionals and the continuing complaints of the users, above Rule 36 is de facto abandoned,[1266] however, a new Rule 38(4) EPC is instead provided with effect from April 1, 2014, i.e. imposing additional fee for second (or subsequent) generation divisional applications.

The legal uncertainty and difficulty of assessing the third parties' positions through the pendency of patent applications are certainly the cause of anxiety. This phenomenon could be amplified by the increased number of second generation patent applications and patents.

1262 *Astropower/Divisional*, G1/05 (2007), para 13.5.

1263 *Astropower/Divisional*, G1/05 (2007), para 13.5 (further mentioning administrative measures, such as giving priority to the examination of divisional applications and bundling and speedily deciding co-pending divisional, in order to minimize the possibility for applicants to keep the subject-matter alive).

1264 *Teschemacher*, IIC 2007, 703, 706.

1265 EPC 2000 Rule 36 [European divisional applications]
"(1) The applicant may file a divisional application relating to any pending earlier European patent application, provided that: (a) the divisional application is filed before the expiry of a time limit of twenty-four months from the Examining Division's first communication in respect of the earliest application for which a communication has been issued, or (b) the divisional application is filed before the expiry of a time limit of twenty-four months from any communication in which the Examining Division has objected that the earlier application does not meet the requirements of Article 82, provided it was raising that specific objection for the first time.".

1266 EPC 2000 Rule 38(4) EPC
"(4) The Rules relating to Fees may provide for an additional fee as part of the filing fee in the case of a divisional application filed in respect of any earlier application which is itself a divisional application."

c) Active movement of the market to new products

In general, once a patent on a product expires, consumers can choose to buy the products at a price lowered by the competition.[1267] Reformulation of products hardly hampers competition in most other markets, since consumers who decide whether the "improved product" deserves a higher price can simply buy a competing product instead.[1268] In the pharmaceutical market, however, the consumers choosing the product (physicians) do not have to pay for it, and those who have to pay for it, the patients or insures, do not choose it.[1269] Even though spending on direct-to-consumer advertisement has been reported as continuing to increase,[1270] the main interaction in this market is between the health care funder and the pharmaceutical industry.[1271] These circumstances may lead this market to suffer from a significant market failure,[1272] especially on new products based on second generation patents.

Efforts to move the market to products covered by second generation patents

In the late 1960s, Kefauver argued that the pharmaceutical industry had made a huge expenditure on marketing and promoting drugs, which was reflected

1267 *Scherer/Ross*, 1990, 624.

1268 *Shadowen/Leffler/Lukens*, IIC 2011, 698, 700.

1269 See subsection III.A.2.b); *see also McGuire/Drummond/Rutten*, 2004, 130-31 (noting "The clinician, acting as the agent for the patient, does not bear full, if any, financial responsibility for the purchase and may be affected by promotional activities of the companies."); *Shadowen/Leffler/Lukens*, IIC 2011, 698, 700; *Kefauver*, 1966, 29 (also noting this peculiar market structure is the reason the drug industry is particularly susceptible to monopoly control).

1270 *Donohue/Cevasco/Rosenthal*, 357 New Eng. J. Med. 673, 677-80 (2007); *Gilbody/Wilson/Watt*, 14 Quality & Safety in Health Care 246, 246 (2005); *United States General Accountability Office*, 2008, 1.

1271 *McGuire/Drummond/Rutten*, 2004, 131.

1272 *Shadowen/Leffler/Lukens*, IIC 2011, 698, 700.

in turn in the prices thereof.[1273] This argument continues to be made.[1274] For example, companies spend money on aggressive promotion of new versions of old drugs before the date of the basic patent expires.[1275] The drug makers typically bring a newly named drug for the same condition at the end of the basic patent's market exclusivity and then launch a huge promotional campaign to convert users to the new drug.[1276] One commentator argues that the pharmaceutical industry is famous for its superior ability to inform physicians about the results of clinical trials.[1277] When the physicians are persuaded to switch their patients to the new versions, such conversion efforts could protect the drug maker from market share erosion after the date of generic entry.[1278] This in turn will result in substantially elevated costs, both directly through their own relatively high prices and indirectly by reducing access to generics.[1279]

Example of Nexium®

One of the most telling stories is the case of AstraZeneca's "purple pill." After its glittering success with racemic Omeprazole (Prilosec®) and shortly before the patent on Omeprazole was about to expire, the company commenced a massive and unprecedented advertising campaign to persuade patients and doctors to move from Prilosec® to Nexium®.[1280] To promote this switch, AstraZeneca priced Nexium® a bit lower than Prilosec®, gave discounts, distributed free samples to doctors, and even offered coupons in newspapers, all of which cost the company half a billion dollars in 2001

1273 *Kefauver*, 1966, 68-97.

1274 *United States General Accounting Office*, 2002, 3 (reporting "[p]harmaceutical companies spend more on research and development initiatives than on all drug promotional activities, including [direct-to-consumer] advertising."); *Gagnon/ Lexchin*, 5 PLOS Med. 29, 32 (2008) (Based on the estimate derived from a research comparing the data from two market research companies, namely, IMS and CAM, *Gagnon* and *Lexchin* argued that "it appears that pharmaceutical companies spend almost twice as much on promotion as they do on R&D", which was contrary to the industry's claim).

1275 *NIHCM*, 2002, 18; *Angell*, 2004, 77; *Harris*, The Wall Street Journal, June 6, 2002; *Hall*, The New York Times, March 11, 2001.

1276 Because of the high loyalty of patients and doctors (see subsection III.A.2.c)), fiercer promotional activity is required to convert.

1277 *See e.g., Privitera,* 68 Epilepsy Res. 52, 56 (2006).

1278 *NIHCM*, 2002, 4, 18.

1279 *NIHCM*, 2002, 4.

1280 *Angell*, 2004, 77; *Harris*, The Wall Street Journal, June 6, 2002.

alone.[1281] Again, AstraZeneca basically cut Prilosec® in half, though not without difficulty. The only important question was whether the new drug would be better than the old. The truth is that the new version is little better or even different.[1282]

This is also a good example of a phenomenon called "chiral-switch," which is often observed in chiral drugs that are already approved as a mixture of optical isomers that have been reevaluated, redeveloped and launched later as a single enantiomer.[1283] This is the line extension of established clinically effective and commercially profitable drugs, which provides a strategy to extend the profitable life of drugs, may result in extended patent protection, and may give an advantage against generic competition.[1284] Obviously, whether one may get a patent on the enantiomer will substantially affect profitability.[1285] It is axiomatic that AstraZeneca would not have invested in switching to S-omeprazole without patent protection. Based on the litigation and settlements in the United States and the appeals in Europe, the generic version of Nexium® seems to be available in some European countries after the ten-year regulatory exclusivity[1286] and will be available in 2014 in the American market at the earliest after the patent expires.[1287] Even if the patent were ultimately invalidated, thanks to the lowered patentability requirements and the patents granted as the result thereof, AstraZeneca suc-

1281 *Angell*, 2004, 77-78; *Harris*, The Wall Street Journal, June 6, 2002.

1282 *Harris*, The Wall Street Journal, June 6, 2002.

1283 *Agranat/Caner*, 4 Drug Discov. Today 313, 313 (1999); *Caldwell*, 16 Hum. Psychopharm. S67, S69-S70 (2001); *Tucker*, 355 Lancet 1085, 1085 (2000); *cf. Pifferi/Perucca*, 20 Eur. J. Drug Metab. Ph. 15, 24 (1995) (arguing these 'chiral switch' can be justified not only in terms of technological innovation and marketing appeal but also, in terms of sound scientific motivations. Otherwise, they warned there would be a clear risk to divert a significant proportion of investment from more innovative research and from areas which are in particular need of therapeutic breakthroughs.).

1284 *Tucker*, 355 Lancet 1085, 1085 (2000); *Hutt/Valentová*, 50 Acta Facultatis Pharmaceuticae Universitatis Comenianae 7, 15 (2003); *BGH/Escitalopram*, GRUR 2010, 123, 126.

1285 *Hutt/Valentová*, 50 Acta Facultatis Pharmaceuticae Universitatis Comenianae 7, 15 (2003).

1286 For example, http://www.shop-apotheke.com/arzneimittel/6456801/esomeprazol-ratiopharm-40mg-hartkapseln.htm?know=search%3Aesomeprazole~. (Last accessed on December 20, 2013).

1287 See subsection V.A.1.b).

cessfully delayed the launches of generic versions for a good number of years.

Example of Clarinex®

Another famous example is the story of Clarinex®, which is a repeat of the Nexium® story. Clarinex®, the metabolite of Claritin® of Schering-Plough successfully replaced its parent drug before its patent expired, thanks in large part to the massive promotional campaign that made the brand ubiquitous.[1288] As Angell properly noted, Clarinex was approved for additional use, i.e. indoor allergies, "only because the company decided to test it for that use. If they had tested Claritin [the parent drug] for indoor allergies, it would undoubtedly have been the same as Clarinex – because it is the same."[1289]

The scope of the patent on enantiomer does not cover the racemate. Thus, generic companies can principally sell the racemate form. However, if the whole market moves to the enantiomers due to the efforts of the company, generics which include the "old" racemate form, are seen as "outdated" or perceived as "less effective" even if no actual benefit results. This market switch to the new version, in turn, is very useful for the innovating company in extending patent exclusivity.

d) Along with very specific patents on the secondary products

Life cycle management strategy for maximizing the period of exclusivity includes a complex combination of patents, which are sometimes too specific and hard to invalidate. The narrow scope of second generation patents often provides ineffective protection, since their limited scope allows generic manufacturers to design around the patent and launch the generic version without infringing the patents.[1290] In addition, these second generation patents are often challenged with regard to validity over their own basic patent disclosures. On the other hand, once the patentee overcomes the challenge, some of these incredibly specific scopes can be extremely valuable in stopping generic entries.

1288 *Angell*, 2004, 78.
1289 *Angell*, 2004, 78-79.
1290 *Roin*, 87 Tex. L. Rev. 503, 548 (2009).

There is a tension between regulatory requirement and patent infringement for generic products. On the one hand, to meet the regulatory requirement, i.e. bioequivalency of the generic version, the product should be as close to the reference drug as possible, since the similarity to the reference drug really matters in the market place. Namely, a generic drug maker may have marketing approval by showing that their versions are the same dosage form, contain the same dose and the same chemical form, and are equivalents of the innovator's drug.[1291] Thus, they will likely copy the reference product exactly to avoid the expense and time of clinical trials required by the FDA for an even slightly different version.[1292] In other words, some slight change in dosage form, route of administration, strength, or the like, which can be normally covered by second generation patents, would most likely trigger clinical trials.[1293]

On the other hand, to avoid a patent infringement, the same generics should be as different as possible. Thus, because the patent covering the new version of a product is too specific to avoid it and survived after the validity challenge, the generic manufacturers will be hard pressed to bring the generic versions to market. One of the most specific claims would be the one claiming certain pharmacokinetic parameters related to the formulation.[1294] In the case of the European Patent No EP0973527, covering the "Extended release formulations of clarithromycin,"[1295] claim 1 is as follows:

1291 *Rosenbaum*, 2011, 195-198 (further explaining the *bioavailability* of a dosage form is the rate, and extent to which, the drug reaches the systemic circulation; *bioequivalence* is a special type of relative bioavailability; and two or more products would be regarded as *bioequivalent* when it is shown that the products have essentially the same bioavailability.).

1292 *Scherer*, 351 New Eng. J. Med. 927, 927 (2004) (noting "[d]rug patents provide particularly strong protection against competition from other companies because even a slightly different molecular variant must undergo the full panoply of clinical tests required by the FDA"); *Voet,* 2011, 62-63.

1293 *See e.g.*, 21 U.S.C. § 505(b)(2) (this application procedure also allows a company to rely, at least in part, on the FDA's finding of safety and/or efficacy for the reference drug, and to save money and time).

1294 *Grubb/Thomsen*, 2010, 268.

1295 European Patent No. EP0973527 (B1) (November 5, 2003, under the title of "Extended release formulations of clarithromycin").

1. A pharmaceutical composition for extended release of clarithromycin in the gastrointestinal tract, to be administered orally, comprising clarithromycin and a pharmaceutically acceptable, hydrophilic, water-soluble polymer,
   which releases clarithromycin so that after a regimen of a single 1000 mg dose on day 1 and a multiple dose regimen of 1000 mg on days 3, 4 and 5, the maximum plasma concentration is reached after 6.9 ± 3.3 hours, and the area under the plasma concentration time curve 0-24 hours is 40.2 ± 13.8 μg·h/mL, or
   which releases clarithromycin so that after a single 500 mg dose, the area under the plasma concentration time curve 0-∞ is 15.0 ± 6.5 μg·h/mL.

The specificity of the claim is apparent, i.e., claim 1 claims the composition of the formulation, its dosage regime, and the pharmacokinetic profiles after the administration of the formulation, such as C_{max}, T_{max},[1296] and AUC[1297]. Since pharmacokinetics includes the study of the mechanisms of absorption and distribution of an administered drug, and the like, if a patent covers not only the composition of the formulation but also what the body does to the drug, it will be very difficult to design around. Thus, once the market is moved to this second generation product, the generic drug of the older version will not sell well, and the launch of the generic of the new version should be postponed until the second generation patents expire. At this point, one clear option for the generic company to launch its product would again be trying to invalidate the second generation patents through litigation.[1298]

4. Analysis and conclusion

Life cycle management or evergreening has been discussed in this section especially in respect of whether it can unfairly hinder a generic's market entry. Such tactics can be deployed on the basis of second generation patents. However, contrary to the prevailing perception, not all kinds of selection inventions can prevent entrance of a generic version once the basic patent expires. To the extent that second generation patents can prevent the entry of generics, a second generation patent granted thanks to the relaxed patentability requirement can prevent the marketing of generics for another some years. The argument on the purposely delayed filing of second generation patent applications to delay the entry of generics was shown not to be justified.

1296 A "C_{max}" is the peak plasma concentration of a drug after its administration, and a "T_{max}" is the time at which the peak plasma concentration of a drug occurs, *see Rosenbaum*, 2011, 164-195.

1297 An "AUC" is a measure of the body's exposure to the drug, and proportional to the effective dose, *see Rosenbaum*, 2011, 196.

1298 See subsection V.A.1.c).

Many serious concerns were found in other fields. The pendency of patent applications on second generation inventions would create much increased legal uncertainty and make it more difficult for the generic companies to assess their positions and legal security. Moreover, the active market shift to the newer version of the product based on second generation patents, along with the very specific scope thereof could make the market for generics unattractive. This is possible with the specificities of the pharmaceutical markets, such as high loyalty, disconnection between the decision-makers and buyers, and the like. In addition, although the case would be limited to the United States, the new list up in the Orange Book could seriously delay generic entry.

E. Summary and conclusion

Lowered patentability requirements on second generation inventions naturally increases the number of second generation patents.[1299] In particular, the relaxed novelty requirement has led to concerns about the patent disclosure depending on the language, reducing the examination of patentability *de facto* to the examination of novelty, and other potential concerns about the applications of disclosure requirements in other fields of patent law. This greatly increased number of second generation patents has amplified the patent exclusivities, thereby creating a more complicated and uncertain landscape. This has also caused companies to incur more costs in their search for the freedom to operate, in the process of obtaining second generation patents, and in the litigation and invalidation of such patents. The relaxed patentability requirements could be one of the reasons why basic patentees greatly increased the spending attributable to line extensions and why short-term priorities encourage marginal inventions that provide more reliable returns on investment at the expense of major changes.[1300] Eventually, the market becomes flooded with second generation products,[1301] which results in more imitative research and fewer breakthroughs and drugs[1302] and which hinders real pharmaceutical innovation and could threaten health.

1299 *Thomas*, 52 Am. U. L. Rev. 771, 773 (2003).
1300 *Munos*, 8 Nat. Rev. Drug Discov. 959, 966 (2009).
1301 *NIHCM*, 2002, 18-19.
1302 *Munos*, 8 Nat. Rev. Drug Discov. 959, 966 (2009).

The increased number of marginal patents with the case law involving the patent term extensions on second generation patents seems to promote more work on the second generation inventions rather than on the basic inventions. Namely, patent term extensions seem to be granted based on the extent to which, if they are patented, they will be distinctive from the basic substances and can enjoy the extensions of terms.[1303] In the end, after the patent term and the SPC of the basic patent, which is desirable, many additional years of patent term on the second generation invention can be obtained. In addition, unlike other patent term extension systems, the calculation system of SPC seems to penalize even the basic inventions, the R&D for which takes longer.[1304] In contrast, since the disclosure requirement does not seem to be lower, there is little influence on the breadth of the second generation patents.

The implications on the competition in the industry were also discussed. Firstly, contrary to the dominant perception, there are fewer cases in which the exploitation of the basic patent was held to infringe the second generation patents. Secondly, only to the extent that second generation patents can prevent a generic's entry can second generation patents stop the marketing of generics for additional periods of years. Thirdly, the common argument on the purposely delayed filing of second generation patent applications was shown to have no merit.

Serious concerns were found in other areas. The automatic thirty-month stay and new list up in the Orange Book in the United States could seriously delay generic entry. The pendency of patent applications on second generation inventions increases legal uncertainty and makes it difficult for the generic companies to assess their legal security. Moreover, the active movement of the market to the new version of the product based on second generation patents, along with the very specific scope thereof, can make the market unattractive for generics.

1303 See subsectionV.C.2..

1304 See *supra* 1173 -1175 and accompanying texts.

VI. PROPOSALS

In the literature on economics, particular emphasis has been placed on the best way to design optimal patent policies.[1305] Much debate about the patent system has focused on the trade-off between the dynamic benefits of innovation and the static costs of monopoly power given to the innovators as rewards.[1306] The status costs are generally measured by "deadweight loss", which is the value of inventions that would be under-used, because a patentee would charge a monopoly price. Consequently, only those buyers willing and financially able to pay the monopoly price could use the inventions.[1307] However, overprotecting intellectual property is as harmful as underprotecting it,[1308] as Kozinski J noted:

> "Creativity is impossible without a rich public domain. Nothing today, likely nothing since we tamed fire, is genuinely new: Culture, like science and technology, grows by accretion, each new creator building on the works of those who came before. Overprotection stifles the very creative forces it's supposed to nurture."[1309]

There has also been a tension between providing strong patent rights to encourage break-through innovations, thereby possibly discouraging the de-

1305 *Luski/Wettstein*, 1 Probl. Perspect. Manage. 31, 31 (2004).

1306 *Gilbert/Shapiro*, 21 RAND J. Econ. 106, 106 (1990); *Arrow*, 1962; *Kamien/Schwartz*, 1982, 195 (noting according to the increase of the reward for innovation, total expected expenditure of participants is raised collectively and increase the expected appearance of the innovation); *Svatos*, 13 Soc. Philos. Policy 113, 119 (1996); *Scherer/Ross*, 1990, 624; *O'Donoghue*, 29 RAND J. Econ. 654, 658 (1998).

1307 *See e.g.*: *Friebel et al.*, 2006, 23.

1308 *White v. Samsung Electronics America, Inc.*, 989 F.2d 1512, 1513 (9th Cir. 1993).

1309 *White v. Samsung Electronics America, Inc.*, 989 F.2d 1512, 1513 (9th Cir. 1993) (Kozinski, J. dissenting); *see also Gordon*, 102 Yale L. J. 1533, 1556-57 (1993); *Matutes/Regibeau/Rockett*, 27 RAND J. Econ. 60, 78-80 (1996) (arguing that it should be expected that the patentee would effectively be granted exclusive rights to the applications of a basic discovery and also could acquire protection on applications which they had not yet worked out.).

velopment of subsequent improvements.[1310] And balancing between two inventors has also been an important issue,[1311] as noted by Lord Mansfield in 1785.[1312]

This tension exists because we live in active investment climates in which companies invest to improve each other's products/innovations in various ways. However, it is not easy to balance the rights of all concerned. For example, if we do not provide broad enough protection to the first innovations, we will hamper the incentive to create in the first place. However, if we provide complete exclusivity to the first generation innovations, we will stifle R&D by second generation inventors.[1313] However, as discussed so far, more weight should be given to the basic inventions in the pharmaceutical industry, which can bring more NMEs to the public. As instruments to this end, many scholars have considered the trade-off among patent breadth, length, and patentability requirements, and so on.[1314] This chapter will present the arguments on each instrument by scholars, which will be followed by the practical proposals on the instruments for pharmaceutical inventions.

1310 *Jaffe/Lerner*, 2004, 50; *Scotchmer*, 5 J. Econ. Perspect. 29-41 (1991); *Friebel et al.*, 2006, 27; *Heller/Eisenberg*, 280 Science 698 (1998); *Merges/Nelson*, 90 Colum. L. Rev. 839, 916 (1990); *Merges/Nelson*, 25 J. Econ. Behav. Organ. 1, 20-23 (1994); *cf. Bessen/Maskin,* 40 RAND J. Econ. 611 (2009) (arguing even patent would inhibit the innovation in complementary and sequential innovation).

1311 *Lemley*, 75 Tex. L. Rev. 989, 989-990 (1997).

1312 *Sayre v. Moore,* 1 East 361 n.(b), 102 Eng. Rep. 139, 140 n.(b) (K.B.1785), cited in *Sony Corp. of Am. v. Universal City Studios, Inc.,*_464 U.S. 417, 480 n. 33 (1984). (on a copyright case against improved navigational chart noting "we must take care to guard against two extremes equally prejudicial; the one, that men of ability, who have employed their time for the service of the community, may not be deprived of their just merits, and the reward of their ingenuity and labour; the other, that the world may not be deprived of improvements, nor the progress of the arts be retarded.").

1313 *Lemley*, 75 Tex. L. Rev. 989, 990 (1997); *Merges/Nelson*, 90 Colum. L. Rev. 839, 871-79 (1990); *see also Sony Corp. of Am. v. Universal City Studios, Inc.,*_464 U.S. 417, 480 n. 33 (1984) in the copyright context, *supra* 1312 .

1314 *See e.g., Friebel et al.,* 2006, 21-23.

A. Introduction

In the art of pharmaceutical sciences, the first issue between the two problems in this dissertation, the dearth of NMEs and the drastic increase of second generation inventions, has generally been of interest. While it has not been easy to overcome or even suggest overcoming the dearth of NMEs, some scholars have suggested that the key would be to increase substantially the number and quality of innovative, cost-effective new medicines, without incurring unsustainable R&D costs.[1315] To do so, many scholars have proposed transiting from "me-too" or "me-slightly better" drugs to highly innovative medicines and re-focusing resources such as money and talent on discovery research.[1316] One chief officer of a pharmaceutical company that has been facing revenue loss announced that the company needed to rely much more on new medicines.[1317] The U.S. government has also attempted to overcome the crisis created by a lack of new medications by implementing the so-called "wild card patent term extension" but this proposal was finally rejected.[1318] How, then, can the patent regime help to bring more new basic medicines to the public?

Providing general patent policy recommendations is difficult, since the framework is dynamic and complicated in nature, and the strategic behaviour of many firms is involved. However, in general, as profit opportunities have expanded, firms have competed to exploit them by increasing R&D investment. [1319] Patents create incentives and chances to explore the known or unknown possibilities that may exist within the scope of the patent.[1320] Prospect theory is in the same vein. According to Kitch's prospect theory, the broad prospect of intellectual property can allocate better resources and

---

1315 *Paul, et al.*, 9 Nat. Rev. Drug Discov. 203, 203 (2010) (noting "our parametric analyses further reveal where the greatest improvements in productivity must occur.").

1316 *Paul, et al.*, 9 Nat. Rev. Drug Discov. 203, 213 (2010).
The recommendations from the scientific point of view were much more improvements in understanding of human (disease) biology, and fostering scientific creativity and being opportunistic for serendipitous scientific and medical findings.

1317 *Armstrong*, Bloomberg, April 12, 2012.

1318 Project Bioshield II Act of 2005. S. 975, 109th Congress (2005–2006); *See supra* 978 and accompanying texts.

1319 *Scherer*, 20 Health Affair. 216, 220 (2001).

1320 *Domeij*, 2000, 90.

activities to innovations once they are made.[1321] This theory recognizes that many patents appear at the beginning of the process that starts with conception and ends with innovation.[1322] Namely, this theory envisages inventions as something made by a single firm as only the first step in a long and expensive process of innovation.[1323] There is always pressure to file a patent application as early as possible, since competition is fierce. Moreover, the patent system only requires something that works and not the end product that is finished and commercially available.[1324] Even though this theory attracts criticism, such as limitation to the scope of patents[1325] and dense thickets of intersecting, overlapping, and cross-blocking patents, the benefits of this theory fit the pharmaceutical industry best.[1326] One thing is clear: Without patent protection, the threat of competition hampers investment in R&D.[1327]

In addition, the evidence that companies terminate many projects on commercial grounds suggests that many more drug candidates may be developed if the markets can be made more economically attractive.[1328] In the following sections, the way to help to increase the new medications and decrease the second generation inventions in the pharmaceutical industry will be analyzed and recommendations will be made. Before that the discussion will focus on the main issues, and the nature and value of selection inventions will be analysed.

1321 *Kitch*, 20 J. Law Econ. 265, 276-280 (1977) (based on Schumpeterian tradition that there is not sufficient incentive to innovate in market place and prospect of realizing monopoly profits would provide with the incentive for innovation); *See also Kamien/Schwartz*, 1982, 189-90 (noting monopolist would make an efficient allocation of fixed level of resources); *Burk/Lemley*, 54 Case W. Res. L. Rev. 691, 726-727 (2003).

1322 *Kitch*, 20 J. Law Econ. 265, 283 (1977).

1323 *Burk/Lemley*, 89 Va. L. Rev. 1575, 1615 (2003).

1324 *Kitch*, 20 J. Law Econ. 265, 270-71 (1977).

1325 *Merges*, 76 Cal. L. R. 803, 840-42 (1988).

1326 *Burk/Lemley*, 54 Case W. Res. L. Rev. 691, 726-728 (2003).

1327 *Machlup*, 1958, 36-37.

1328 *Cockburn*, 2006, 26.

B. Nature of selection inventions

1. Different natures of selection inventions

The definition of each selection invention was provided in chapter 2. Here, the nature and value of species selection invention will be further explained in comparison with other selection inventions.

a) Species selection invention

The value of a species selection invention exists in the choice of one compound out of a range of candidates (sometimes millions). A similar situation exists in the invention of a DNA sequence. Apart from the issue of whether a DNA sequence is a patentable subject matter,[1329] the existence thereof in nature, or of a DNA library, including the multitude of DNA sequences, does not automatically render the sequence non-novel, unless the sequence concerned had recognisably been made available.[1330] Like the genus claim, a DNA library of many gene fragments, does not enable a person skilled in the art to *locate* the gene in question.

In *Association for Molecular Pathology v. U.S. Patent and Trademark Office*, Bryson J used his leaf analogy to argue that a gene simply isolated from the body cannot be patentable subject matter just as a naturally grown

---

1329 There are some jurisdictions, where the patentable subject matter is mattered on the DNA sequence invention. *See e.g., Association for Molecular Pathology et al. v. Myriad Genetics Inc. et al.* 133 S.Ct. 2107, 2109 (2013) ("A naturally occurring DNA segment is a product of nature and not patent eligible merely because it has been isolated, but cDNA is patent eligible because it is not naturally occurring.").

1330 *Biogen/Alpha interferons*, T301/87, OJ EPO 1990, 335, 351.

leaf cannot be patentable simply because it was snapped from the tree.[1331] To this dissent, the majority argued as follows:

> "With respect, no one could contemplate that snapping a leaf from a tree would be worthy of a patent, whereas isolating genes to provide useful diagnostic tools and medicines is surely what the patent laws are intended to encourage and protect. Snapping a leaf from a tree is a physical separation, easily done by anyone. Creating a new chemical entity is the work of human transformation, requiring skill, knowledge, and effort."[1332]

The majority's opinion seems to differentiate a DNA sequence from a leaf based on the difficulty of isolation and the usefulness of genes. It could have been relatively difficult to isolate a DNA at the time of this invention. However, the separation was already very well known and was not difficult to a person skilled in the art, once he knew the sequence of the DNA. The majority values more highly and differentiates the usefulness of the DNA invention from a leaf, thus arguing that the DNA invention must have been encouraged and protected. In this sense, it would be fair to say that, if a snapped leaf from the whole forest were useful, say to cure breast cancer, which the Myriad's DNA invention tried to diagnose, no one would argue that a patent should not be granted on the leaf. Consequently, the majority appears to distinguish the inventions according to their value and thereby tries to grant a patent to encourage and protect the invention.

The extreme undue burden that would have been necessary to enable a person skilled in the art to locate and to make practical use either of the genetic sequence or of the species compound and the particular beneficial use thereof rendered this type of selection invention novel and/or patentable.

1331 *Association for Molecular Pathology v. U.S. Patent and Trademark Office*, 689 F.3d 1303, 1352 (Fed. Cir. 2012) ("[E]xtracting a gene is akin to snapping a leaf from a tree. Like a gene, a leaf has a natural starting and stopping point. It buds during spring from the same place that it breaks off and falls during autumn. Yet prematurely plucking the leaf would not turn it into a human-made invention. That would remain true if there were minor differences between the plucked leaf and the fallen autumn leaf, unless those differences imparted "markedly different characteristics" to the plucked leaf."), aff'd in part, rev'd in part, *Association for Molecular Pathology et al. v. Myriad Genetics Inc. et al.* 133 S.Ct. 2107 (2013).

1332 *Association for Molecular Pathology v. U.S. Patent and Trademark Office*, 689 F.3d 1303, 1332 (Fed. Cir. 2012), aff'd in part, rev'd in part, *Association for Molecular Pathology et al. v. Myriad Genetics Inc. et al.* 133 S.Ct. 2107 (2013).

b) Other selection inventions

The other selection inventions discussed, i.e. optical isomers, crystalline forms, or metabolites are selected from a much smaller group. The size of a group from which an enantiomer is chosen depends on the number of chiral carbon atoms in the molecule, and the optical isomers can be selected out of two options. Crystalline forms are selected out of a couple of forms,[1333] unless they are a newly synthesized form. Metabolites are also screened out of a couple of substances, which are acquired after analyzing and profiling the sample of the subject who received the parent drug. Thus, the nature of other selection inventions seems to relate more to the difficulty of separation/ isolation from the previous mixtures.

2. Selection inventions from the era of penicillin to the 21th century

a) Early medications and the novelty requirement

Lack of novelty was already the major hurdle that early medications had to overcome to secure patents. One very early case was *aspirin* (acetyl salicylic acid). Patents on it were filed in Germany,[1334] the United States, and the United Kingdom.[1335] However, only the patent[1336] filed in the United States in 1898 managed to survive after an infringement suit in 1909.[1337] Considering that the compound is simple and was already available on the market, the results are not surprising. The cases of early antimicrobial drugs were not much different from that of aspirin. Neither *sulphanilamide,* whose appearance in 1935 foreshadowed the technological change in the drug industry, nor *penicillin,* which was the first antibiotic, was patented.[1338] The for-

---

1333 However, the novelty requirement seems to be higher than other selection inventions.

1334 *Dutfield*, 2009, 18 (noting the German application was granted but rejected later because only processes were patentable and the compound was not new).

1335 *Dutfield*, 2009, 18 (noting the British application was filed in 1898 but invalidated in 1905 in an infringement case based on the lack of novelty).

1336 U.S. Patent No. 644,077 (February 27, 1900, under the title of "acetyl salicylic acid").

1337 *Kuehmsted v. Farbenfabriken of Elberfeld Co.*, 179 F. 701 (7th Cir. 1910).

1338 *Temin*, 10 Bell J. Econ. 429, 435 (1979).

mer was a previously known substance, and the latter was a known natural substance.[1339]

b) "Made available to the public" for the first time

The infringement cases of two patents[1340] on adrenaline[1341] in 1911 appear to be the first to require a court to consider the patentability of a "purified form" of natural products extracted from living organisms.[1342] The decision delivered by the renowned Hand J held that the novelty of such extracts was not destroyed by the fact that it was merely an extracted product without change. Consequently, he upheld the patentability thereof.[1343] More importantly, he further noted,

> "Takamine was the first to make it available for any use by removing it from the other gland-tissue in which it was found, and, while it is of course possible logically to call this a purification of the principle, it became for every practical purpose a new thing commercially and therapeutically."[1344]

Streptomycin was the second antibiotic that came to the market after penicillin and the first to be effective against tuberculosis. In 1948, Streptomycin was covered by two patents. One was granted to the Rutgers Research and Endowment Foundation and was related to methods of extraction and production.[1345] The other one was granted to Merck and covered complex salts

---

1339 *Temin*, 10 Bell J. Econ. 429, 435 (1979); for the penicillin, *see also Dutfield*, 2009, 141 (noting "penicillin was not patented, as aspirin should probably not have been on account of its already being known about"); *American Cyanamid Co. v. F.T.C.,* 363 F.2d 757, 760 (6th Cir. 1966).

1340 U.S. Patent No. 730,176 (June 2, 1903, under the title of "Glandular extract product"); U.S. Patent No. 753,177 (February 23, 1904, under the title of "Glandular extract compound").

1341 This is a hormone produced by adrenal glands and which increases heart rate, constricts blood vessels, dilates air passages and participates in the fight-or-flight response of the sympathetic nervous system.

1342 *Dutfield*, 2009, 108-09.

1343 *Parke-Davis & Co. v. H.K. Mulford Co.*, 189 F. 95, 103 (C.C.N.Y., 1911); reversed in part in Parke-Davis & Co v. H K Mulford & Co, 196 F. 496 (2nd Cir. 1912) (reversed to the extent that the claim didn't have the limitation such as "of product of the suprarenal glands.").

1344 *Parke-Davis & Co. v. H.K. Mulford Co.*, 189 F. 95, 103 (C.C.N.Y., 1911).

1345 U.S. Patent No. 2,449,866 (September 21, 1948, under the title of "streptomycin and the process of preparation").

of streptomycin containing inorganic salts.[1346] Even though streptomycin was also a natural product, the patent claimed to the satisfaction of the examiner that "for the first time streptomycin is available in the form which not only has valuable therapeutic properties but also can be produced, distributed, and administered in a practicable way."[1347] Patents were also granted in 1951 on the invention of *Vitamin* B_{12}, which was indeed the extraction of a pure substance[1348] and in 1955 on the composition containing VtB_{12} and the process to prepare it.[1349] The validity of these patents was attacked. The Appeals Court upheld the validity of the first patent entirely based on the Court's determination that the invention provided the world with a medication for the first time that could successfully treat pernicious anemia without having the unfavourable reaction from the earlier liver extracts, and that the isolated form had not existed in nature.[1350] *In the United States*, therefore, at least a naturally occurring substance either in the composition or in less purified form does not anticipate the claims directed to the pure material.[1351] The patents on the substances isolated or purified from the mixture were granted because they made the medication available to the public for the first time.

In Germany, precedents were established in the *Reichspatentamt*[1352] in the 1920s and 1930s by granting patents on hormones, and were used to consolidate the notion that purified biological products could generally be-

1346 U.S. Patent No. 2,446,102 (July 27, 1948, under the title of "complex salts of streptomycin and process for preparing same"); *Temin*, 10 Bell J. Econ. 429, 436 (1979) (noting "the chemical modifications made to streptomycin to enable it to be purified created a new product and both this new product and the process by which it was made were patentable.").

1347 *Dutfield*, 2009, 23 (citing the words of the U.S. patent No. 2,449,886).

1348 U.S. Patent No. 2,563,794 (August 7, 1951, under the title of "Vitamin B_{12}").

1349 U.S. Patent No. 2,703,302 (March 1, 1955, under the title of "Vitamin B_{12}-active composition and process of preparing same").

1350 *Merck & Co. v. Chase Chemical Co.*, 273 F.Supp. 68, 84 (D.N.J. 1967) (noting "the patentees of the '794 patent have given to the world, for the first time, a medicine that can be used successfully in treating all patients suffering with pernicious anemia, a medicine that is subject to accurate standardization, and avoids the unfavorable reactions of the earlier liver extracts. It did not exist in nature in the form in which the patentees produced it, and nothing in the prior art either suggested or anticipated it.").

1351 *In re Kratz*, 592 F.2d 1169, 1174 (C.C.P.A. 1979); *In re Bergstrom*, 427 F.2d 1394, 1401-02 (C.C.P.A. 1970).

1352 German Imperial Patent Office.

come proprietary.[1353] However, until recent years the important difference from the American practice was that, as in most of continental Europe,[1354] only process patents to manufacture a drug could be granted in Germany.[1355]

3. Analysis and conclusion

The nature of selection inventions is different. Namely, their nature is to locate and characterise one out of numerous, sometimes millions, of candidates. The nature of the rest of the selection inventions exist in their isolation or the separation from the mixture. As discussed, isolated or separated chemical compounds were patented. However, these decisions[1356] were decided a century ago when the pharmaceutical industry was arguably not yet a research-based industry but a manufacturing industry.[1357] The knowledge of the average skilled person in the pharmaceutical art has dramatically increased yearly ever since.[1358] Furthermore, patents were granted to isolated compounds, based mainly on the fact that the compounds *were available for the first time* in the form that could cure the disease therapeutically and commercially.

One may doubt whether subsequent selection inventions have also made something available to the public for the first time. Even if they have, however, the public already had the older versions, which usually were covered by the basic patent. One may also doubt whether it is proper to apply the

---

1353 *Gaudillière*, 24 Hist. Technol. 107, 125 (2008).

1354 For example, the U.K. has interesting history of development, i.e. it prohibited claims to the chemical substance in 1919 and removed this prohibition in 1949. In addition, the Section 4 (7) of UK 1949 Patents Act had stated that a claim to a new substance shall be construed to as not extending to the substance when found in nature.

1355 For example, product patents on pharmaceuticals and chemicals had been granted in Germany from1968, in Japan from 1976, in Switzerland from 1977, and in Italy from 1978 and in Spain and in Portugal from 1992; *See e.g.,ter Meer*, 57 J. Pat. Off. Soc'y 763, 763 (1975) (noting "there have been changes in the German patent law, particularly in the chemical field, in large measure due to the change of the Patent Law in 1967 which abolished the prohibition against the claiming of chemical products, *per se*."); *Nastelski*, IIC 1972, 267, 267.

1356 *See supra* 1340 -1353 and accompanying texts.

1357 *Dutfield*, 2009, 59-60.

1358 *Hansen/Hirsch*, 1997, 51.

patentability requirement of a century ago to the inventions in the present highly developed technological era. One may also doubt whether the absolute product protection afforded by a patent is appropriate for second generation inventions. Usually, the patentability of these inventions was acknowledged because of the difficulty of separation. If the technical contribution to the art were the method of separation of something out of the mixture that already existed and provided the therapeutic contribution to the public, the protection of the method to manufacture the substance would be enough. Some scholars argue that the various second generation patents do not have that much value, because they function only to protect the fundamental innovations, and these scholars even argue that these kinds of activities are obviously be wasteful from a societal point of view.[1359] This is different from species selection inventions that make a new medicine available to the public. More importantly, the difference between species selection invention and the rest is that the former would be the NMEs that could open an entirely new field of second generation inventions and the latter would be IMDs.

Considering the different values of selection inventions and the needs of the society, the proper ways for the patent law to help bring more NMEs to the public will now be discussed.

C. *Proposals on the breadth of patents*

1. Arguments on the breadth of patents

Although it should not be taken for granted that better protection necessarily leads to more innovation,[1360] the allowable breadth of the claims is decisive for the consequences of the patent system,[1361] and is one of the key means to incentivize innovation.[1362] Thus, many arguments have been brought forward regarding the proper scope of the patent to send messages to the industry to help to foster more useful innovations.

1359 *Hopenhayn/Mitchell*, 32 RAND J. Econ. 152, 163 (2001).
1360 *Levin et al.*, 1987 Brookings Paper on Econ. Activity, 783, 787 (1987).
1361 *Lerner*, 25 RAND J. Econ. 319 (1994).
1362 *Scotchmer*, 5 J. Econ. Perspect. 29, 30 (1991).

a) Arguments for a broader patent scope

Many arguments have been brought forward regarding the broader scope of patents. The scope of protection conferred by patents can be broadened to increase rewards for basic inventions.[1363] Many scholars claim that a broader scope in patents would increase the power of the patentee to *exclude competition,* which would lead to more innovations for various reasons here adduced. For example, Kitch argues that broad patent rights were mandatory, basically because enhanced breadth would provide incentives to develop technology by allowing the inventors to appropriate the full benefits of the development.[1364] Harrelson contends that broader and stronger exclusivity must be given, because the underprotection of patent rights would decrease the quantity and quality of new products beneficial to society in the long run.[1365] Along with Klemperer, Gilbert and Shapiro argue that broadening the scope of patents increases the per-period profit for the innovator, because a broader patent protection would allow the innovator to charge a high premium or would prevent competitors from selling close substitutes, respectively.[1366] Green and Scotchmer argue that the broader scope of the patents in sequential innovations would determine the division of profit between them rather than the level of per-period profit.[1367]

Eisenberg and Strandburg also contend that based on a reduction of the strength of patent monopolies, the use of patented invention would increase, however, to put existing technologies into use – i.e., the *investment* itself - would be undermined.[1368] Scotchmer further argues that the patentee of the

1363 *Avorn*, 309 Science 669, 669 (2005).

1364 *Kitch*, 20 J. Law Econ. 265 (1977).

1365 *Harrelson*, 7 Wid. L. Symp. J. 175, 187-88 (2001).

1366 *Gilbert/Shapiro*, 21 RAND J. Econ. 106, (1990) (defining breadth as anything increasing the flow rate of innovator's profits uniformly during the period of protection); *Klemperer*, 21 RAND J. Econ. 113 (1990) (defining breadth as a quality advantage conferred on the patentee); cf. *Green/Scotchmer*, 26 RAND J. Econ. 20 (1995) (arguing that broader patents in the sequential innovations would determine not the level of per-period profit, but the division of profit between them.).

1367 *Green/Scotchmer*, 26 RAND J. Econ. 20 (1995) (defining scope protecting innovator from quality improvements).

1368 *See e.g., Eisenberg*, 56 U. Chi. L. Rev. 1017, 1036-44 (1989); *Strandburg*, 1 UC Irvine L.R.,265, 276 (2011).

original invention will collect a larger share of the profit if second generation products are not patentable.[1369]

Other arguments arising from the nature of intellectual assets provide further support for broader scope of rights. Namely, the broader upstream patents would be *helpful for SMEs*. Lerner argues that this is so, because increasing the patent's scope increases the value of the firm, as the result of which broader patents help to attract capital investment.[1370] In addition, based on Lerner and Merges' report that the allocation of control rights to the smaller parties at the time of licensing increases with its financial health,[1371] one can argue that the broader patent scope can be useful if it confers bargaining power either directly or by facilitating financing that enhances SMEs' bargaining power.

Grady and Alexander also maintain that granting broader patent rights to a nascent invention, which is in early development and can signal many various improvements, would avoid the possibility of races to patent the improvements, but would likely induce a rush to patent the original concepts.[1372] Scotchmer and Chang urge that broad patent protection could provide a necessary spur to further innovation, because it would motivate R&D investment in the initial basic technologies, the stand-alone values of which are less than their subsequent innovations.[1373] O'Donoghue and Friebel *et al.*, claim that to induce a large target innovation, larger rewards for larger innovations or some protection against future innovations must be

1369 *Scotchmer*, 27 RAND J. Econ. 322 (1996); *Chang*, 26 RAND J. Econ. 34, 48-49 (1995) (arguing that broadest protection should be provided not only to those that are very valuable relative to possible improvements, but also those that have very little value relative to the improvements (=which has relatively low stand-alone value)).

1370 *Lerner*, 25 RAND J. Econ. 319, 325-28 (1994) (by noting that the increase in patent scope leads to increase in the firm's valuation).

1371 *Lerner/Merges*, 1997, 27-28.

1372 *Grady/Alexander*, 78 Va. L. Rev. 305, 318 (1992).

1373 *Scotchmer*, 5 J. Econ. Perspect. 29, 31 (1991); *Chang*, 26 RAND J. Econ. 34, 48-49 (1995) (further argued that broadest protection should be provided not only to those that are very valuable relative to possible improvements, but also those which has relatively low stand-alone value because it may also be a breakthrough innovation in the sense that it might generate great spillovers in the form of improvements.).

provided by the patent system.[1374] Acording to O'Donoghue *et al.*, without some leading breadth of patents, the effectiveness of the patent system to promote innovation will be seriously impeded.[1375]

For the *biopharmaceutical field*, Mazzoleni and Nelson believe that granting patents in the biotechnology field, in which there is a long way to go to reach practical applications, has helped spur research specialist firms.[1376] In addition, they contend that a patent holder with a monopoly on the basic innovation will develop the basic innovation and some of the improvements as well,[1377] not only because the original inventors would earn the entire profit from the improvements,[1378] but also because they have more and better (or perhaps the most and best) knowledge of and experience with the basic substances in this sector.[1379] Burk and Lemley distinguish the pharmaceutical industry from other industries, such as the software and most semiconductor industries, in which inventions were characterized by more incremental improvements.[1380] While insisting that those incremental improvements would not be entitled to the broader scope of the protection, they claim that inventions in the pharmaceutical industry should be entitled to it, because innovations in this industry were likely to take the form of discrete new inventions that usually open up an entire field of inquiry.[1381]

b) Arguments against a broader patent scope

To the contrary, Merges and Nelson argue that allowing and enforcing broader patent rights would tend to hinder technical progress, harass the

---

1374 *O'Donoghue*, 1996, 49-50; *See also Friebel et al.,* 2006, 26 (noting that some protection against future innovations should be provided to the basic inventions, for early inventors to fully consider the value of his contribution to future R&D or to allow them to compete with future inventors).

1375 *O'Donoghue/Scotchmer/Thisse*, 7 J. Econ. Manage. Strat. 1, 3 (1998).

1376 *Mazzoleni/Nelson*, 27 Res. Policy, 273, 282 (1998).

1377 *Merges/Nelson*, 90 Colum. L. Rev. 839, 873 (1990).

1378 *Scotchmer*, 5 J. Econ. Perspect. 29, 32-33 (1991) ("under broad patent protection, the incentive for the first innovator to develop a second generation product will be stronger than for an outside firm (provided the first innovator has expertise to develop the new product, and thinks of it), since the first innovator will earn the entire incremental profit.").

1379 *Landes/Posner*, 2003, 330.

1380 *Burk/Lemley*, 89 Va. L. Rev. 1575, 1657 (2003).

1381 *Burk/Lemley*, 89 Va. L. Rev. 1575, 1657 (2003).

competitors out of the field, and cut down diversity and creativity of the development.[1382] Following this, Nelson with Mazzoleni repeat that stronger patent protection might hinder both technological and economic progress in the field of industries, such as semiconductors, computers, telecommunication, and so forth, because it would induce more litigation and increase costs, and it would hinder the entry of new players.[1383]

Barnett even argues that imperfect patent protection would generate as much incentive to develop as those generated by broader patent protections, because it would encourage upstream researchers, who work on research that is relatively far removed from a commercial end product, to collaborate with downstream firms to appropriate at least some of the spillover applications of the patented research.[1384] Landes and Posner are concerned that broad protection might result in an excessive return of the inventor's fixed costs of invention. [1385]

For the biopharmaceutical field, Rai also maintains that patents on early-stage, nascent biopharmaceutical inventions should not be given broad protection because the protection on those inventions is different from the protection on the end-product drugs, and most cumulative innovation in the industry occurs before a drug is produced.[1386] Heller and Eisenberg claim that strengthening IPR would impede and discourage research rather than promote it; the so-called "anticommon problem."[1387] The "anticommon" is characterized by fragmented property rights. Only by aggregating these rights is it possible to make effective use of the property.[1388] To aggregate the fragmented property rights, high search and negotiation costs are necessary to locate and bargain with the many right holders.[1389]

1382 *Merges/Nelson*, 25 J. Econ. Behav. Organ. 1, 20-23 (1994) (however, noting that a strong patent may be essential if the inventor of a new chemical product is to profit from the invention); *Merges/Nelson*, 90 Colum. L. Rev. 839, 843-44 (1990) (noting "[w]ithout extensively reducing the pioneer's incentives, the law should attempt at the margin to favor a competitive environment for improvements, rather than an environment dominated by the pioneer firm").

1383 *Mazzoleni/Nelson*, 27 Res. Policy, 273, 280-83 (1998) (noting also broad and strong patent rights would benefit some industries, though they didn't give separate examples.).

1384 *Barnett*, 37 San Diego L. Rev. 987, 1031-32 (2000).

1385 *Landes/Posner*, 2003, 323.

1386 *Rai*,16 Berkeley Tech. L. J. 813, 818, 836-38 (2001).

1387 *Heller/Eisenberg*, 280 Science 698, 700 (1998).

1388 *Heller*, 111 Harv. L. Rev. 621, 670-72 (1998).

1389 *Burk/Lemley*, 89 Va. L. Rev. 1575, 1611 (2003).

c) Arguments on patent scope with consideration of other relevant factors

Value dependent

While stressing the heterogeneity of innovations, Hopenhayn and Mitchell contend that the courts could give a broader scope of protection to fundamental breakthroughs.[1390] Merges and Nelson seem to admit the argument to grant a broad set of claims for breakthrough innovations. They note that, "since the inventor may have enabled a broad new range of applications, courts reason, it is unfair to limit her to the precise embodiment through which she discovered the broader principle claimed."[1391]

Situation dependent

Patent breadth has an impact on the difficulty and cost of inventing around the patent and, thereby, on the entrance of competitive products onto the market. Taking Bell's invention of the telephone as an example, Grady and Alexander explain as follows: If we were to grant a very narrow protection on it, an incremental improvement would not infringe Bell's patent, and a second generation improver could enjoy not only the revenue derived from the improved portion but also the entire revenue from Bell's basic telephone invention. This kind of system would punish the first innovator and reward only the second, and revenue dissipation at the level of second generation invention would get worse.[1392] On the other hand, with a broad protection, Bell would control all opportunities for developing new communication devices, thereby reducing revenue dissipation at the improvement stage. However, granting such a large reward to Bell, who introduced a nascent and generally crude device to society, would lead to revenue dissipation at the pioneer level of innovation.[1393] Finally, they contend that the courts might reconcile these effects by adjusting patent scope on a case-by-case basis. For example, when the improvement-stage revenue dissipation is serious, it will

1390 *Hopenhayn/Mitchell*, 32 RAND J. Econ. 152, 162-64 (2001) (arguing so in a special setting where the patent authorities can offer a menu of patent types with different lengths and breadths).
1391 *Merges/Nelson*, 90 Colum. L. Rev. 839, 848 (1990); *Hoffman*, 89 Cornell L. Rev. 993, 1041-42 (2004).
1392 *Grady/Alexander*, 78 Va. L. Rev. 305, 307-308 (1992).
1393 *Grady/Alexander*, 78 Va. L. Rev. 305, 307-308, 316-321 (1992).

give broad protection to the original patents, thereby effectively eliminating the possibility of revenue-dissipating rushes to the modifications.[1394]

Landes and Posner point out that the patent system makes no effort to match the degree of patent protection to the variables, such as fixed cost or R&D, ease of inventing around, or the degree of patent protection to create adequate incentives to invest.[1395] Posner insists that the cost of inventing must be compared to the cost of copying in order to determine the optimal patent protection for an inventor, while comparing the software industry where the cost of invention is relatively low with the pharmaceutical industry, where it is very high.[1396]

There is also an interesting suggestion that the patent breadth should be determined by the cost of R&D and the type of invention.[1397] Specifically, when the R&D cost is low, protection of the product should be narrow and protection of the process should be broader. When the R&D cost is high, protection of the product should be high, and the protection of the process innovation should be narrow. However, this argument seems intended to protect process invention more efficiently.[1398]

2. Interim conclusion

Granting broad protection to basic inventions would provide basic inventors with maximum incentives, but could discourage improvements, because the probability of infringing the original patent by an improvement inventor would be higher.[1399] As shown in the previous chapter, many arguments have been advanced for and against a broader scope of patents. Among the argu-

---

1394 *Grady/Alexander*, 78 Va. L. Rev. 305, 318 (1992); *cf. Matutes/Regibeau/Rockett*, 27 RAND J. Econ. 60, 79 (1996).

1395 *Landes/Posner*, 2003, 300.

1396 *Posner*, Sep, 30, 2012.

1397 *Eswaran/Gallini*, 27 RAND J. Econ. 722 (1996).

1398 *Eswaran/Gallini*, 27 RAND J. Econ. 722 (1996).

1399 *Jaffe/Lerner*, 2004, 48-51; *Scotchmer*, 5 J. Econ. Perspect. 29, 30-35 (1991); *Levin et al.*, 1987 Brookings Paper on Econ. Activity, 783, 788 (1987) (noting strong protection of individual achievement may retard the advance of technology, since technological development is often an interactive and cumulative process); *cf. Gilbert/Shapiro*, 21 RAND J. Econ. 106 (1990) (discussing breadth of patent protection in the context of single innovation with hardly focusing on cumulative innovation).

ments against a broader scope of patents, Nelson with Mazzoleni repeat that stronger patent protection might hinder progress, however, they insist that this could happen in certain fields of industry, such as semiconductor, computer, telecommunication,[1400] but not in the field of biopharmaceutical industry. Barnett could have argued so, because he does not address the downstream inventors' incentives.[1401] In other words, even though upstream inventors may try to collaborate with downstream inventors, the downstream inventors will be less willing to collaborate with the upstream inventors, since they have more and better room to research because of the narrower scope of patents on the upstream inventions. Landes' and Posner's concern does not apply to pharmaceuticals, because the fixed costs of pharmaceutical inventions, if they are NMEs, are among the highest in any industries, and because these costs must embrace all of the failures that enabled the product to reach the market.[1402]

There are also specific arguments for the narrow scope of protection for the biopharmaceutical patents. However, Rai's hierarchy given to cumulative inventions is one level higher than the one on which this dissertation focuses; i.e. the early stage invention in the scope of this dissertation is the end-product drug, and the later stage inventions are improvements on that drug. A word about the "anticommon problem" is necessary. The problem with the anticommon theory is not necessarily the scope of the patent but rather the number of rights held by different owners.[1403] Furthermore, Rader Chief J argued in his blistering dissent that this problem just did not happen because of little commercial value of experiments and the increased need for cooperation.[1404] Moreover, there was no empirical research substantiating these alleged concerns.[1405] Finally, since in the field of the pharmaceutical art usually one, not many, basic invention is required to exploit second generation inventions, the IPRs in this art are not that fragmented.

1400 *Mazzoleni/Nelson*, 27 Res. Policy, 273, 280-83 (1998) (noting also broad and strong patent rights would benefit some industries, though they didn't give separate examples.).

1401 *Rai*,16 Berkeley Tech. L. J. 813, 829-30 (2001).

1402 See subsection III.A.1.c).

1403 *Burk/Lemley*, 89 Va. L. Rev. 1575, 1613 (2003).

1404 *Momenta Pharmaceuticals, Inc. v. Amphastar Pharmaceuticals, Inc.*, 686 F.3d 1348, 1375 (Fed. Cir. 2012) (Rader Chief J. dissenting).

1405 *Momenta Pharmaceuticals, Inc. v. Amphastar Pharmaceuticals, Inc.,* 686 F.3d 1348, 1375 (Fed. Cir. 2012) (Rader Chief J. dissenting); See also e.g., *Caulfield*, 84 Chi.-Kent L. Rev. 133, 137 (2009).

The question ultimately returns to what kind of invention we need, and the answer for this industry was already given in chapter III.B, i.e. encouraging more breakthrough innovations. Thus, as many scholars have insisted, to obtain more basic inventions in the pharmaceutical field of technology, it would be advisable to provide them with a broader scope of protection. This broader scope of a patent's power to exclude others in turn "forces other firms, if they want to compete in the broad product field, to work on alternatives that may be very different from what is already presented."[1406] Thus, on the one hand, broad patent protection might reduce patent racing as pointed out by Kitch's critics; on the other hand, it could shift the race to the earlier period of invention, i.e. the race for the broad patent.[1407]

Since a breakthrough invention would have less prior arts in the new field that it has just opened, it would have a broad scope of protection. However, how can we practically grant the broad scope of patent in the field of pharmaceutical inventions? The doctrine of equivalents can be applied to accomplish this goal. In practice, however, it can hardly be applied to the pharmaceutical art. The way that the doctrine of equivalents is applied in Germany provides an example.[1408] In brief, the alleged embodiment would not be found to infringe the patent under the literal infringement, because the alleged embodiment is "modified." At this point, the unpredictability of pharmaceutical art is an important factor.[1409] Because of this lack of predictability in the activity, pharmacokinetics and efficacy of compounds, which leads one atom modification of a known compound to be ineffective or promisingly effective, the second condition[1410] would be very difficult to meet, i.e. the person skilled in the art would not be able to find the modified element as having the same effect. Thus, equivalent protection for this industry is neither easily nor properly applied.[1411] Infringement under this doctrine could still be found if the patent is claiming a process invention[1412] or if there is a relationship between prodrugs and metabolites, such

1406 *Mazzoleni/Nelson*, 27 Res. Policy, 273, 275 (1998).

1407 *Landes/Posner*, 2003, 324.

1408 See *supra* 1071 -1073 and accompanying texts.

1409 See subsection III.A.1.c)(1).

1410 "Whether a person skilled in the art by means of his specialist knowledge is able to identify the modified means as having the same effect.".

1411 *Hansen/Hirsch*, 1997, 326.

1412 *See e.g., BGH/Metronidazol*, GRUR 1975, 425 (holding the infringement of a process patent by equivalent means, in the case where the infringing embodiment differed from the wording of the claim).

as in the hetacillin case in the United Kingdom.[1413] Therefore, granting a broader scope of patent claims for selection inventions is not a proper tool for the promotion of pioneering innovations.

Although granting a broad scope of patent does not help to promote basic invention in this art, the already broad scope of genus patent could be a problem because of the overlapping scope of patents with species selection inventions. In the next section, the solutions that can minimize this problem will be discussed.

3. Solutions to the overlapping scope with species selection invention

While a patent on the basic invention, such as an NME, is still in force, second generation patents will be subservient to the earlier patent. A patent in this situation can be called a "blocking patent,"[1414] i.e. each patentee may block the other from using second generation patents without a license.[1415] The absolute product protection and the broad claim, such as the Markush type claim, make this blocking effect possible. Suggested solutions to this problem include licensing, the doctrine of reverse equivalents, and a compulsory license.[1416]

1413 *Hansen/Hirsch*, 1997, 343.

1414 It is important to distinguish the concept of "blocking patents" in this thesis from that described in the Pharma Sector Inquiry. DG Competition defined the "blocking patents" as follows: "[Another originator company] filed several "paper" patent applications related to [our company's molecule]. The only objective was to impede [our company] from developing [our company's molecule], as far as (i) no research laboratory data and/or work exists related to this paper patent applications, and (ii) [the other company] has no right on [our compound] compound, protected by patents owned by [our company] A letter […] was received by [our company] from [the other company], […] stating that [the other company] is not ready to achieve any settlement at all regarding the blocking patents." *See DG Competition,* 2009, 391.

1415 *Jackson*, 9 J. Tech. L. & Pol'y, 117, 119 (2004); *Merges/Duffy*, 2011, 398.

1416 *Merges/Nelson*, 90 Colum. L. Rev. 839, 904 (1990); *O'Donoghue*, 29 RAND J. Econ. 654, 658 (1998). (noting strength of leading breadth could be determined by the interpretation of "use of technology", the doctrine of equivalents, and the doctrine of reverse equivalents.); *Merges*, 62 Tenn. L. Rev. 75 (1994).

a) Voluntary licensing agreements

Licensing is certainly one way to solve this problem. The second generation inventor will try to secure a license from the controlling patentee. Licensing is also advantageous to the basic patentee, because transactions that involve patents are important in monetizing the value of the patent. The basic patentee knows that his patent's value is constantly declining because of its limited term and the threat of new competing technologies, especially considering the limited ways to extract value from an asset that awards only a right to exclude, not a right to use.[1417]

Licensing agreements can occur at two stages: *ex ante* or *ex post*. The difference is whether the second inventor has already incurred the R&D cost for the second generation invention at the time of the license negotiation. Both inventors can negotiate at *ex ante* license before second generation inventors invest any R&D costs. Green and Scotchmer argue that *ex ante* licensing is proper with the wide patent breadth of a basic patent.[1418] Conversely, in *ex-post* licensing, where the second inventor can bargain only after he has incurred the cost and finished the R&D project, firms may underinvest in the second generation inventions, since they know that they will have less bargaining power, because they have incurred costs.[1419] However, these second generation inventions in the pharmaceutical art usually follow the success of a product covered by the basic patent, i.e., either the basic patentee or the secondary inventor will try to pursue these kinds of inventions. Consequently, the order between licensing and the investment does not make a significant difference. *Ex ante* licensing is especially difficult and is typically excluded from consideration.[1420]

Licensing agreements also occur in mutual directions. Cross-licensing between two patentees can be a solution in the situation where the patents block each other and the most efficient invention is to be employed. [1421] Along with Scotchmer, Chou and Haller suggest that the basic patentee

1417 *Kieff*, 2008, 16.

1418 *Green/Scotchmer*, 26 RAND J. Econ. 20 (1995); *see also Gallini/Scotchmer*, 2002, 72.

1419 *Friebel et al.*, 2006, 27.

1420 *Denicolò*, 31 RAND J. Econ. 488, 488 (2000); *Heller/Eisenberg*, 280 Science 698, 699-700 (1998).

1421 *Landes/Posner*, 2003, 317; *Merges/Nelson*, 90 Colum. L. Rev. 839, 865-66 (1990).

might be able to extract more of the profit facilitated by the basic innovation by offering a licensing contract that the subsequent inventor can accept;[1422] and the improvers can use their inventions without being concerned about infringement.

However, problems have arisen regarding licensing agreements.[1423] Firstly, because licensing lessens competition, raises antitrust concerns, and may retard innovation.[1424] Secondly, *ex ante* licensing will prevent innovations from appearing in the patent race.[1425] Thirdly, *ex post* licensing can create incentives for inefficient entry by imitators, who seek to "invent around" the original patent.[1426] Fourthly, if the transaction cost is high, it might limit the use of contracts.[1427] Lastly, but importantly, obtaining licenses may not be always possible, because the patentees may prefer to have exclusivity either to avoid competition or sometimes even to attempt to dominate the industry, if they are able.[1428] Since patents matter more in the pharmaceutical industry, companies in these fields might be even less willing to participate in patent pools that would undermine their exclusivity.[1429] In the same manner, they might not be willing to license out to their competitors.

b) Non-voluntary licenses

If the second generation patentee fails to acquire a license, he could try to ask the competent authorities to grant a license against the basic patentee's

---

1422 *Chou/Haller*, 1995; *Scotchmer*, 27 RAND J. Econ. 322 (1996); *Chang*, 26 RAND J. Econ. 34, 43-48 (1995); *Green/Scotchmer*, 26 RAND J. Econ. 20 (1995) (also arguing it can be achieved by broadening the first inventor's patent protection); *Matutes/Regibeau/Rockett*, 27 RAND J. Econ. 60, 77-78 (1996).

1423 *Merges/Nelson*, 90 Colum. L. Rev. 839, 874 (1990) (noting general problems in licensing, e.g. steep transaction costs.).

1424 *Chang*, 26 RAND J. Econ. 34, 49 (1995) (arguing the lax antitrust scrutiny of collusion despite reducing the dead weight loss, both because such collusion would be unnecessary and because collusion between holders of competing patents would be desirable only in limited circumstances).

1425 *Gallini/Scotchmer*, 2002, 68.

1426 *Chang*, 26 RAND J. Econ. 34 (1995).

1427 *Mazzoleni/Nelson*, 27 Res. Policy, 273, 279-80 (1998).

1428 *Svatos*, 13 Soc. Philos. Policy 113, 120 (1996).

1429 *Heller/Eisenberg*, 280 Science 698, 700 (1998); Patent pools may be more needed for industries with a strong need of standardization to achieve compatibility amongst various devices.

will, if it is available in his jurisdiction. Under this title, the area of non-voluntary licensing agreement will be explored to try to find solutions.

(1) Compulsory licenses

As Ann noted, compulsory licenses would be the only exception to the general rule, i.e. patents should do no more than reward and promote innovative activity and encourage the disclosure of the results of their innovative activities.[1430] This exceptional measure of a license authorized by a governmental body to a third party for working the patent without the patentee's consent can be granted for various reasons.[1431] The three most prevalent circumstances under which compulsory licensing provisions are applied are when a dependent patent is blocked, when a patent is not worked, and when an invention is related to food or medicine. [1432] In addition, compulsory licensing can be applied as a remedy in antitrust or misuse situations.[1433] The most relevant ground for this dissertation is that a compulsory license can be granted on dependent patents.[1434] Among the selected jurisdictions, the patent acts of Germany,[1435] the United Kingdom,[1436] and Korea[1437] provide provisions for compulsory licensing of dependent patents. The United States Patent Act does not include an explicit authority for a court to order a compulsory license.[1438] Even in the selected jurisdictions, relatively few such compulsory licenses have actually been granted.[1439] Since these provisions are rarely used, a German case concerning gamma-interferon will be reviewed to explore the possibility of granting a compulsory license for a dependent patent.

1430 *Ann,* 2009, 361.

1431 *Reichman/Hasenzahl*, 2003, 12-15; *See also Haracoglou*, 2008, 50; TRIPS Agreement, Art. 31 (1) (providing the grounds for the grant of compulsory license, determined by the member states, but not binding).

1432 *See in general*, *Julian-Arnold*, 33 IDEA 349 (1993).

1433 *See in general*, *Julian-Arnold*, 33 IDEA 349 (1993).

1434 This is because the older form of medication is available in the public, thus the reason for the medicine would be hardly applied.

1435 GPA Art. 24(2).

1436 U.K. Patents Act of 1977, §§ 48, 48A(1)(b)(i), (4).

1437 Korean Patent Act Art. 138, para. 1.

1438 *Reichman*, 46 Hous L. Rev. 1115, 1139 (2009).

1439 *Reichman*, 46 Hous L. Rev. 1115, 1139 (2009).

From 1961 to 2003, twelve applications for compulsory license were filed with the BPatG, only one of which was granted.[1440] This grant allowed the German company Bioferon to produce, to offer, and to market "Polyferon" containing recombinant human gamma-interferon for the new medical indication - chronic polyarthritis, which was widespread in Germany. Bioferon had developed Polyferon. This decision was interpreted in a way that the BPatG desired to stimulate the development of new medical uses of known products and enhanced medical care by granting compulsory licenses.[1441] It was further interpreted that the acknowledged necessary "public interest" under § 24(1) German Patent Act ("GPA")[1442] could be i) a drug at issue showing characteristics which were not shown by an already marketed drug, or ii) a drug avoiding undesired side effects of a marketed drug.[1443] However, BGH revoked this license, mainly based on the lack of sufficient "public interest" to justify granting a compulsory license.[1444] On this decision, *Thomas* comments that "a German court will not grant a compulsory license in order to redress the private interest conflict between the parties, but if exploitation of the invention is in the public interest, then a German court may consider granting a compulsory license."[1445] However, it appears that the BGH decided the way it did because the basis of the original decision was § 24(1), not § 24(2) GPA.

Considering that the product was for a new medical indication, one may wonder if the conclusion would have been different had a compulsory license under the GPA § 24(2) argued before the same court. Namely, in a case like *Olanzapine,* if the two patentees had been different, would the second patentee have had recourse to § 24(2) GPA to allow the grant of a compulsory license for a dependent patent, which cannot be exploited without using another invention protected by a previous patent? § 24(2) GPA clearly provides the opportunity to obtain a compulsory license under the condition that the

---

1440 *Buhrow/Nordemann*, GRUR Int 2005, 407, 409.

1441 *Jaenichen*, 11 Biotechnol. Law Rep. 369, 375 (1992).

1442 GPA § 24(1): A non-exclusive authorization to commercially use an invention shall be granted by the Patent Court in individual cases in accordance with the following provisions (compulsory license) if 1. the person seeking a license has unsuccessfully endeavored during a reasonable period of time to obtain from the patentee consent to use the invention under reasonable conditions usual in trade; and 2. public interest commands the grant of a compulsory license.

1443 *Jaenichen*, 11 Biotechnol. Law Rep. 369, 375 (1992).

1444 *BGH/Polyferon*, GRUR, 190, 1996.

1445 *Thomas*, 23 Santa Clara Computer & High Tech. L. J. 347, 364-65 (2007).

improvement patent contain an important technical advance of considerable economic significance, in comparison with those of the basic patent.[1446] As Straus commented, § 24(2) GPA would play a role in preventing hindrance of the innovation by blocking patents[1447] as well as in improving technological development. Moreover, one can consider this impact in regard to the SPC system in Europe. The SPC not only grants the same rights as conferred by the basic patents, but the granted SPC is also subject to the same limitations and the same obligations.[1448] If the compulsory licenses for the SPC could also be issued as the British Patents Court once held,[1449] when the basic patent acquired the SPC, the blocking effect would not be prolonged. Therefore, even though the difficulty in setting the right royalty rate is fully understandable, the preferable solution would be to enact or implement compulsory licensing provisions for the dependent patent.[1450]

(2) Case law relevant to compulsory licenses

In the United States: eBay Inc. v. MercExchange, L.L.C.

An injunction is an effective way of enforcing a patentee's right.[1451] Before the *eBay* case, injunctive relief was regularly granted in an infringement case. In *eBay v. MercExchange*, however, the U.S. Supreme Court unanimously rejected the claim that as a "general rule a permanent injunction will

---

1446 GPA Sec. 24(2) ("If the applicant for a license is unable to exploit an invention for which he holds protection under a patent of later date without infringing a patent of earlier date, he shall be entitled within the framework of subsection (1) to request the grant of a compulsory license with respect to the owner of the patent of earlier date *if his own invention comprises*, in comparison with that under the patent of earlier date, *an important technical advance of considerable commercial significance*. The patentee may require the applicant for a license to grant him a counter license under reasonable conditions for the exploitation of the patented invention of later date.").

1447 *Straus*, 1 J.E.C.L. & Pract. , 189 (2010).

1448 Council Regulation 469/2009, Art. 5.

1449 *Research Corp's Supplementary Protection Certificate* [1994] R.P.C. 667, 674.

1450 *See also Reichman/Dreyfuss*, 57 Duke L. J. 85, 116 (2007) (addressing when necessary, compulsory licenses to unblock dependent patents and enable improvers to reach the market could also be enacted, a solution that remains fully consistent with the TRIPS Agreement.); for the public interest, see *Thomas*, 23 Santa Clara Computer & High Tech. L. J. 347, 365 (2007).

1451 *cf. eBay Inc. v. MercExchange, L.L.C.*, 547 U.S. 388 (2006).

issue once infringement and validity have been adjudged"[1452] and formalized the notion that a court should consider the public impact before granting an injunction to stop infringement. Even though the Supreme Court did not mention a compulsory license as a remedy to the denial of an injunction, many lower courts have granted such relief, i.e. "ongoing royalties" after the denial of a permanent injunction.[1453]

In the *eBay* case, the Supreme Court held that the plaintiff claiming injunctive relief must demonstrate (i) that he had suffered an irreparable injury, (ii) that remedies available at law were inadequate to compensate for that injury, (iii) that considering the balance of hardships between the plaintiff and the defendant, a remedy in equity was warranted, and (iv) that the public interest would not be disserved by a permanent injunction.[1454] This sort of a compulsory license is not a necessary remedy, and, indeed, on remand in the *eBay* case, the District Court did not impose a compulsory license.[1455] Instead, the Court warned that there could be a "real potential for enhanced damages" for the possible post-trial infringement.[1456]

Damage awards for infringements and injunctive relief to prevent infringement through judicial orders to shut down the infringers' production or sales are fundamentally different remedies.[1457] The potentially continued infringement is serious. Without the threat of an injunction, the patentee would be forced to negotiate with the infringing party about granting a license. The risk of incurring treble damages under American law is a strong inducement to the allegedly infringing party to negotiate in good faith. Of course, a myriad of various factors should be considered before granting this kind of remedy. However, this could resolve the mutual blocking problem.

In Germany: Orange Book Standard case

The blocking effect of basic patents in the competition law area may be attacked by claiming a so-called "compulsory license objection" or the "Eu-

---

1452 *eBay Inc. v. MercExchange, L.L.C.*, 547 U.S. 388, 394-395 (2006).

1453 *See e.g., z4 Technologies, Inc. v. Microsoft Corp.*, 434 F.Supp.2d 437 (E.D.Tex. 2006); *Finisar Corp. v. DirecTv Group, Inc.*, 2006 WL 2709206 (E.D.Tex. 2006), reversed in part with different ground, *Finisar Corp. v. DirecTV Group, Inc.*, 523 F.3d 1323 (Fed. Cir. 2008); *Merges/Duffy*, 2011, 952-53.

1454 *eBay Inc. v. MercExchange, L.L.C.*, 547 U.S. 388, 391 (2006).

1455 *MercExchange, L.L.C. v. eBay, Inc.*, 500 F.Supp.2d 556, 585 (E.D.Va.,2007).

1456 *MercExchange, L.L.C. v. eBay, Inc.*, 500 F.Supp.2d 556, 581 n.23 (E.D.Va.,2007).

1457 *Ann*, 2009, 362.

ro-defense"[1458] against a suit for patent infringement. If an attack succeeds, the plaintiff will not receive the benefit of an injunction and cannot claim it. The BGH held its decision on the *Orange Book Standard* case, in this regard.[1459]

At issue was a patent on the "Orange Book Standard" and was related to the manufacture of writable CDs. The primary issue was whether the patentee had abused a dominant position contrary to Art. 102 TFEU[1460] by refusing to grant a license. The Court provided significant prerequisites for this compulsory license defense. The defendant had to act like a "true licensee," which required that i) the party seeking a license should have made to the patentee an unconditional offer which the patentee cannot refuse and remains bound by said offer, ii) if the alleged infringer has already used the subject matter of the patent before the patentee has accepted the offer, the alleged infringer must pay or guarantee the payment of the license fees resulting from the contract,[1461] and he can do so by rendering accounts about the extent of his acts of use and by complying with the payment obligation, such as depositing the license fees.[1462] The dominance of an essential patent is similar to the dominance of the basic patent over second generation inventions. However, it would be better to wait some time before applying this defense in dependent patent cases. Many questions remain to be answered by the Court, including what is a reasonable amount of royalty, about which the

1458 *See Hays*, 91 Trademark Rep. 675, 679 (2001) (addressing the "Euro Defense" as follows: "Euro Defense" is a legal tactic akin to alleging "unclean hands". A defendant asserts that, while it may have infringed upon an intellectual property right under other circumstances, enforcement of that right would be a violation of the EC's competition laws, particularly of EC Treaty Articles 81 and 82 (now EFTU Articles 101 and 102)).

1459 *BGH/Orange Book-Standard*, GRUR 2009, 694.

1460 Article 102 of TFEU: "Any abuse by one or more undertakings of a dominant position within the common market or in a substantial part of it shall be prohibited as incompatible with the internal market in so far as it may affect trade between Member States." Such abuse may, in particular, consist in: (a) directly or indirectly imposing unfair purchase or selling prices or other unfair trading conditions; (b) limiting production, markets or technical development to the prejudice of consumers; (c) applying dissimilar conditions to equivalent transactions with other trading parties, thereby placing them at a competitive disadvantage; (d) making the conclusion of contracts subject to acceptance by the other parties of supplementary obligations which, by their nature or according to commercial usage, have no connection with the subject of such contracts.".

1461 *BGH/Orange Book-Standard*, GRUR 2009, 694, 696.

1462 *BGH/Orange Book-Standard*, GRUR 2009, 694, 697.

patent holder and the alleged infringer are likely to disagree, whether a running royalty, which was apparently featured by the BGH, is proper, whether the defendant can still raise a non-infringement argument, and others. Unlike the *eBay* case in the United States, however, the German court appears to grant the injunction if the infringement is confirmed and the existence of market dominance or the abuse thereof is denied.[1463]

c) Reverse doctrine of equivalents

A judicially devised counterpart to the doctrine of equivalents is the "reverse doctrine of equivalents." As some scholars have argued, improvers could escape liability under this doctrine.[1464] The source of this doctrine is the following statement in the *Graver Tank* case.[1465]

> "The wholesome realism of this doctrine is not always applied in favor of a patentee but is sometimes used against him. Thus, where a device is so far changed in principle from a patented article that it performs the same or a similar function in a substantially different way, but nevertheless falls within the literal words of the claim, the doctrine of equivalents may be used to restrict the claim and defeat the patentee's action for infringement."[1466]

This doctrine can be a good remedy in the situation where a dependent patentee and a dominant patentee are unable to reach a license agreement, and the introduction of the invention to the market can be facilitated. Once a patentee establishes literal infringement, the alleged infringer can try to establish noninfringement under the reverse doctrine of equivalents.[1467] As Merges argues, this doctrine can be used to influence reluctant patent holders

1463 *BGH/Orange Book-Standard*, GRUR 2009, 694, 697 (holding "Just as the proposed licensee cannot be denied the possibility to defend himself first of all against the accusation of infringement, the consequence being that the action has to be dismissed in its entirety if the accusation of infringement turns out to be unjustified, the patent holder cannot be prohibited from first of all asserting the claim for injunctive relief based on the patent, the consequence being that this claim must be adjudged if the infringement is confirmed and if the court negates a dominant position on the market or an abuse of the same.").

1464 *Lemley*, 75 Tex. L. Rev. 989, 1010-13 (1997); *Merges/Nelson*, 90 Colum. L. Rev. 839, 911 (1990); *Merges*, 62 Tenn. L. Rev. 75, 91-99 (1994).

1465 *Graver Tank & Mfg. Co. v. Linde Air Products Co.*, 339 U.S. 605, 608-09 (1950).

1466 *Graver Tank & Mfg. Co. v. Linde Air Products Co.*, 339 U.S. 605, 608-09 (1950).

1467 *SRI Intern. v. Matsushita Elec. Corp. of America*, 775 F.2d 1107, 1023-24 (Fed. Cir. 1985).

who considered using "holdup rights" against improvers,[1468] and it can be valuable, since it can help to maintain a balance in infringement cases by mitigating the impact of literal infringement.[1469] Lemley also insists that this doctrine will serve as a crucial release valve that will prevent the patentees from stifling improvements.[1470]

Most importantly, the doctrine will be applied in the cases where there is a "considerable added value" in the contested embodiment.[1471] According to Lemley, the radical improver is the inventor of an improvement sufficiently different to constitute a departure from all that came before it.[1472] Landes and Posner also note that, "if the contribution made by the improvement greatly exceeds the contribution made by the original patented invention, the improver is allowed to practice his invention without being deemed an infringer, even though he is making use of the prior invention without a license from the patentee." [1473] This is permitted because the degree of the blocking problem is dependent on the situations. The problem will be more significant if the contribution of the prior inventor is of very little value compared to the improvement; the problem will be less significant if the contribution of prior invention is of the same or greater value than the selection patent.[1474]

The application of this doctrine should be limited,[1475] and, indeed, courts have rarely applied it.[1476] One of the biggest concerns is that both patents should be evaluated to confirm the additional contribution by a species selection invention. However, considering that a species selection invention can be developed into another NME, the species selection inventions could be at least as valuable as the genus patent if a medicine covered by the basic patent was developed; it could be even more valuable if no medicine covered by the basic patent was developed. Thus, this doctrine is more likely to be

---

1468 *Merges*, 62 Tenn. L. Rev. 75 (1994).

1469 *Merges*, 73 J. Pat. & Trademark Off. Soc'y 878, 880 (1991).

1470 *Lemley*, 75 Tex. L. Rev. 989, 1010-13 (1997).

1471 *Domeij*, 2000, 129.

1472 *Lemley*, 75 Tex. L. Rev. 989, 1010 (1997).

1473 *Landes/Posner*, 2003, 317.

1474 *Merges/Nelson*, 90 Colum. L. Rev. 839, 865-66 (1990).

1475 *Domeij*, 2000, 129 (noting like the uncertainty caused by the doctrine of equivalence, there is uncertainty to interpret the claims and the case is exceptional).

1476 *Durham*, 1999, 148-419.

applied for species selection inventions,[1477] because there is less concern about assessing the values of both patents. Moreover, since this assessment would be made not before the patent office but before a court, which would have a greater opportunity to consider evidence as the patent lives, one may not need to worry too much about the difficulty in applying this doctrine. Therefore, it would advisable for courts to apply this doctrine when a broader prior genus patent holds up the sale of a new medication or at least to try applying it actively to encourage manufacturers to invest their resources in the products that are literally covered by the broader earlier patent.

d) Conclusion

There have been many proposals by scholars[1478] about voluntary license agreements. Since the pharmaceutical companies usually do not want to undermine their exclusivities by licensing, apart from the license agreements with academia or SMEs, voluntary license agreements do not seem to be of practical use. Among the judicially acknowledged compulsory licenses, the *eBay* case appears to be the most applicable to dependent patents. Most properly, either an implementation of the statutory compulsory license or an improved use of the reverse doctrine of equivalence would be desirable to solve the problem created by using the dominant patent to block the exploitation of a dependent patent. The same approach could be applied to the situation in which the basic patent blocks the use of inventions on dosage forms, combinations of active ingredients, or especially new medical uses.

1477 This situation is different from the doctrine of equivalents can scarcely be applied for the chemical selection inventions; or also different from other selection inventions would be still difficult to be applied this doctrine because of their comparably low value.

1478 *See supra* 1418 -1422 and accompanying texts.

D. Proposals on the length of patents

1. Arguments on the length of patents

The breadth and length of a patent are often contrasted, but they are substitutes.[1479] The limited patent term is one of the devices employed to minimize the social cost of patent exclusivity.[1480] Empirical research has shown that the economic benefit of having patents often vanishes before they expire.[1481] It is also reported that the *de facto* term is chosen by the patentee in return for renewal fees.[1482] Indeed, reportedly no more than 50% of patents are maintained longer than 10 years across technologies and countries.[1483] The effective economic life of a patent ends at the moment when any non-infringing but competitive improvements emerge in the market.[1484] Again, there are substantial inter-industry variations. Unlike in industries in which the life cycle of a product is very short and its turnover is frequent, such as electronics, the lifetime of a patent is more relevant in the pharmaceutical industry.[1485] The value of patent protection in this industry is clearly demonstrated by the market erosion that occurs when generic versions are introduced after a patent expires.

In contrast to the breadth of patents, their duration is not hotly debated, probably because many patent systems set a statutory 20-year patent term. While disagreeing with the uniform patent life, Cornelli and Schankerman assert that "differentiated patent lives can be welfare improving because of an 'incentive effect': allowing firms with high R&D capabilities to choose longer patent lives gives these firms an incentive to invest more R&D re-

---

1479 *Landes/Posner*, 2003, 331.

1480 *Landes/Posner*, 2003, 302.

1481 *Hunt*, 1999, 2; *See for instance, Mansfield/Schwartz/Wagner*, 91 Econ. J. 907 (1981).

1482 *Scotchmer*, 30 RAND J. Econ. 181 (1999); *Cornelli/Schankerman*, 30 RAND J. Econ. 197 (1999).

1483 *Scotchmer*, 30 RAND J. Econ. 181, 182 (1999); *Cornelli/Schankerman*, 30 RAND J. Econ. 197, 197 (1999); *O'Donoghue/Scotchmer/Thisse*, 7 J. Econ. Manage. Strat. 1, 2 (1998).

1484 *Scotchmer/Green*, 21 RAND J. Econ. 131 (1990) (noting "the effective life of the patent is the time until it is superseded by a superior technology."); *Friebel et al.*, 2006, 30; *O'Donoghue/Scotchmer/Thisse*, 7 J. Econ. Manage. Strat. 1 (1998) (defining "effective patent life as a life which is "the expected time until a patented product is replaced in the market").

1485 *Levin et al.*, 1987 Brookings Paper on Econ. Activity, 783, 816 (1987).

sources."[1486] While arguing that the patents used for good inventions live much longer than the existing statutory maximum term, they contend that it might be optimal to grant a zero patent life for inventions with low value, and an infinite life for inventions with high value.[1487] Under the circumstances of cumulative inventions, Green and Scotchmer argue that a longer duration of a patent should be attributed, especially to the first inventor, if a sequence of innovations was provided by different inventors rather than by the concentrated effort of one company. They reason that it is difficult to divide profit between the first and second inventors and that the incentive to undertake basic research will inevitably be too weak.[1488] Other scholars discuss this issue in consideration of other factors. Gilbert and Shapiro argue that the optimal patent life should be infinite, while the patent breadth should be narrow.[1489] Alternatively, as O'Donoghue *et al.,* maintain, although the statutory life of a patent and its effective economic life differ, both can coincide when the breadth of the patent is so broad as to cover every subsequent innovation in a product that infringes the basic patent.[1490]

As Nordhaus shows, however, a longer patent life brings a more inventive input to society, but it also prolongs the deadweight loss of such inventions.[1491] Thus, the optimal life of a patent should be finite and should end at the point at which the increased number of inventions and the length of the monopoly are in balance.[1492] The determination of this point remains unsolved.

1486 *Cornelli/Schankerman*, 30 RAND J. Econ. 197, 197 (1999).
1487 *Cornelli/Schankerman*, 30 RAND J. Econ. 197, 198, 209 (1999).
1488 *Green/Scotchmer*, 26 RAND J. Econ. 20, 20-21 (1995).
1489 *Gilbert/Shapiro*, 21 RAND J. Econ. 106, 111-112 (1990) (But also mentioning that "overly-long patent would retard subsequent innovation by establishing monopoly rights to an entire line of research").
1490 *O'Donoghue/Scotchmer/Thisse*, 7 J. Econ. Manage. Strat. 1,2 (1998).
1491 *Nordhaus*, 1969, 70-75.
1492 *Nordhaus*, 1969, 76-86.

2. Proposals on the length of patents

a) Proposal on the length of basic patents

(1) Introduction

Since the pharmaceutical industry is very susceptible to the terms of patents, the patent term can be certainly and efficiently applied to basic pharmaceutical patents to incentivise the drug companies to invest more in the R&D targeting NMEs. The current term of a patent, however, does not serve this purpose well.

The uniform patent term starts to run from the patent filing date, but the effective patent term runs from the date when the product reaches the market. The latter date varies highly from industry to industry and from product to product. Generally, the longer it takes to bring a drug to market, the greater the investment that must be made will be, and the better the protection provided to the product will need to be in order to justify incurring the R&D cost. This is quite the reverse of what it should be. First, without consideration of a patent term extension, the drugs containing NMEs that take longer than ten years to get to market could enjoy fewer than ten years of exclusivity. In contrast, second generation inventions or even dosage regimes, such as "once a day prior to sleep" can theoretically enjoy at least 17 years of exclusivity if the patent examination is completed within three years.[1493] Therefore, there have been significant deadweight losses by second generation patents, and the uniform patent term has not provided enough incentives for basic innovations. In this sense, the patent system seems to provide *de facto* reverse-discriminatory protection to basic inventions, because it takes so long time to get each invention to market.

Even if the patent term extension, which aims to compensate the reduced exclusivity period because of the long R&D [1494] is considered, the situation is not significantly improved. As the preamble to the Council Regulation 469/2009 clearly states, the purpose of this system is to encourage research, especially long and costly research on medicinal products.[1495] In the United States, one-half of the time during which the drug is evaluated as an inves-

1493 Of course, it is not possible to note that this kind of invention does not deserve the 17 years' exclusivity.

1494 *See e.g., Rai,* Ill. L. Rev. 173, 182-83 (2001).

1495 Council Regulation 469/2009, Preamble (3).

tigational new drug, plus the time during which the drug is pending approval at FDA, would be compensated.[1496] In Europe, neither the date of the patent grant nor the duration of clinical trials is relevant to the duration of the SPC, because only the date of first marketing approval in the community matters.[1497] The medication that gains first marketing approval between five and ten years from the patent filing date, is most likely covered by second generation inventions, and could enjoy fifteen years of maximum effective patent life. However, those medications that are launched ten years after the filing date can never enjoy the maximum effective life[1498] (see Figure 9). In Korea, the situation is comparably better, since the whole period necessary for the clinical trial and the regulatory approval can be extended. However, the extension period still has a five year cap, as do the systems in other jurisdictions. The basic reason for this is probably that the patent term extension system was not originally meant to compensate for the loss of exclusivity because of the long R&D period, but was instead meant to offset the accelerated generic entry into the market. Some scholars point out that the effective patent terms for inventions having unduly long R&D periods might not be effective enough to convince manufacturers to invest in such inventions, which can cause society to lose these innovations.[1499]

(2) Proposed term of basic patents

How can this problem be remediated? Ideally, the system must award each invention in accordance with the extent that it contributes to society or in an amount that will compensate the cost and time of R&D. However, calculating the amount of such an award would be very difficult and, even if possible, would incur significant administrative costs.[1500] Considering the discrepancies discussed above and the shortage of basic medications, therefore, it would be advisable to include a provision on the patent term of the basic invention as follows:

1496 35 U.S.C. § 156.

1497 Council Regulation 1768/92, Article 13.

1498 See subsectionV.C.3..

1499 *White*, 38 J. Pat. Off. Soc'y 839, 853 (1956).

1500 In addition, there could be an invention which comes just out of the brilliance of inventor, even though it does hardly apply to the pharmaceutical inventions.

"The term of a patent, which covers a product containing an active ingredient that has not been subject to the marketing approval process related to the first commercial marketing of the active ingredient, shall be the later of either i) 15 years after the marketing approval date or ii) 20 years after the patent filing date."

(3) The basis of the proposal

According to the proposal, an NME that gains marketing approval from the regulatory authority would enjoy fifteen years of effective term,[1501] but, if it fails to gain marketing approval, it would still enjoy the conventional patent term. The fifteen year effective term is based on the maximum effective patent term with SPC protection,[1502] and considers the regulatory exclusivity available in Europe, which is eight to ten years for the new medical entities,[1503] and which is longer than the one in the United States. The second option, which is to set the patent term at 20 years after the patent filing date, was added in consideration of the decision in *Canada – Term of Patent Protection*. In this dispute, the Panel, and afterwards the Appellate Body of the WTO, reviewed Canada's patent term calculation based on seventeen years after the grant of the patent. They found a violation of Art. 33 TRIPS, because this calculation failed to provide a patent term of at least twenty years from the patent application filing date, regardless of the fact that the calculation would often lead to a longer term.[1504] Since the TRIPS Agreement sets out the minimum standards of protection to be provided by each member,[1505] further protection could be provided.

1501 *Domeij*, 2000, 283.

1502 In fact, considering the R&D for the chronic diseases, Alzheimer's disease, or cancers, it would be much advisable to provide longer protection, however, it was found very difficult to propose something without any further basis.

1503 Council Directive 87/21/EEC of 22 December 1986 amending Directive 65/65/EEC on the approximation of provisions laid down by law, regulation or administrative action relating to proprietary medicinal products.

1504 *WTO-Panel Report*, Canada-Term of Patent Protection, WT/DS170/R (May 5, 2000); *WTO-Appellate Body Report*, Canada-Term of Patent Protection, WT/DS170/AB/R (Sep 18, 2000).

1505 TRIPS Art. 1(1) "Members shall give effect to the provisions of this Agreement. Members may, but shall not be obliged to, *implement in their law more extensive protection than is required by this Agreement*, provided that such protection does not contravene the provisions of this Agreement." [Emphasis added].

TRIPS compliance must be considered further. Canada challenged the same issue before the WTO-Panel contending that the SPC regulation was incompatible with the obligation of the non-discrimination principle based on the field of technology (Art. 27(1)),[1506] since it is available only for pharmaceuticals and for agricultural chemical products. [1507] However, this request was not pursued by Canada. In the same manner as this SPC regulation, the German Patent Act[1508] and the British Patents Act,[1509] the American Patent Act[1510] and the Korean Patent Act contain provisions that benefit only the pharmaceutical and agrochemical industries.

Many scholars have discussed the scope of this non-discrimination principle according to Art. 27(1) TRIPS and argued that Art. 27(1) did not require a single level of protection for all technologies and that it must be distinguished from "differentiation" for legitimate reasons.[1511] This principle was also considered by the WTO Panel in *Canada-Patent Protection of Pharmaceutical Products.*[1512] The Panel noted that "[t]he ordinary meaning of the word 'discriminate' is potentially broader than these more specific definitions." It certainly extends beyond the concept of differential treat-

---

1506 TRIPS Art. 27(1): "inventions, whether products or processes, in all fields of technology, provided that they are new, involve an inventive step and are capable of industrial application. Subject to paragraph 4 of Article 65, paragraph 8 of Article 70 and paragraph 3 of this Article, *patents shall be available and patent rights enjoyable without discrimination as to the place of invention, the field of technology and whether products are imported or locally produced.*" (Emphasis added).

1507 Request for Consultations by Canada, *European Communities - Patent Protection for Pharmaceutical and Agricultural Chemical Product*, December 7, 1998, WT/DS153/1. This dispute was indeed initiated by Canada as a kind of a counter-claim against the dispute initiated by the EC on the provisions of Canadian Patent Act (*Canada-Patent Protection of Pharmaceutical Product*, March 17, 2000, WT/DS114/R), however, it have not been pursued by Canada.

1508 GPA Sec. 49a.

1509 U.K. Patents Act, Sec. 128B and Schedule 4A.

1510 35 U.S.C. § 156; *see also* 35 U.S.C. § 103(b) (2000).

1511 *Correa*, 3 Tul. J. Tech. & Intell. Prop. 1, 7 (2001) (noting "differential treatment does not necessarily mean discriminatory treatment, because different technologies might require different treatment."); *Dinwoodie/Dreyfuss*, 13 Mich. Telecomm. Tech. L. Rev. 445, 452 (2007) ("We suggest that those defending an exclusion as compliant with Article 27 should be permitted to rebut a showing of disparate treatment by demonstrating a legitimate purpose."); *Berger*, 17 Conn. J. Int'l L. 157, 200 (2002).

1512 *WTO-Panel Report*, Canada - Patent Protection of Pharmaceutical Products, WT/DS114/R (Mar 17, 2000).

ment. It is a normative term, pejorative in connotation, referring to results of the unjustified imposition of differentially disadvantageous treatment."[1513] This could be interpreted as allowing members to treat different fields of patent protection differently if they do so for a legitimate regulatory purpose.[1514] The panel further noted that "Article 27 does not prohibit bona fide exceptions to deal with problems that exist only in certain product areas."[1515] This further suggests that the members may adopt different rules if the differences are adopted for bona fide purposes and if such measures are consistent with other provisions of TRIPS.[1516] Thus, this proposed provision should be interpreted as not violating the TRIPS Agreement. Even if it does, since the existing industry-specific provisions have encountered little challenge, the threat of such an attack would likely be limited.[1517]

(4) Expected effects

The guaranteed effective patent term proposed by the proffered provision could motivate the pharmaceutical industry to incur the investment of the R&D of new medical entities with less concern about the period to recover the R&D costs. Furthermore, ample litigation and invalidity actions have already occurred with regard to the validity of patent term extensions. By adapting this provision, the unnecessary waste of resources through litigation would be substantially reduced. Additionally, the manufacturers could invest the saved resources in R&D as long as the patentee is confident about the patentability of the ultimate invention. This optimized effective patent term would also provide the SMEs with more bargaining power and would help them to attract funding. In the end, and most importantly, this could increase the number of NMEs and ultimately the health of society.

One may argue that this proposal may delay access to medicine. However, it is undeniable that medicine must first be available before access can be taken into consideration.

1513 *WTO-Panel Report*, Canada - Patent Protection of Pharmaceutical Products, WT/DS114/R (Mar 17, 2000), para 7.94.

1514 *Gervais*, 2012, 2.369.

1515 *WTO-Panel Report*, Canada - Patent Protection of Pharmaceutical Products, WT/DS114/R (Mar 17, 2000), para 7.92.

1516 *Gervais*, 2012, 2.369.

1517 *Roin*, 87 Tex. L. Rev. 503, 558 (2009).

b) Proposal on the patent term extension of second generation patents

As Landes and Posner worry, protection might realize a return vastly in excess of the inventor's fixed cost of innovation. This would be especially true if the inventor could effectively extend his patent term by obtaining improvement patents.[1518] In fact, a patentee could enjoy the patent term of a selection invention plus its SPC in addition to those of the basic patent. These proliferating patent rights and SPCs on second generation patents have signalled the manufacturers to invest more in second generation inventions.

Following the same logic that supports protecting basic inventions, it would be proper to provide a shorter protection period to the second generation patents. However, since the TRIPS Agreement sets out the minimum standards of protection that should be provided by each member,[1519] it would be absurd to do so.

However, the patent term extension on second generation patents could be limited in two ways. Firstly, it could be reduced through the heightened patentability requirements, which will be discussed in the next chapter, and the reduced number of second generation patents that would result. Secondly, until the effect of heightened patentability requirements is established, grants of patent term extensions could be restricted. As long as a biologically active moiety is the same, the patent term extension would be granted to the first substance applied, as in the *Doxorubicin-sulfate* case in Germany. This could further be applied to granting a patent term extension to salts or esters.

1518 *Landes/Posner*, 2003, 323.
1519 *See* TRIPS Art. 1(1).

E. Proposals on the patentability requirements

Patents should be granted to the extent necessary to encourage the innovation that otherwise would not reach the public,[1520] and that are socially desirable.[1521] These can be controlled through the patentability requirements.

1. Introduction: Technology specific patentability standards

The Imperial Supreme Court of Germany has held that the question of whether an invention exists cannot be answered differently for an invention in the field of the chemical industry than for an invention in the field of the mechanical industry.[1522] As some scholars note, the law must be the same for all patents and types of inventions.[1523] Certainly, in the past, the inventions were more homogeneous than they are today, and it made more sense to have a unified set of rules for inventions.[1524] Some scholars also advocate for a uniform patent system, because of the difficulty of implementing differential treatment.[1525] Jaffe and Lerner argue for a uniform system, because as soon as patentees in a particular category receive the better treatments, there would be an inevitable tendency for people to position themselves to

---

1520 *Lessig*, 11 St. John's J. Legal Comment. 635, 638 (1996) (noting "while we protect real property to protect the owner from harm, we protect intellectual property to provide the owner sufficient incentive to produce such property. 'Sufficient incentive,' however, is something less than 'perfect control'."); *Lemley*, 83 Tex. L. Rev. 1031, 1065 (2005) (noting "[g]ranting intellectual property rights imposes a complex set of economic costs, and it can be justified only to the extent those rights are necessary to provide incentives to create."); *Roberts v. Sears, Roebuck & Co.*, 723 F.2d 1324, 1345-46 (7th Cir. 1983) (Posner, J. concurring in part and dissenting in part, especially noting "[t]he inherent problem was to develop some means of weeding out those inventions which would not be disclosed or devised but for the inducement of a patent.").; *Burk/Lemley*, 89 Va. L. Rev. 1575, 1598-99 (2003).

1521 *Roin*, 87 Tex. L. Rev. 503, 512 (2009).

1522 *Kongo-Rot*, Decision of the Reichsgericht (Imperial Supreme Court) of May 8, 1889, Patentblatt 1889, 209, 212.

1523 *Harmon/Homan/McMahon*, 2010, 14.

1524 *Allison/Lemley*, 82 B.U.L.Rev. 77 (2002). Considering this, one may doubt whether it is still appropriate to apply the same rules in today's increasingly complex landscape of inventions.

1525 *Jaffe/Lerner*, 2004, 203-05.

get the most favourable treatment.[1526] At the same time, however, they acknowledge the differences between the technologies and the specificities of the pharmaceutical industry and further admit that it is vitally important to resolve the problems with patenting in different areas.[1527] Regarding these inter-industry differences, Wagner argues there need be no concern, because they are merely factual differences.[1528] However, "'[o]ne-size-fits-all' ultimately fits few",[1529] and this approach has been repeatedly challenged.[1530]

We have a uniform patent system, which provides technology-neutral protection to all kinds of inventions.[1531] However, although technology-neutral in theory, patent law is technology-specific in application.[1532] For example, for software patents in the United States, a series of decisions has not only eliminated the enablement and best mode requirements, but has also found that a high-level functional description is sufficient to meet these requirements.[1533] In contrast, for patents in biotechnology, the courts have focused on the unpredictability of the arts, and emphasized proof of the

---

1526 *Jaffe/Lerner*, 2004, 203-05.

1527 *Jaffe/Lerner*, 2004, 205 ("[…] the problems in business methods, software, and biotechnology derive from the unique properties of these technologies.").

1528 *Wagner*, 50 Adv. Genet. 367 (2003).

1529 *Crews*, 49 J. Copyright Soc'y U.S.A. 549, 564 (2001).

1530 *Hilty*, 2009, 92.

1531 *Burk/Lemley*, 17 Berkeley Tech. L.J. 1155, 1156 (2002).

1532 *Burk/Lemley*, 89 Va. L. Rev. 1575, 1577 (2003); *Burk/Lemley*, 17 Berkeley Tech. L.J. 1155, 1156 (2002). (also noting the legal rules were the same, but the application of those to different industries were different from each other); cf. *Moba, B.V. v. Diamond Automation, Inc.*, 325 F.3d 1306, 1323-27 (Fed. Cir. 2003) (noting but criticizing technology specific requirements between the biotechnology (*Reagents of the University of California v. Eli Lilly & Co.*, 119 F.3d 1559, 1566-69 (Fed. Cir. 1997)) and software invention (e.g.: *Northern Telecom, Inc. v. Datapoint Corp.*, 908 F.2d 931, 941-43 (Fed. Cir. 1990), *cert denied,* 498 U.S. 920 (1990)); *See also Klemperer*, 21 RAND J. Econ. 113, 127 (1990) (noting optimal patent policies vary across different classes of products).

1533 *Burk/Lemley*, 17 Berkeley Tech. L.J. 1155, 1162 (2002); *e.g., Fonar Corp. v. General Electric Co.*, 107 F.3d 1543, 1549 (Fed. Cir. 1997) ("[…] writing code for such software is within the skill of the art, not requiring undue experimentation, once its functions have been disclosed."); *see also Mahajan*, 67 Fordham L. Rev. 3297, 3317 (1999) (noting, for example, it was not mandatory to disclose the source code of the patented program).

structure of the invention.[1534] As is noticeable from the name itself, a person skilled in the art is very specific to the particular technology in which the inventions are involved. This imaginary person is involved in determining many doctrines in the patent law, such as non-obviousness, enablement disclosure, definiteness of patent claims, claim construction, doctrine of equivalents, and others. Thus, the assessments of these doctrines are already technology specific. A skilled person in the software industry is so skillful as to need little guidance from the prior art to implement a new idea in software. However, a skilled person in the biotechnology industry is apparently less skillful, and so needs much more information from the prior art to enable an invention. If one imagines that the same standard were applied in biopharmaceutical inventions and software inventions, it would be tantamount to requiring disclosure of the entire source code, symbol by symbol, including all source code permutations that would not alter the function of the software.[1535] Indeed, this concept of an imaginary person leaves the discretion to the courts or patent offices, and proper exploitation of this concept will allow the flexible tailoring of the law to the different fields of technology.

Some scholars suggest adopting technology specific patent rules to deal with the specific attributes of different technologies.[1536] As a representative characteristic, the field of biotechnology is considered less "predictable" than the fields of mechanics or electronics.[1537] The Federal Circuit perceived unpredictability in the pharmaceutical field that might distinguish pharmaceutical inventions from mechanical inventions in its assessment of obviousness.[1538] In the *Eli Lilly* case, the Federal Circuit heightened the written

---

1534 *See e.g., Reagents of the University of California v. Eli Lilly & Co.*, 119 F.3d 1559, 1568 (Fed. Cir. 1997) ("A definition by function, […] does not suffice to define the genus because it is only an indication of what the gene does, rather than what it is.[…] It is only a definition of a useful result rather than a definition of what achieves that result. Many such genes may achieve that result. The description requirement of the patent statute requires a description of an invention, not an indication of a result that one might achieve if one made that invention. […] Accordingly, naming a type of material generally known to exist, in the absence of knowledge as to what that material consists of, is not a description of that material.").

1535 *Moba, B.V. v. Diamond Automation, Inc.*, 325 F.3d 1306, 1325 (Fed. Cir. 2003).

1536 *See e.g., Long*, 55 Fed. Law. 44, 49 (2008); *Meurer,* 8 Wash. U. J. L. & Pol'y 309 (2002) (arguing the scope of business method patents should be construed narrowly).

1537 *See, e.g., In re Vaeck*, 947 F.2d 488, 496 (Fed. Cir. 1991).

1538 *Sanofi-Synthelabo v. Apotex, Inc.*, 550 F.3d 1075, 1090 (Fed. Cir. 2008).

description requirement specifically for biotechnological inventions,[1539] which received heavy criticism from many scholars.[1540] Considering the heterogeneity of inventions and technologies and the developments thereof, the uniform application of patent requirements would not only be difficult, but also unfair. Instead, they contended that industries must be treated differently through the existing patent law provisions and doctrines.[1541] Based on these *de facto* technology specific patentability standards, the proposals on the patentability of pharmaceutical inventions including the way to implement this principle will be analyzed and provided.

2. Proposals on the novelty requirement

a) Arguments on the novelty requirement

Many scholars argue that a more demanding patentability requirement would result in a higher level of innovations. Luski and Wettstein contend that lowering the novelty requirement would result in lowering the levels of R&D and innovation and that heightening the novelty requirement would prevent firms from pursuing sub-optimally small innovations and increase R&D expenditures and social welfare.[1542] Scotchmer and Green caution against a weak novelty requirement, which would induce firms to patent even incremental inventions.[1543] They further argue that, with a strong novelty requirement, the market would be more concentrated (e.g. possibly only competition between advanced innovation and the base-level technology) by softening post-innovation competition. Thus, the innovators would realize a better profit flow at the second stage, and a strong requirement would

---

1539 *Reagents of the University of California v. Eli Lilly & Co.*, 119 F.3d 1559 (Fed. Cir. 1997).

1540 See *supra* 899 .

1541 *Burk/Lemley*, 89 Va. L. Rev. 1575, 1638-68 (2003); *see also Long*, 55 Fed. Law. 44, 49 (2008).

1542 *Luski/Wettstein*, 1 Probl. Perspect. Manage. 31, 40-42 (2004); *See also La Manna*, 10 Int'l. J. Indus. Org. 81, 81-82 (1992) (noting that a high minimum patentability standard would be more optimal instrument than setting patent life, and would demand the patentees to develop his idea into a well-defined form with specifically beneficial properties to be granted as patents).

1543 *Scotchmer/Green*, 21 RAND J. Econ. 131 (1990).

induce more innovators to enter into the race.[1544] Van Dijk coins a new term, "patent height," which is mainly determined by the stringency of the novelty requirements and defines the degree of protection against rival improvements.[1545] He explains that patent height could be deployed as a policy instrument to incentivize certain types of research, thus high protection would stimulate basic research.[1546]

Abramowicz and Duffy maintain that it could even be considered as a way of permitting patents to issue on products that are not technologically novel if they do not exist in the market place.[1547] Roin argues for relaxing the novelty requirement for basic inventions in the pharmaceutical art and proposes amending the novelty requirement to allow patenting drugs that have not yet been developed and are not otherwise covered by a valid patent or a pending patent application.[1548] At the same time, he recommends applying the traditional patentability standards to drugs that are derived from certain minor changes to existing drugs.[1549]

b) Proposal on the novelty requirement of species selection invention

(1) Meaning of something "made available to the public" in the pharmaceutical industry

Owing to the cumulative nature of technologies, some patents granted today can hinder the follow-on inventions,[1550] as long as they are still valid and can exclude others from exploiting their inventions. However, after patent term expiration, these inventions are available to the public, and the public must be free to use them. The U.S. Supreme Court held as follows:

> "First, patent law seeks to foster and reward invention; second, it promotes disclosure of inventions, to stimulate further innovation and to permit the public

1544 *Scotchmer/Green*, 21 RAND J. Econ. 131 (1990) (*cf.* In the same literature, they also argued the weak patentability would be attractive as well, since it would permit the technologies to be patented and this is also socially valuable.).
1545 *Van Dijk*, 44 J. Ind. Econ. 151, 152 (1996).
1546 *Van Dijk*, 44 J. Ind. Econ. 151, 165-66 (1996).
1547 *Abramowicz/Duffy*, 83 N.Y.U. L. Rev. 337, 398 (2008).
1548 *Roin*, 87 Tex. L. Rev. 503, 558, 567 (2009) (further distinguishing the one which did not need to go through the clinical trials from those which needed to do so.).
1549 *Roin*, 87 Tex. L. Rev. 503, 558, 567 (2009).
1550 *See* subsection II.A.

> to practice the invention once the patent expires; third, the stringent requirements for patent protection seek to assure that ideas in the public domain remain there for the free use of the public."[1551]

In other words, the information already disclosed to the public must keep providing free access to them and cannot be subject of further patent protection.[1552] To accomplish this, those inventions that have been made available to the public constitute the prior art and claims to identical inventions would lack novelty. As Merges notes, "[t]he logic behind [the novelty requirement] is fairly straightforward, [since, if] information is already in the public domain when the 'inventor' seeks to patent it; society has no need to grant a patent to get this information."[1553] In addition, denying an invention a patent because of the lack of novelty could mean that an idea has been available to the public. This is proper for such industries as mechanics, where, once the idea, like the structure of a wheel, is available, the public can easily exploit the idea and enjoy the product.

However, what is the meaning of an idea being available to the public in the pharmaceutical art? One may look at one genus invention claimed as a Markush type claim[1554] and consider what kind of invention the public can practice once the patent expires, or what kinds of ideas become public domain and remain for the free use of the public. A person skilled in the art may have a fairly good idea about the structures and expected potential therapeutic effects of millions of compounds, and he could work on them for future development. However, the public could hardly benefit from a new medication, unless someone has invested and succeeded in gaining market-

---

1551 *Aronson v. Quick Point Pencil Co.*, 440 U.S. 257, 262 (1979); *see also Ann*, 2009, 361 (noted "[p]atents, as a rule, shall do no more than reward and promote innovative activity and encourage the disclosure of its results.").

1552 *Eisenberg*, 53 Vand. L. Rev. 2081, 2088 (2000) ("Granting patents on technologies that are not new would impose the social costs of monopolies without the countervailing benefits of promoting development and introduction of welfare-enhancing inventions."); *Merges*, 7 High Tech. L. J. 1, 12-13 (1992).

1553 *Merges*, 7 High Tech. L. J. 1, 12-13 (1992); see also Art. 54(2) EPC ("The state of the art shall be held to comprise ***everything made available to the public*** by means of a written or oral description, by use, or in any other way, before the date of filing of the European patent application." [Emphasis added]); *See also* 35 U.S.C. 2011 Art. 102(a) ("A person shall be entitled to a patent unless—(1) the claimed invention was patented, described in a printed publication, or in public use, on sale, or ***otherwise available to the public*** before the effective filing date of the claimed invention." [Emphasis added]).

1554 See e.g. *supra* 110 and accompanying texts.

ing approval for it as a drug.[1555] In this sense, the novelty requirement seems to treat the pharmaceutical field more strictly than it does other technical fields, since novelty is judged based on whether the idea of the invention is new, not on whether the product is or has been accessible to the public.[1556] Put differently, the mere earlier disclosure of an idea, not the accessibility of a product, can keep the invention from being patented, thereby possibly depriving the pharmaceutical companies of opportunities to invest in launching a product. The situation has been getting worse because of the over and immature disclosure problem,[1557] which has prevented more potential drugs from becoming patentable. The same would be true for any industry where the itinerary from the invention to the product is long and costly, and investment is unlikely to be decided upon without the patent protection.

(2) A patent as a double-edged sword to NMEs

In contrast to what has been observed hitherto, a patent can be a double-edged sword to NMEs, because patent law better protects tangible products and processes than it does information. A medication is rich in information, which costs time and money.[1558] This could also be because the patent is not granted in exchange for subsequent investments,[1559] but for the creation and disclosure of inventions, which is secured through the novelty requirement. On the one hand, many pharmaceuticals could not have reached the public without a patent protecting them from the copycats; on the other hand, the prior arts which are mainly the prior patents, and the stricter novelty requirement in this industry have potentially prevented medicines from being further developed, because the basic idea was disclosed somewhere. This simply results in much reduced health gains as compared to those that could have been produced by the medications.

A more liberalized approach to the patentability requirements of species selection inventions, therefore, would provide more opportunities for com-

---

1555 *See also*, *Straus*, 2009, 482.
1556 *Roin*, 87 Tex. L. Rev. 503, 517-518 (2009).
1557 See subsection III.B.2.c)(3).
1558 *See* subsection III.A.1.
1559 *Kitch*, 20 J. Law Econ. 265, 276 (1977) ("[...] the development of patented inventions generally requires significant investments that lead to unpatented information.").

panies to conduct research. This approach would be in line with earlier cases in which courts have held to grant patents on the medications that were purified from a mixture of natural products, because the inventions made the medications available for the first time for any uses.[1560] How, then we can reach the goal? This will be reviewed in light of statutory examples, proposals, and the implications of the *Olanzapine* decisions.

(3) Statutory exceptions to the novelty requirement and considerations thereof

According to the UK Patents Act 1949, an invention was not deemed to have been anticipated solely because it was published in the United Kingdom either in a specification filed in pursuance of an application for a patent made there more than fifty years earlier or in a specification describing the invention for the purposes of an application for protection in any country outside the United Kingdom made more than 50 years earlier.[1561] This provision means that an inventor who unearths lost technology might make a significant contribution to scientific progress.[1562]

There are also a few existing exceptions in the form of industry specific provisions, such as Art. 54(4) and (5) EPC (special novelty provision for 1st and 2nd medical use) and 35 U.S.C. § 103(b) (special non-obviousness provision for biotechnological invention). The former provides statutory exceptions to novelty to the extent that, even if a substance is not new, it is still patentable for any medical method if the use for any medical method was not comprised in the state of the art. In addition, even if the substance was patented for one medical use, it is still patentable for a new use of the same substance. By now it should be easy to be noticed that the novelty exceptions provided by the EPC seem to have a similar basis to the decisions on the early medications, i.e. "made it available to the public for the first time as a medication." In any case, it seems to be possible to make an exception in the patentability standards for drugs. However, there are further concerns. Firstly, dramatic alterations to the patentability standards would likely produce unexpected results given this industry's creative litigation

1560 See subsection VI.B.2.b); *see e.g., Parke-Davis & Co. v. H.K. Mulford Co.*, 189 F. 95, 103 (C.C.N.Y., 1911).
1561 UK Patents Act, 1949, Section 50(1).
1562 *Keeling*, 2003, 41.

tactics.[1563] Secondly, it would be difficult to implement specifically different treatment, and even if it could be done, it is doubtful whether the law can keep pace with the real progress in the development of technology. Thirdly, there is still concern about violating Art. 27(1) TRIPS.[1564]

Some scholars also argue against industry-specific patent legislation.[1565] Instead, they contend that industries must be treated differently through the existing patent law provisions and doctrines.[1566] As Long maintains, tailoring the application of different rules to the relevant circumstances can be done without the intervention of Congress.[1567] This would provide a degree of flexibility in the patent system for pharmaceutical inventions without involving legislative changes. Therefore, possible applications to pharmaceutical inventions will now be explored and suggested.

(4) Proposed novelty requirement for NMEs

Many scholars contend that a strong novelty requirement would bring more robust and advanced inventions and less incremental inventions. However, most of them do not seem to consider the specificities of the pharmaceutical art, such as the broad disclosure of the Markush type claim, the attrition rate of drug candidates, the easy and over-disclosure problem, and the unpredictability in this art. Roin, however, specifically discusses the problems in the industry and proposes increasing the amount of information necessary to make a drug not novel, such that a prior disclosure would not be adequate unless the disclosure were sufficient to support the invention as a drug ("his proposal").[1568] He further contends that Congress would be justified in reforming patent law as above to ensure that such doctrines would no longer deter the development of socially valuable drugs.[1569] In the same article, however, he rejects his own proposal for the following reasons: that it could be a violation of the Constitution, namely, the two doctrines - (i) Congress can use the patent system only to "promote the progress of … useful

1563 *Roin*, 87 Tex. L. Rev. 503, 559 (2009).
1564 See *supra* 1506 -1517 and accompanying texts.
1565 *Burk/Lemley*, 89 Va. L. Rev. 1575, 1634-38 (2003).
1566 *Burk/Lemley*, 89 Va. L. Rev. 1575, 1638-68 (2003); *see also Long*, 55 Fed. Law. 44, 49 (2008).
1567 *Long*, 55 Fed. Law. 44, 49 (2008).
1568 *Roin*, 87 Tex. L. Rev. 503, 560 (2009).
1569 *Roin*, 87 Tex. L. Rev. 503, 560 (2009).

arts,"[1570] (ii) based on this Congress may not "authorize the issuance of patents whose effects are to remove existent knowledge from the public domain",[1571] that it could be misused to evergreen the old drugs, that it could not solve the problems caused by the non-obviousness standard,[1572] and that it could violate Art. 27(1) TRIPS.[1573]

In light of this concern about overcoming non-obviousness hurdle, he gives up his proposal too early, if this was the reason for the rejection. Overcoming the novelty requirement is impossible as long as the invention is anticipated by the prior art. However, once it is different from the prior art, there are many grounds upon which to argue that the invention involves an inventive step. In addition, according to his proposal, the amount of prior art would be greatly reduced. Since non-obviousness is assessed over the prior art, this standard would not be that problematic. Instead, it is important to provide applicants with room to argue by relaxing the novelty requirement.

The real concern regarding his proposal arises from his intention to substantially reduce the prior art to only that which discloses the information which provides sufficient support for a drug. This would involve regarding something as novel that is not novel. This justifies his concern about the potential violation of the Constitution. In addition, as discussed, the amount of potential prior art would be substantially reduced. Since this provision could open the patent door too wide, which would increase the opportunity for double patenting. Further, as he mentions, this provision could be misused, since, as long as there is no prior art disclosing that the invention was available as a drug, the possibility of receiving a patent would be raised. In the end, the enforceability of these potentially overlapping patents would naturally create serious problems. Thus, while his apprehensions about the unpatentable drug are understandable, the proposal is somewhat at odds with patent law.

In fact, some of these problems appear to be solved by the *Olanzapine* decision within the realm of patent law, and it is therefore advisable to appreciate and apply it.

1570 U.S. Const. Art. I, § 8, cl. 8.

1571 *Graham v. John Deere Co.*, 383 U.S. 1, 6 (1966).

1572 *Roin*, 87 Tex. L. Rev. 503, 559-60 (2009).

1573 *Roin*, 87 Tex. L. Rev. 503, 558 (2009). Regarding this concern, see subsection VI.D.2.a)(3).

(5) Appreciation of the Olanzapine decision and its expected results

The *Olanzapine* decision[1574] may be the result of efforts to try to solve this problem. While giving up its earlier efforts to reconcile the discrepancy between the scope and the disclosure of the invention (See Figure 11), the BGH finally held that, unless the prior art disclosed the claimed invention clearly and unambiguously, the prior art does not deprive the novelty of the invention. Namely, contrary to its traditional position of denying selection inventions, the BGH increased the amount of information necessary to anticipate the later claimed invention. Therefore, this decision solved the problem sagely without changing the fundamental framework of the patent system.

Since the earlier disclosure of the genus claim is too broad, it is hardly possible to realize the full scope of invention. Thus, it would certainly be beneficial to provide an invention to find a narrower subgroup having particular properties which might have been difficult to find by trial and error.[1575] Even if the much relaxed novelty requirement in the *Olanzapine* decision raises some concerns,[1576] it enhances the possibility of resuscitating an invention in the lists of thousands of theoretically generated and published compounds.

Furthermore, a species invention does not create the situation in which a prior user unexpectedly identifies a new patent stopping him from continuing the work that he has long been undertaking. In *In re Cruciferous Sprouts Litigation*, the Federal Circuit reinforced the basic rule that a patentee must not have gained exclusive rights over something that was previously in the prior art.[1577] A species patent could prevent the genus patentee from working on the very species invention, but the species patent would not stop someone who has been working so far, because a species invention could have been patented, since no one appreciated the invention. On the contrary, a species patent could increase the possibility of making a new medication available to the public, which would allow society to benefit from further medications that would otherwise hardly have garnered investment and reached the market.[1578]

1574 *See e.g., BGH/Olanzapine,* IIC 2009, 596.
1575 *Grubb/Thomsen*, 2010, 335.
1576 See subsection V.A.2.
1577 *In re Cruciferous Sprout Litigation*, 301 F.3d 1343, 1350 (Fed. Cir. 2002).
1578 *See also, Straus*, 2009, 483.

c) Discussion on the novelty requirement of other selection inventions

Novelty of selection inventions is mainly based on the identification, purification, or selection of the invention. As Lord Neuberger stated, the technical contribution of selection invention is to make a selected invention – in this case, an enantiomer - available for the first time.[1579] One may recall the earlier meaning of "make available to the public." Patents were granted on the early medications that were products of extraction and purification from mainly natural sources when the nature of this industry was more a manufacturing industry than a research-based industry.[1580] These early medications were indeed made available to the public for the first time, as the result of which they could cure disorders for the first time. In a similar fashion, selection inventions, such as enantiomers, polymorphs, and metabolites, were also made available for the first time. However, the public already had access to the older ones, such as racemates, a group of polymorphs, or parent drugs.

Even though the level of contribution of other selection inventions is much lower, they were enabled for the first time. In addition, the anticipation has required both the specifically clear and unambiguous disclosure and enablement, and the prior art generally did not enable the selected ones. Therefore, it would be absurd to argue in favour of applying a different novelty requirement to other selection inventions.

3. Proposals on the inventive step requirement

The importance of the non-obviousness doctrine accords with the difficulty of the inquiry because this requirement attempts to measure technical accomplishment, which is a quality more abstract than novelty or utility.[1581] Thus, non-obviousness is described as a "nontriviality" requirement in patent law.[1582]

1579 *Generics Ltd. v. Lundbeck* [2009] UKHL 12, para 83.
1580 *Dutfield*, 2009, 59-60.
1581 *Merges/Duffy*, 2011, 620.
1582 *Merges/Duffy*, 2011, 620.

a) Arguments on the inventive step requirement

(1) Arguments for a strict inventive step requirement

Many scholars contend that the demanding inventive step requirements would work better to promote R&D on advanced and major inventions. O'Donoghue shows that, when there are transaction costs, a patent system based on strict non-obviousness requirements is a better regime, which can stimulate R&D investment and increase dynamic social welfare.[1583] He explains that this is because, when an improvement is patentable only if it meets a stricter patentability requirement (or its size is large enough), inventors must pursue more ambitious projects, which will take longer to realize.[1584] In other words, a higher patentability requirement would stimulate R&D investment without significantly increasing market power and would provide forward protection by delaying the next patentable innovation and slowing down the market turnover.[1585] Similarly, Hunt argues that increasing the standard of non-obviousness would stimulate R&D investment or increase the average flow profit of patentable discoveries and the economically effective life of patents.[1586] Avorn contends that patent laws could take a more conservative view to determine whether a minor change of an existing molecule, such as one-atom changes or isomerisations, warrant patent exclusivity.[1587] Burk and Lemley also mention that lowering the obviousness threshold would make marginal inventions more likely be patented, but this would do nothing to encourage inventions that would have met the non-obviousness standard anyway.[1588] Merges similarly maintains that the strict non-obviousness requirement was to encourage companies to engage in "risky" R&D projects, where there is "relatively" high uncertainty of com-

1583 *O'Donoghue*, 29 RAND J. Econ. 654, 664 (1998) (noting this is so because weaker patentability requirement might retard R&D because it provide less protection from future innovators); *See also Hunt*, 1999, 37-38.

1584 *O'Donoghue*, 29 RAND J. Econ. 654 (1998).

1585 *O'Donoghue*, 29 RAND J. Econ. 654, 673 (1998); *Hunt*, 1999.

1586 *Hunt*, 1999 11, 30-35 (also noting that lowered non-obviousness requirement would be less likely to raise R&D activity in industries that already innovate rapidly).

1587 *Avorn*, 309 Science 669, 669 (2005); *See also, Angell*, 2004, 240.

1588 *Burk/Lemley*, 89 Va. L. Rev. 1575, 1682 (2003).

mercial success.[1589] Scotchmer argues that a strong patentability requirement would weaken the incentives of subsequent inventors, and even that patents should not be granted on the applications and other second generation products.[1590]

(2) Arguments for a strict inventive step requirement together with broader protection

Some scholars recommend higher patentability requirements in the consideration of the broad scope of a basic patent. To protect basic inventions against future inventions, either the patent protection for second generation inventions could be denied or made harder through a high patentability requirement, or second generation inventions could infringe the patents of basic innovations by granting a broad patent scope of basic innovations.[1591] Both policies have a blocking effect on second generation inventions, since the second generation inventor would hesitate to invest or would not invest in them, either because the invention would be hard to obtain a patent for, or because the inventor would have less bargaining power. Denicolò and Zanchettin argue that granting a broader patent scope on the first invention would nevertheless be better, since, as long as the second innovation was patentable, it creates mutual blocking which might be solved through an *ex post* licensing agreement that would have a sharing effect.[1592]

However, a broader scope of patent would increase the market power and deadweight loss, thus, a higher patentability requirement would a better tool to achieve the goal with fewer side effects.

1589 *Merges*, 88 Cal. L. Rev. 2187, 2225-2226 (2000) (noting "high-cost research justifies a less stringent standard of purely technical nonobviousness."); *Merges*, 7 High Tech. L. J. 1, 3-4 (1992) (argued moderate lowering of patentability standards are required for the very high-cost research.).

1590 *Scotchmer*, 27 RAND J. Econ. 322, 323 (1996) (further arguing that the first innovators can collect more profit even by denying patents on second generation products than by granting some of them).

1591 *Friebel et al.*, 2006, 26; *Denicolò/Zanchettin*, 20 Int'l. J. Indus. Org. 801, 801-802 (2002); *Denicolò*, 31 RAND J. Econ. 488, 489 (2000); *Gallini/Scotchmer*, 2002, 66.

1592 *Denicolò/Zanchettin*, 20 Int'l. J. Indus. Org. 801, 825-826 (2002).

(3) Arguments against a strict inventive step requirement

In contrast, some scholars warn that too high a hurdle on the patentability requirement would prevent desirable secondary innovations from occurring.[1593] Denicolò explains that this is because, when the second invention was seldom patentable, on the one hand only the first inventor would be willing to develop the second invention and fully internalize the benefit of the future innovation; on the other hand, the second innovation would be underinvested, because R&D competition would be eliminated.[1594] Lemley also notes that it would discourage improvements too strongly, thus freezing development at the first generation of products.[1595] As Friebel *et al,*. point out, demanding patentability requirements would weaken the second inventors' incentives only when (i) the prior art patents are still in force and (ii) where the inventions take place in more than two stages.[1596] Theoretically, this might result in so-called 'patent-thicket problems.'[1597]

(4) Arguments for the relaxed inventive step requirement in risky and expensive R&D fields

Regardless of their basic positions, some scholars have justified a relaxed standard of non-obviousness in the field of technology, because its R&D is very risky and expensive.[1598] Merges especially urges that a moderate lowering of patentability standards, such as the non-obviousness requirement, would be required for the very high-cost research.[1599] Roin considers lowering the non-obviousness requirement to patent drugs that have not yet been

---

1593 *Denicolò*, 31 RAND J. Econ. 488 (2000); *Friebel et al.,* 2006, 29.

1594 *Denicolò*, 31 RAND J. Econ. 488 (2000).

1595 *Lemley*, 75 Tex. L. Rev. 989, 990 (1997).

1596 *Friebel et al.,* 2006, 29.

1597 *Friebel et al.,* 2006, 29; *Denicolò/Zanchettin,*20 Int'l. J. Indus. Org. 801, 803 (2002) (noting demanding patentability requirement would not have blocking effect on second generation inventions when the original innovator obtains the second generation innovation.).

1598 *Boyd*, 12 Berkeley Tech. L. J. 311, 337-343 (1997); *Merges*, 7 High Tech. L. J. 1, 3-4 (1992); *Merges*, 88 Cal. L. Rev. 2187, 2225-2226 (2000).

1599 *Merges*, 7 High Tech. L. J. 1, 3-4 (1992); *Merges*, 88 Cal. L. Rev. 2187, 2225-2226 (2000) (noting "high-cost research justifies a less stringent standard of purely technical nonobviousness.").

developed.[1600] Boyd also asserts that a lowered standard of non-obviousness is required to permit the industry to overcome the risk aversion that is otherwise problematic.[1601]

Many scholars comment on the post-invention costs and the uncertainty of commercializing inventions in the assessment of non-obviousness, although these considerations are not relevant to the determination of obviousness.[1602] Benjamin and Rai argue that, where the economic expense or the risk of development of an invention is substantial, allowing a patent on even an obvious invention could be useful.[1603] Shavell also notes that, if an invention tends to fail the non-obviousness requirement, but its development cost is high and would clearly not be covered by the profits in the absence of patent protection, not awarding a patent on that invention would be a mistake under an economic analysis.[1604] Burk and Lemley also contend that, for patents to drive innovation and not merely invention, courts must consider the cost and uncertainty of post-invention testing and development.[1605] Abramowicz and Duffy argue that it makes sense to weaken the non-obviousness standards to encourage the commercialization of new products,[1606] or even to extend this theory to permit patents to issue on products that are technologically non-novel if they do not exist in the market place. Considering that these assertions were for inventions with high post-invention costs or uncertainty, the same can be argued for the basic patents on the pharmaceuticals which are the inventions themselves.

1600 *Roin*, 87 Tex. L. Rev. 503, 558, 567 (2009) (further distinguishing the one which did not need to go through the clinical trials from those which needed to do so).

1601 *Boyd*, 12 Berkeley Tech. L. J. 311, 339 (1997).

1602 *Graham v. John Deere Co.*, 383 U.S. 1,11 (1966) (providing outline of basic non-obviousness test).

1603 *Benjamin/Rai*, 95 Geo. L. J. 269, 278 (2007); *Kitch*, 20 J. Law Econ. 265, 265-67, 269 (1977) (advocating development as a significant consideration for granting patent rights).

1604 *Shavell*, 2004, 152-53, fn 31.

1605 *Burk/Lemley*, 89 Va. L. Rev. 1575, 1678 (2003); *see also Merges*, 7 High Tech. L. J. 1, 47, 33-34 (1992) (noting to consider the commercial uncertainty to assess non-obviousness).

1606 *Abramowicz/Duffy*, 83 N.Y.U. L. Rev. 337, 398 (2008).

b) Proposal on the inventive step of species selection inventions

There are further considerations on the expenditure of money on the creation of inventions to assess the inventive step. In the United States, several decisions noted that the expenditure of a large amount of money to make the invention tended to show that the invention was non-obvious.[1607] Commercial success has long been to be one of the secondary considerations in establishing an inventive step. Consideration of commercial success while judging obviousness helps to foster technological innovation.[1608] Post-invention costs are in the same vein as these considerations.

Expensive research alone, however, has not been regarded as an important indicator of patentability, and courts have considered this factor in a limited class of cases.[1609] Critics have also noted that commercial success is not a good indicator of patentability, because it is indirect and depends on a long chain of inferences that are weak,[1610] and because commercial success might instead indicate "sales promotion ability, manufacturing technique, ready access to markets, consumer appeal design factors, and advertising budget."[1611] Simply put, the weak point of these arguments rests upon whether there is causal relationship between these factors and the technical value of the invention.

However, it would be still advisable to consider *post-invention costs* or *high-uncertainty in the course of development* as among the *secondary con-*

1607 *See for instance, Panduit Corp. v. Dennison Mfg.*, 774 F.2d 1082, 1099 (Fed. Cir. 1985) (fact that patentee took a couple of years and spent millions of dollars is one of the evidence that the invention is non-obvious); *Edoco Technical Products, Inc. v. Peter Kiewit Sons' Co.*, 313 F. Supp. 1081, 1086 (C.D. Cal. 1970) (the fact that a long and expensive period of experimentation was required to solve the problem was an important evidence of non-obviousness); *see also Sanofi-Synthelabo v. Apotex, Inc.*, 470 F.3d 1368, 1379 (Fed. Cir. 2006), *reh'g denied* (Jan. 19, 2007) (the extensive time and money [the patentee] spent developing the racemate before redirecting its efforts toward the enantiomer was one of the indicators of non-obviousness); *cf. United States v. Ciba-Geigy Corp.*, 508 F. Supp. 1157, 1168 (D.C.N.J. 1979) (a costly research undertaken should be rewarded with a product patent).

1608 *Merges*, 76 Cal. L. R. 803, 837-388 (1988).

1609 *Merges*, 7 High Tech. L. J. 1, 55 (1992).

1610 *Kitch*, 1966 Sup. Ct. Rev. 293, 330-35 (1966) (also noting courts should even more cautious to hold the patents valid, since commercially successful patents can truly impose a monopoly tax on the market).

1611 *Kitch*, 1966 Sup. Ct. Rev. 293, 332 (1966); *see also Landes/Posner*, 2003, 305.

siderations for the following reasons. Firstly, the patent system aims to promote not only the invention but also the innovation. If high post-invention costs are incurred to bring an invention to the innovation or uncertainty in the same course, fewer innovations will be realized without patent protection. Commercial success has been used to transform the patentability doctrine partially into an instrument that rewards innovation rather than invention.[1612] Secondly, the benefit of the invention to the patients who are awaiting new medications must be considered. If an invention regarding a new drug failed to acquire a patent based on its relatively weak inventive step, the invention could hardly reach the market as a medicine. In the end, the loss of even one NME may be seen as a loss.

When considering post-invention costs or uncertainty, there appears to be a greater opportunity to argue that the basic invention establishes the inventive step which allows the patentee to secure a patent on it. Thus, the increased incentives could bring more NMEs to the public, which could in turn provide new opportunities to save or prolong life, or to improve the quality of life. On the other hand, the impact may not be so dramatic, since this factor can be considered only by the courts, not by the patent offices. The courts are in a better position to consider this factor basing their decisions on the evidence gathered in the period of time up to and during the litigation.

c) Proposal on the inventive step of other selection inventions

(1) Introduction

Many scholars argue that a heightened inventive step requirement would result in better and advanced inventions, while too high a hurdle could stifle second generation inventions.[1613] Thus, a demanding inventive step requirement is to be recommended to encourage the manufacturers to work more on basic inventions. However, no proposal has been advanced to suggest how to raise the inventive step requirement, especially for the pharmaceutical art.

1612 *Merges*, 76 Cal. L. R. 803, 876 (1988).
1613 See subsection VI.E.3.a).

(2) Proposed standard to assess the inventive step

"Therapeutic contribution" as a secondary indicia

The inventive step requirement prevents granting patents on inventions that are likely to reach the public without the inducement of the patent system and excludes such slight advances from the patent protection.[1614] Since patent exclusivity can be justified by this technical advance or contribution to the art, when there was no real technical advance in art, the objection of obviousness must be made.[1615] Therefore, the measurement of the technical contribution to the art is important in assessing the inventive step.

It is advisable to assess the level of "therapeutic contribution" of pharmaceutical inventions as a consideration of the technical contribution in this field. The value of a patent is calibrated by structural features; however, the value of a pharmaceutical patent is the therapeutic effect itself.[1616]

(3) Basis of the proposal

Technical contribution of inventions

The patentability requirement of computer-implemented inventions is defined in the EPO glossary as follows: "To be patentable, they must have technical character and solve a technical problem, be new and involve an *inventive technical contribution* to the prior art."[1617] [Emphasis added]. However, it does not further define the inventive technical contribution to the prior art, which seems to refer to the inventive step of the computer-implemented invention. While distinguishing "inventive concept," which was concerned with the "identification" of the core of the invention, the House of Lords held that "technical contribution" was concerned with the evaluation of its inventive concept, i.e. how far forward had it carried the

---

1614 *Eisenberg*, 19 Berkeley Tech. L.J. 885 (2004).

1615 *Dr Reddy's Laboratories Ltd v. Eli Lilly & Company Ltd*, [2009] EWCA Civ 1362, paras 40-52; *Agrevo/Triazoles*, T 939/92, OJ EPO 309, 319-20 (1996), point 2.4.2. ("it has for long been a generally accepted legal principle that the extent of the patent monopoly should correspond to and be justified by the technical contribution to the art […].").

1616 *Domeij*, 2000, 87.

1617 *EPO glossary*, available at: http://www.epo.org/service-support/glossary.html. (Last accessed on December 20, 2013).

state of the art.[1618] The European Examination Guidelines also note that, if an invention is shown to have considerable technical value, which provides a new and surprising technical advantage, this technical advantage is of great importance in assessing the inventive step.[1619] In turn, the test of inventive step is directly linked to the social practical value of the invention that is newly created by the inventor.[1620]

This technical contribution is also the basis for determining the breadth of a claimed invention, since the extent of exclusivity should not exceed the technical contribution to the art made by the invention as described in the specification.[1621] In other words, a patent should not be granted if the benefits do not exceed the costs.[1622] The provision of a product, such as other species inventions, is also one of the technical contributions to the art. According to the case laws, contributions of other species inventions lie more in the identification and purification of the claimed inventions. As Kitchin J properly pointed out, however, the inventive idea connected with an enantiomer is neither the discovery of the enantiomer nor its medicinal effect, only the process required to synthesize it.[1623] Although the exclusivity should not exceed the technical contribution to the art, instead of granting a patent on the process to manufacture the enantiomer, a further absolute compound protection is provided to these inventions. As a result, both old and new versions of the same drugs, i.e. enantiomer and racemate, polymorphs, metabolites and the parent drugs are concurrently available in a number of countries.[1624]

The genuine technical contribution of drug patents: Therapeutic contribution

The genuine technical contribution of a drug invention to the pharmaceutical art should be the "therapeutic contribution." This has been more often required in other regimes than the patent system. For example, some scholars

1618 *Generics Ltd. v. Lundbeck* [2009] UKHL 12, para 30.

1619 EPO Examination Guidelines G-VII, 8.

1620 *Domeij*, 2000, 205.

1621 *Biogen Inc v. Medeva Plc* [1996] UKHL 18, point 80.

1622 *Mazzoleni/Nelson*, 27 Res. Policy, 273, 275 (1998).

1623 *Lundbeck v. Generics Ltd.* [2008] EWCA Civ 311, para 26; *Generics (UK) Ltd & Ors v. Lundbeck A/S* [2007] EWHC 1040 (Pat), paras64-66.

1624 *Hutt/Valentová*, 50 Acta Facultatis Pharmaceuticae Universitatis Comenianae 7, 8 (2003).

propose the contribution of innovations, which is a therapeutic contribution in the case of a pharmaceutical innovation, as a ground for awarding a "prize,"[1625] which is a kind of a reward to the innovator as a lump sum payment and is an incentive to invest in the invention.[1626] The therapeutic contribution is also considered as an important factor in reimbursement schemes, such as controlling costs of the newer and costly drug, the therapeutic contribution of which may be small,[1627] in contrast to the innovative drugs which offer major therapeutic advances.[1628] The Korean Supreme Court has considered whether the claimed technical contribution of selected inventions also contribute to showing the *pharmaceutical effects (benefits)* over the basic inventions.[1629] It would be also highly advisable to require pharmaceutical inventions to prove their therapeutic contributions over the prior art. Such therapeutic contributions could also consist in the enhancement of absorption of a substance, prolongation of the duration of effects, mitigation of the side effect of main substance, and the like.

Therapeutic contributions of other selection inventions

One may need to consider the extent to which the other selection inventions contribute to the treatment as a medicine over their older versions. Higgins and Graham contend that even though those new products which are covered by improvement patents reach the market sooner, they are much less likely to provide improvement over previous products.[1630] Rai also insists that there are drugs that provide little or even no therapeutic advantage over existing drugs.[1631] These non-NMEs do little to increase the length of human life.[1632] Some new drugs covered by secondary fresh patents are frequently associated with higher potential monopoly costs, without providing measurable economic and/or clinical advantages.[1633] Many scholars doubt the clinical benefits of the enantiomer inventions over the racemates. Some sci-

1625 *Arbex*, 2009, 3; *Abramowicz*, 2003, 91-118.
1626 *Rockett*, 2010, 355-56.
1627 *Schweitzer*, 2007, 126; *see also Rucker*, 1996, 73.
1628 *Schweitzer*, 2007, 146.
1629 *Korean Supreme Court/Lercanidipine*, 2010Hu2872, Jul. 14, 2011, para 2.; *Korean Supreme Court/ Ibandronate*, 2010Hu3554, Sept. 8, 2011, para 2.
1630 *Higgins/Graham*, 326 Science 370, 370 (2009).
1631 *Rai*, Ill. L. Rev. 173, 205-06 (2001).
1632 *Lichtenberg*, 5 Int. J. Health Care Fi. 47, 70 (2005).
1633 *Zhang/Soumerai*, 26 Health Affair. 880, 884 (2007).

entists note “some new chemical entities[1634] might be minor modifications of older agents without offering measurable clinical benefits, such as esomeprazole (Nexium) versus omeprazole (Prilosec).”[1635] Other scientists also observe that the overall degree of clinical improvement that could be expected from the purified preparation of one isomer might be limited unless the total dose was correspondingly increased.[1636] They add that there is no published evidence to indicate any advantage of esomeprazole 40mg over omeprazole 40mg.[1637] Although the different physical properties of polymorphs could contribute the characteristics required to handle the substances, such as filterability or drying properties, it could hardly provide better therapeutic effects. The only action that could contribute to the clinical benefit of the metabolites would be to onset the therapeutic effects slightly earlier.

Regarding the two crystalline forms of atorvastatin, the BOA made it clear that although not every crystalline form provides improved filterability or drying characteristics, trying this carries a reasonable expectation of success.[1638] Therefore, the provision of crystalline forms that present nothing more than the obvious advantages of crystalline forms based on their improved physical and/or physicochemical properties would not be sufficient to find as an inventive. However, crystalline forms could be found non-obvious, if they provided unexpected pharmaceutical activity. Likewise, separation of enantiomer from the racemate or identification of a metabolite would provide virtually expected results.

(4) Expected effects

Consideration of the therapeutic contribution as one of the secondary indications would provide drugs with improved effects, could discourage inventors from working on the rather obvious modifications and variations of

---

1634 According to the criteria provided by this dissertation, Es-omeprazole is not a new chemical entity, but a second generation product.

1635 *Zhang/Soumerai*, 26 Health Affair. 880, 884 (2007).

1636 *Sachs/Shin/ Howden*, 23 (Suppl. 2) Aliment Pharm. Ther. 2, 7 (2006).

1637 *Sachs/Shin/ Howden*, 23 (Suppl. 2) Aliment Pharm. Ther. 2, 7 (2006) (For example, although esomeprazole 40 mg has been shown in some trials to be superior to omeprazole 20 mg, there is no published evidence to indicate any advantage of esomeprazole 40 mg over omeprazole 40 mg.).

1638 *Warner-Lambert/Atorvastatin polymorphs,* T 0777/08 (2011).

existing medications, and lead them to carry out research on more ambitious projects. Furthermore, since there is little monopoly situation in the pharmaceutical market,[1639] once an inventor acquired the patents on second generation inventions that show therapeutically advanced effects, these patents would provide them with more competitiveness in the market place as well.

In addition, the loss of these second generation inventions should not be of too much concern. Firstly, with some effort, work on second generation inventions can be performed without the help of a patent. Secondly, even if this leads to the loss of these inventions, since these kinds of inventions have followed successful basic inventions, the public would still have the "older" versions. In this regard, Roin notes that "this effect may be rather benign, such as when patent protection is denied to drugs that are so closely related to an older drug that they are unlikely to provide any additional therapeutic benefits."[1640] Indeed, these criteria would not foreclose the patent grant on second generation inventions. For example, if it mitigates the toxic effect of the racemate, the choice of an enantiomer will be patentable. If the parent drug is too much of a burden to the patient's metabolism and could be toxic, and a metabolite without this toxicity is found, this metabolite should be allowed patent protection. Therapeutic contribution could be further acknowledged when a new dosage form enables a certain group of patients to take the basic medication. Examples of such improvements are oral dosage forms when the original form was a parenteral drug, or combinations of active ingredients showing a synergistic effect, thereby allowing the dose of a drug to be lowered.

The adaptation of these secondary criteria could be expedited under the recent decision of Federal Circuit holding that evidence of secondary considerations must be considered as part of all of the evidence, not just when the decision maker remains in doubt after reviewing the art. [1641]

1639 *See* subsection III.A.2.d).

1640 *Roin*, 87 Tex. L. Rev. 503, 537 (2009).

1641 *Transocean Offshore Deepwater Drilling, Inc. v. Maersk Drilling USA, Inc.*, 699 F.3d 1340, 1349 (Fed. Cir. 2012).

4. Discussions on the sufficiency requirement

a) Discrepancy between the scope of and the disclosure of a genus claim

In the *Fluoran* decision, the Court clarified that, even if the compound falls under a general formula in the prior art, nothing was said about the disclosure of the individual compound.[1642] In other words, the disclosure of a general chemical formula is not equivalent to the disclosure of all of the individual compounds that fall within the scope of the formula. However, all of these individual compounds literally infringe the claim that is characterised by the same general formula.[1643]

Similarly, the BOA noted that the question of the scope of the claims was distinct from the question of disclosure of these claims.[1644] According to the Board, there is a distinction between the extension of the concept and the intention of the concept, which extended from the individual examples and depended upon the person skilled in the art.[1645] (1) The maximum scope would be the full extent of the claim, (2) the next largest scope would be that which can be derived from the sum of individual examples by the person skilled in the art, and (3) the minimum scope would be the one indicated by the individual examples. It can be better understood by the following diagram.

1642 *BGH/Fluoran*, GRUR 1988, 447, 449 (holding it was more essential whether the skilled person could have produced the compound).

1643 *Hansen/Hirsch*, 1997, 336.

1644 *Amazonen-Werke/Zustreicher*, T 378/94, 1996, point 3.1.1.

1645 *Amazonen-Werke/Zustreicher*, T 378/94, 1996, point 3.1.1. ("The scope of protection is related to the "extension" of the concept defined in the claim, ie the sum of all individual objects that show all the features of the concept. In comparison, the disclosure is associated with the "intention" of the concept, i.e. all the features that allow an intellectual summary of individual objects. [...] If a claim is concerned with general concepts, then it discloses only these general concepts and does not all of specific examples which come under these general concepts.").

Figure 11: Discrepancy between the scope of and the disclosure of a genus claim[1646]

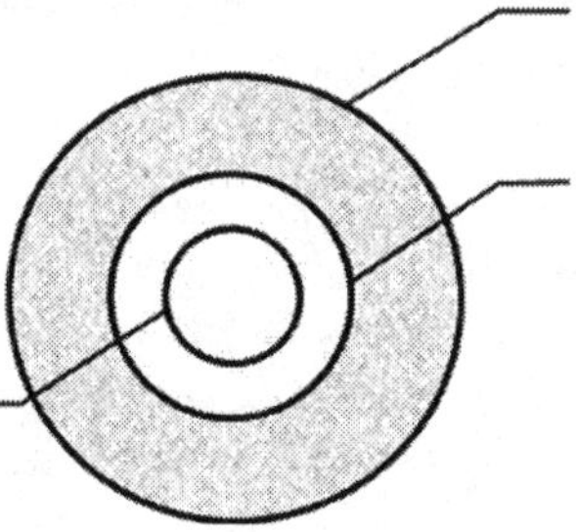

This discrepancy is hardly observed in other fields. The BGH's earlier approaches before its *Olanzapine* decision were that the disclosure was a simplified representation, as a result of which either the individual compounds in the compound selection[1647] or the intermediate values in the range selection (e.g., see Figure 6),[1648] which fall within the scope of disclosure, must be regarded as disclosed. Therefore, a patent on the selection could not be granted. Some scholars interpret the BGH's earlier general tendency not to grant the selection patents by broadening the content of disclosure of the generic formula as an effort to solve the discrepancy,[1649] i.e. to make the gray area in Figure 11 narrower by extending the area of middle circle to the outer circle. However, the end of this approach was declared through the novelty doctrine in the *Olanzapine* decision. Even if this approach may no longer be possible, one may still try to resolve the discrepancy by shrinking the biggest circle to reach the middle one, i.e. restricting the scope of the claim by applying the stricter disclosure requirement.

b) Stringent disclosure requirement of the basic invention

Patentability requirements, such as non-obviousness and enablement, rarely relate to the patent scope,[1650] but a stringent disclosure requirement would

1646 This figure is prepared by the author.
1647 *BGH/Fluoran*, GRUR 1988, 447.
1648 *BGH/Inkrustierungsinhibitoren (Incrustration inhibitors)*, GRUR 2000, 591, 593-94.
1649 *Hansen/Hirsch*, 1997, 336.
1650 *Chisum*, 15 AIPLA Q. J. 57, 58 (1987).

lead to patents with narrower scopes. Burk and Lemley argue that written description and enablement doctrines need to be recalibrated (reduced) to permit broader claiming of inventions.[1651] In contrast, Merges and Nelson maintain that more consistent and stricter interpretation of enablement and equivalents doctrines is necessary to achieve sounder policy.[1652]

The disclosure requirement is divided between the written description and the enablement. One may first consider applying a stricter enablement requirement. However, the enablement issue in respect of compounds is rarely raised. For example, olanzapine is a relatively simple chemical compound and is easily synthesized by the traditional method of manufacture. Thus, enablement was never drawn into question in this case. Next, in considering the written description, the specification must disclose the structure of the compounds and the claiming effects thereof that are commensurate with the scope of the claimed invention. As discussed in chapter III.B.2.c)(3), it is relatively easy to draw the structure, and there is a relatively fair relation between the structure and the technical effects. The unpredictability of inventions can play a role here, such that, if one can prove that some claimed compounds, for which a technical effect has not been demonstrated explicitly, do not show the predicted effects, part of the claim can be revoked. The examiners are hardly in a position to prove this and have to rely on third party observations in the course of the proceedings or during the opposition period after grant. However, once the scope of the basic invention becomes an issue, the selection patentee could test the compounds, invoke the lack of this requirement, and limit the scope of claims. One thing to note here is that the same scenario could not be realized in certain jurisdictions, such as the EPO, where violation of Art. 84 EPC, second sentence[1653] matters only during the original examination. Indeed, the non-availability of this in the revocation grounds has been well criticized,[1654] especially in the context of the allegedly overly broad claims in the field of chemistry and biotechnology.[1655] Some decisions by the BOA illustrate that the circumstances that

1651 *Burk/Lemley*, 89 Va. L. Rev. 1575, 1681-83 (2003).

1652 *Merges/Nelson*, 25 J. Econ. Behav. Organ. 1, 22-23 (1994).

1653 The claims shall [...] be supported by the description.

1654 *Brandi-Dohrn*, GRUR Int 1995, 541; *Wibbelmann*, EIPR, 1997, 515.

1655 *Roberts*, EIPR, 1994, 371, 371, 373 (also arguing that European law must be changed to include Art. 84 lack of support objections in opposition grounds before EPO).

were relevant to Art. 84 EPC might also be relevant to Art. 83 EPC, and, therefore, the claim could be revoked.[1656]

c) Conclusion

If one could prove that a part of a claimed invention in the basic patent was not sufficiently disclosed in the specification, to the extent that the claim would be nullified, the discrepancy (See Figure 11) would be resolved to the same extent and more freedom to operate would be created. However, proving that some compounds claimed in the basic invention do not show the claimed effect would not help the patentee of a species selection invention to exploit the invention without concerns, because the species invention must show the expected technical effects. Thus, although consideration of a stringent disclosure requirement for the basic invention would help to solve the discrepancy, it would not help the selection patentee to acquire the freedom to operate.

F. Conclusion

A species selection invention is importantly distinguished from the other selection inventions in the sense that it can be developed to the product that is available for the first time in the form of medication. The technical contribution of other selection inventions lies mainly in the isolation or the separation thereof from the mixture in the prior art. The patents on earlier med-

---

1656 *Exxon/Fuel oils*, T 409/91, OJ EPO 1994, 653, 662 (noting "the reasons why the invention defined in the claims does not meet the requirement of Article 83 EPC are in effect the same as those that lead to their infringing Article 84 EPC as well, namely that the invention extends to technical subject-matter not made available to the person skilled in the art by the application as filed, since it was not contested by the appellant that no information was given to perform the claimed invention successfully without using the structurally defined class of additives."); *Genentech/Human t-PA*, T 923/92, OJ EPO 1996, 564, 584 (holding "in order to fulfill the requirement of Article 83 EPC, the application as filed must contain sufficient information to allow a person skilled in the art, using common general knowledge, to carry out the invention within the whole area that is claimed. Claims which by omission of an essential feature extend to subject-matter which, after reading of the description, would still not be at the disposal of the person skilled in the art, are objectionable under both Article 83 and Article 84 EPC.").

ications that were generally purified or isolated were also granted on the basis that they were available for the first time in a therapeutic and commercial manner. However, one may doubt whether it is proper to apply similar standards a century later. The proposals from the various perspectives were made to promote the R&D on the more ambitious projects and thereby to bring more NMEs and fewer second generation inventions to the public.

The findings and proposals on species selection inventions were as follows: Firstly, providing the broader scope of patents to species selection inventions does not appear to be appropriate to promote R&D, because the equivalent protection in this industry is neither easy nor properly applicable, and because granting a broader scope of patent would increase the deadweight loss. Secondly, in contrast, the already broad scope of the genus patent could stop the species selection patentee from exploiting his invention. Application of the lesson from the *eBay* case, implementation of the statutory compulsory license system or improved use of the reverse doctrine of equivalence would be desirable to resolve this blocking issue. Thirdly, considering that the pharmaceutical industry is sensitive to the term of protection, and that the patent term extension system is more favourable to second generation inventions, the R&D for which take a shorter period of time than the basic invention, a provision guaranteeing a fifteen year effective patent term was proposed for the species selection inventions to promote research on NMEs. Fourthly, regarding the novelty requirement, the appreciation and application of the requirement in the *Olanzapine* decision of "clear and unambiguous" prior art disclosure to destroy a claimed invention, was recommended. Lastly, in consideration of some of the specificities in the pharmaceutical industry, such as high uncertainty along the way to marketing approval and high post-invention costs, both factors were recommended as secondary considerations in assessing the inventive step of species selection inventions.

The following proposals were made on the other selection inventions. Firstly, since the case law on the patent term extension seems to encourage more investment in second generation inventions, it was proposed that, if the biologically active moiety is the same and the first one enjoyed a patent term extension, no further patent term extension should be granted. Secondly, to judge the inventive step requirement, it was suggested that the therapeutic contribution of other selection inventions be one of the secondary considerations. Other systems, such as prizes or reimbursement schemes for medication, consider the genuine technical contribution of a drug invention as the therapeutic contribution. Similarly, in assessing the inventive step, the

Korean Supreme Court considered whether the claimed invention contributed to showing the pharmaceutical effects over the basic inventions. Thus, it was recommended that the therapeutic contribution be considered in judging the inventive step of other selection inventions.

The discrepancy between the scope and the disclosure of the genus claim that was firmly established by the *Olanzapine* decision, was discussed. Even though the stringent disclosure requirement of the basic invention can help to decrease this discrepancy, it will not help the species selection patentee to acquire the freedom to operate because the selection invention must show the expected result claimed in the basic patent.

VII. FINAL CONCLUSIONS

A steady supply of new medications is vital to public health. The patent system and patent exclusivity have been among the most important incentives in encouraging continuing investment in the research and development ("R&D") of innovative medications. In addition, to ensure an efficient flow of medicines to society, competitive pressure plays an important role in lowering drug prices.

Pharmaceutical inventions are generally divided into basic inventions, which can be further developed into new medical entities, and second generation inventions. The latter include species selection inventions, optical isomers, crystalline forms, metabolites, prodrugs, esters, salts, dosage forms, combinations of active ingredients, new uses or new methods of treatment, dosage regimes, processes, intermediates, and more.[1657] Products in the pharmaceutical field fall into the categories of new medical entities, me-too products, second generation products and generic drugs.[1658] This dissertation has focused mainly on chemical selection inventions, such as species selection inventions, optical isomers, crystalline forms, and metabolites, as representatives of second generation inventions. Species selection inventions can also represent basic inventions, since, unlike other second generation inventions, they can be the basis for further improvements or applications, as long as they are developed to New Medical Entities ("NMEs").

The pharmaceutical industry differs from other industries in various ways. It is one of the few industries that bears high regulatory burdens, especially on initial innovations. The development process of these innovations is long and costly, and it includes production of the information needed to meet regulatory requirements. Transforming an invention into an NME involves enormous scientific, regulatory, and market uncertainties.[1659] These uncertainties raise the cost of developing new medications even further, since manufacturers must also absorb the costs incurred by all of their failures. In contrast, imitation involves negligible costs and significantly reduced risks.

1657 See subsection II.C.
1658 See subsection II.D.
1659 See subsection III.A.1.c).

This is one of the main reasons why the pharmaceutical industry depends so greatly on patent protection.[1660]

Despite the existing patent system, the number of NMEs has decreased, especially during the last decade, which has been the most technologically advanced period in history.[1661] This has caused great concern, since NMEs have made important contributions to reductions in morbidity and mortality of the population. In comparison to the declining number of new medical entities, the number of second generation inventions and products has increased dramatically over the same period.[1662] The industry is accused not only of neglecting its real mission of providing new medications while it generates second generation inventions, but also of preventing less expensive generic products from entering the market. Thus, this dissertation has reviewed and analyzed whether these concerns are justified.

To begin with, this dissertation analyzed whether the patent system has changed, especially in conjunction with chemical selection inventions. The novelty requirements of a species selection invention and optical isomer inventions were found to have become less stringent. For species selection inventions, Germany and the United Kingdom have changed their earlier strict ways of assessing novelty according to the *Fluoran* decision and the *IG Rule* respectively.[1663] In the United States, the size of the genus in the prior art from which the species selection was made, has become an important factor in the assessment of novelty. Assessment of novelty of these inventions seems to be based on the difficulty of identifying and selecting a specific species which has a therapeutic effect distinguishing it from the rest of the genus.[1664] For optical isomers, based on the enablement requirement for assessing anticipation of the prior art,[1665] novelty is established over racemic mixtures, if purification of one isomer from the racemate is not disclosed, and this is difficult, even if the structure is clearly disclosed. In the past novelty standards of inventions were based on the difficulties of isolation or separation just as they are today, however, more advanced techniques have now incomparably decreased those difficulties, and the isolation of isomers is made out of a well-known targeted mixture. Thus, the novelty

---

1660 See subsection III.A.3.b).
1661 See subsection III.B.2.
1662 See subsection III.B.5.
1663 See subsections IV.A.4.a).
1664 See supra 558 - 559 and accompanying texts.
1665 See subsections IV.A.3. and IV.C.2.b)(1).

standards of inventions connected with purification, such as the isolation of an optical isomer have relaxed over the past century. For crystalline forms, the issue of novelty arises mainly when the claimed crystalline forms are produced according to the process disclosed in the prior art, in which case novelty generally is not found. Similarly, though their reasoning was different, the courts in the United Kingdom and in the United States both held that metabolite invention was not novel.[1666] To some extent, the ruling in this case is natural, because the patent on the metabolite is a repetition of the prior art, insofar as it precludes the use of the parent drug as an anti-histamine treatment.[1667] Therefore, except for the crystalline forms, this thesis concludes that satisfaction of the novelty requirement for selection patents has become less demanding.

Furthermore, the inventive step requirement for selection inventions was found to have been significantly reduced. For species selection inventions, the courts in each jurisdiction acknowledged advantageous effects over the prior art. In addition, the size of the genus from which the selection invention is made is important for establishing the inventive step. Due to the changed inventive step requirement, however, the superior effects do not need to be shown over the whole scope of the prior art. For optical isomers, the early rulings held that the different effects of one enantiomer from the other were known, and that it was routine both to produce an enantiomer and to test its activity. Thus, even advanced effects were not considered evidence of the inventive step.[1668] However, the BOA held that an enantiomer invention establishes the inventive step based on a radically different problem and a solution disclosed by the original patent specification; the BGH held the same based on the difficulty of separating the racemate, and the decision was similarly reached in the United Kingdom. The earlier decision held that the enantiomer was obvious because resolution of a racemate was common knowledge.[1669] However, unless there was enough motivation to resolve the racemate or the separation was predictable, the Court found an inventive step in the enantiomer invention.[1670] In the United States, even acknowledging that there was ample motivation to separate an enantiomer, an inventive step

1666 Because of the bifurcate system in Germany, the Court on the same metabolite issue held only the non-infringement of selling the parent drug.

1667 *Jacob*, IIC 1996, 170, 171.

1668 See *supra* 790 and accompanying texts.

1669 See *supra* 803 -804 and accompanying texts.

1670 See *supra* 809 -811 and accompanying texts.

of the enantiomer was found based on the difficulty of separation. However, the Korean Supreme Court ruling contrasted sharply with those in other jurisdictions. For example, the Federal Circuit found one enantiomer to be inventive, because the fact that one enantiomer was responsible for the biological activity and the other for the side effect was not predictable. In the corresponding case, the Korean Supreme Court held that the invention was obvious, because a two-fold superiority in therapeutic effect and the 1.6-fold superiority in acute toxicity in comparison with the racemate were not significantly better than the activity of the racemate.[1671] For crystalline forms, the inventive step was denied either because of a reasonable expectation of success or because of a clear expectation that a crystalline form would provide more desirable characteristics. The Korean Supreme Court held that the properties of crystalline forms were well known, that it was a common practice to confirm the existence of polymorphism of a substance, and specifically the Court could not acknowledge the improved "pharmaceutical effect" achieved by the improved physical characteristics of a crystalline form.[1672] For metabolite inventions, novelty was the central issue, and the inventive step was not. Therefore, except for the crystalline form, the inventive step requirements of species selection inventions in the selected jurisdictions have been lowered or are lower than the standard in Korea.

For these reasons, it was concluded that the patentability standards of second generation inventions in selected jurisdictions have a tendency toward a lowered novelty requirement and a significantly relaxed inventive step requirement. In a certain sense, the case law seems to be more harmonized, although the observed direction of the changes may be worrisome.

These lowered patentability requirements have led to an increased number of superfluous second generation patents and to greater uncertainties on the landscape of exclusivities. Moreover, considering that manufacturers have finite resources, these lowered requirements may siphon off resources and divert them away from breakthrough drug developments, thus potentially hindering future pharmaceutical innovations. Furthermore, they result in

---

1671 See *supra* 836 and accompanying texts (with the comparison that the administration of one enantiomer gave around 2-fold better effects than that of a racemate which is a 1:1 mixture of enantiomers).

1672 See *supra* 863 -867 and accompanying texts.

higher cost for searches, prosecutions, and especially litigations,[1673] which are incurred both in the attack and the defence of these patents. Since second generation patents are also eligible for patent term extensions, this provides further incentives for those companies whose drugs contain older active ingredients to extend their R&D efforts, marketing resources, and capital on second generation inventions.

The scope of patent term extensions on second generation patents seems to encourage R&D efforts to focus more on second generation inventions. Since, another SPC or patent term extension can be granted if the derivatives are covered by the patent,[1674] this can lead the original patentee to work more on trivial modifications of those active moieties which were already authorized in previous products. This concentration on trivial modifications is exacerbated by the fact that lowered patentability requirements make it easier to patent derivatives.

Furthermore, the patent term extension system apparently compensates for the cost and period of R&D more on second generation inventions than on NMEs.[1675] This is especially so for medications that require more extensive safety testing, toxicity testing, or both. For example, for medicines to treat chronic diseases, Alzheimer's disease, or cancers, the maximum cap of five years to an extension risks discouraging the companies from pursuing research in these fields.[1676] The situation in Europe may be more serious, because the calculation system for the SPC is much more favourable to secondary products than to new medical entities. Unlike medications that take five to ten years from the patent application date to acquire market approval, those that need more than ten years can never enjoy fifteen years of the maximum effective patent term.[1677] The gap between the two dates should be much shorter for second generation products, ideally less than ten years,

---

1673 For example, in the United States, litigation costs to take a patent case through to appeal range from $650,000 to $4.5 million. In Germany, the overall cost for each party of a small to middle-scale patent case ranges €50,000 to €250,000 at first instance, and ranges €90,000 to €190,000 at second instance for both validity and infringement. In the U.K., the cost of a similar case ranges from €150,000 to €1.5 million at first instance and €150,000 to €1 million at second instances, and an average patent case in the U.K. lies well over €1 million. *EPO*, 2006, 10-12; *see also Holderman/Guren*, 2007 U. Ill. J.L. Tech. & Pol'y 101, 110 (2007).

1674 See subsection V.C.2.

1675 See also subsection VI.D.2.a)(1).

1676 *Domeij*, 2000, 282.

1677 See subsection V.C.3.

which would increase the chances for them to enjoy maximum effective patent term.[1678]

The impacts of increased second generation patents on generic manufacturers, which are referred to as life cycle management or evergreening, must also be mentioned. Against the grain of prevailing perceptions, only in a few specific cases can selection inventions impact the entry of generic versions of older products.[1679] To the extent that second generation patents can prevent the entry of generics, the patent term and term extension of second generation patents can cause delays. What is more noteworthy is the manufacturers' augmented legal uncertainty and insecurity in the preparation of its generic versions because of the increased patent pendency of second generation inventions. Furthermore, although the case has limited application in the United States, the automatic thirty-month stay and the new listing in the Orange Book, which are usually based on second generation patents, effectively delay the entry of generics. In addition, the active market movement to second generation versions in conjunction with the very specific scope of second generation patents make the market for the older version very unattractive. The disconnect between decision-makers and payers for a medicine may also help to diminish the attractiveness of older medications, considering that there is probably no other industry where quality is so disparaged on account of lower prices.[1680]

The nature of a species selection invention is different from that of other selection inventions because the former can be developed into NMEs. In addition, whereas the value of the former is that it has been identified from among millions of candidates, the nature of the latter is in the isolation or separation from a mixture. Isolated or separated inventions have been patented for over a century. However, many of these decisions were taken a century ago[1681] when the pharmaceutical industry was arguably not yet research-based but a manufacturing industry. In addition, the average skilled person has since become dramatically more knowledgeable. More importantly, even if other selection inventions were available to the public for the first time, the public already has access to older versions developed from the basic inventions. In addition, patentability of the majority of the other selection inventions is based on the difficulty of separation from a well-known mix-

1678 See subsection V.C.3.
1679 See subsection V.B.3.
1680 *Steele*, 5 J. Law Econ. 131, 142 (1962).
1681 See subsection VI.B.2.b).

ture. Accordingly, one might doubt whether the absolute product protection afforded by a patent is appropriate for second generation inventions. On the basis of the different sets of values inherent in selection inventions and the needs of society, this dissertation has analyzed and proposed optimal ways for patent law to help bring more NMEs to the public.

Firstly, to move research capacity and investments from second generation research to basic research on NMEs, the main arguments for granting a broader scope of patent protection to the basic invention were explored. However, because of the unpredictable character of selection inventions, the granting of a broader scope of patent protection is not regarded as a proper tool for the promotion of pioneering innovations.[1682] Because of the problem presented by the already broad scope of the genus patent, several possible solutions were explored for acquiring the freedom to operate the species selection invention. Although scholars have offered many proposals for voluntary license agreements,[1683] pharmaceutical companies usually do not want to undermine their exclusivities based on licensing. Consequently, licensing does not seem to be of practical use. Instead, application of the lesson from the *eBay* case, implementation of the statutory compulsory license system or improved use of the reverse doctrine of equivalence were put forward as more desirable solutions to resolving the blocking issue. The same solutions can be applied to the situation in which the basic patent stops the use of new dosage forms, combinations of active ingredients, or especially new medical uses. Secondly, given that the pharmaceutical industry is one of the few that is sensitive to the term of protection, and that the patent term extension system is more favourable to second generation inventions, a provision that guarantees fifteen year patent exclusivity from the time of market approval is proposed for new medical entities.[1684] Thirdly, in order to assess the novelty requirement of species selection inventions, application of the teaching in the *Olanzapine* decision is recommended, which requires "clear and unambiguous" prior art disclosure to destroy a claimed invention.[1685] This recommendation is based on the observation that a patent system is a double-edged sword for the pharmaceutical industry, which differs from the prevailing conception. Fourthly, this dissertation recommends that post-invention costs and uncertainties in the course of product development be

1682 See subsection VI.C.2.
1683 See subsection VI.C.3.a).
1684 See subsection VI.D.2.a).
1685 See subsection VI.E.2.b).

considered as secondary considerations in accessing the inventive step requirement of basic inventions such as species selection inventions.[1686]

For other second generation inventions, it is firstly proposed that, if the biologically active moiety is the same and the earlier one enjoyed a patent term extension, no further patent term extension should be granted.[1687] Secondly, the therapeutic contribution of these inventions is recommended as a secondary consideration in judging the inventive step.[1688]

Even though these observations were made for selection inventions, the same rationale could be applied to other second generation inventions. Through these efforts, much R&D could be directed toward new medical entities, and more new medications could be offered to patients who are awaiting them at this very moment.

Further research directions

This dissertation also proposes a series of additional research questions. Crucial among these are detailed evaluation and refinement of proposals that were made in chapter 6. Further, an in-depth study on competition issues, including movement of the market to second generation products would be desirable.

Considering that pharmaceuticals are information-rich substances, changes in other regimes that protect the information itself, such as regulatory exclusivities,[1689] could be further researched and compared with the protection provided by patent law. In particular, further exploration and analysis would be warranted to determine whether it would be proper to extend exclusivity in the regulatory regime and, if so, how the non-disclosure problem in "data protection" could be resolved, or even, in the end, whether both systems should be run parallel but in a different manner from existing ones.

Pharmaceutical companies are facing an increasing number of challenges from private and governmental health systems, which put companies under pressure to reduce prices.[1690] These intensified price controls, including changing reimbursement mechanisms, significantly reduce the funding

1686 See subsection VI.E.3.b).
1687 See subsection VI.D.2.b).
1688 See subsection VI.E.3.c).
1689 *Roin*, 87 Tex. L. Rev. 503, 564-68 (2009).
1690 *Wilson*, The New York Times, March 6, 2011.

available for R&D,[1691] and they may also add to the already substantial costs involved in bringing new products onto the market.[1692] For instance, curtailing reimbursement impacts on the company's marginal rate of return on innovation, and reduces R&D expenditure on future projects. [1693] Considering the high failure rate in developing new medical entities, the decrease in reimbursement could significantly affect innovations which would otherwise have market potential.[1694] The effect would be even greater since lower profits for pharmaceutical companies discourage investment in R&D and clog the pipeline for new drug treatments, which in turn shortens expected life spans.[1695] Considering the fact that the two largest pharmaceutical markets, i.e. the United States and Germany, are not, or were not until recently, subject to price controls by the government, it also would be interesting to study the relationship between pharmaceutical innovation and price regulation. Therefore, it would be advisable to research the relationship between pharmaceutical R&D and reimbursement mechanisms in order to propose measures such as pricing schemes that would promote R&D on both basic inventions and second generation inventions.

1691 *Vernon*, Regulation, 22, 25 (2002-2003, Winter); *U.S. Department of Commerce International Trade Administration*, 2004, x.

1692 *McGuire/Drummond/Rutten,* 2004, 131-32.

1693 *McGuire/Drummond/Rutten,* 2004, 131-32; *U.S. Department of Commerce International Trade Administration*, 2004, x-xi.

1694 *McGuire/Drummond/Rutten,* 2004, 131-32.

1695 *Lakdawalla, et al.*, 28 Health Affairs w138, w148-w149 (2009); *Holmes*, 379 Lancet 1863, 1864 (2012).

List of Statutory Instruments

Council Directive 2001/83/EC of 6 November 2001 on the Community code relating to medicinal products for human use, as amended.

Council Directive 87/21/EEC of 22 December 1986 amending Directive 65/65/EEC on the approximation of provisions laid down by law, regulation or administrative action relating to proprietary medicinal products, as amended.

Council Regulation (EEC) 1768/92 of 18 June 1992 concerning the Creation of a Supplementary Protection Certificate for Medicinal Products, as amended.

Directive 98/44/EC of the European Parliament and of the Council of 6 July 1998 on the legal protection of biotechnological inventions, as amended.

European Patent Convention (as amended).

German Patent Act (as amended).

Implementing Regulations to the Convention on the Grant of European Patents (as amended).

Indian Patents Act (as amended).

Korean Patent Act (as amended).

Protocol on the Interpretation of Article 69 EPC.

Regulation (EC) No 1610/96 of the European Parliament and of the Council of 23 July 1996 concerning the Creation of a Supplementary Protection Certificate for Plant Protection products, as amended.

Regulation (EC) No 469/2009 of the European Parliament and of the Council of 6 May 2009 concerning the Supplementary Protection Certificate for Medicinal Products, as amended.

The Agreement on Trade Related Aspects of Intellectual Property Rights of April 15, 1994.

The Constitution of the United States of America (as amended).

The Treaty on the Functioning of the European Union.

U.S. Food, Drug, and Cosmetic Act, 21 U.S.C. (as amended).

U.S. Patent Act, 35 U.S.C. (2007).

U.S. Patent Act, 35 U.S.C. (2011).

UK Patents Act 1977 (as amended).

Examination Guidelines for Patent

Examination Guidelines for Patent and Utility Model in Korea (January 2011).

Guidelines for Examination in the European Patent Office (June 2012).

Manual of Patent Office Practice and Procedure in India (March 2011).

Manual of Patent Practice - UK Patents Act 1977 (October 2012).

List of Case Laws

EUROPEAN UNION

Case C-457/10, AstraZeneca AB v. European Commission, 2012.

Case C-181/95, Biogen v. Smithklein Beecham [1997] ECR I-357.

Case C-428/08, Monsanto Technology LLC v. Cefetra BV and Others, [2010] ECR I-06765.

Case C-34/10, Oliver Brüstle v. Greenpeace e.V., 2011.

BOARD OF APPEAL OF THE EUROPEAN PATENT OFFICE

Abbott Respiratory/Dosage Regime, G 2/08 (2010).

Agrevo/Triazoles, T 939/92, OJ EPO 1996, 309.

AKZO/Bleaching activators, T 133/92, 1994.

Alcan/Aluminium alloys, T 465/92, OJ EPO 1996, 32.

Amazonen-Werke/Zustreicher, T 378/94 (1996).

AstraZeneca/Hexal et al., T 1760/11 (2012).

Astropower/Divisional, G1/05 (2007).

Bayer/Carbonless copying paper, T 1/80, OJ EPO 1981, 206.

Bayer/Diastereomer, T 12/81 OJ EPO 1982, 296.

Bayer/E-Isomers of N-alpha-(2-Cyan-2-alkoximino-acetyl)-amino acid derivatives and peptides, T12/90 (1990).

Bayer/Plant growth regulating agent, G 6/88, OJ EPO 1990, 114.

Biogen/Alpha interferons, T301/87, OJ EPO 1990, 335.

Ciba-Geigy/Benzothiopyran derivatives, T 20/83, OJ EPO 1983, 419.

Ciba-Geigy/Spiro compounds, T 181/82, OJ EPO 1984, 401.

Collaborative/Preprorennin, T81/87, OJ EPO 1990, 250.

CPC/Flavour concentrates, T 303/86 (1988).

Diener/Shear, T305/87, OJ EPO 1991, 419.

Draco/Xanthines, T 7/86, OJ EPO 1988, 381.

Dupont/Copolymer, T 124/87, OJ EPO 1989, 491.

Eisai/Second medical indication, G 5/83, OJ EPO 1985, 64.

Eli Lilly/Enantiomer, T 600/95 (1996).

Exxon/Fuel oils, T 409/91, OJ EPO 1994, 653.

Genentech/Human t-PA, T 923/92, OJ EPO 1996, 564.

Hoechst/Diastereomers of 3-cephem-4-carboxylic acid-1-(isopropoxycarbonyloxy) ethyl ester, T 940/98 (2003).

Hoechst/ Enantiomers, T296/87, OJ EPO 1990, 195.
Hoechst/Thiochloroformates, T198/84, OJ EPO 1985, 209.
ICI/Herbicides, T 206/83, OJ EPO 1987, 5.
Kos Lifesciences/ Dosage regimen, T 1319/04, OJ EPO 2009, 36.
Merck/Finasteride, T605/02 (2005).
MIT/Biopolymers, T639/95 (1998).
Mobil Oil /Friction Reducing Additives, G2/88, OJ EPO 1990, 93.
Molecular Biosystems/Oligonucleotide therapeutic agent, T 994/95 (1999).
Mycogen/Modifying plant cells, T 694/92, OJ EPO 1997, 408.
Nippon/Crystalline dye, T 0051/97 (2000).
Pfizer/Penem Derivatives, T1048/92 (1994).
Richter Gedeon/Famotidine, T 226/98, OJ EPO 2002, 498.
Seiko/Sequences of Divisionals, G1/06 (2007).
Smithkline Beecham/Paroxetine methanesulfonate, T 0885/02 (2004).
Texaco/Novelty, T279/89 (1991).
Toshiba/Thickness of Magnetic Layers, T 26/85, OJ EPO 1990, 22.
Unilever/Stable bleaches, T 0226/85, OJ EPO 1988, 336.
Unilever/Washing Composition, T 666/89, OJ EPO 1993, 495.
Warner-Lambert/Atorvastatin polymorphs, T 0777/08 (2011).
Warner-Lambert/Atorvastatin, T 0229/97 (2000).
Warner-Lambert/Polymorphic Atorvastatin, T 1066/03 (2006).
Xerox/Amendments, T 133/85, OJ EPO 1988, 441.
Zeneca/Enantiomer, T1046/97 (1999).

GERMANY

Imperial Court of Justice

Kongo-Rot (Kongo-Red), Patentblatt 1889, 209, 212.
Methylenblau (Methyleneblue), 22 Reichsgerichts in Zivilsachen 8.

Federal Supreme Court of Germany

BGH/ Betrieb einer Sicherheitseinrichtung (Operating a Safety Device), GRUR 2009, 746.
BGH/ α-aminobenzylpenicillin, GRUR 1978, 696.
BGH/7-Chlor-6-demethyltetracyclin, GRUR 1978, 162.
BGH/Bierklärmittel (Beer Fining Agent), GRUR 1984, 425.
BGH/Calcipotriol-Monohydrat, GRUR 2012, 803.
BGH/Crackkatalysator (Cracking catalyst), GRUR 1990, 510.
BGH/Doxorubicin-Sulfate, GRUR 2009, 41.

BGH/Dreinahtschlauchfolienbeutel (Three-Seam Tubular Sachet), GRUR 2010, 44.

BGH/Elektrische Steckverbindung (Electronic Plug-in connection), GRUR 1995, 330.

BGH/Escitalopram, GRUR 2010, 123.

BGH/Fluoran, GRUR 1988, 447.

BGH/Formstein, GRUR 1986, 803.

BGH/Inkrustierungsinhibitoren (Incrustration inhibitors), GRUR 2000, 591.

BGH/Klinische Versuche (Clinical Trials), GRUR 1996, 109.

BGH/Metronidazol, GRUR 1975, 425.

BGH/Olanzapine, GRUR 2009, 382.

BGH/Olanzapine, IIC 2009, 596.

BGH/Orange Book-Standard, GRUR 2009, 694.

BGH/Polyferon, GRUR, 1996, 190.

BGH/Schmierfettzusammensetzung(Grease composition), GRUR 2000, 296.

BGH/Schneidermesser I (Cutting blade I), GRUR 2002, 515.

BGH/Textilgarn, GRUR 1959, 125.

Federal Patent Court of Germany

BPatG/Atorvastatin, BeckRS 2007, 18183.

BPatG/Escitalopram II, 3 Ni 22/10, 29.03.2011. available at: http://www.juris.de/jportal/portal/t/1581/page/jurisw.psml/screen/JWPDFScreen/filename/MPRE134660964.pdf

BPatG/Escitalopram, BeckRS 2007, 14624.

BPatG/Kristallformen(Crystal forms), BpatGE 20, 6.

Higher Regional Court

OLG München/Terfenadine, GRUR, 1994, 746.

INTERNATIONAL

WTO-Appellate Body Report, Canada-Term of Patent Protection, WT/DS170/AB/R.

WTO-Panel Report, Canada - Patent Protection of Pharmaceutical Products, WT/DS114/R.

WTO-Panel Report, Canada-Term of Patent Protection, WT/DS170/R.

ITALY

Corte di Cassazione/Cimetidin, GRUR Int 1991, 497.

Pfizer v. Italian Competition Authority et al., Regional Administrative Court for Latium, N. 07467/2012, Sept. 3, 2012.

Ratiopharm v. Pfizer, Italian Competition Authority, p23194, Jan 11, 2012.

KOREA

Supreme Court

Korean Supreme Court/Atorvastatin, 2008Hu3469, Mar. 25, 2010.

Korean Supreme Court/Bayer Aktiengesellschaft v. Union Quimico Famaceutica, S.A, 97Hu2200, Jul. 28, 2000.

Korean Supreme Court/Clopidogrel, 2008Hu736 & 2008Hu743, Oct. 15, 2009.

Korean Supreme Court/Ibandronate, 2010Hu3554, Sept. 8, 2011.

Korean Supreme Court/Lercanidipine, 2010Hu2872, Jul. 14, 2011.

Korean Supreme Court/Olanzapine, 2010Hu3424, Aug. 23, 2012.

Patent Court

Korean Patent Court/A combining method, 98Heo8397, Apr. 23, 1999.

Korean Patent Court/Kimchi fridge, 2002Heo8424, Sept. 04, 2003.

Korean Patent Court/Olanzapine, 2010Heo371, Nov. 11, 2010.

UNITED KINGDOM

The House of Lords

Beecham Group v. Bristol Laboratories Ltd. [1978] RPC 153, 192.

Biogen Inc v. Medeva Plc [1996] UKHL 18.

Catnic Components Limited and another v. Hill & Smith Limited [1982] R.P.C. 183.

Conor Medsystems Inc v.Angiotech Pharmaceuticals Inc & Ors [2008] UKHL 49.

Electric & Musical Industries Ltd v. Lissen Ltd [1939] R.P.C. 23.

General Tire v. Firestone [1972] RPC 457.

Generics Ltd. v.Lundbeck [2009] UKHL 12.

I.G. Farbenindustrie's AG's Patent [1930] R.P.C. 289.

Merrell Dow Pharmaceuticals Inc v.HN Norton & Co Ltd [1995] UKHL 14.

Synthon BV v.SmithKline Beecham plc, [2005] UKHL 59.

Court of Appeal

Actavis UK Ltd v. Novartis AG [2010] EWCA Civ 82.

Dr Reddy's Laboratories Ltd v. Eli Lilly & Company Ltd, [2009] EWCA Civ 1362.

Generics (UK) Ltd v. Daiichi Pharmaceutical [2009] EWCA Civ 646.

Green Lane Products Ltd v. PMS International Group Plc & Ors [2008] EWCA Civ 358.

Laboratoires Servier v. Apotex [2008] EWCA Civ 44.

Leo Pharma v. Sandoz Ltd [2009] EWCA Civ 1188.

Lundbeck v.Generics Ltd. [2008] EWCA Civ 311.

Napp Pharmaceuticals v. Ratiopharm [2009] EWCA Civ 252.

Occlutech GmbH v. AGA Medical Corp [2010] EWCA Civ 702.

Pozzoli v. BDMO [2007] EWCA Civ 588.

Ranbaxy (UK) v.Warner-Lambert [2006] EWCA Civ 876.

Smith Kline & French Laboratories v. Evans Medical [1989] F.S.R. 561.

Societe Technique de Pulverisation Step v. Emson Europe Ltd. and others [1993] R.P.C. 513.

Windsurfing International Inc. v. Tabur Marine (GB) Ltd. [1985] R.P.C. 59.

Patents Court

Dr Reddy's Laboratories (UK) Ltd v. Eli Lilly & Company Ltd [2008] EWHC 2345.

Generics (UK) Ltd & Ors v. Lundbeck A/S [2007] EWHC 1040 (Pat).

Generics (UK) v. Daiichi Pharmaceutical [2008] EWHC 2413 (Pat).

Ranbaxy UK & Anor v. Warner-Lambert [2005] EWHC 2142.

Research Corp's Supplementary Protection Certificate [1994] R.P.C. 667.

Teva v. Merrell [2007] EWHC 2276 (Ch).

UNITED STATES

Supreme Court

Aronson v. Quick Point Pencil Co., 440 U.S. 257 (1979).

Association for Molecular Pathology et al. v. Myriad Genetics Inc. et al., 133 S.Ct. 2107, 2109 (2013).

Bonito Boats, Inc. v. Thunder Craft Boats, Inc., 489 U.S. 141 (1989).

Caraco Pharmaceutical Laboratories, Ltd. v. Novo Nordisk A/S, 132 S.Ct. 1670 (U.S. 2012).

eBay Inc. v. MercExchange, L.L.C., 547 U.S. 388 (2006).

Evans v. Eaton, 20 U.S. 356 (1822).

Festo Corp. v. Shoketsu Kinzoku Kogyo Kabushiki Co., Ltd., 535 U.S. 722 (2002).

Graham v. John Deere Co., 383 U.S. 1 (1966).

Graver Tank & Mfg. Co. v. Linde Air Products Co., 339 U.S. 605 (1950).

Illinois Tool Works Inc. v. Independent Ink, Inc., 547 U.S. 28 (2006).

J.E.M. AG Supply, Inc. v. Pioneer Hi-Bred Intern., Inc., 534 U.S. 124 (2001).

Kewanee Oil Co. v. Bicron Corp., 416 U.S. 470 (1974).

KSR Int'l Co. v. Teleflex Inc., 127 U.S. 1727 (2007).

LabCorp v. Metabolite, Inc., 548 U.S. 124 (2006).

Mayo Collaborative Services v. Prometheus Laboratories, Inc., 132 S.Ct. 1289 (2012).

Pfaff v. Wells Electronics, Inc., 525 U.S. 55, 63 (1998).

Sony Corp. of Am. v. Universal City Studios, Inc., 464 U.S. 417 (1984).

United States v. Dubilier Condenser Corp., 289 U.S. 178 (1933).
Warner-Jenkinson Co., Inc. v. Hilton Davis Chemical Co., 520 U.S. 17 (1997).

Courts of Appeals

Abbott Laboratories v. Geneva Pharmaceuticals, Inc., 182 F.3d 1315 (Fed. Cir. 1999).
ACS Hosp. Systems, Inc. v. Montefiore Hosp., 732 F.2d 1572 (Fed. Cir. 1984).
Advanced Display Sys., Inc. v. Kent State Univ., 212 F.3d 1272 (Fed. Cir. 2000).
Alza Corp. v. Mylan Labs. Inc., 388 F. Supp. 2d 717 (N.D. W. Va. 2005).
American Cyanamid Co. v. F.T.C. 363 F.2d 757 (6th Cir. 1966).
Ariad Pharmaceuticals, Inc. v. Eli Lilly and Co., 598 F.3d 1336 (Fed. Cir. 2010).
Association for Molecular Pathology v. U.S. Patent and Trademark Office, 689 F.3d 1303 (Fed. Cir. 2012).
Atlas Powder Co. v. Ireco, Inc., 190 F.3d 1342 (Fed. Cir. 1999).
Aventis Pharma Deutschland GmbH v. Lupin, Ltd., 499 F.3d 1293 (Fed. Cir. 2007).
Bristol-Myers Squibb Co. v. Ben Venue Labs., Inc., 246 F.3d 1368 (Fed. Cir. 2001).
Capon v. Eshhar, 418 F.3d 1349 (Fed. Cir. 2005).
CFMT, Inc. v. Yieldup Intern. Corp., 349 F.3d 1333 (Fed.Cir. 2003).
Chester v. Miller, 906 F.2d 1574 (Fed. Cir. 1990).
Chiron Corp. v. Genentech, Inc., 363 F.3d 1247 (Fed. Cir. 2004).
Continental Can Co. USA, Inc. v. Monsanto Co., 948 F.2d 1264 (Fed. Cir. 1991).
Corning Glass Works v. Sumitomo Elec. U.S.A., Inc., 868 F.2d 1251 (Fed. Cir. 1989).
Custom Accessories, Inc. v. Jeffrey Allan Industries, Inc., 807 F.2d 955 (Fed. Cir. 1986).
Dewey & Almy Chemical Co v. Mimex Co., 124 F.2d 986 (2nd Cir. 1942).
DyStar Textilfarben GmbH & Co. Deutschland KG v. C.H. Patrick Co., 464 F.3d 1356 (Fed. Cir. 2006).
Elan Pharmaceuticals., Inc. v. Mayo Foundation, 346 F.3d 1051 (Fed. Cir. 2003).
Eli Lilly & Co. v. Barr Labs., 251 F.3d 955 (Fed. Cir. 2001).
Eli Lilly and Company v.Zenith Goldline Pharmaceuticals. Inc., 471 F.3d 1369 (Fed. Cir. 2006).
Environmental Designs, Ltd. V. Union Oil Co., 713 F.2d 693 (Fed. Cir. 1983).
Enzo Biochem, Inc. v. Gen-Probe Inc., 323 F.3d 956 (Fed. Cir. 2002).
Finisar Corp. v. DirecTv Group, Inc., 523 F.3d 1323 (Fed. Cir. 2008).
Fonar Corp. v. General Electric Co., 107 F.3d 1543 (Fed. Cir. 1997).
Forest Labs., Inc. v. Ivax Pharms., Inc., 501 F.3d 1263 (Fed. Cir. 2007).
Glaxo Operations UK Ltd. v. Quigg, 894 F.2d 392 (Fed. Cir. 1990).
Hoechst-Roussel Pharmaceuticals, Inc. v. Lehman, 109 F.3d 756 (Fed. Cir. 1997).
In re Bergstrom, 427 F.2d 1394 (C.C.P.A. 1970).
In re Bergy, 596 F.2d 952 (C.C.P.A. 1979).

In re Brown, 329 F.2d 1006 (C.C.P.A. 1964).
In re Cruciferous Sprout Litigation, 301 F.3d 1343 (Fed. Cir. 2002).
In re Dillon, 919 F.2d 688 (Fed. Cir. 1990).
In re Donohue, 632 F.2d 123 (C.C.P.A. 1980).
In re Donohue, 766 F.2d 531 (Fed. Cir. 1985).
In re Durden, 763 F.2d 1406 (Fed. Cir. 1985).
In re Gardner, 475 F.2d 1389 (C.C.P.A., 1973).
In re GPAC, 57 F.3d 1573 (Fed. Cir. 1995).
In re Hafner, 410 F.2d 1403 (C.C.P.A.1969).
In re Kratz, 592 F.2d 1169 (C.C.P.A. 1979).
In re LeGrice, 301 F.2d 929 (C.C.P.A. 1962).
In re Lukach, 442 F.2d 967 (C.C.P.A. 1971).
In re May, 574 F.2d 1082 (C.C.P.A. 1978).
In re Payne, 606 F.2d 303 (C.C.P.A. 1979).
In re Petering, 301 F.2d 681 (C.C.P.A. 1962).
In re Piasecki, 745 F.2d 1468 (Fed. Cir. 1984).
In re Ruschig, 379 F.2d 990 (C.C.P.A. 1967).
In re Schaumann, 572 F.2d 312 (C.C.P.A.1987).
In re Schoenwald, 964 F.2d 1122 (Fed. Cir. 1992).
In re Schreiber, 128 F.3d 1473 (Fed. Cir. 1997).
In re Sullivan, 498 F.3d 1345 (Fed. Cir. 2007).
In re Vaeck, 947 F.2d 488 (Fed. Cir. 1991).
In re Wands, 858 F.2d 731 (Fed. Cir. 1988).
In re Wiggins, 488 F.2d 538 (C.C.P.A. 1973).
In re Williams, 171 F.2d 319 (C.C.P.A. 1948).
In re Wright, 866 F.2d 422 (Fed. Cir. 1989).
In re Wright, 999 F.2d 1557 (Fed. Cir.1993).
Integra Lifesciences I, Ltd. v. Merck KGaA, 331 F.3d 860 (Fed. Cir. 2003).
Kuehmsted v. Farbenfabriken of Elberfeld Co., 179 F. 701 (7th Cir. 1910).
Martek Biosciences Corp. v. Nutrinova, Inc., 579 F.3d 1363 (Fed. Cir. 2009).
Merck & Co., Inc. v. Biocraft Laboratories, Inc., 874 F.2d 804 (Fed. Cir. 1989).
Merck v. Kessler, 80 F.3d 1543 (Fed.Cir.1996).
Merck v. Teva Pharmaceuticals USA, 347 F.3d 1367 (Fed. Cir. 2003).
Metabolite Laboratories, Inc. v. Laboratory Corporation of America Holdings, 370 F.3d 1354 (Fed. Cir. 2004).
Metallizing Engineering Co. v. Kenyon Bearing & Auto Parts Co., 153 F.2d 516 (2nd Cir, 1946).
Moba, B.V. v. Diamond Automation, Inc., 325 F.3d 1306 (Fed. Cir. 2003).

Momenta Pharmaceuticals, Inc. v. Amphastar Pharmaceuticals, Inc., 686 F.3d 1348 (Fed. Cir. 2012).

Mylan Pharmaceuticals, Inc. v. Thompson, 268 F.3d 1323 (Fed. Cir. 2001).

National Recovery Technologies, Inc. v. Magnetic Separation Systems, Inc., 166 F.3d 1190 (Fed. Cir. 1999).

Newell Companies, Inc. v. Kenney Mfg. Co., 864 F.2d 757 (Fed. Cir. 1988).

Northern Telecom, Inc. v. Datapoint Corp., 908 F.2d 931 (Fed. Cir. 1990).

Novo Nordisk A/S v. Caraco Pharmaceutical Laboratories, Ltd., 601 F.3d 1359 (Fed. Cir. 2010).

Ortho-McNeil Pharmaceutical v. Lupin Pharms., 603 F.3d 1377 (Fed. Cir. 2010).

Panduit Corp. v. Dennison Mfg., 774 F.2d 1082 (Fed. Cir. 1985).

Parke-Davis & Co. v. H.K. Mulford Co., 189 F. 95 (C.C.N.Y., 1911).

Pfizer Inc. v. Dr. Reddy's Laboratories, Ltd., 359 F.3d 1361 (Fed. Cir. 2004).

Pfizer, Inc. v. Apotex, Inc, 480 F.3d 1348 (Fed. Cir. 2007).

Pfizer, Inc. v. Ranbaxy Laboratories Ltd., 457 F.3d 1284 (Fed. Cir. 2006).

PhotoCure v. Kappos, 603 F.3d 1372 (Fed. Cir. 2010).

Picard v. United Aircraft Corp., 128 F.2d 632 (2nd Cir. 1942).

Rasmusson v. SmithKline Beecham Corp., 413 F.3d 1318 (Fed.Cir.2005).

RCA Corp. v. Applied Digital Data Systems, Inc., 730 F.2d 1440 (Fed. Cir. 1984).

Reagents of the University of California v. Eli Lilly & Co., 119 F.3d 1559 (Fed. Cir. 1997).

Roberts v. Sears, Roebuck & Co., 723 F.2d 1324 (7th Cir. 1983).

Royal Typewriter Co. v. Remington Rand, Inc., 168 F.2d 691 (2nd Cir. 1948).

Sanofi-Synthelabo v. Apotex, Inc., 470 F.3d 1368 (Fed. Cir. 2006).

Sanofi-Synthelabo v. Apotex, Inc., 550 F.3d 1075 (Fed. Cir. 2008).

Schering Co. v. Geneva Pharmaceuticals, 339 F.3d 1373 (Fed. Cir. 2003).

SmithKline Beecham Corp. v. Apotex Corp., 403 F.3d 1331 (Fed. Cir. 2005).

SRI Intern. v. Matsushita Elec. Corp. of America, 775 F.2d 1107 (Fed. Cir. 1985).

Stratoflex, Inc. v. Aeroquip Corp., 713 F.2d 1530 (Fed. Cir. 1983).

Tafas v. Doll, 559 F.3d 1345 (Fed. Cir. 2009).

Titanium Metals Corp. v. Banner, 778 F.2d 775 (Fed. Cir. 1985).

Toro Co. v. Deere & Co., 355 F.3d 1313 (Fed. Cir. 2004).

Transocean Offshore Deepwater Drilling, Inc. v. Maersk Drilling USA, Inc., 699 F.3d 1340 (Fed. Cir. 2012).

Tronzo v. Biomet, Inc., 156 F.3d 1154 (Fed. Cir. 1998).

Vas-Cath Inc. v. Mahurkar, 935 F.2d 1555 (Fed. Cir. 1991).

White v. Samsung Electronics America, Inc., 989 F.2d 1512 (9th Cir. 1993).

Yamanouchi Pharm. Co., Ltd. v. Danbury Pharmacal, Inc., 231 F.3d 1339 (Fed. Cir. 2000).

Zenith Laboratories, Inc. v. Bristol-Myers Squibb Co., 19 F.3d 1418 (Fed. Cir. 1994).

District Court

Brenner v. Ladd, 247 F.Supp. 51, 56 (D.D.C. 1965).

Cardiac Pacemakers, Inc. v. St. Jude Med., Inc., No., 96-1718-c H/G, 2001 U.S. Dist. LEXIS 5753, 26 (S.D. Ind. 2001).

Edoco Technical Products, Inc. v. Peter Kiewit Sons' Co., 313 F. Supp. 1081 (C.D. Cal. 1970).

Finisar Corp. v. DirecTv Group, Inc., 2006 WL 2709206 (E.D.Tex. 2006).

In re Buspirone Patent Litigation, 185 F. Supp. 2d 340 (S.D.N.Y. 2002).

MercExchange, L.L.C. v. eBay, Inc., 500 F.Supp.2d 556 (E.D.Va. 2007).

Merck & Co. v. Chase Chemical Co., 273 F.Supp. 68 (D.N.J. 1967).

Ortho-McNeil Pharm., Inc. v. Mylan Labs., Inc., 348 F. Supp. 2d 713 (N.D.W.Va. 2004).

Pfizer Inc. v. Ranbaxy Laboratories Ltd. 405 F.Supp.2d 495 (D.Del. 2005).

Pfizer, Inc. v. Ranbaxy Laboratories, Ltd., 525 F.Supp.2d 680 (D.Del. 2007).

Sanofi-Synthelabo v. Apotex Inc., 492 F.Supp.2d 353 (S.D.N.Y. 2007).

Tafas v. Dudas, 541 F.Supp.2d 805 (E.D.Va. 2008).

United States v. Ciba-Geigy Corp., 508 F. Supp. 1157. (D.C.N.J. 1979).

Zenith Lab. Inc. v. Bristol-Myers Squibb Co., 1992 WL 340761 (D.N.J.1992).

Marion Merrell Dow Inc. v. Baker Norton Pharmaceuticals, Inc., 948 F.Supp. 1050 (S.D.Fla.1996).

z4 Technologies, Inc. v. Microsoft Corp., 434 F.Supp.2d 437 (E.D.Tex. 2006).

Bibliography

Abbott, Alison, Europe Rules Against Stem-Cell Patents, 471 Nature 280 (2011).

Abramowicz, Michael, Perfecting Patent Prizes, Law and Economics Working Paper Series No 01-29, Arlington: George Mason University School of Law (2003).

Abramowicz, Michael/Duffy, John F., Intellectual Property for Market Experimentation, 83 N.Y.U. L. Rev. 337 (2008).

Abramowicz, Michael/Duffy, John F., The Inducement Standard of Patentability, 120 Yale L.J. 1590 (2011).

Agranat, Israel/Caner, Hava, Intellectual Property and Chirality of Drugs, 4 Drug Discov. Today 313 (1999).

Agranat, Israel/Wainschtein, Silvya R., The Strategy of Enantiomer Patents of Drugs, 15 Drug Discov. Today 163 (2010).

Alazraki, Melly, The 10 Biggest-Selling Drugs that are about to Lose Their Patents, DailyFinance, February 27, 2011.

Allison, John R./Lemley, Mark A., The Growing Complexity of the United States Patent System, 82 B.U. L. Rev. 77 (2002).

Angell, Marcia, The Pharmaceutical Industry: To whom Is It Accountable?, 342 New Eng. J. Med. 1902 (2000).

Angell, Marcia, The Truth about the Drug Companies: How They Deceive Us and What to Do about It, New York: Random House (2004).

Ann, Christoph, Patent Trolls – Menace or Myth? in: Zu Waldeck und Pyrmont, Wolrad P., Adelmann, Martin J., Brauneis, Robert, Drexl, Joseph, Nack, Ralph (eds), Patents and Technological Progress in a Globalized World, Liber Amicorum Joseph Straus, Berlin, Heidelberg: Springer (2009).

Anonymous, Bigger isn't Always Better, 418 Nature 353 (2002).

Anonymous, Daiichi Sankyo to Buy Control of Ranbaxy of India for up to $4.6 Billion, New York Times, June 11, 2008.

Anonymous, The Disclosure Function of the Patent System (or Lack Thereof), 118 Harv. L. Rev. 2007(2005).

Anten, Lewis, What's new with novelty - Section 102 of S. 643, 54 J. Pat. Off. Soc'y 75 (1972).

Arbex, Danieli S. Costa, Essay on Incentives for Pharmaceutical Research: A Double Push-Pull Program, Ann Arbor: Proquest LLC (2009).

Ariëns, Everhardus J./Wuis, Eveline W., Bias in Pharmacokinetics and Clinical Pharmacology, 42 Clin. Pharmacol. & Ther. 361 (1987).

Armstrong, Drew, Eli Lilly CEO Says Cost Cutting Won't Solve Drug Sales Loss, Bloomberg, April 12, 2012, available at: http://www.bloomberg.com/news/2012-04-12/eli-lilly-ceo-says-cost-cutting-won-t-solve-drug-revenue-losses.html.

Arora, Ashish/Ceccagnoli, Marco/Cohen, Wesley M., R&D and the Patent Premium, 26 Int. J. Ind. Organ. 1153 (2008).

Arrow, Kenneth, Economic Welfare and the Allocation of Resources for Invention, in The Rate and Direction of Inventive Activity 609, 619-22, Princeton: Princeton University Press ofNati'l Bureau of Econ. Research (1962).

Arrowsmith, John/Harrison, Richard, Drug Repositioning: The Business Case and Current Strategies to Repurpose Shelved Candidates and Marketed Drugs, in: Barratt, Michael J. and Frail, Donald E. (eds), Drug Repositioning: Bringing New Life to Shelved Assets and Existing Drugs, New Jersey: John Wiley & Sons, Inc (2012).

Arundel, Anthony/Kabla, Isabelle, What Percentage of Innovations are patented? Empirical Estimates for European Firms, 27 Res. Policy, 127, 138 (1998).

AstraZeneca, AstraZeneca Annual Report 2010, available at: http://www.astrazeneca-annualreports.com/AZ_AR_100311_single.pdf.

AstraZeneca, AstraZeneca Annual Report 2011, available at: http://www.astrazeneca-annualreports.com/2011/documents/pdfs/annual_report_pdf_entire.pdf.

AstraZeneca, AstraZeneca Annual Review 2000, available at: http://www.astrazeneca.com/cs/Satellite?blobcol=urldata&blobheader=application%2Fpdf&blobheadername1=Content-Disposition&blobheadername2=MDT-Type&blobheadervalue1=inline%3B+filename%3DAnnual-Review.pdf&blobheadervalue2=abinary%3B+charset%3DUTF-8&blobkey=id&blobtable=MungoBlobs&blobwhere=1285635038761&ssbinary=true.

Avorn, Jerry, Sending Pharma Better Signals, 309 Science 669 (2005).

Bacher/Melullis, in: Benkard, Georg, et al., Patentgesetz, Gebrauchsmustergesetz, 10th Ed. München: C. H. Beck (2006).

Barnett, Jonathan M., Cultivating the Genetic Commons: Imperfect Patent Protection and the Network Model of Innovation, 37 San Diego L. Rev. 987 (2000).

Barratt, Michael J./Frail, Donald E.(eds), Drug Repositioning: Bringing New Life to Shelved Assets and Existing Drugs, New Jersey: John Wiley & Sons, Inc (2012).

Bartfai, Tamas/Lees, Graham V., Drug Discovery: From Bedside to Wall Street, Burlington: Elsevier Academic Press (2006).

Barth, Gerhard/Zimmer, Franz-Josef, The Olanzapine Patent Dispute: German Court Grants a Preliminary Injunction on a Patent Invalidated by the First-Instance Federal Patent Court, 28 Biotechnology L. Rep. 532 (2008).

Barton, John H./Abbott, Frederick M./Correa, Carlos M./Drexl, Josef/Foray, Dominique/Marchant Ron (eds), Views on the Future of the Intellectual Property System, Geneva: ICTSD (2007).

Beary, John F., Chirality and Drug Development, 339 Lancet 495 (1992).

Belenzon, Sharon, Knowledge Flow and Sequential Innovation: Implications for Technologz diffusion, R&D and Market Value, Discussion Paper Series No 256, Oxford: Oxford University (2006).

Benjamin, Stuart M./Rai, Arti K., Who's Afraid of the APA? What the Patent System Can Learn from Administrative Law, 95 Geo. L. J. 269 (2007).

Benkard, Georg/Asendorf, Claus Dietrich/Rogge, Rüdiger/Bacher, Klaus/Schäfers, Alfons/Goebel, Frank Peter/Scharen, Uwe/Grabinski, Klaus/ Schmidt, Christof/Melullis, Klaus-Jürgen/Ullmann, Eike (eds.), Patentgesetz, Gebrauchsmustergesetz, 10th Ed. München: C. H. Beck (2006).

Berger, Jonathan M., Tripping over Patents: AIDS, Access to Treatment and the Manufacturing of Scarcity, 17 Conn. J. Int'l L. 157 (2002).

Berndt, Ernst R., Pharmaceuticals in U.S. Health Care: Determinants of Quantity and Price, 16 J. Econ. Perspect. 45 (2002).

Bernstein, Joel, Polymorphism in Molecular Crystals, New York: Oxford University Press (2002).

Bessen, James/Maskin, Eric, Sequential Innovation, Patents and Imitation, Working Paper No 11/99, Massachusetts: MIT (1999).

Bessen, James/Maskin, Eric, Sequential Innovation, Patents, and Imitation, 40 RAND J. Econ. 611 (2009).

Bessen, James/Meurer, Michael J., Patent Failure: How Judges, Bureaucrats, and Lawyers Put Innovators at Risk, Princeton: Princeton University Press (2008).

Blair, Roger D./Cotter, Thomas F., Rethinking Patent Damages, 10 Tex. Intell. Prop. L. J. 1 (2001).

Blanco White, Thomas A., Patents for inventions and the protection of industrial designs, London: Stevens & Sons, 5th Ed. (1983).

Bohsem, Guido, Wie Medikamente Billiger Werden Sollen, Süddeutsche Zeitung, January 23, 2012, available at: http://www.sueddeutsche.de/wirtschaft/pharmaindustrie-wie-medikamente-billiger-werden-sollen-1.1264493.

Bond, Ronald S./Lean, David F., Sales, Promotion, and Product Differentiation in Two Prescription Drug Markets, Washington, DC: U.S. Federal Trade Commission. Bureau of Economics (1977).

Boyd, Karen I., Nonobviousness and the Biotechnology Industry: A Proposal for a Doctrine of Economic Nonobviousness, 12 Berkeley Tech. L.J. 311 (1997).

Brandi-Dohrn, Matthias, Der zu weite Patentanspruch, GRUR Int 1995, 541.

Brandt, Karsten, Die Schutzfrist des Patents, Munich: C.H. Beck (1996).

Bresalier, et al., Cardiovascular Events Associated with Rofecoxib in a Colorectal Adenoma Chemoprevention Trial, 352 New Eng. J. Med. 1092, 1098 (2005).

Brittain, Harry G, Theory and Principles of Polymorphic Systems, in: Brittain, Harry G. (ed), Polymorphism in Pharmaceutical Solids, New York: Informa Healthcare, 2nd Ed. (2009).

Brown, Lucille J., The Markush Challenge, 31 J. Chem. Inf. Comp. Sci. 2 (1991).

Bublak, Wolfgang/Coehn, Markus., Offenbarungsgehalt der Vorveröffentlichung einer chemischen Strukturformel (Disclosure in the Prior Publication of a Chemical Structural Formula), GRUR 2009, 382.

Buhrow, Astrid/Nordemann, Jan B., Grenzen ausschließlicher Rechte geistigen Eigentums durch Kartellrecht (Q 187), GRUR Int 2005, 407.

Burgess, Lesley J./Terblanche, Marli, The Future of the Pharmaceutical, Biological and Medical Device Industry, 3 Open Access J. Clin. Trials 45 (2011).

Burk, Dan L./Lemley Mark A., Biotechnology's Uncertainty Principle, 54 Case W. Res. L. Rev. 691 (2003).

Burk, Dan L./Lemley Mark A., Is Patent Law Technology-Specific?, 17 Berkeley Tech. L.J. 1155 (2002).

Burk, Dan L./Lemley Mark A., Policy Levers in Patent Law, 89 Va. L. Rev. 1575 (2003).

Cadot, Olivier/Lippman, Steven, Barriers to Imitation and the Incentive to Innovate", Working Paper No. 434, Los Angeles: Western Management Science Institute (1995).

Caira, Mino R., Crystalline Polymorphism of Organic Compound, in: Weber, Edwin, Design of Organic Solids, Berlin: Springer (1998).

Caldwell, John, Do Single Enantiomers Have Something Special to Offer?, 16 Hum. Psychopharm. S67 (2001).

Carmichael, Begley S., Desperately Seeking Cures, News Wk. May 15, 2010, available at: http://www.newsweek.com/id/238078.

Chakrabarti, Jiban K./Horsman, Linda/Hotten Terrence M/Pullar Ian A./Tupper David E./Wright Francesca C., 4-Piperazinyl-10H-thieno[2,3-b][1,5]benzodiazepines as potential neuroleptics, 28 J. Med. Chem. 874 (1980).

Chandy, Rajesh/Hopstaken, Brigitte/Narasimhan, Om/Prabhu, Jaideep, From Invention to Innovation: Conversion Ability in Product Development, 43 J. Marketing Res. 494 (2006).

Chang, Howard F., Patent Scope, Antitrust Policy, and Cumulative Innovation, 26 RAND J. Econ. 34 (1995).

Chisum, Donald S., Chisum on Patents, Newark: LexisNexis (2012).

Chisum, Donald S., Comment: Anticipation, Enablement and Obviousness: An Eternal Glden Braid, 15 AIPLA Q. J. 57 (1987).

Chou, Teyu/Haller, Hans, The Division of Profit in Sequential Innovation Reconsidered, Department of Economics Working Paper no. E95-02, Blacksburg: Virginia Polytechnic Institute and State University (1995).

Christie, Andrew F./Dent, Chris/McIntyre, Peter/Wilson, Lachlan/Studdert, David M., Patents Associated with High-Cost Drugs in Australia, 8 PLoS Med 1 (2013).

Cockburn, Iain M., Is the Pharmaceutical Industry in a Productivity Crisis?, in: Jaffe, Adam B., Lerner Josh, and Stern, Scott (eds), Innovation Policy and Economics, volume 7, Cambridge: MIT press (2006).

Coggio, Brian D./Cerrito, Francis D., The Application of the Patent Laws to the Drug Approval Process, 52 Food & Drug L.J. 345 (1997).

Cohen, Mesley M./Nelson, Richard R./Walsh, John P., Protecting Their Intellectual Assets: Appropriability Conditions and Why U.S. Manufacturing Firms Patent (or Not), NBER Working Paper No. 7552. Cambridge: NBER (2000).

Comanor, William S., Research and Competitive Product Differentiation in the Pharmaceutical Industry in the United States, 31 Economia, 372 (1964).

Cornelli, Francesca/Schankerman, Mark, Patent renewals and R&D Incentives, 30 RAND J. Econ. 197 (1999).

Cornish, William R./Llewelyn, David/Aplin, Tanya, Intellectual Property : Patents, Copyright, Trade marks and Allied Rights, London: Sweet & Maxwell, 7th Ed. (2010).

Correa, Carlos M., Public Health and Patent Legislation in Developing Countries, 3 Tul. J. Tech. & Intell. Prop. 1 (2001).

Correa, Carlos, Guidelines for the Examination of Pharmaceutical Patents:Developing a Public Health Perspective - A Working Paper, Geneva: ICTSD, WHO, UNCTAD (2006).

Crews, Kenneth D., Looking Ahead and Shaping the Future: Provoking Change in Copyright Law, 49 J. Copyright Soc'y U.S.A. 549 (2001).

Crouch, Dennis D., Nil: the Value of Patents in a Major Crisis such as an Influenza Pandemic, 39 Seton Hall L. Rev. 1125 (2009).

Crouch, Dennis D., The Patent Lottery: Exploiting Behavioral Economics for the Common Good, 16 Geo. Mason L. Rev. 141 (2008).

Dam, Kenneth W., The Economic Underpinnings of Patent Law, 23 J. Legal Stud. 247 (1994).

Daniels, Jonathan M./Nestmann, Earle R./Kerr, Alex, Development of Stereoisomeric (Chiral) Drugs: A Brief Review of Scientific and Regulatory Considerations, 31 Drug Info. J. 639 (1997).

Danzon, Patricia M./Epstein, Andrew/Nicholson, Sean, Mergers and Acquisitions in the Pharmaceutical and Biotech Industries, 28 Manage. Decis. Econ. 307 (2007).

Darrow, Jonathan J., The Patentability of Enantiomers: Implications for the Pharmaceutical Industry, 2 Stan. Tech. L. Rev. 1 (2007).

Dasgupta, Partha, Patents, Priority and Imitation or the Economics of Races and Waiting Games, 98 Econ. J. 66 (1988).

Davis, Steven J./Murphy, Kevin M./Topel, Robert H., Entry, Pricing and Product Design in an Initially Monopolized Market, NBER Working Paper No. 8547, Cambridge: NBER (2001).

den Exter, André, The Pharmaceutical Sector Inquiry:'Hamlet' in a Nutshell, 17 Eur. J. Health L. 125 (2010).

Denicolò, Vincenzo, Patent Races and Optimal Patent Policy, 44 J. Ind. Econ. 249 (1996).

Denicolò, Vincenzo, Two-Stage Patent Races and Patent Policy, 31 RAND J. Econ. 488 (2000).

Denicolò, Vincenzo/Zanchettin, Piercarlo, How should forward patent protection be provided?, 20 Int'l. J. Indus. Org. 801 (2002).

Dessemontet, François, The Legal Protection of Know-How in the United States of America, Geneva: Librairie Droz, H.W. Clarke trans., 2nd Ed. (1976).

DeStevens, George, Lead Structure Discovery and Development, in: Hansch, Corwin, Sammes, Peter G., and Taylor, John B. (eds.), Comprehensive Medicinal Chemistry: The Rational Design, Mechanistic Study and Therapeutic Applications of Chemical compounds, Oxford: Pergamon Press (1990).

Deutsches Patent- und Markenamt, Jahresbericht 2007, München: DPMA (2008).

DG Competition, Pharma Sector Inquiry - Final Report (2009), available at http://ec.europa.eu/competition/sectors/pharmaceuticals/inquiry/staff_working_paper_part1.pdf.

Dickson, Michael/Gagnon, Jean Paul, Key Factors in the Rising Cost of New Drug Discovery and Development, 3 Nat. Rev. Drug Discov. 417 (2004).

Dickson, Michael/Gagnon, Jean Paul, The Cost of New Drug Discovery and Development, 4 Discov. Med. 172 (2004).

DiMasi, Joseph A./Hansen, Ronald W./Grabowski, Henry G., Cost of Innovation in the Pharmaceutical Industry, 10 J. Health. Econ. 107 (1991).

DiMasi, Joseph A./Hansen, Ronald W./Grabowski, Henry G., The Price of Innovation New Estimates of Drug Development Costs, 22 J. Health Econ. 151 (2003).

Dinwoodie, Graeme B./Dreyfuss, Rochelle C., Diversifying without Discriminating: Complying with the Mandates of the TRIPS Agreement, 13 Mich. Telecomm. Tech. L. Rev. 445 (2007).

Doi, Teruo, The Territoriality Principle of Patent Protection and Conflict of Laws: A Review of Japanese Court Decisions, 26 Fordham Int'l L.J. 377 (2002).

Domeij, Bengt, Pharmaceutical patents in Europe, Hague: Kluwer Law International (2000).

Donohue, Julie M/Cevasco, Marisa/Rosenthal, Meredith B., A Decade of Direct-to-Consumer Advertising of Prescription Drugs, 357 N. Eng J. Med. 673 (2007).

Drexl, Josef, Responding to the Challenges for Development with a Competition-Oriented Approach, in: Barton, John H., Abbott, Frederick M., Correa, Carlos M., Drexl, Josef, Foray, Dominique, and Marchant Ron (eds), Views on the Future of the Intellectual Property System, Geneva: ICTSD (2007).

Drexl, Josef/Hilty, Reto M./Boy, Laurence/Godt, Christine/Remiche, Bernard (eds), Technology and Competition : Contributions in Honour of Hanns Ullrich, Bruxelles: Larcier (2009).

Duffy, John F., Rethinking the Prospect Theory of Patents, 71 U. Chi. L. Rev. 439 (2004).

Duffy, John F., Rules and Standards on the Forefront of Patentability, 51 Wm. & Mary L. Rev. 609 (2009).

Durham, Alan L., Patent Law Essentials: A Concise Guide, Westport: Praeger (1999).

Dutfield, Graham, Intellectual Property Rights and the Life Science Industries, London: World Scientific Publishing Co., 2nd Ed. (2009).

Dutfield, Graham/Suthersanen, Uma, The Innovation Dilemma: Intellectual Property and the Historical Legacy of Cumulative Creativity, 8 Intell. Prop. Q. 379 (2004).

Eidson, B. Scott, How Safe Is the Harbor? Considering the Economic Implications of Patent Infringement in Section 271(e)(1) Analysis, 82 Wash. U. L. Rev. 1169 (2004).

Eisenberg, Rebecca S., Analyze This: A Law and Economics Agenda for the Patent System, 53 Vand. L. Rev. 2081 (2000).

Eisenberg, Rebecca S., Obvious to Whom? Evaluating Inventions from the Perspective of PHOSITA, 19 Berkeley Tech. L.J. 885 (2004).

Eisenberg, Rebecca S., Patents and the Progress of Science: Exclusive Rights and Experimental Use, 56 U. Chi. L. Rev. 1017 (1989).

Eisenberg, Rebecca S., The Problem of New Uses, 5 Yale J. Health Pol'y L. & Ethics 717 (2005).

Eisenberg, Rebecca S., The Role of the FDA in Innovation Policy, 13 Mich. Telecomm. Tech. L. Rev. 345 (2007).

Ellery, Tony/Hansen, Neal, Pharmaceutical Lifecycle Management: Making the Most of Each and Every Brand, New Jersey: John Wiley & Sons, Inc (2012).

Engelberg, Alfred B., Special Patent Provisions for Pharmaceuticals: Have they Outlived Their Usefullness - A Political Legislative and Legal History of U.S. Law and Observations for the Future, 39 IDEA 389 (1999).

Engelberg, Alfred B./Kesselheim, Aaron S./Avorn, Jerry, Balancing Innovation, Access, and Profits--Market Exclusivity for Biologics, 361 New Eng. J. Med. 1917 (2009).

Eswaran, Mukesh/Gallini, Nancy, Patent Policy and the Direction of Technological Change, 27 RAND J. Econ. 722 (1996).

European Federation of Pharmaceutical Industries and Associations, The Pharmaceutical Industry in Figures, 2012, available at: http://www.efpia.eu/sites/www.efpia.eu/files/EFPIA%20Figures%202012%20Final.pdf.

EvaluatePharma, World Preview 2014, (2009) available at: http://www.evaluatepharma.com/pdf/EvaluatePharma%20World%20Preview%202014.pdf.

FDA, FY 2011 Innovative Drug Approvals, (2011), available at: http://www.fda.gov/downloads/aboutfda/reportsmanualsforms/reports/ucm278358.pdf.

Federal Trade Commission, Generic Drug Entry Prior to Patent Expiration, an FTC Study, 2002, available at: http://www.ftc.gov/os/2002/07/genericdrugstudy.pdf.

Federsel, Hans-Jürgen, Process R&D under the Magnifying Glass: Organization, Business Model, Challenges, and Scientific Context, 18 Bioorgan. Med. Chem. 5775 (2010).

Fitt, Robert, Selection Patents and Markush Claims in Europe, 20 Biotechnol. Law Rep. 17 (2010).

Frank, Richard G., Behavioral Economics and Health Economics, NBER Working Paper No. 10881. Cambridge: NBER (2004).

Frank, Richard. G., Editorial: New Estimates of Drug Development Costs, 22 J. Health Econ. 325 (2003).

von der Freien, Klaus Roth, Von Vollmilch bis Bitter, edelste Polymorphie, 39 Chemie in Unserer Zeit 416 (2005).

Friebel, Guido/Koch, Alexander K./Prady, Delphine/Seabright, Paul, Objective and Incentives at the european Patent Office, Toulouse: Institut d'Economie Industrielle (2006).

Gagnon, Marc-André/Lexchin, Joel, The Cost of Pushing Pills: A New Estimate of Pharmaceutical Promotion Expenditures in the United States, 5 PLOS Med. e1 (2008).

Gallini, Nancy/Scotchmer, Suzanne, Intellectual Property: When Is It the Best Incentive System,in: Jaffe, Adam B., Lerner, Josh, Stern, Scott (eds), Innovation Policy and the Economy, Vol. 2, Massachusetts: MIT Press (2002).

Gaudillière, Jean-Paul, Professional or Industrial Order? Patents, Biological Drugs, and Pharmaceutical Capitalism in Early Twentieth Centry Germany, 24 Hist. & Tech. 107 (2008).

Gaudry, Kate S, Evergreening: a Common Practice to Protect New Drugs, 29 Nature Biotech. 876 (2011).

Germinario, Claudio, Double Patenting in the Practice of the European Patent Office, IIC 2011, 387.

Gervais, Daniel, The TRIPS Agreement: Drafting History and Analysis, London: Sweet & Maxwell, 4th Ed. (2012).

Ghofrani, Hossein A./Osterloh, Ian H./Grimminger, Friedrich, Sildenafil: from Angina to Erectile Dysfunction to Pulmonary Hypertension and Beyond, 5 Nat. Rev. Drug Discov. 689 (2006).

Gilbert, Richard/Shapiro, Carl, Opimal patent length and breadth, 21 RAND J. Econ. 106 (1990).

Gilbody, Simon/Wilson, Paul/Watt, Ian, Benefits and harms of direct to consumer advertising: a systematic review, 14 Quality & Safety in Health Care 246 (2005).

Gilfillan, S. C., The Root of Patents, or Squaring Patents by Their Roots, 31 J. Pat. & Trademark Off. Soc'y 611 (1949).

Giron, Danielle, Chracterisation of Salts of Drug Substances, 73 J. Thermal Analysis & Calorimetry 441 (2003).

Glasgow, Lara J., Stretching the Limits of Intellectual Property Rights: Has the Pharmaceutical Industry Gone Too Far?, 41 IDEA 227 (2001).

GlaxoSmithKlein, GSK's Position on Evergreening, 2011 available at: http://www.gsk.com/policies/GSK-and-evergreening.pdf.

Gordon, Wendy J., A Property Right in Self-Expression: Equality and Individualism in the Natural Law of Intellectual Property, 102 Yale L. J. 1533 (1993).

Grabowski, Henry G./Kyle, Margaret, Generic Competition and Market Exclusivity Periods in Pharmaceuticals, 28 Manage. Decis. Econ. 491 (2007).

Grabowski, Henry G./Kyle, Margaret, Mergers and Alliances in Pharmaceuticals: Effects on Innovation and R&D productivity, in: Gugler, Klaus and Yurtoglu, B. Burcin (eds.), The Economics of Corporate Governance and Mergers, Cheltenham: Edward Elgar (2008).

Grabowski, Henry G./Vernon, John M., Brand Loyalty, Entry, and Price Competition in Pharmaceuticals after the 1984 Drug Act, 35 J. Law Econ. 331 (1992).

Grabowski, Henry/Vernon, John, Longer Patents for Increased Generic Competition in the US. The Waxman-Hatch Act after One Decade,10 Suppl 2 Pharmacoeconomics 110 (1996).

Grady, Mark F./Alexander, Jay I., Patent Law and Rent Dissipation, 78 Va. L. Rev. 305 (1992).

Green, Jerry R./Scotchmer, Suzanne, On the division of Profit in Sequential Innovation, 26 RAND J. Econ. 20 (1995).

Grubb, Philip W./Thomsen, Peter R., Patents for Chemicals, Pharmaceuticals and Biotechnology : Fundamentals of Global Law, Practice and Strategy, Oxford: Oxford Univ. Press, 5th Ed. (2010).

Günzel, Brigitte, Die Anhängigkeit der Stammanmeldung als Voraussetzung für die Einreichung einer Teilanmeldung – ein Bericht und viele Fragen, IIC Int 2008, 644.

Gugler, Klaus/Yurtoglu, B. Burcin (eds.), The Economics of Corporate Governance and Mergers, Cheltenham: Edward Elgar (2008).

Hall, Bronwyn H./Rosenberg, Nathan (eds.), Handbook of The Economics of Innovation, Oxford: Elsevier B.V. (2010).

Hall, Stephen S., The Claritin Effect; Prescription for Profit, The New York Times, March 11, 2001, available at:http://www.nytimes.com/2001/03/11/magazine/the-claritin-effect-prescription-for-profit.html?pagewanted=all&src=pm.

Hansch, Corwin/Sammes, Peter G./Taylor, John B. (eds.), Comprehensive Medicinal Chemistry:The Rational Design, Mechanistic Study and Therapeutic Applications of Chemical compounds, Oxford: Pergamon Press (1990).

Hansen, Bernd/Hirsch, Fritjoff, Protecting Inventions in Chemistry - Commentary on Chemical Case Law under the European Patent Convention and the German Patent Law, Weinheim: Wiley-VCH (1997).

Haracoglou, Irina, Competition Law and Patents: a Follow-on Innovation Perspective in the Biopharmaceutical Industry,Cheltenham: Edward Elgar (2008).

Harhoff, Dietmar, Economic Cost-benefit Analysis of a Unified and Integrated european Patent Litigation System, Tender No MARKT/2008/06/D, Munich: Ludwig-Maximilians-Universität München (2009).

Harmon, Robert L./Homan, Cynthia A./McMahon, Charles M., Patents and the Federal Crcuit, Arlington: BNA Books, 10th Ed. (2010).

Harrelson, John A., Trips, Pharmaceutical Patents, and the HIV/AIDS Crisis: Finding the Proper Balance between Intellectual Property Rights and Compassion, 7 Wid. L. Symp. J. 175 (2001).

Harris, Gardiner, Prilosec's Maker Switches Users To Nexium, Thwarting Generics, The Wall Street Journal, June 6, 2002, available at: http://online.wsj.com/article/0,,SB1023326369679910840,00.html

Hays, Thomas, An application of the European Rules on Trademark Exhaustion to Extra-market Goods, 91 Trademark Rep. 675 (2001).

Heilman RD, Drug development history, "overview," and what are GCPs?, 4 Quality Assurance, 75 (1995).

Heller, Michael A., The Tragedy of the Anticommons: Property in the Transition from Marx to Markets, 111 Harv. L. Rev. 621 (1998).

Heller, Michael A./Eisenberg, Rebecca S., Can Patents Deter Innovation? The Anticommons in biomedical Research, 280 Science 698 (1998).

Hemphill, C. Scott/Sampat, Bhaven N., Evergreening, Patent Challenges, and Effective Market Life in Pharmaceuticals, 31 J. Health Econ. 327 (2012).

Hemphill, C. Scott/Sampat, Bhaven N., Drug Patents at the Supreme Court, 339 Science 1386 (2013).

Henderson, Rebecca/Cockburn, Iain, Scale, Scope, and Spillovers: The Determinants of Research Productivity in Drug Discovery, 27 RAND J. Econ. 32 (1996).

Henkel, Joachim/Jell, Florian, Alternative Motives to File for Patents: Profiting from Pendency and Publication (2009), Working paper, available at: http://ssrn.com/abstract=1271242.

Herper, Matthew, Solving The Drug Patent Problem, Forbes, February 5, 2002, available at: http://www.forbes.com/2002/05/02/0502patents.html.

Higgins, Matthew J.,/Rodriguez, Daniel, The Outsourcing of R&D through Acquisitions in the Pharmaceutical Industry, 80 J. Financ. Econ. 351 (2006).

Higgins, Matthew J./Graham, Stuart J. H., Balancing Innovation and Access: Patent Challenges Tip the Scales, 326 Science 370 (2009).

Hilty, Reto M., The Role of Patent Quality in Europe, in: Drexl, Josef, Hilty, Reto M., Boy Laurence, Godt, Christine, Remiche, Bernard (eds), Technology and Competition : Contributions in Honour of Hanns Ullrich, Bruxelles: Larcier (2009).

von Hippel, Eric, The Sources of Innovation, New York: Oxford University Press (1988).

Hoffman, David C., A Modest Proposal: Toward Improved Access to Biotechnology Research Tools by Implementing a Broad Experimental Use Exception, 89 Cornell L. Rev. 993 (2004).

Holbrook, Timothy R., Possession in Patent Law, 59 SMU L. Rev. 123 (2006).

Holmes, David, Skies Darken over Drug Companies, 379 Lancet 1863 (2012).

Hopenhayn, Hugo A./Mitchell, matthew F., Innovation Variety and Patent Breadth, 32 RAND J. Econ. 152 (2001).

Hopkins, Andrew L./Groom, Colin R., The Druggable Genome, 1 Nature Rev. Drug Discov. 727 (2002).

Horton, Richard, Vioxx, the implosion of Merck, and aftershocks at the FDA, 364 Lancet 1995 (2004).

Hovenkamp, Herber/Janis, Mark D./Lemley, Mark A./Leslie, Christopher R., IP and Antitrust - An Analysis of Antitrust Principles Applied to Intellectual Property Law, Austin: Wolters Kluwer Law & Business, Aspen Publ, 2nd Ed. (2010).

Howard, Leighton, Use of Patents in Drug Lifecycle Management, 4 J. Generic Med 231 (2007).

Hunt, Robert M., Nonobviousness and the Incentive to Innovate: An Economic Analysis of Intellectual Property Reform, Working Paper No. 99-3, Philadelphia: Federal Reserve Bank Of Philadelphia (1999).

Hutt, A.J./Valentová, J., The Chiral Switch: The Development of Single Enantiomer Drgs from Racemates, 50 Acta Facultatis Pharmaceuticae Universitatis Comenianae 7 (2003).

IMAP, Global Pharma and Biotech M&A Report-2012 (2012), available at: http://www.imap.com/imap/media/resources/Pharma_Report_2012_FINAL_2F6C8ADA76680.pdf.

IMS Health, Top 20 Global Products(2010), available at: http://imshealth.com/deployedfiles/imshealth/Global/Content/StaticFile/Top_Line_Data/Top_20_Global_Products.pdf.

Ionescu, Corina/Caira, Mino R., Drug Metabolism - Current Concepts, Dordrecht: Springer (2005).

Jack, Andrew, Drugs Groups Forced to Put Squeeze on R&D, Fin. Times, October 17, 2011.

Jackson, Richard T., A Lockean Approach to the Compulsory Patent Licensing Controversy, 9 J. TECH. L. & POL'Y, 117 (2004).

Jacob, Robin, Novelty of Use Claims, IIC 1996, 170.

Jacob, Robin, Patents and Pharmaceuticals – a Paper given on 29th November at the Presentation of the Directorate-General of Competition's Preliminary Report of the Pharma-sector Inquiry, December, The Chartered Institute of Patent Attorneys 711 (2008).

Jacob, Robin, Some Recent Cases of Significance in the UK, IIC 1997, 880.

Jaenichen, Hans-Rainer, The Grant of a Compulsory License for Recombinant γ-IFN in Germany, 11 Biotechnol. Law Rep. 369 (1992).

Jaffe, Adam B., Lerner Josh, and Stern, Scott (eds), Innovation Policy and Economics, volume 7, Cambridge: MIT press (2006).

Jaffe, Adam B., The U.S. Patent System in Transition: Policy Innovation and the Innovation Process, 29 Res. Policy 531 (2000).

Jaffe, Adam B./Lerner, Josh, Innovation and Its Discontents - How Our Broken Patent System Is Endangering Innovation and Progress and What To Do About It, Princeton: Princeton University Press (2004).

Janis, Mark D., On Courts Herding Cats: Contending with the "Written Description" Requirement (and Other Unruly Patent Disclosure Doctrines), 2 Wash. U. J. L. & Pol'y 55 (2000).

Janis, Mark D., Second Tier Patent Protection, 40 Harv. Int'l L. J. 151 (1999).

Jantzen, Gwen M./Robinson, Joseph R, Sustained- and Controlled- Release Drug-Delivery System, in: Banker, Gilbert S and Rhodes Christopher T.(eds), Modern Pharmacetics, 4th Ed. New York: Marcel Dekker (2002).

Johnson-Laird, Andrew, Software Reverse Engineering in the Real World, 19 U. Dayton L. Rev. 843 (1994).

Julian-Arnold, Gianna, International Compulsory Licensing: The Rationales and the Reality, 33 IDEA 349 (1993).

Karmien, Morton I./Schwartz, Nancy L., Market Structure and Innovation, Cambridge: Cambridge University Press (1982).

Kash, Don E/Kingston, William, Patents in a world of complex technologies, 28 Sci. & Pub. Pol'y 11 (2001).

Katzenberger, Paul, Mannheim Conference on fundamental Questions of Patent Protection for Chemical Inventions, IIC 1972, 357.

Keeling, David T., Intellectual Property Rights in Eu Law: Free Movement and Competition Law, Oxford: Oxford University Press (2003).

Kefauver, Estes, In a few hands : Monopoly power in America, Harmondsworth: Penguin Books (1966).

Kieff, Scott F., On the Ecnonomics of Patent Law and Policy, in: Toshiko Takenaka (ed), Patent Law and Theory, Cheltenham: Edward Elgar Publishing Limited (2008).

Kieff, Scott F., Property Rights and Property Rules for Commercializing Inventions, 85 Minn. L. Rev. 697 (2001).

Kieff, Scott F., The Case for Registering Patents and the Law and Economics of Present Patent-Obtaining Rules, 45 B.C.L.Rev., 55 (2003).

Kieff, Scott F./Schwartz, Herbert F./Newman, Pauline, Principle of Patent Law, New York: Foundation Press, 5th Ed. (2011).

Kilger, Christian/Feldges, Joachim/Jaenichen, Hans-Rainer, The Erosion Of Compound Protection In Germany: Implementation Of The EU Directive On The Legal Protection Of Biotechnological Inventions -- The German Way, 87 J. Pat. & Trademark Off. Soc'y 569 (2005).

Kitch, Edmund W., Graham v. John Deere Co.: New Standards for Patents, 1966 Sup. Ct. Rev. 293 (1966).

Kitch, Edmund W., The Nature and Function of the Patent System, 20 J. Law Econ. 265 (1977).

Klemperer, Paul, How Broad should the Scope of Patent Protection Be?, 21 Rand J. Econ. 113 (1990).

Kling, Jim, From Hypertension to Angina to Viagra, 1 Modern Drug Discov. 31 (1998).

Klöpsch, Gerald, The Patentability of Pharmaceuticals According to the European Patent Collection (EPC), IIC 1982, 457.

Knowles, Jonathan/Gromo, Gianni, Target Selection in Drug Discovery, 2 Nat. Rev. Drug Discov. 63 (2003).

Kola, Ismail/Landis, John, Can the pharmaceutical industry reduce attrition rates?, 3 Nat. Rev. Drug Discov. 711 (2004).

Kraßer, Rudolf, Patentrecht, 6th Ed. München: C. H. Beck (2009).

La Manna, Manfredi, M.A., Optimal Patent Life vs Optimal patentability standards, 10 Int'l. J. Indus. Org. 81 (1992).

Lakdawalla, Darius N./Goldman, Dana P./Michaud, Pierre-Carl/Sood, Neeraj/Lempert, Robert/Cong, Ze/Vries, Han de/Gutierrez, Italo, U.S. Pharmaceutical Policy In A Global Marketplace, 28 Health Affairs w138 (2009).

Landes, William M./Posner, Richard A., The Economic Structure of Intellectual Property Law, Cambridge: The Belknap Press of Harvard University Press (2003).

Langreth, Robert/Murphy, Victoria, Perennial Patents, Forbes, Apr. 2, 2001, available at: http://www.forbes.com/forbes/2001/0402/052_print.html.

Lanjouw, Jean O./Schankerman, Mark, Patent Quality and Research Productivity: Measuring Innovation with Multiple Indicators, 114 Econ. J. 441 (2004).

Lemley, Mark A., Rational Ignorance at the Patent Office, 95 Nw. U. L. Rev. 1495 (2001).

Lemley, Mark A., The Economics of Improvement in Intellectual Property Law, 75 Tex. L. Rev. 989 (1997).

Lerner, Joschua, The Importance of Patent Scope: An Empirical Analysis, 25 RAND J. Econ. 319 (1994).

Lerner, Josh/Merges, Robert P., The Control of Strategic Alliances: An Empirical Analysis of Biotechnology Collaborations, NBER Working Paper No. 6014. Cambridge: NBER (1997).

Lessig, Lawrence, Intellectual Property and Code, 11 St. John's J. Legal Comment. 635 (1996).

Levin, Richard C./Klevorick, Alvin K./Nelson, richard R/ Winter, Sidney G., Appropriating the Returns from Industrial Research and Development, 1987 Brookings Paper on Econ. Activity, 783 (1987).

Lichtenberg, Frank R., Are The Benefits Of Newer DrugsWorth Their Cost? Evidence From The 1996 MEPS-The newer the drug in use, the less spending on nondrug items, 20 Health Affair. 241 (2001).

Lichtenberg, Frank R., The Impact of New Drug Launches on Longevity: Evidence from Longitudinal, Disease-Level Data from 52 Countries, 1982–2001, 5 Int. J. Health Care Fi. 47 (2005).

Lichtman, Douglas/Baker, Scott/Kraus, Kate, Strategic Disclosure in the Patent System, 53 Vand. L. Rev. 2175 (2000).

Lindgardt, Zhenya/Reeves, Martin/Wallenstein, Judith, Waking the giant: business model innovation in the drug industry, 26 In Vivo: Bus. Med. Rep. 1 (2008).

Long, Clarisa, Our Uniform Patent System, 55 Fed. Law. 44 (2008).

Luski, Israel/Wettstein, David, An Optimal Patent Policy in a Dynamic Model of Innovation, 1 Probl. Perspect. Manage. 31 (2004).

Machlup, Fritz, An Economic Review of the Patent System : Study No. 15 of the subcommittee on Patents, Trademarks, and Copyrights of the Committee on the Judiciary, United States Senate, 85th Congress, 2nd Sess. / Fritz Machlup. - Washington : G P O (1958).

Macomber, Roger, Organic Chemistry, Sausalito: University Science Books (1996).

Mahajan, Anthony J., Note, Intellectual Property, Contracts and Reverse Engineering after ProCD: A Proposed Compromise for Computer Software, 67 Fordham L. Rev. 3297 (1999).

Mahato, Ram I./Narang, Ajit S., Pharmaceutical Dosage Forms and Drug Delivery, Boca Ranton: CRC Press, 2nd Ed (2012).

Mahn, Terry G., Patenting Drug Products: Anticipating Hatch-Waxman Issues during the Claims Drafting Process, 54 Food & Drug L.J. 245 (1999).

Mann, Ronald D./Andrews, Elizabeth B, Introduction, in: Mann, Ronald D., and Andrews, Elizabeth B (eds), Pharmacovigilance, Chichester: John Willey & Sons, Ltd. (2007).

Mansell, Peter, Who is afraid of the patent cliff? 1 Scrip Executive Briefing 1 (2008).

Mansfield, Edwin, Patents and Innovation: An Empirical Study, 32 Manage. Sci. 173 (1986).

Mansfield, Edwin/Schwartz, Mark/Wagner, Samuel, Imitation Costs and Patents: an Empirical Study, 91 Econ. J. 907 (1981).

Mansfield, Peter/Henry, David/Tonkin, Anne, Single-Enantiomer Drugs: Elegant Science, Disappointing Effects,43 Clin. Pharmacokinet. 287 (2004).

Martin, Ben R./Nightingale, Paul (eds.), The Political Economy of Science, Technology, and Innovation, Cheltenham: Edward Elgar Publishing Limited (2000).

Martinez, Barbara/Mathews, Anna Wilde/ Lublin, Joann S./Winslow, Ron, Merck Pulls Vioxx from Market After Link to Heart Problems, Wall St. J., Oct. 1, 2004, available at: http://online.wsj.com/article/0,,SB109654671320932405,00.html.

Matutes, Carmen/Regibeau, Pierre/Rockett, Katharine, Optimal Patent Design and the diffusion of Innovation, 27 RAND J. Econ. 60 (1996).

Mauer, Stephen M./Scotchmer, Suzanne, The Independent-Invention Defense in Intellectual Property, 69 Economica 535 (2002).

Mazzoleni, Roberto/Nelson, Richard R, The Benefits and Costs of Strong Patent Protection: A Contribution to the Current Debate. 27 Res. Policy, 273 (1998).

McGuire, Alistair/Drummond, Michael/Rutten, Frans, Reimbursement of pharmaceuticals in the European Union, in: Mossialos, Elias, Mrazek, Monique F. and Walley, Tom (eds.), Regulating pharmaceuticals in Europe: striving for efficiency, equity, and quality. European Observatory on health systems and policies . Maidenhead: Open University Press (2004).

Meier-Beck, Peter, Die Rechtsprechung des Bundesgerichtshofs zum Patent und Gebrauchsmusterrecht im Jahr 2008, GRUR 2009, 893.

Merck, Merck Press Release, Merck Settles Thousands of Vioxx Claims for $4.85 Billion, Nov. 9, 2007, available at: http://www.officialvioxxsettlement.com/documents/Offical%20Press%20Release%20-%20Vioxx%20Settlement.pdf.

Merges, Robert P., A Brief Note on Blocking Patents and Reverse Equivalents: Biotechnology as an Example, 73 J. Pat. & Trademark Off. Soc'y 878 (1991).

Merges, Robert P., Commercial Success and Patent Standards: Economic Perspectives on Innovation, 76 Cal. L. R. 803 (1988).

Merges, Robert P., Intellectual Property Rights and Bargaining Breakdown: the Case of Blocking Patents, 62 Tenn. L. Rev. 75 (1994).

Merges, Robert P., One Hundred Years of Solicitude: Intellectual Property Law, 88 Cal. L. Rev. 2187 (2000).

Merges, Robert P., Uncertainty and the Standard of Patentability, 7 High Tech. L. J. 1 (1992).

Merges, Robert P./Duffy, John F., Patent Law and Policy: Cases and Materials, Newark: LexisNexis, 5th Ed. (2011).

Merges, Robert P./Nelson, Richard R., On Limiting or Encouragine Rivalry in Technical Progress: The Effect of Patent Scope Decision, 25 J. Econ. Behav. Organ. 1 (1994).

Merges, Robert P./Nelson, Richard R., On the Complex Economics of Patent Scope, 90 Colum. L. Rev. 839 (1990).

Meurer, Michael J., Business Method Patents and Patent Floods, 8 Wash. U. J. L. & Pol'y 309 (2002).

Michele Boldrin/David K. Levine., Against Intellectual Monopoly, Cambridge: Cambridge Univ. Press (2010).

Miller, Christ P./Evans, Mark J. The Chemist's Companion Guide to Patent Law, New Jersey: John Wiley & Sons, Inc (2010).

Morgan, Steven G/Bassett, Kenneth L/Wright, James M/Evans, Robert G/Barer, Morris L/Caetano, Patricia A/Black, Charlyn D, "Breakthrough" Drugs and Growth in Expenditure on Prescription Drugs in Canada, 331 Brit. Med. J. 815 (2005).

Mueller, Janice M., The Evolving Application of the Written Description Requirement to Biotechnological Inventions, 13 Berkeley Tech. L.J. 615 (1998).

Mueller, Janice M./Chisum, Donald S., Enabling Patent Law's Inherent Anticipation Doctrine, 45 Hous. L. Rev. 1101 (2008).

Munos, Bernard, Lessons from 60 Years of Pharmaceutical Innovation, 8 Nat. Rev. Drug Discov. 959 (2009).

Nastelski, Karl, Product Protection for Chemical Inventions in Germany, IIC 1972, 267.

Nathan, Carl/Goldberg, Frederick M., The Profit Problem in Antibiotic R&D, 4 Nat. Rev. Drug Discov. 887 (2005).

National Institute for Health Care Management Research and Educational Foundation, Changing patterns of pharmaceutical innovation. Washington, DC;NIHCM (2002). Available at: http://nihcm.org/pdf/innovations.pdf.

Nelson, Richard R., The Simple Economics of Basic Scientific Research, in: Martin, Ben R./Nightingale, Paul (eds.), The Political Economy of Science, Technology, and Innovation, Cheltenham: Edward Elgar Publishing Limited (2000).

Nelson, Richard, R./Winter, Sidney G., An Evolutionary Theory of Economic Change Cambridge: The Belknap Press of Harvard University Press (1982).

Nordhaus, William D., Invention, Growth, and Welfare - A Theoretical Treatment of Technological Change, Massachusetts: MIT Press (1969).

Norrby, S. Ragnar/Nord, Carl Erik/Finch, Roger, Lack of Development of New Antimicrobial Drugs: a Potential Serious Threat to Public Health, 5 Lancet Infect. Dis. 115 (2005).

O'Donoghue, Ted, A Patentability Requirement for Sequential Innovation, 29 RAND J. Econ. 654 (1998).

O'Donoghue, Ted, Patent Protection When Innovation is Cumulative, Ann Arbor: UMI Company (1996).

O'Donoghue, Ted, Suzanne Scotchmer, and Jacques-François Thisse, 7 J. Econ. Manage. Strat. 1 (1998).

Oellerich, Michael/Armstrong, Victor W., Prodrugs Metabolites: Implications for Therapeutic Drug Monitoring, 47 Clin. Chem. 805 (2001).

Osterrieth, Christian/Köhler, Martin/Haft, Klaus (eds), Patentrecht, Festschrift für Thomas Reimann zum 65. Geburtstag, Köln: Carl Hezmanns Verlag (2009).

Outterson, Kevin/Samora,Julie B./Keller-Cuda, Karen, Will Longer Antimicrobial Patents Improve Global Public Health?, 7 Lancet Infect. Dis. 559 (2007).

Owen-Smith, Jason/Powell, Walter W, To Patent or Not: Faculty Decisions and Institutional Success at Technology Transfer, 26 J. Technol. Transfer 99 (2001).

Pagenberg, Jochen, Beweisanzeichen auf dem Prüfstand Für eine objektive Prüfung auf erfinderische Tätigkeit, GRUR Int 1986, 83.

Parthasarathy, R/Goddar, Heinz, Patentability of Pharmaceutical Products in India - The Novartis Case, IIC 2009, 38.

Patented Medicine Prices Review Board, Annual Report 2004, Ottawa: PMPRB (2005).

Paul, Steven M./Mytelka, Daniel S./Dunwiddie, Christopher T./Persinger, Charles C./ Munos, Bernard H./Lindborg, Stacy R./Schacht, Aaron L., How to Improve R&D Productivity: the Pharmaceutical Industry's Grand Challenge, 9 Nat. Rev. Drug Discov. 203 (2010).

Peterson, John M., Finite Mathematics, New York: Holt, Rinehart and Winston (1974).

Pfizer, Annual Review 2009, (2009), available at: http://www.pfizer.com/files/annual-report/2009/annual/review2009.pdf.

Pifferi, G./Perucca, E., The Cost Benefit Ratio of Enantiomeric Drugs, 20 Eur. J. Drug Metab. Ph. 15 (1995).

Pisano, Gary P., Science Business: the Promise, the Reality, and the Future of Biotech, Boston: Harvard Business School Press (2006).

Power, Eddie, Impact of Antibiotic Restrictions: the Pharmaceutical Perspective, 12 Clin. Microbiol. Infec. 25 (1998).

Privitera, Michael, Large Clinical Trials in Epilepsy: Funding by the NIH versus Pharmaceutical Industry, 68 Epilepsy Res. 52 (2006).

Rai, Arti K., Fostering Cumulative Innovationin the Biopharmaceutical Industry: The Role of Patents and Antitrust 16 Berkerly. Tech. L. J. 813 (2001).

Rai, Arti K., Intellectual Property Rights in Biotechnology: Addressing New Technology 34 Wake Forest L. Rev. 827 (1999).

Rai, Arti K., The Information Revolution Reaches Pharmaceuticals: Balancing Innovation Incentives, Cost, and Access in the Post-Genomics Era, 2001 Ill. L. Rev. 173 (2001).

Rautio, Jarkko/Kumpulainen, Hanna/Heimbach, Tycho/Oliyai, Reza/Oh, Dooman/Järvinen, Tomi/Savolainen, Jouko, Prodrugs: Designs and Clinical Applications, 7 Nat. Rev. Drug Discov. 255 (2009).

Reichman, Jerome H., Intellectual Property in the Twenty-First Century: Will the Developing Countries Lead or Follow? 46 Hous L. Rev. 1115 (2009).

Reichman, Jerome H./Hasenzahl, Catherine, Non-Voluntary Licensing of Patented Inventions: Historical Perspective, Legal Frame-work under TRIPS, and an Overview of the Practice in Canada and the USA1-2, (2003), Issue Paper, Geneva: ICTSD-UNCTAD, available at: http://ictsd.net/downloads/2008/ 06/cs_reichman_hasenzahl.pdf.

Reichman,Jerome H./Dreyfuss, Rochelle C., Harmonization without Consensus: Critical Reflections on Drafting a Substantive Patent Law Treaty, 57 Duke L. J. 85 (2007).

Roberts, Tim, Broad Claims for Biotechnological Inventions, EIPR, 1994, 371.

Robinson, Christopher, Patent Protection for Chemical Products in Canada, Great Britain and the United States, IIC 1972, 139.

Rockett, Katharine, Property Rights and Inventions, in: Hall, Bronwyn H./Rosenberg, Nathan (eds.), Handbook of The Economics of Innovation, Oxford: Elsevier B.V. (2010).

Roin, Benjamin N., Unpatentable Drugs and the Standards of Patentability, 87 Tex. L. Rev. 503 (2009).

Rose, Carol M., Possession as the Origin of Property, 52 U. Chi. L. Rev. 73 (1985).

Rosenbaum, Sara E., Basic Pharmacokinetics and Pharmacodynamics, An Integrated Textbook and computer Simulations, New Jersey: John Wiley& Sons, Inc (2011).

Rucker, T. Donald, Public Policy and Drug Cost: Legitimate and Bastard Options, in: Smith Mickey C (ed), Studies in Pharmaceutical Economics, Binghamton: The Haworth Press, Inc (1996).

Russ, Andreas P./Lampel, Stefan, The Druggable Genome: an Update, 10 Drug Discov. Today. 1607 (2005).

Sachs, George/Shin, Jai M./Howden, Collin W., Review Article: the Clinical Pharmacology of Proton Pump Inhibitors, 23 (Suppl. 2) Aliment Pharm. Ther. 2 (2006).

Safir, Peter O., Current Issues in the Pioneer Versus Generic Drug Wars, 50 Food & Drug L. J. 335 (1995).

Sampson, Margaret, The Evolution of the Enablement and Written description Requirements under 35 U.S.C. § 112 in the Area of Biotechnology, 15 Berkeley Tech. L.J. 1233 (2000).

Satchell, Ralph D., Chemical Product Patent Practice in the United Kingdom, IIC 1970, 179.

Scherer, Frederic M./Ross, David, Industrial market structure and economic performance, Boston: Houghton Mifflin Co., 3rd Ed. (1990).

Scherer, Frederic M., Innovation and Growth: Schumpeterian Perspectives, Cambridge: The MIT Prress (1984).

Scherer, Frederic M., Pharmaceutical Innovation, Massachusetts: John F.Kennedy School of Government (2007).

Scherer, Frederic M., The Link Between Gross Profitability and Pharmaceutical R&D Spending, 20 Health Affair. 216 (2001).

Scherer, Frederic M., The Pharmaceutical Industry — Prices and Progress, 351 New Eng. J. Med. 927 (2004).

Schmied-Kowarzik, Volker, Chemical Inventions According to the New German Patent Act, IIC 1970, 190.

Schneider, Dieter R., Patenting of Pharmaceuticals – Still a Challenge?, IIC 2008, 511.

Schumpeter, Joseph A., Kapitalismus, Sozialismus und Demokratie, Bern: Verlag A. Francke AG. (1942).

Schumpeter, Joseph, Business Cycle, New York: McGraw-Hill Book Company (1939).

Schumpeter, Joseph, Theorie der Wirtschaftlichen Entwicklung, Berlin: Duncker & Humbolt (1964).

Schuster, Daniela/Laggner, Christian/Langer, Thierry, Why Drugs Fail - A Study on side Effects in New Chemical Entities, 11 Current Pharmaceutical Design 3545 (2005).

Schweitzer, Stuart O., Pharmaceutical Economics and Policy, Oxford: Oxford University Press (2007).

Scotchmer, Suzanne, On the Optimality of the Patent Renewal System, 30 RAND J. Econ. 181 (1999).

Scotchmer, Suzanne, Protecting Early Innovators: Should Second-Generation Products be Patentable?, 27 Rand J. Econ. 322 (1996).

Scotchmer, Suzanne, Standing on the Shoulders of Giants: Cumulative Research and the Patent Law, 5 J. Econ. Perspect. 29 (1991).

Scotchmer, Suzanne/Green, Jerry, Novelty and Disclosure in Patent Law, 21 RAND J. Econ. 131 (1990).

Scudellari, Megan, Teaching an Old Drug New Tricks, The Scientist, April 1, 2011, available at: http://www.the-scientist.com/?articles.view/articleNo/29617/title/Teaching-an-Old-Drug-New-Tricks/.

Seager, Spencer L./Slabaugh, Michael R., Chemistry for Today - General, Organic, & Biochemistry, Belmont: Brooks/Cole (2010).

Seißer, Goetz, Perfecting Imperfect Competition, Economics Discussion Papers No 2008-28, Kiel Institute for the World Economy (2008), available at: http://www.economics-ejournal.org/economics/discussionpapers/2008-28

Seymore, Sean B., Rethinking Novelty in Patent Law, 60 Duke L. J., 919 (2011).

Shadowen, Steve D./Leffler, Keith B./Lukens, Joseph T., Bringing Market Discipline to Pharmaceutical Product Reformulations, IIC 2011, 698.

Shavell, Steven, Foundations of Economic Analysis of Law, Cambridge: Belknap Press of Harvard Univ. Press (2004).

Singer, Romuald/Singer, Margarete, The European Patent Convention : a Commentary / Raph Lunzer, rev. English, London: Sweet & Maxwell (1995).

Smith, Austin, 'No' to Ban on Stem-Cell Patents, 472 Nature 418 (2011).

Somaya, D. 2012. Patent Strategy and Management. 38 J. Manage. 1084 (2012).

Spellberg, Brad/Miller,Loren G./Kuo, Melissa N./Bradley, John/Scheld, William M./Edwards, John E., Societal Costs Versus Savings from Wild-Card Patent Extension Legislation to Spur Critically Needed Antibiotic Development, 35 Infection 167 (2007).

Spenner, Jonathan M., Obvious-to Try Obviousness of Chemical Enantiomers in View of Pre-and Post-KSR Analysis, 90 J. Pat. & Trademark Off. Soc'y, 477 (2008).

Stafford, Randall S., Regulating Off-Label Drug Use —Rethinking the Role of the FDA, 358 N Engl J Med, 1427 (2008).

Steele, Henry, Monopoly and Competition in the Ethical Drugs Market, 5 J. Law Econ. 131 (1962).

Strandburg, Katherine J., Patent Fair Use 2.0, 1 UC Irvine L.R.,265 (2011).

Straus, Joseph, Patent Application: Obstacle for Innovation and Abuse of Dominant Position under Article 102 TFEU? 1 J. E. C. L. & Pract. 189 (2010).

Straus, Joseph, Zur Rolle klinischer Versuche beim Zustandekommen von so genannten Auswahlerfindungen, in: Osterrieth, Christian, Köhler, Martin, Haft, Klaus (eds), Patentrecht, Festschrift für Thomas Reimann zum 65. Geburtstag, Köln: Carl Hezmanns Verlag (2009).

Svatos, Michele, Biotechnology and the Utilitarian Argument for Patents, 13 Soc. Philos. Policy. 113 (1996).

Sweet, Miles J., The Patentability of Chiral Drugs Post-KSR: The More Things Change, the More They Stay the Same, 24 Berkeley Tech. L.J. 129 (2009).

Szabo, George S. A, The Problem and Solution Approach in the European Patent Office, IIC 1995, 457.

Talbot, George H./Bradley,John/Edwards, John E./Jr., Gilbert, David/Scheld, Michael/ Bartlett, John G., Bad Bugs Need Drugs: An Update on the Development Pipeline from the Antimicrobial Availability Task Force of the Infectious Diseases Society of America, 42 Clin Infect Dis. 657 (2006).

Teece David J., Profiting from technological innovation: Implications for integration, collaboration, licensing and public policy, 15 Res. Policy 285 (1986).

Temin, Peter, Technology, Regulation, and Market Structure in the Modern Pharmaceutical Industry, 10 Bell J. Econ. 429 (1979).

ter Meer, Nicolaus, German Chemical Patent Law 1965-1975, 57 J. Pat. Off. Soc'y 763 (1975).

Teschemacher, Rudolf, Enlarged Board of Appeal of the EPO Restores Legal Certainty for Divisional Applications – Established Practice Confirmed, IIC 2007, 703.

The Association of the British Pharmaceutical Industry, Did you know? Facts and Figures about the Pharmaceutical Industry in the UK, 2nd Ed. (2011).

The Infectious Diseases Society of America (IDSA), Bad Bugs, no Drugs: as Antibiotic Discovery Stagnates, a Public Health Crisis Brews, Alexandria: ISDA (2004), available at: http://cdm266901.cdmhost.com/cdm/singleitem/collection/p266901coll4/id/801/rec/14.

Thomas, John R., Formalism at the Federal Circuit, 52 Am. U. L. Rev. 771 (2003).

Thomas, Katie, Pfizer Races to Reinvent Itself, The New York Times, May 1, 2012, avilable at: http://www.nytimes.com/2012/05/02/business/pfizer-profit-declines-19-after-loss-of-lipitor-patent.html.

Thomas, Kimberly M. , Protecting Academic and Non-Profit Research: Creating a Compulsory Licensing Provision in the Absence of an Experimental Use Exception, 23 Santa Clara Computer & High Tech. L. J. 347 (2007).

Thomson Reuters, Top 100 Global Innovators (2011), available at: http://blogs.reuters.com/mediafile/files/2011/11/analysis.pdf.

Thomson Reuters, Top 100 Global Innovators (2012), available at: http://img.en25.com/Web/ThomsonReutersScience/1001639.pdf.

Tilmann, Winfried, Validity of Selective Product Claims – Venice Conferences III and V, Lundbeck and Olanzapine, IIC 2010, 149.

Tucker, Geoffrey T., Chiral Switches, 355 Lancet 1085 (2000).

Tuominen, Nicoleta, Patenting Strategies of the EU Pharmaceutical Industry Crossroad between Patent Law and Competition Policy, Research Papers in Law 1/2011, Belgium: European Legal Studies (2011).

U.S. Department of Commerce International Trade Administration, Pharmaceutical Price Controls in OECD Countries - Implications for U.S. Consumers, Pricing, Research and Development, and Innovation, Washington, DC: USITA (2004), available at: http://www.ita.doc.gov/td/chemicals/drugpricingstudy.pdf.

UK Office of Fair Trading, The Pharmaceutical Price Regulation Scheme, London: Crown Copyright (2007), available at: http://www.oft.gov.uk/shared_oft/reports/comp_policy/oft885.pdf.

UNCTAD-ICTSD, Resource Book on TRIPS and Development, Cambridge: Cambridge University Press (2005).

United States General Accountability Office, Prescription Drugs: Trends in FDA's Oversight of Direct-to-Consumer Advertising (2008) available at: http://www.gao.gov/new.items/d08758t.pdf.

United States General Accounting Office, Prescription drugs: FDA oversight of direct-to-consumer advertising has limitations (2002) available: http://www.gao.gov/new.items/d03177.pdf.

Valance, Edward H., Understanding the Markush Claim in Chemical Patents, 1 J. Chemical Documentation, 87 (1961).

Van Dijk, Theon, Patent Height and Competition in Product Improvements, 44 J. Ind. Econ. 151 (1996).

Vernon, John A, Drug Research and Price Controls, Winter, Regulation, 22 (2002-2003).

Vivian, Michael F., Novelty and Selection Inventions, IIC 1989, 303.

Voet, Martin A., The Generic Challenge- Understanding Patents, FDA and Pharmaceutical Life Cycle Management, Florida: Brown Walker Press, 3rd Ed. (2011).

Vossius, Corinna/Vossius, Tilman/Vossius, Volker, Der Terfenadin-Verletzungsstreit; zum Standard der Neuheitsprüfung, GRUR 1994, 472.

Vossius, Volker, Selection Inventions in Chemistry According to German Patent Law - A Problem of Novelty, 59 J. Pat. Off. Soc'y 180 (1977).

Vossius, Volker, Stoffschutz für Auswahlerfindungen auf dem Gebiet der Chemie, GRUR 1976, 165.

Wagner, R. Polk, (Mostly) against Exceptionalism, 50 Adv. Genet. 367 (2003).

zu Waldeck und Pyrmont, Wolrad P./Adelmann, Martin J./Brauneis, Robert/Drexl, Joseph/Nack, Ralph (eds), Patents and Technological Progress in a Globalized World, Liber Amicorum Joseph Straus, Berlin, Heidelberg: Springer (2009).

zu Waldeck und Pyrmont, Wolrad Prinz, BGH: Enantiomer eines bekannten Razemats kann patentiert warden- „Escitalopram“, GRUR-Prax, 2010, 13.

Weaver, Mark/Perakis, Nikolaos/Riolo, Joseph, Novelty-Current Trends in the Jurisprudence of the boards of Appeal of the European Patent Office, 15 World Pat. Info. 81 (1993).

Weissman, Robert, A Long, Strange Trips: The Pharmaceutical Industry Drive to Harmonize Global Intellectual Property Rules, and the Remaining WTO Legal Alternatives Available to Third World Countries, 25 U. Pa. J. Int'l Econ. L. 1079 (2004).

Wermuth, Camille G., Strategies in the Search for New Lead Compounds or Original Working Hypotheses, in: Wermuth, Camille G. (ed), The Practice of Medicinal Chemistry, Burlington: Elsevier Ltd, 3rd Ed. (2008).

Wertheimer, Albert I./Santella, Thomas M./Chaney, Nicole M., The World Health Organization's Essential Medicines List: An Endorsement of Incremental Innovation and Follow-On Research, 17 J. Pharmaceut. Marketing Manage. 25 (2005).

Wertheimer, Albert/Levy, Richard/O'Connor, Thomas, Too many drugs? The Clinical and Economic Value of Incremental Innovations, in: Farquhar, Irina, Summers, Kent and Sorkin, Alan (eds), Investing in Health: The Social and Economic Benefits of Health Care Innovation, Oxford: Elsevier Science Ltd. (2001).

Whalen, Jeanne/Stovall, Sten, AstraZeneca Plans to cut 7300 Jobs, the Wall Street Journal, February 2, 2012, available at: http://online.wsj.com/article/SB10001424052970203711104577198264263381758.html.

White, C. Michael, Why a Seventeen Year Patent, 38 J. Pat. Off. Soc'y 839 (1956).

Wibbelmann, Jobst, Broad Claims: a Nuisance, EIPR 1997, 515.

William, Johnson. A., Invitation to Organic Chemistry, Sudbury: Jones and Barlett (1999).

Willkens, Robert F./Segre, Eugene J., Combination Therapy with Naproxen and Aspirin in Rheumatoid Arthritis, 19 Arthritis & Rheumatism 677 (2006).

Wilson, Duff, Drug Firms Face Billions in Losses in '11 as Patents End, The New York Times, March 6, 2011, available at: http://www.nytimes.com/2011/03/07/business/07drug.html?pagewanted=all.

WIPO, PCT, The International Patent System, Yearly Review, Development and Performance in 2012, (2012), available at: http://www.wipo.int/freepublications/en/patents/901/wipo_pub_901_2012.pdf.

Witherspoon, John F. (ed), Nonobviousness:The Ultimate Condition of Patentability: Papers Compiled in Commemoration of the Silver Anniversary of 35 USC 103,Washington: The Bureau of National Affairs, Inc (1980).

World Bank, The World Bank Legal Review: Law and Justice for Development, Washington D.C.: Inc. World Bank (2003).

Yu, Yu/Sachin,Gupta, Pioneering Advantage in Generic Drug Competition, Johnson School Research Paper Series No. 37-06, Ithaca: The Johoson School at Cornell University (2008).

Zentiva, Zentiva the Unifying Brand for Sanofi-aventis' European Generics Business, Zentiva Press Release, Apr. 4, 2011, available at: http://www.zentiva.com/media-centre/press-releases/pages/press-release-detail.aspx?ItemId=6.

Zhang, Yuting/Soumerai, Stephen B., Do Newer Prescription Drugs Pay For Themselves? A Reassessment Of The Evidence, 26 Health Affair. 880 (2007).

Zins, Gerald D., The History of the Development of Minoxidil, 6 Clin. Dermatol. 132 (1988).

OTHER SOURCES

EPO glossary, available at: http://www.epo.org/service-support/glossary.html.

Espacenet, available at: http://worldwide.espacenet.com.

European Patent Register, available at: https://register.epo.org/espacenet/regviewer.

FDA, Drugs@FDA Glossary of Terms, available at: http://www.fda.gov/Drugs/ResourcesForYou/Consumers/QuestionsAnswers/ucm100100.htm

FDA, Generic Drugs: Same Medicine, Lower Cost, available at: http://www.fda.gov/downloads/ForConsumers/ConsumerUpdates/UCM340458.pdf

FDA, Information for Consumers, available at: http://www.fda.gov/ Drugs/ResourcesForYou/Consumers/BuyingUsingMedicineSafely/UnderstandingGenericDrugs/ucm144456.htm.

O'Hagan, P/Farkas, Charles, Bringing pharma R&D back to health. Bain Insights [online], (2009) available at: http://www.bain.com/Images/BB_Managing_RandD_HC.pdf.

Orange Book: Approved Drug Products with Therapeutic Equivalence Evaluations, available at: http://www.accessdata.fda.gov/scripts/cder/ob/default.cfm.

Posner, Richard A., Do Patent and Copyright Law Restrict Competition and Creativity Excessively?, Sep, 30, 2012, available at: http://www.becker-posner-blog.com/2012/09/do-patent-and-copyright-law-restrict-competition-and-creativity-excessively-posner.html

Teva, Teva Completes Acquisition of Cephalon, Teva News Release, October 14, 2001, available at: http://ir.tevapharm.com/phoenix.zhtml?c=73925&p=irol-newsArticle&ID=1617357&highlight=

USPTO, USPTO Press Release #09-21 (Oct. 8, 2009), available at: http://www.uspto.gov/ news/09_21.jsp.

WHO, International nonproprietary name, available at: http://www.who.int/medicines/services/inn/en/.

WHO, Pharmaceutical products, available at: http://www.who.int/topics/pharmaceutical_products/en/.